T0244315

Tubby

Raymond O. Barton and the US Army, 1889–1963

Stephen A. Bourque

Number 24 in the North Texas Military Biography and
Memoir Series

University of North Texas Press
Denton, Texas

10 9 8 7 6 5 4 3 2 1

Permissions:
University of North Texas Press
1155 Union Circle #311336
Denton, TX 76203-5017

The paper used in this book meets the minimum requirements of the
American National Standard for Permanence of Paper for Printed Library
Materials, z39.48.1984. Binding materials have been chosen for durability.

Library of Congress Cataloging-in-Publication Data

Names: Bourque, Stephen A. (Stephen Alan), 1950- author.
Title: Tubby : Raymond O. Barton and the US Army, 1889-1963 / Stephen A.
    Bourque.
Other titles: North Texas military biography and memoir series ; no. 24.
Description: Denton : University of North Texas Press, [2024] | Series:
    Number 24 in the North Texas military biography and memoir series |
    Includes bibliographical references and index.
Identifiers: LCCN 2024022949 (print) | LCCN 2024022950 (ebook) | ISBN
    9781574419436 (cloth) | ISBN 9781574419535 (ebook)
Subjects: LCSH: Barton, Raymond Oscar, 1889-1963. | United States. Army.
    Infantry Division, 4th--Biography. | Generals--United States--Biography.
    | Hürtgen Forest, Battle of, Germany, 1944. | Operation Cobra, 1944. |
    World War, 1939-1945--Campaigns--Europe. | BISAC: HISTORY / Wars &
    Conflicts / World War II / European Theater | BIOGRAPHY &
AUTOBIOGRAPHY
    / Military | LCGFT: Biographies.
Classification: LCC E745.B37 B68 2024 (print) | LCC E745.B37 (ebook) |
    DDC 355.0092 [B]--dc23/eng/20240725
LC record available at https://lccn.loc.gov/2024022949
LC ebook record available at https://lccn.loc.gov/2024022950

Tubby is Number 24 in the North Texas Military Biography and Memoir Series.

The electronic edition of this book was made possible by the support of the
Vick Family Foundation. Typeset by vPrompt eServices.

An AUSA Book. Published in cooperation with the Association of the
United States Army.

Contents

Abbreviations

AEF	American Expeditionary Force (US Army in Europe during World War I)
AFG	American forces in Germany (1919–1923)
AGF	Army Ground Forces
CCC	Civilian Conservation Corps
CGSS	Command and General Staff School, Fort Leavenworth, KS
COSSAC	Chief of Staff, Supreme Allied Commander (planning staff before Eisenhower)
ETO	European theater of operations
G-1	assistant chief of staff, personnel
G-2	assistant chief of staff, intelligence
G-3	assistant chief of staff, operations and training
G-4	assistant chief of staff, supply and logistics
GHQ	US Army General Headquarters
HQ	headquarters
LST	landing ship, tank (large amphibious landing craft)
R. O.	Raymond Oscar Barton Jr. (son)
ROTC	Reserve Officers Training Corps
SHAEF	Supreme Headquarters, Allied Expeditionary Force
USMA	United States Military Academy

Maps and Illustrations

4th Infantry Division Organization, June–December 1944

Combat Units
8th Infantry
12th Infantry
22nd Infantry
4th Reconnaissance Troop (Mechanized)
4th Engineer Combat Battalion

Combat Support
4th Medical Battalion
4th Division Artillery
    20th Field Artillery Battalion (155 mm howitzer)
    29th Field Artillery Battalion (105 mm howitzer)
    42nd Field Artillery Battalion (105 mm howitzer)
    44th Field Artillery Battalion (105 mm howitzer)

Special Troops
704th Ordnance Light Maintenance Company
4th Quartermaster Company
4th Signal Company
Military Police Platoon
Headquarters Company
Band

Units Habitually Attached
377th Anti-Aircraft Artillery Automatic Weapons Battalion (mobile)
70th Tank Battalion
87th Chemical Mortar Battalion
801st Tank Destroyer Battalion (self-propelled)

Preface

Writing in the 4th Infantry Division's yearbook at the end of the Second World War, its commander, Major General H. W. Blakeley, noted, "It is hoped that a complete history of the Division's participation in World War II may be published in the not too distant future."[1] Unfortunately, it did not happen, and almost eighty years after the end of the war, the details of its soldiers' experiences continue to slip into history's lacuna, with little hope of resurrection. Forgotten are the feats of its officers and men who struggled in some of America's most intense combat, save the occasional plaque remembering those to whom the nation awarded the Congressional Medal of Honor. However, this is not the 4th Infantry Division's combat history; that has yet to be written. This is the story of its remarkable commander, Major General Raymond O. Barton, who led the division from Georgia to the German border during the Second World War.

My original intention was to write a history of the US VII Corps during the first two months of Operation OVERLORD. My first book was an operational history of this organization during Operation Desert Storm, so I naturally desired to return to its earlier years. Contributing to my interest in expanding this story was the corps' battle flag with its many combat streamers I walked past each day at the army's School of Advanced Military Studies at Fort Leavenworth, Kansas. Therefore, soon after finishing my previous book, *Beyond the Beach: The Allied War Against France* (2018), I began to gather the organization's documents, archived at several locations including the Combined Arms Research Library at Fort Leavenworth, the Dwight David Eisenhower Presidential Library in Abilene, Kansas, and the National Archives at College Park, Maryland.

However, beyond the official records and the unofficial narrative so successfully created by its commander, J. Lawton Collins, we know little about many senior officers, colonels, brigadier generals, and division commanders who ran its staff sections and commanded its subordinate units. As a result of a massive fire at the St. Louis National Personnel Records Center in 1973, most of these officers' official personnel records are gone. This absence of documents was the case for the corps' chief of staff, Richard G. McKee. The officer that signed off on almost every order and plan issued by Collins from March through September 1944 had disappeared from history. After an extensive search, I located his daughter, Nancy McKee Smith. She helped me fill in details about her father—most importantly, his role as commander of the 8th Infantry Regiment in the Hürtgen Forest.[2]

I continued to run into the same problems concerning McKee's commander, Major General Barton. While the army's official historians have summarized what he did during the war, I could find little about his personal or professional background before June 6, 1944. However, Barton's records at Saint Louis survived the fire, and in 2018 the government released his official military personnel file with details about his career. These include all his officer efficiency reports and medical records, which provide a picture of why he left command in the middle of the 1944 Ardennes battle and why he did not achieve command of a corps. At about the same time, I located his grandson, Rocky Barton, and his granddaughter, Cathy Barton Clarke. By chance they told me they had a collection of his letters that Cathy had retrieved in 2005 as the Barton home in Augusta was being sold. Without considering the implications, someone had dumped most of Raymond's surviving papers in the street for the next trash pickup.

Among this amazing collection was his correspondence with his parents from 1908 until his mother died in 1943. In his own words, he provides us with a series of intimate snapshots beginning with his journey to West Point and taking us sequentially through his time at the academy and his subsequent progression through his career from lieutenant to colonel. For his parents he describes the military aspects of America in the first third of the twentieth century. It is a journey that takes him from West Point to Alaska, from upstate New York to the Rio Grande Valley and then to Georgia. It continues to the post–World War I Rhineland, marriage, and postings at Fort Leavenworth, Omaha, Washington, DC, and then back to Georgia. There the letters become fewer as his parents pass away, but he continues writing to his daughter until the eve of the Second World War. At that point a second collection of papers centers on correspondence with his fellow officers and, most importantly, his war diary. Maintained by his aide de camp, it provides a detailed rendering of his activities from March 1944 through January 1945. It answers fundamental questions about what a division commander was doing before, during, and after each battle. Therefore, along with the official US Army records available at the National Archives at College Park and the War Department Microfilm Collection, I had more than enough material to prepare a complete bibliography.

Readers should note that each chapter reflects only an abbreviation of events from the perspective of one person. Most significantly, there is no comprehensive history of the 4th Infantry Division during the Second World War. The scope of its operations before and after D-Day, including the capture of Cherbourg, its combat in the Bocage, Operation COBRA, the liberation of Paris, and the intense combat in the Hürtgen Forest, certainly require one. Therefore, sadly, there is no space to present in detail a comprehensive record of the division's battles, and this narrative, focusing on the division commander, can only hint at the combat operations of the 8th, 12th, and 22nd Infantries.

As the title of this book indicates, "Tubby" was Raymond Barton's nickname, awarded to him by his peers while at West Point. Unlike modern usage, the term had nothing to do with his size or weight but was probably more about his prowess on the wrestling mat. He embraced this moniker, and for the rest of his life, superior officers, friends, and family all called him Tubby. In this manuscript I have limited its use to personal interactions.

It is essential to remind the reader that the American officer corps in the first half of the twentieth century was exclusively male and almost exclusively white. Barton's wife, Clare Fitzpatrick, like most officers' wives, actively participated in her husband's career, and her and Raymond's letters to the Barton family provide us with much information on their family life. Unfortunately, the letters that might provide details of Clare's life during the war have essentially disappeared.

I should also note that Barton, like most of his peers, grew up in the shadow of Reconstruction and shared a bias against African Americans. With only a few exceptions, the US Military Academy was an all-white school, and Barton's class had no Black officers. The influence of the sons of the Confederacy on the academy, of which Barton was one, was profound and only in the twenty-first century beginning to wane. The same was true concerning the 4th Infantry Division of the Second World War. It was officered by white men from the south, many from Georgia, Florida, and South Carolina. Clare and Raymond lived in a culturally different time and place from modern America, and this difference is always in this story's background.[3]

Finally, officers do not simply show up on the battlefield but grow within a framework of peers, seniors, and subordinates. In the small army of the pre–World War II era, officers knew most of those within their branch, either in person or by reputation. Friendships formed at schools, isolated posts, or in Washington remained. Barton came in contact with so many officers, famous and obscure, over his thirty-seven-year career that identifying these connections emerged as a significant focus of this book. Readers will note many names appearing throughout the book, such as Bull, Flint, Ord, Weaver, Haislip, and Singleton. These formed the core of his mentors and friends.

Acknowledgments

My completion of this five-year journey has been possible only through the kindness and support of many friends, archivists, librarians, and scholars. Most important is the Barton family, especially Rocky Barton and Cathy Clarke, who shared their time, stories, and Raymond's personal documents. Without their help I would not have written this book. Others with relations in the 4th Infantry Division include Nancy McKee Smith, the daughter of the VII Corps chief of staff and later 8th Infantry Regiment commander, who was a big supporter in the early stages of this manuscript and shared many important documents and photographs from the period. Beth Reiman, niece of Barton's chief of staff and, later, deputy commander, shared a collection of documents and insights into her uncle's role with the 4th Division. George Mabry III and Stephen Cano also shared material from their distinguished family members.

Many of the great soldiers I have described in this book have, essentially, disappeared from history. Fortunately, genealogy web services have performed a great service in copying and making massive document collections available to researchers and historians. These include passport applications, transportation manifests, military unit personnel returns, birth records, obituaries, and other government documents. Although I usually cite the original archive and collection, behind the scenes in many cases was a search on Ancestry.com. Especially during the COVID lockdown, the web page proved an amazing research tool and well worth the subscription price for researching historians.

As mentioned, I researched this manuscript during the COVID pandemic, with all important archives closed to scholars. In several cases the archivists performed well beyond their required duties to either provide me materials or ensure they were waiting for me as soon as their visiting restrictions ended. These included Elizabeth Dubuisson, John Dubuisson, and Rusty Raferty at the Combined Arms Research Library, Fort Leavenworth, Kansas; Mary Burtzloff at the Dwight David

Eisenhower Presidential Library; Susan M. Lintelmann at United States Military Academy Library; and Tim Nenninger at National Archives and Records Administration, College Park, who provided me many important documents on the eve of the pandemic, as did Holly Rivet and the staff at the National Personnel Records Center in Saint Louis.

Other scholars, archivists, and librarians who supported my work include Bryan Hockensmith, Jessica Sheets, LeeAnn Caldwell and Wendy Turner, Phillip (Matt) Hart, Frank Shirer, Steve Lofgren, Florian "Flo" Kardoskee, Helen Nerska, Debra Kimok, Mike Burges, Tina Monaco, Genoa R. Stanford, Steve Rauch, Sammy Way, Sepp Scanlin, Mathilde Rouquet, Carol Lechartier, Lisa Smith, Lynn Conway, Augie Lorio, David K. Butler, Lisa Keith-Lucas, Manuel Gass, Michele Willbanks, Tyler Reid, Sarah Jones, Katherine Howry, Melissa Davis, Amy Vaughn, Jerome Brubaker, Connie Barone, Courtney Burns, Dusty Finley, Elizabeth Cook, Jay Defillipo, Jerry Martin, André Rakoto, Cara McCormack, Michael Belis, Reiner Sauer, David Capps-Tunwell, Valentin Schneider, and David Livingstone.

Brian North and Peter Kindsvatter read and commented on earlier versions of this manuscript. Robert Rush reviewed this biography from the 22nd Infantry Regiment's perspective and provided great comments to improve the text's mechanics. Mark Calhoun from the World War II Museum in New Orleans gave this book its first external review, and I appreciate his sound advice and prescient comments. Steven Ossad, Bradley's biographer, reviewed the entire manuscript, provided great comments, and motivated me to get this book into print. Probably no one knows more about the division's history than Bob Babcock, historian and often commander of the 4th Infantry Division Veterans Association. His archive is a gold mine of details about the division's veterans, and he personally met some of the officers mentioned in these pages. His assistance, support, and comments have been invaluable.

At the University of North Texas Press, Director Ron Chrisman has been a source of sound advice and motivation since I embarked on this journey. Amy Maddox worked miracles as my stylistic editor, forcing me to be precise about notes and documentation and discovering my writing errors.

Bobby Wright proved especially creative and adaptive in helping me create the appropriate maps to illustrate Barton's career.

Finally, special thanks to my partner for more than thirty-five years, Debra Anderson. She has joined me in following Barton's trail from Oklahoma to the Hürtgen, and has read every word of this manuscript several times, pointing out my many repetitions and vague references. I deeply appreciate the love, support, and critical advice that helped make this project a personal joy. However, I know that despite all of the help and assistance I received, readers will discover errors or questionable interpretations. These, of course, belong solely to me.

Introduction

It was the eve of the most significant operation in the history of the US Army. Pinned for six weeks on the Norman coast, General Omar Bradley's First Army was ready to break through the German defenses and into the heart of France. A massive air bombardment by almost the entire Eighth and Ninth Air Forces would support the army's assault. Bradley had massed a reinforced VII Corps of three infantry, one motorized, and two armored divisions in the assault area—six divisions in all. On either flank was a standard three-division corps designed to hold the shoulders of the main effort. Behind the First Army was Lieutenant General George S. Patton's Third Army, ready to exploit the breach and take command of part of the growing American combat force.[1]

The 4th Infantry Division, nicknamed the Ivy Division, was at the center of the breach zone, and James S. Rodwell's 8th Infantry Regiment would lead its penetration of the Nazi defenses. Ernie Pyle, the celebrated war correspondent, was in the 8th Infantry Regiment's command post that evening as the staff and commanders discussed their orders. Rodwell, a cavalryman who had been with the division since it organized for combat back in Georgia, first as chief of staff and now as regimental commander, stood up and began giving last-minute instructions. His staff chiefs and the battalion commanders looked at their maps and copied his words into their small army-issued notebooks. Then, just as the colonel finished introducing Pyle to his officers and letting them know he would be with them for the attack, another officer entered the room. The correspondent captured the moment in one of his noted dispatches:

> Then Maj. Gen. Raymond O. Barton, 4th Division Commander, arrived. The colonel called, "Attention!" And everybody stood rigid until the general gave them, "Carry on," he barked.
> An enlisted man ran to the mess truck and got a folding canvas stool for the general to sit on. He sat listening intently while the colonel wound up his instructions.

Then the General stepped into the center of the circle. He stood at a slouch on one foot with the other leg far out like a brace. He looked all around him as he talked. He didn't talk long. Then, finally, he said something like this:

"This is one of finest regiments in the American Army. It was the last regiment out of France in the last war. It was the first regiment into France in this war. It has spearheaded every one of the division's attacks in Normandy. It will spearhead this one. For many years this was my regiment and I feel very close to you, and very proud."

The General's lined face was a study in emotion. Sincerity and deep sentiment were in every contour, and they shone from his eyes. Gen. Barton is a man of deep affections. The tragedy of war, both personal and impersonal, hurts him. At the end, his voice almost broke, and I for one had a lump in my throat. He ended: "That's all. God bless you and good luck."[2]

With that, Major General Raymond O. Barton moved on to visit another of his three regiments.

The children of the World War II generation might know a little about Barton because of a scene from the 1962 movie *The Longest Day*. Brigadier General Theodore Roosevelt Jr., assigned to the 4th Infantry Division as an extra officer (portrayed by Henry Fonda), limps down the hall to see his boss, Major General Barton (played by Edmond O'Brien). In this scene Roosevelt asks Tubby, the name Barton earned years ago as a West Point wrestler, permission to accompany the first wave ashore. After some banter explaining to the audience that Barton's reluctance to grant permission is because he is the son of the former president, the division commander relents, and Roosevelt limps out of the office. The next time we encounter Roosevelt is on Utah Beach, where he is deciding to continue the assault after discovering the lead regiment had arrived at the wrong landing site. The audience never sees Barton again. Other than in the world of military historians and World War II history buffs, the 4th Infantry Division commander has mostly disappeared from public view. Of course, most of this on-screen dialogue is contrived for the audience. It did not take place on the ship in the last few hours, as Barton had decided earlier. This invasion was not Roosevelt's first combat experience, as combat in North Africa and Sicily had tested him earlier in the war. It is also doubtful that either of them, while aboard, would be wearing anything other than their combat uniforms. Indeed, the actual Roosevelt was much more casual about his appearance than Fonda's portrayal.[3]

Although eighty years have passed since the landings that June morning, and the extensive combat that followed in the summer and fall of 1944, there is surprisingly little written about Barton the man or about his record as a division commander. What has been conveyed by the US Army's historians in the official history, best known as the Green Books, are all the details about Barton known to modern historians. These authors tell us that he led the 4th Infantry while landing on Utah Beach, although some have ignored that fact and credit Roosevelt as the division's leader that day. He then directed his forces to capture the eastern portion of Cherbourg before the end of June. In early July the division continued to advance south through the waterlogged Bocage country. At the end of the month, the Ivy Division broke through the German lines as part of Operation COBRA and helped block the German counteroffensive at Mortain. In August it joined the 2nd French Armored Division in the liberation of Paris, after which the division advanced north and crossed into Germany along the Siegfried Line. It moved to the Hürtgen Forest in November and fought through some of Europe's most inhospitable terrain. Finally, in early December Barton's unit moved to Luxembourg—a more restful portion of the front lines—only to encounter attacking German troops during the Battle of the Bulge. When the Americans stopped the German forces, Barton could go no further since a stomach ulcer was ravishing his body, and he asked his corps and army commander to send him home in December 1944.

This description, however, leaves many questions unanswered. How did his assignments contribute to his performance as a division commander? Who were his mentors, and what was his relationship with his superiors throughout his career? Who were his friends, and how did they affect his military and personal life? Why was he was given command of one of the two divisions to land on D-Day? Who was he as a person, beyond what is found in his official records? How effective was he as a division commander? Why was he not selected for corps command? What is his legacy?

Thankfully, we now have answers to many of these questions. The Saint Louis National Personnel Records Center recently released his military personnel records file, which survived the 1973 fire. Fortunately, his grand-children saved almost one thousand letters and his war diary. Thus, we now have a better picture of this distinguished American warrior. What follows is Barton's journey from a small city in Oklahoma through the ranks of the professional officer corps while maintaining solid relationships with his family and friends. Because of his competence, and the trust of his superiors, he became one of the few officers ever to command a division in combat. Ultimately, the physical cost of seven months of intense fighting and mental stress of losing so many of his officers and men took a toll from which he could not recover. His was a path familiar to many who rose to division command. But to understand his unique story, we must travel back to Texas, Colorado, and Oklahoma at the end of the nineteenth century.

Chapter 1

Growing Up, 1889–1912

> *[Raymond] will make a mark in his class.*
> —Principal to Mrs. Barton, March 1898[1]

Ada to West Point, 1889–1908

Raymond's father, Conway O. Barton Jr. (b. 1857), grew up in the shadow of the Confederacy. His father, Conway O. Barton Sr. (b. 1805), and his mother, Martha J. Cox (b. 1810), were both born in South Carolina but married in 1827 in Montgomery, Alabama. The couple migrated west, probably with a contingent of slaves, to Texas soon after it joined the United States in 1845. By the beginning of the Civil War, Conway Sr.'s wealth had grown, and he now owned a large plantation near Calvert, halfway between Waco and College Station, with seven slaves working his fields.[2] Martha gave birth to eleven children, the last one Conway O. Barton Jr., in June 1856. Four years later, at the beginning of the Civil War, at least two of his three brothers, Josiah and John, joined the Texas Brigade, initially commanded by John B. Hood. As students of Civil War history know, this unit was at the center of almost all the conflict's significant engagements in the eastern theater.

1

Most likely Thomas also served. Surprisingly, all three brothers survived the war but at least one returned home severely wounded.[3]

During Reconstruction the family remained relatively wealthy, and Conway Jr. attended a private school in Port Sullivan, a town south of Calvert. Since no public education existed, the local planters established their school, importing instructors from England to teach some of the lessons. He spent his secondary school years at the Texas Military Academy in Austin. Finally, in 1876, when he was 20 years old, he headed east to study law at the University of Virginia, in a state still coming to grips with the reality of war, Union occupation, and the death and legacy of Robert E. Lee. After graduating from law school, he returned to Cameron, about twenty-five miles west of his family's home. He was as educated and well-read as anyone in that part of the country.[4] He married 20-year-old Mary Blanch Crow from Saint Louis, Missouri, the following year. Their daughter, Maude, was born a year later, in 1879. In 1882 they returned to Saint Louis to give birth to their second daughter, Ann. Unfortunately, Mary did not survive the experience. Since Conway had no roots or connections in Saint Louis, he temporarily left his children with Mary's family and returned to Cameron.[5]

There is evidence that Conway had partially given up the law and was working on the telegraph line along the rail route. By 1885 he was working on the old military trail in southern Colorado, today US Route 50. He lived in Granada, a waypoint on the Santa Fe Trail along the Arkansas River and a base for the army's ongoing war against the Indigenous tribes. Troops and commerce moving from Fort Dodge in Kansas could either continue west toward Fort Lyon and Pueblo or head south on the military road to Fort Union in New Mexico territory.[6] The Atchison, Topeka & Santa Fe Railroad arrived in 1873, and Granada became a growing stop on the expanding line. Heading west from Granada, the next significant town was La Junta, on another crossroads connected to the Santa Fe Trail.

Probably searching for provisions while stringing wire nearby, Conway walked into George Mosher's grocery store. Originally from Vermont, George had fought with the 6th Ohio Regiment during the Civil War. When it was over, he and his family moved west and lived in Abington, Illinois, until the early 1880s. By 1885 they had moved again and set up a new store in La Junta.[7] When the lonely 29-year-old Conway walked into the store to purchase provisions one day, he discovered 24-year-old Carrie Mosher working behind the counter. Whatever the details of the courtship may be, Conway and Carrie married on January 4, 1887, at the old Bent County courthouse in Las Animas, halfway between La Junta and Granada.[8]

The newlyweds moved back to Conway's dwellings in Granada. Conway's daughter Maude moved in with her grandmother's family in Travis, Texas, while Ann moved in with him and his new wife.[9] That October Carrie gave birth to their daughter Myra, named after her mother. Sadly, the baby died almost immediately. Then, on August 22, 1889, the couple welcomed their first son, Raymond, into the family.[10] After Raymond's birth the family moved back to Texas, and Carrie urged Conway to resume his career as a lawyer. They moved for a short time to Wellington, the county seat of Hollingsworth County, located between Amarillo and Wichita Falls. Then, looking for better opportunities, they relocated to Gainesville, north of Dallas near the Oklahoma border and the county seat of Cooke County. While in Texas the couple lost three children, Winnie, Ernest, and Conway, during childbirth. In addition to losing three children, Carrie's family's situation in Colorado was now causing her concern. Her 13-year-old sister, Daughter, died at the same time as her father's store was suffering during the Panic of 1896.[11] Overwhelmed by it all, her father committed suicide by asphyxiation, leaving his wife, Myra, to manage the family business.[12] Sons Dom, Harry, and Jessie stepped in, saved the grocery, and renamed it in honor of their father: George F. Mosher's Sons, Groceries and Provisions. The Mosher family would be a strong influence during Raymond's school years.[13]

Meanwhile, Conway discovered opportunities across the border as Oklahoma opened up to non-Indigenous settlers. The Santa Fe Railway began pushing through the Chickasaw National area and completed a track between Kansas and the Gulf Coast in 1887. As a result of the growing population, the federal government established a courthouse in Pauls Valley, Garvin County, in 1895 to provide legal administration for the territory. The creation of this new jurisdiction looked like an excellent opportunity to join a developing system, so Conway moved the family to Pauls Valley later that same year. Two years later (February 11, 1897) the couple welcomed their son Percy into

Myra Mosher, Raymond, and Carrie Barton. Taken in La Junta, Colorado, about 1890. Courtesy Barton family.

their family that included Ann, now 15.[14] Meanwhile, 9-year-old Raymond was progressing in his education. A note from his principal in March 1898 discussing his reading concludes with the prophetic message, "Raymond is a good student and will make a mark in his class."[15]

Another opportunity for Conway arose in 1902 when the US government established a court in nearby Ada. Founded in 1890 on land formerly belonging to the Chickasaw Nation, Ada, Oklahoma, emerged as the seat of Pontotoc County. With the arrival of regular rail service, the town rapidly enlarged. So the family again moved so Conway could practice law at the new county court.[16] It was still a relatively primitive town, and banks, shops, city government, and schools would emerge in the next few years. Its first elementary school, the Scarborough Institute, opened in 1901, and Raymond was one of its original students. One of his classmates in that small class was Charles Chauncey, who would become a major general in the air force and serve as chief of staff for the Mediterranean Allied Air Forces. Another was Orel Busby, who would room with him at the University of Oklahoma, serve with Raymond's father on the bar in Ada, and end his career as a justice for the Oklahoma Supreme Court.[17]

Conway prospered in his new environment, and soon after his arrival became a member of the county's first legal bar. The county appointed him as a judge and then as mayor from 1906 to 1908.[18] He became well-connected with the county's political structure and was also a community leader in a harsh, almost lawless, town. Judge Barton appeared to all but his closest friends as a tough and determined community member. A photograph of the first county officers shows him in the front row as an intimidatingly stocky man, frowning intensely and displaying his prominent mustache. Orel Busby, Raymond's friend who knew the judge better than anyone outside his family, reminds us that he was also a caring and wonderful father and deeply in love with Carrie.[19]

Ada was striving to develop a civilized character and soften its rough frontier edge. The town's women formed several ladies' clubs encouraging the improvement of educational facilities in the community. These clubs, especially the Sorosis Club, of which Carrie was a member, sought to bring noted speakers to the community and organized a library. When the president called the club roll, members would reply with "quotations from the works of Tennyson, Bryon, Shakespeare, and other classics."[20] A photograph from 1912 shows Mrs. Barton as a member of a group of fifteen ladies who were all leaders in the community.[21] The Bartons represented the best in the region of education and civility, and their son, Raymond, would begin his progression as a leader, following in his parent's footsteps.

Unfortunately, Ada was not a particularly healthy place, and young Raymond became quite sick in 1905. It was likely an allergy, and the prescription was to send him back to Carrie's family in La Junta, where the fresh mountain air would help. Her brothers, Dom Pedro and Jessie, treated her son like a prince. First, they took him on excursions around the area and exposed him to the beauties of the local mountains and sights, such as Pike's Peak, the Pillars of Hercules in Cheyenne Canyon, and the Devil's Slide in the Garden of the Gods. Next, Jessie took him to Denver and spent several days exploring one of America's most dynamic and growing cities. This trip went so well that the brothers tried to convince Raymond to stay and finish school in La Junta. The 15-year-old liked the idea but deferred to his parents, who wanted him home. He also exhibited writing ability and sent Conway and Carrie detailed letters of his explorations and experiences. These letters display his love of travel and exploring his environment.[22] He also wrote to his brother Percy, giving advice and asking what he wanted him to bring from the Colorado mountains.[23] The vacation did him good as his cough cleared up, and he gained weight, from 124 to 136 pounds. But a fear of excessive spending also crept into his letters, reflecting the financial insecurity that haunted Conroy and Carrie.[24] His parents loved his reports and often shared his letters with the local newspaper, which commented after one such posting, "For a boy of fourteen [fifteen] he has a precocious literary ability and shows a marked appreciation of the beauties of nature, and for the handiwork of man as well."[25]

Returning to Ada, Raymond did well in his small high school. Learning from his father, he earned spending money as a lineman for the local telegraph company. Early 1907 the principal realized he had seven students, five boys and two girls, with enough credits to graduate, and selected the young Barton as his valedictorian. He titled his valedictory speech on June 12 "Good Citizenship."[26] It was several months before classes started at the University of Oklahoma, so Barton busied himself with various tasks besides laying wire for the telegraph company. In addition, he was a Presbyterian Church Educators society member and represented Ada at the organization's state convention in June.[27] He helped organize a young men's literary club to "afford its members an opportunity to get practice in the art of public speaking and the essentials of parliamentary law."[28] He also spent a few weeks collecting information for the Bureau of the Census, getting four dollars daily for his labor.[29]

Finally, he was at school in Norman, Oklahoma, rooming with his friend Orel Busby. His letter of September 10, 1907, is the first one in which he addresses his parents as "Dear Folx," a salutation he continued until his father's death.[30] This letter and others describe his academic progress, which was generally good, except for German, with which he struggled. He joined the freshman football team and enjoyed it. He sensed that athletics was essential and a way for him to succeed on campus and later in life. But one issue appears regularly in his letters: money. He knew he was putting a strain on his family by attending school. His uncle Dom sent him twenty-five dollars a month, a large sum in 1907, to help with his expenses.[31] Writing in November to his father, he confides, "The only thing which discourages me from going to school is that it will be so long before I become a producer. That I am now only a drag [on the family]."[32]

As judge and mayor, his father was connected with the young state's political class. When Raymond went home at Christmas, the two discussed his future. Conway's friend Charles D. Carter was the state's representative for the Fourth Congressional District. With his father's support, Raymond wrote Carter, asking him for an appointment to Annapolis. After further discussions with his father, the young man wrote again, on December 30, to Carter, asking him for an appointment first to West Point and then, if not possible, to the Naval Academy. He directly mentions in his letter that one reason for his application is to become "productive" sooner.[33] Indicating that Mayor Barton's influence was involved, Carter announced only three days later (January 3, 1908) that he was appointing Raymond as an alternate for West Point for 1908 and guaranteed an appointment for the following year.[34]

The appointment was not inevitable, so Raymond returned to Norman in January. Now he had another focus: to prepare for the West Point entrance exam. However, first Barton had to pass the courses in his current semester, which included botany, English, economics, history, and that dreaded German. He knew he had to do well if the military academy appointment failed. So on January 25 Barton began taking his final exams to finish the semester. He passed all his courses and was ready for whatever transpired, but he chose not to come home just yet. As much as Raymond missed his family, he was not in a hurry to return to Ada as he knew he would be less distracted living on campus studying for his examinations. Instead, he asked his parents to send him some books and reviewed algebra, geometry, geography, and history, which made up the core of his forthcoming examination. Fortunately, it looked as if he could afford the journey to New York, as his uncle Harry joined his brother Dom in sending him money to cover the cost. Barton's letters reflect his appreciation to all his family for helping him succeed. Later, when he was on a sound financial footing, he would pass on this kindness to others.[35]

Finally, on February 6 he returned to Ada to finish his preparation and spend time with his family. He realized that he would be away for a long time, most likely more than a year, after he signed into the academy.[36] The local newspaper, the social media mode in 1908, announced his departure to his friends and neighbors:

> Raymond Barton left on last Sunday morning for West Point for the purpose of standing an examination for a possible cadetship. We say a possible cadetship for the reason that there is another appointee, who if he passes the examination, has the senior claim on the place; but in the event the first appointee fails in his examination the place is open to the boy from Ada, and in both examination and qualifications Raymond will make good. A young man of clear brains, a student of more than ordinary ability, of fine physique and exemplary habits, and with a high sense of honor, and courteous demeanor, Raymond Barton's friends in his hometown are limited only by the extent of his acquaintance, and the best wishes of everyone go with him on his trip. He will stop off and see the sights in the cities of Saint Louis and Washington on his way to West Point.[37]

Nineteen-year-old Raymond departed Ada on Sunday, February 16, 1908. His trip, which he chronicled in a very detailed letter to his parents, is something to marvel at over one hundred years later. From Oklahoma City on Sunday, he traveled by train to Saint Louis. Although only there for a few hours, he had time to see a few sights and walk over the Eads Bridge across the Mississippi River, one of the nation's engineering marvels at the time. He then took the night train to Pittsburgh, arriving on Tuesday morning in time to get out and look at the big city. Catching the train to Washington the following day, he got off at Harper's Ferry and played tourist. His mission was to procure souvenir pebbles from the river for two of his favorite teachers. Catching the next train, he arrived at Washington's Union Station, opened only a year earlier, by ten o'clock on the evening of February 18. He checked into a hotel only a block from the US Capitol.

The following morning he walked around Washington, which he had only been able to imagine. He later wrote his parents, "The next day I spent in the capitol, and it surpassed all I had expected. The beauty and elegance cannot be adequately described."[38] His unhindered access to officials and sites is striking for those living in the twenty-first century. He climbed the Capitol dome but could not see much because of the fog. He looked for his US senators, Robert L. Owen and Thomas P. Gore. He found Gore, and they talked pleasantly about home and parents. The senator was blind, so Raymond walked past him later and chose not to disturb him in his travels through the Capitol halls. He looked, with no success, for Senator Charles A. Culberson from Texas, his father's friend from his University of Virginia law school days.

He started his second full day in the capital on Thursday morning by climbing to the top of the Washington Monument. There he could see and marvel at the view of the entire city. He then strolled the short distance to the Smithsonian Institute; all of its exhibits were then contained in the historic Castle, built in 1847. His next stop was the Library of Congress in the recently completed Thomas Jefferson Building. That afternoon he went to the Congressional Office Building to visit his congressman and the source of his West Point appointment, Charles D. Carter. Carter appeared fully engaged but stopped what he was doing and asked him to sit down.

From Carter's perspective Barton was well-connected back home, and spending a half hour with this young man made great sense. In addition to Conway, many of Ada's most prominent citizens had urged the congressman to appoint Raymond to the academy, so it was a good investment of his time. Carter assured Raymond that he would get an appointment next year if things did not work out this time. He also offered to take the young man in to see President Taft if he wanted to make his case for a presidential appointment in person, an offer Barton turned down since he had to depart the next day.

He departed Washington early Friday morning, arriving in New York a little after three o'clock in the afternoon. It was another world of wonders for a young man from the middle of the United States. He walked up Broadway and then took a streetcar around the city. He crossed the Brooklyn Bridge and returned to the station, wondering about the skyscrapers, such as the recently completed forty-two-story Singer Building. He thought the city hotels were too expensive, more than two dollars a night, so he began hiking to West

Point, fifty-six miles away. Although he does not mention it in his letter home, we must assume he managed to get a ride partway since he arrived by nine o'clock that evening. Unfortunately, the hotel he found was still expensive, costing him about three dollars a night. What a journey![39]

On Monday, February 24, Barton reported with about sixty other cadets to West Point. He moved out of the hotel into a two-room barracks along with Sidney V. Bingham. Sid came from a military family, with his grandfather serving in the Union Army during the Civil War and his father being an infantry colonel. He was a quiet student with a great singing voice.[40] Their room was about as large as the Barton parlor in Ada, with the cots separated by a wooden partition. Raymond told his parents in a letter:

> There are no carpets, but we have steam heat and a fireplace. The furnishings are plain but ample and of the best material, and lights, well, I should say. In our room we have 6 electric lights and two gas. All rooms are just alike. The dormitory is a new one that we have. It, like the old one is 4 stories high and is divided into sections of 4 rooms, 4 stories up, making 16 rooms, and four halls to each section. In the hall of each floor is a sink and hot and cold water. Our slop buckets are carried down, but we have to sweep etc. and make up our beds and also gather-up all bed clothes in the morning. The rooms are inspected each morning. . . .
> The grub is served in course, and they have silver plates of all kinds. In fact it is more like I imagine wealthy persons (would use). The food is good too. Since being here, we have not had the same meat for dinner, nor the same soup. I am what they call "gunner" at our table. It corresponds to host, and to serve, carve, and have all dishes kept full.[41]

He concluded his long letter with a postscript: he had passed his examinations. Eleven candidates to West Point from Oklahoma took these exams, but only three passed. One of those failing was Carter's original appointment. Hedging his bets, and because of political pressure, the congressman had also selected another alternate who was unable to show up for the test. Seventy-four young men from across the country had taken these examinations, but only nineteen qualified for admission. The successful completion of tests was quite an achievement, as the local newspaper boasted, "Not only does it [Barton's success] bear witness to his natural ability and diligence as a student, but also speaks well for the thoroughness and efficiency of the Ada schools."[42] Raymond O. Barton was ready to begin his four years as a military academy cadet. Ultimately, he would remain in a United States Army uniform for thirty-eight more years.

West Point, 1908–1912

West Point was a relatively small but influential institution in the first decade of the twentieth century. For the class entering 1908, the academic faculty included four colonels, six lieutenant colonels, one major, twenty-two captains, and sixty-two lieutenants. After adding the civilian instructors in language, music, fencing, broadsword, and gymnastics, the institution's total faculty totaled 111.[43] These instructors profoundly influenced the cadets and conveyed a sense of military duty. One only needs to consider the effect Dennis Hart Mahan had on the pre–Civil War classes, much of this mentoring off duty, to appreciate the power of these connections.[44] West Point's superintendent, future Army Chief of Staff Hugh L. Scott, was born before the Civil War. His first assignment was in a troop in the 7th Cavalry, filling a vacancy opened when the previous occupant perished at the Battle of the Little Big Horn. He participated in several operations against Native American tribes, most notably Wounded Knee, in 1890. Before arriving at West Point, his last combat was against the Moros in the Philippines in 1903.[45]

Only 411 students comprised the entire corps of cadets, all four classes in 1908. The senior class, called firsties, graduating the following June had only 108 remaining members. Among them were Jacob L. Devers, George S. Patton Jr., Robert L. Eichelberger, John C. H. Lee, and William H. Simpson. James G. Ord was also in that class and would profoundly influence Barton's career. The junior class (1910), called Cows, included future 4th Infantry Division commanders Oscar Griswold and Fred C. Wallace. Finally, the sophomore class (1911), referred to as Yearlings, also had a group of cadets that Raymond would work with later in his career, including Ira T. Wyche, William Morris, Paul Baade, Carroll Bagby, and John P. Lucas.[46] With the small numbers of students and cadre, the average student knew, directly or indirectly, every other officer and cadet on post during his four years of attendance. These cadets existed within an ever-changing complex web of instructors, upperclassmen, subordinates, and peers. These relationships constantly changed as the newly commissioned seniors, who survived all four years, departed and the new plebes arrived in the spring.

Raymond arrived with 137 other plebes. Only 95 remained to receive their commissions at the end of four years. One went absent without leave (AWOL), and the army dismissed him from the service after a general court-martial. Four died early, within a few years of graduation. Several others found their way leading soldiers in combat during the First World War, such as the highly decorated D'Alary Fechet and Wade (Ham) Haislip. Two became Olympic athletes: Karl (Joe) Greenwald (equestrian, 1920) and Harold Rayner (fencing, 1920 and 1928). After flying pursuit aircraft on the western front, Edgar (Nap) Gorrell continued his ways as an innovator in aviation and automobiles, becoming president of Stulz Motor Car Company and later the Air Traffic Association. Out of that group of young men who learned to "brace" that year and learned the ways of the army, Haislip and Walton Walker would ultimately pin on the rank of four-star general. Stephen "Chamby" Chamberlin, who became Douglas MacArthur's G-3 (operations), and Millard "Miff" Harmon Jr., who commanded the Twelfth Air Force in the Pacific, became lieutenant generals.

Seventeen other classmates joined Barton in ending their careers as major generals leading corps and divisions, including Gilbert "Doc" Cook, Franklin "Si" Sibert, Walter Robertson, John S. "P" Wood, Bill Weaver, Harry J. Malony, Albert E. Brown, and Archibald Arnold. Logisticians included Bob Littlejohn, who served as the chief of quartermaster in the European theater, working for Eisenhower in London. Russell Maxwell was the American military mission North Africa leader at the beginning of the war. He later became the army's G-4 (logistics) chief, working directly for George C. Marshall. Thomas J. Hayes Jr. became chief of industrial service (Ordnance Department) in June 1942. He remained in that position until the war's end, supervising the production of over $30 billion worth of ordnance material to support American soldiers and the Allies. James Kirk ended up as the Ordnance Corps' chief of the small arms branch, supervising the design and production of the M-1 Garand rifle and the various machine guns used in the army. One other group member that year, who ended World War II as a major general, was Terry de La Mesa Allen, recycled from the previous class. However, he would not make it to graduation because of his problems with mathematics. Leaving the academy in 1911, he gained his degree from a civilian college and passed the army's entrance examinations in 1912.[47]

Other class members who became major generals include Phil Faymonville, who joined the Siberian Expedition in 1918 and later became the first military attaché to the Soviet Union and supervised the nation's Lend-Lease support to Russia. Alongside Faymonville, Sidney Spaulding attended the details of the US military mission to the Soviet Union's chief of supply. David Crawford spent World War II coordinating communications for the Combined Chiefs of Staff. In addition to Harmon and Gorrell, Davenport Johnson became an aviator and ended his service as commander of the Eleventh Air Force in the Pacific. Engineers included Roscoe Crawford, who commanded the engineer school and became the US Army's deputy chief engineer. Eleven other class members retired as brigadier generals and thirty-eight as colonels. Notably, Charles Drake and Brad Chynoweth fought in America's first battles with the Japanese in Asia. After the American surrender at Corregidor in 1942, they survived the war as prisoners. Paddy Flint and Millard Harmon died in combat. Finally, Will Wilbur received one of the first Congressional Medals of Honor for his bravery during Operation TORCH in 1942.[48] No matter what their final life destination, these four years introduced these cadets to a brotherhood, mostly a friendly one, that would continue for the rest of their lives.

During his four years at the academy, Barton came across about one thousand fellow cadets, and we should not underestimate the importance of the West Point experience in developing the early twentieth-century army officer. As in combat, replacements (plebes) arrived and found themselves the subject of the veteran's ribbing and harassment. As time went by, most rose in the ranks while others disappeared. The survivors, now the veterans, welcomed in yearly cohorts of new replacements until it was time for them to depart. For four years each group attended classes and fired on ranges together. They participated in tactical camps and attended assemblies, parades, and other activities particular to a military school. They interacted with their seniors and subordinates, so this narrative includes the names of those Barton probably got to know. Each cadet formed an opinion of the cadets he encountered, and others did the same to him. Because few personal records exist, giving a window to student emotions, biographers often write about their subjects as if they were among the few on campus.[49]

This situation is unfortunate since these feelings toward others, good and bad, were there, affecting assignments and promotions long into their military careers. Historian Carlo D'Este noted that "Eisenhower placed his personal stamp of approval on every division commander or higher. His criteria were unambiguous: No officer was selected whom he did not know personally. Numerous West Point classmates, along with veterans of the North African and Italian Campaigns, were among those tapped to fill the roster of jobs."[50] Personal connections were a vital career consideration in the era of decentralized promotion. In this small officer corps, these perceptions began the day they reported to the officer of the day. Before the Reserve Officer Training Corps (ROTC) expanded the officer base, it was the primary bonding experience of most of the officer corps, and the connections cannot be overlooked.

Beginning a Career

However, Barton's plebe (freshman) year would not begin until that summer. As a member of D Company, he spent the next three months in what we would call in the twenty-first century a military preparatory school. Unlike Sid, his roommate, who had watched soldiers all his life, he was new to the army's ways. Since he was under little pressure, he could spend some time enjoying his environment. He and Sid joined the cadets who lived across the hall, Ham Haislip and Paddy Flint, for long horseback riding excursions in the New York countryside. Local families were already sizing up these potential officers and trying to match them with young ladies they knew would be available. One invited Barton over one Saturday afternoon for refreshments and to hear a Miss Van Curry sing. Since that relationship did not work out, the local matron asked him to visit later to meet other young ladies. But he was not ready to settle down and knew that a relationship at this time would be a drain on him. "I am letting the married question alone. It will take care of itself. I've not yet seen a female that I would consider for a wife, and I guess when the right one comes along, I'll have time for her. So much for that."[51] His letters during these months are full of details of living at the academy— like being the "milk" or "coffee corporal" at dinner, and the Saturday hops where girls from Vassar and New York City, all chaperoned, came to meet potential partners.[52]

He stayed in touch with his friends, who sometimes sent excerpts of his letters to the local newspaper:

> Between drill, recitations, and meal formations, I am only able to change clothes and to clean up. At other times I have either to work on equipment (by order of upper-Class), thus letter writing is confined to a while Sunday morning or a little stolen time as tonight. This is being written during time between tattoo and taps. I am sitting at a table ready to hit the bed on the run at taps, while the weather outside is below freezing and there is a blanket of snow on the ground. The Hudson is a pretty sight now; immense cakes of ice and snow are floating down it, and the stream being as wide as it is here is all right.[53]

The cadets took remedial English and math courses, and Barton let his parents know he was doing well. He was impressed with his instructors, all army officers, who were strict and patient. In addition, he was enjoying the athletic environment and watching as the West Point baseball team competed against Yale, Fordham, William and Mary, and the University of Virginia.

And he learned the basics of military maneuvers, which were still a game to the young cadet. "Yesterday we had a dandy drill. It was a sham battle. Three companies, 'D,' 'E,' and 'F,' were divided up into two forces (I am in 'D' Company) and fought all over the mountain in back of us. We used blanks. It was lots of fun."[54]

Raymond was a prolific letter writer, and several hundred he sent to his parents during his West Point years have survived. Most are chatty, discuss family matters, and provide details on some of the routines he accepted during his academy years. He made a serious effort to educate his correspondents about the nature of the school and how it was so different from his previous school experiences. Although bouts of homesickness sometimes appeared, he was generally proud of his accomplishments. He was an intense reader and pestered his parents for books by Shakespeare, Milton, and Chaucer, as well as novels by Scott and George Elliot.[55]

On June 13, 1908, the corps of cadets, minus those who had just graduated, marched off the post to Camp Thomas H. Ruger, named after a former officer and superintendent who died in 1907. The cadets lived in shelter-half pup tents that were still being used into the 1990s. Although subjected to hazing from the new senior class, Barton and his peers enjoyed the experience. "We plebes have a lot of fun, even though we are treated like Puritan children. It is exciting to take chances in getting caught."[56]

Like most students at the academy, Barton got a nickname. A couple of different options seemed to be going through his classmates' minds. Some called him Sitting Bull because of his link to Indian Territory. Others called him Bart. But the one that seemed to be gaining favor that July was Tubby.[57] The origins are obscure, but it probably started in the wrestling gym, which is where he spent most of his free time. It was certainly not intended as an insult, since he was not by any measure a chubby young man. He liked it, and soon it became the name used by all of his friends.

While most of their daytime schedules focused on tactical problems, the cadets had some free time to experience the local area. A religious young man, he joined a Bible study class at the Warner House on Constitution Island, across from West Point. Little did the cadet realize that the Warner sisters who owned the property and taught the classes (Susan Bogert Warner and Anna Bartlett Warner) were two of the nineteenth century's most significant American women writers. Appreciating the lessons, Barton was impressed with the quality and variety of the artwork everywhere.[58]

The summer camp that year finished with a so-called "practice march." On August 24 the cadets were in a combat formation with cavalry, infantry, and artillery. For the next week, the cadets practiced tactical problems, including the conduct of a rearguard, the protection of a railroad, the attack of a convoy, and the defense of a defile. They practiced conducting forced marches to relieve a defensive position under an attack and then how to assume responsibility for its defense. At the end of each day, the cadets gathered to discuss the day's problems with the opposing commanders and umpires. As the firsties' historian notes, "It was generally impossible to convince the loser that he had been licked."[59] Then it was over, and by September 1 Barton was back on the academy grounds and ready to begin his year as a plebe. He surprised his parents by telling them he intend not to play football but to join the new wrestling club.[60] At the end of August, he settled down into his plebe routine, and sent his parents a detailed letter describing his intense daily schedule:

- 5:45 Reveille, make bed
- 6:00 Clean up room and make toilet
- 6:25 Breakfast
- 7:15 Study
- 9:20 Recite (in class)
- 10:40 Study
- 11:00 Recite (in class)
- 12:10 Wash up for dinner
- 12:20 Dinner
- 1:00 "30 Minutes all my own (Usually Study)"
- 1:30 Drawing or mechanics
- 3:30 Change into drill uniform
- 3:35 Drill
- 4:35 Change into full dress
- 4:45 Parade ground and guard mounting
- 5:45 Fifteen minutes share time
- 6:00 Supper
- 6:40 More share time
- 7:15 Study
- 9:30 Bathe and make down beds
- 10:00 Sleep

He wrote, "How's this for a busy day? No other college on earth could exist with so little time for recreation." From a teaching perspective, one wonders how much learning occurred during this hurried schedule.[61]

He did well in his courses and was in the top half of his cohort. He worried about some of his friends and expected the school to dismiss at least ten by midyear. He was in awe of those who grew up in the cities and fine homes of the East Coast and was amazed that anyone from Boston would have difficulty in class.[62] Midyear examinations began on December 21, and as he predicted the academic boards dismissed fifteen firsties from the academy.[63] During the holidays Barton remained on post performing guard duty and the other tasks required of first-year students. Then, with everyone back in January, studies and the routine resumed. Recognition Day for the class of 1912 was on February 28, a significant event in the life of a plebe. Now promoted to cadet private first class, these first-year students migrated from their isolated existence and a separate group to becoming full-fledged but still junior members of the corps of cadets. Then, finally, they could consider upperclassmen as friends and not simply tormentors.[64]

The corps of cadets headed south to participate in William Howard Taft's presidential inauguration in March. Unfortunately, the trip occurred during a snowstorm, and the railroad tracks were impassable. Accepting the condition as a challenge, without hesitation the cadets dismounted, grabbed whatever tools were available, and cleared about forty miles of track to the Washington, DC, train station. Barton noted in his letter home that the corps of cadets became a "corps of pioneers." On arrival they cleaned up and marched in the parade as scheduled.[65] The rest of the year was without difficulty as he continued and remained in the top half of his class. Somehow, he read and commented to his parents how much he enjoyed the *Rubaiyat* by Omar Khayyám. He was surprised by how much he enjoyed this poetry. He suspected he would be lucky to have the chance to do this relaxed reading again.[66]

Adjusting to Army Routine: West Point, 1909–1912

In 1909 a new group of ninety-three cadets, the class of 1913, replaced the recently commissioned upperclassmen. Only one year apart, Barton, now a Yearling, would get to know most of this group and stay in touch with many for the rest of his career. Alexander "Sandy" Patch, Geoffrey Keyes, and Willis Crittenberger would all command corps and leave the service as lieutenant generals. After Patch's untimely death, the War Department posthumously promoted him to full general. Charles "Pete" Corlett, Oliver Lunsford, William Schmidt, and Louis Craig all commanded divisions. Another cadet who attained the rank of major general was Henry Balding, who became a personnel officer and served as G-1 for Omar Bradley's Twelfth Army Group.

One searches the 1910 *Howitzer*, the military academy's annual yearbook, in vain for an indication that Raymond Barton was an active participant in class events during his sophomore year. He appears on none of the team lists, such as football and wrestling. Other than the class roster at the beginning of the yearbook, the only time we read a reference to Barton is when the editor lists him among the "Area Birds," those with so many demerits that year that they deserved recognition for all of the time they spent in the yard walking them off. Thirty-four members of the Yearling class, including Allen, Haislip, and Walker, achieved this unflattering achievement.[67] Recognition Day the previous year did not end the scrutiny of Barton's class by upperclassmen and faculty. By the end of November, Barton had accumulated over eighty demerits. Then, as the holiday season approached, he wrote to his parents to tell them he would not be home.[68]

Outside the routine of classes, and Barton walking the area, was the corps of cadets' participation in the Hudson-Fulton Celebration. This two-week-long event, beginning the last week in September, commemorated the three hundredth anniversary of Henry Hudson's discovery of the river that bears his name and the centennial anniversary of Robert Fulton's first successful application of the paddle steamer. It was also an opportunity for New York City to show off its place as one of the world's premier cities. On October 6, 1909, a naval parade passed West Point, where the cadets rendered a variety of salutes. The next day transports arrived, and the cadets boarded them for New York. It was Barton's first trip on a boat, and he had a wonderful time. After lunch onboard the cadets disembarked on the island's northern end and formed for the parade. They marched through the crowded streets for about seven miles, with people cheering on both sides. When they reached the end of the route, the boats were waiting again. They filed onboard, and the ship chugged up the Hudson back to West Point with everyone in the barracks by 22:30. The whole event impressed Barton, who was, by his account, able to see over seventy warships in the harbor. This trip was quite an experience for the young man from Oklahoma, who had never seen the ocean until the previous year.[69] Other activities he wrote home about included dating an upperclassman's sister, which may explain some of his demerits, and a visit by his brother, Percy, who "made a good impression on the officers here."[70] As the year went on, he struggled with his transgressions, spent some time in "confinement," and was in danger of not coming home for summer leave. Somehow, he managed to get it all sorted out and came home at the end of the year.[71]

In the fall of 1910, Barton was now a Cow and greeted the 132 plebes, the class of 1914. Among the most successful of this group was Brehon Somervell, who became the commanding general of the Army Service Forces and supervised the Pentagon's construction. His classmate, Carl Spaatz, became a pioneer aviator and would command the US Strategic Air Forces–Europe, in World War II. Both retired as four-star generals. Frank Milburn and Harold Bull, Eisenhower's G-3 (operations) during the war, became lieutenant generals. Eleven in this group left the service as major generals, including Jens Doe, James L. Bradley, John B. Anderson, and Orlando Ward, who after the war became chief of the US Army Historical Division and supervised the early stages of the official army history, generally known as the Green Books. Air Force officers included Ralph Royce and also William O. Ryan, who had the misfortune to command the 4th Fighter Command in Hawaii during the Japanese attack on December 7, 1941.

When Barton returned to West Point that year, he experienced what sociology professor Morris Massey called a "significant emotional event," which changed his attitude and determination to take his last two years seriously.[72] In the view of the cadet leadership, one of the tactical officers had overstepped his bounds and exceeded what they believed appropriate by humiliating students. In one significant case, the students observed the officer berating a sick cadet who had just returned from his brother's funeral. The last straw was to make the area birds, those walking the yard to work off demerits, march in the pouring rain, resulting in rusty weapons and ruined clothing. The new senior class leaders met secretly and decided to "silence" the officer. While the practice of silencing a cadet is well-known, especially regarding Black students, it was not common for the corps to take such action against a superior regular officer. This act, of course, was a mutiny. The superintendent convened a board of inquiry and began interviewing cadets. By the end of October, the board implicated more than fifteen men in the silencing incident, including four cadet lieutenants and the first captain. The court-martials began, and cadets disappeared from the academy or found themselves in some confinement or other punishment. The entire first class had its senior privileges withdrawn. All the other cadets received severe punishment.[73]

The experience made quite an impression on young Barton, who had just turned 21. He realized this was not an adolescent game, and challenging the system had severe consequences. Although he would still accumulate his share of demerits, he became part of the school's system. He went out for football and made the second team. Rather than eating with the other cadets, he had dinner with the team at the training table. He was now an active part of a leadership laboratory where athletes challenged themselves and each other. His first game was on November 5 against Springfield, where he played halfback. He became engrossed in international relations and attended lectures on possible war with Japan.[74] In the late winter, he joined the wrestling club. It was a relatively new sport at the academy, still in the developmental stages, and they were not yet competing with other colleges. Nevertheless, he enjoyed the training atmosphere and the activity and camaraderie.[75] He was also good at it. In March he wrote, "I threw Cook yesterday afternoon, and I am now the champion wrestler of the academy."[76] His class performance was respectable, and he now enjoyed his studies.

One of the year's significant events was the funeral of Wesley Merritt. The West Point graduate (1860), Civil War cavalryman, former West Point superintendent, and first American governor of the Philippines, had retired from the army in 1900 and chose to be buried at the academy cemetery. While important, it was a trying experience for the cadets as they stood outside for hours in the extreme cold and then had to march to the cemetery at a slow funeral pace. Everyone was frozen, and Barton wrote home, "I resolved right then not to get any northern or Alaskan service if I could help it."[77]

After Barton returned for his senior year, 273 new cadets, the largest class in West Point's history, reported to plebe camp. Fourteen more showed up after camp in August because congressmen could appoint additional cadets. This group became the most famous class in the academy's history because of the many graduates who became general officers during the Second World War. The most renowned class members include Dwight D. Eisenhower and Omar N. Bradley, who received the rare rank of five-star general. Joseph T. McNarney and James Van Fleet both became full generals. Seven others reached the rank of lieutenant general, and twenty-four others, major generals. Barton's activities and impending graduation consumed him; therefore, he says little about this large class in his letters. However, since he would cross paths with many of these officers in the future, especially Van Fleet, they were part of his long-term social memory. Junior cadets would also remember how they were treated by the upperclassmen long after they left the academy.[78]

He was now known as Tubby to all his classmates. Contrary to the modern era, it was a term of endearment, not judgment, and he would sign his name that way in correspondence to his classmates and good friends for the rest of his life. He was certainly not fat but highly fit. He was the backup halfback on the football team and managed to get into all but two of the academy's games, injuring his ankle in a November scrimmage. Nevertheless, he had enough playing time to earn his athletic letter. And for the second year in a row, he was the school's heavyweight champion wrestler and the club's captain. He was a leading advocate for making it a varsity intercollegiate sport, which it would become in 1920. The yearbook confirms the tenor of his letters home:

Off the football field no one ever saw Tubby get really mad,—no one wants to. They much prefer good natured fat men tho' they not be very fat. In spite of his easy going ways he has proven himself worthy, whether it be in playing football, walking the area, spooning, or muckering in Tom's studio. He emerged from that place with the heavy weight wrestling championship tucked under his arm and commenced

Barton's formal photograph for the 1912 *Howitzer*. US Military Academy.

to stir up interest in the sport in the Corps, with how much success remains to be seen. He is very much in evidence when the band begins to play over at Cullum. Indeed, the leader of the orchestra always looks to see if Tubby is present before he starts the ball.[79]

Barton's class ranking was sixty-eight out of the ninety-five cadets who survived the course. His best marks were in mathematics and engineering. In addition, he had a fair ability to speak and read Spanish.[80] After graduation he signed out of the post and spent some time in New York City, visiting friends before returning to Ada to start his three-month leave. Despite his dislike of cold weather, he was going to Alaska and the 30th Infantry Regiment. Classmates Ed Gorrell, Duke Edwards, and Charles Sawyer would join him that fall.[81]

Chapter 2

30th Infantry and the First World War, 1912–1919

Alaska and San Francisco, 1912–1914

After West Point Raymond spent the early part of his three-month leave visiting his sister Ann in Texas and his parents in Ada. Toward the end of his vacation, he headed west to visit his mother's family in Colorado. He spent the last days of his free time visiting one of his uncles in the mining town of Leadville, about thirty-five miles south of the modern ski resort at Vail. From there Raymond caught a train on Sunday evening, September 1, with his first stop being Salt Lake City. The following day, he took a fast train to Ogden, Utah.

From Ogden Barton headed northwest, visiting his Uncle Harry Mosher in Portland and Aunt Blanch, his mother's sister, in Tacoma. Then, along with thirty other passengers, he boarded the side-wheeled ferry *City of Seattle* on September 12. Soon after midnight the ferry pulled away and headed north into Canadian waters, sailing up the east side of Vancouver Island. Navigating the often-traveled ferry route, the vessel plodded north, weaving in and out of the dozens of large islands that characterize the continent's northwest coast. Besides the occasional village, there was little to see on either side of the water.

Second Lieutenant Raymond O. Barton while home on leave, summer 1912.
Courtesy Barton family.

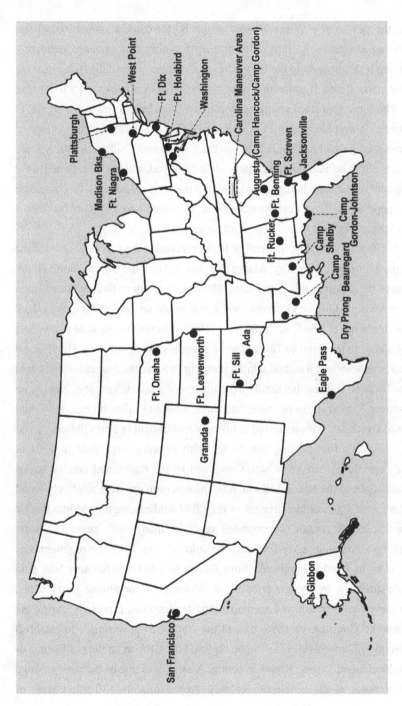

Raymond O. Barton in the United States, 1889–1963

But the views and wildlife were spectacular. Barton could see schools of whales moving alongside the ferry almost every morning and evening, apparently paying little attention to the ferry. The large number of seagulls flying near the boat amused him. If something went overboard, they all dove to try to retrieve it. The ferry continued chugging north past the Alaskan territory's capital at Juneau. It first stopped at Fort William H. Seward, located at the village of Haines on a small peninsula between the Chilkat and Chilkoot Inlets. Seward was the 30th Infantry's headquarters while deployed, and Barton reported to the adjutant in the time-honored tradition of American soldiers. As he completed the paperwork, the officer assured Barton he would love Fort Gibbon since it was one of the best places to go hunting and fishing.[1]

The following day, September 17, he reboarded the *City of Seattle* for the eight-hour trip to Skagway, Alaska. He checked into the Golden North Hotel, one of the oldest hotels in the state. The town's claim to fame was as a main port for the Klondike Goldrush, and it was made somewhat famous by Jack London's novel *The Call of the Wild* (1903). Barton had to wait a few days for a boat to take him to Tanana, so he spent his time exploring. He visited a nearby glacier and watched salmon jumping in a stream. Somehow he caught one by hand and sent his family a picture to document his exploit. Finally, on October 7, after a trip of more than three thousand miles by rail, ferry, and small riverboat, Barton arrived at his new assignment at Fort Gibbon.[2]

Barton's first posting was to the 30th Infantry, organized in 1901 at the Presidio of San Francisco. Compared to the regimental combat teams that fought in the Second World War, these regiments were relatively small units, with a peacetime strength of only 959 soldiers, organized into twelve companies. A captain commanded each company with several officers and approximately sixty-five enlisted soldiers.[3] In 1912 the regiment was on duty in Alaska. Purchased from Russia in 1867, the territory was paid little attention by the government in Washington for almost thirty years. However, gold rushes and accompanying lawlessness, especially during the Klondike Goldrush of 1896, caused the American government to establish several military installations in the region. Fort Gibbon, at the confluence of the Yukon and Tanana Rivers in central Alaska, was one of the most isolated army posts of the nineteenth century. Approximately 130 miles west of

Fairbanks, the small town of Tanana had about 350 residents, and its only link to the remainder of Alaska was by boat on the Yukon River, which froze during the winter. Even in the twenty-first century, no paved roads connect Tanana with other Alaskan towns, and visitors must travel from Fairbanks by air. The 1896 Gold Rush did not last much beyond the fort's completion and occupation in 1899. However, in addition to demonstrating federal control of central Alaska, Gibbon's importance was as a critical node of the Washington-Alaska Military Cable and Telegraph System, or WAMCATS, that passed through the post. Companies A and D, and a company from the Signal Corps, occupied this isolated facility. With Barton's arrival the post had only eleven officers.[4]

Major Leon S. Roudiez was the battalion and post commander. As a lieutenant he was the University of North Dakota's first ROTC commander from 1890 to 1894. He spoke French and was at home in an academic environment. Gibbon was certainly not that place, and Barton did not like him. Writing to his parents nine months into his tour he said, "I despise him yet military courtesy requires that I hide my feelings in all official relations with him. Thank goodness he has not much longer to stay here."[5] During World War I, Roudiez would command the 47th Infantry Regiment and serve on the 4th Infantry Division's quartermaster staff. After the war he served until 1921 as the chief trainer for the South Carolina National Guard. He then returned to Paris, working for American banks. His son, Leon Jr., became a well-known author and chair of Columbia University's French Department.[6]

Captain Halsey E. Yates, Barton's company commander, was an 1899 Military Academy graduate. His father was a railroad official and managed to have Halsey, Nebraska, named in his honor. Yates's wife, Julie, was an accomplished sculptor and studied under the great Rodin. After service with the 5th Infantry Regiment in Cuba and the Philippines, Yates returned to the academy as a military law instructor. Before arriving at Fort Gibbon, he was the commandant of cadets at the University of Nebraska.[7]

One realizes how slow early twentieth-century promotions were when among the senior company officers was Second Lieutenant Asa L. Singleton, who received a direct commission in the Philippines in 1901. An avid hunter, his exploits in the Alaskan backcountry were legendary within the regiment. Barton wrote, "Singleton had been able to go out on a two-month hunting expedition and returned with eight mountain sheep, two grizzly bears, and a bunch of caribou, more than he could carry."[8] The post surgeon was Captain Robert H. Pierson. He and his wife were good friends with his West Point roommate Sid Bingham's parents. Mrs. Bingham wrote the Piersons a long letter about how wonderful Raymond was, and when he arrived on the post, they took care of him like he was one of their own. James G. "Sunny" Ord and Delos C. "Nemo" Emmons, both from the class of 1909, were his two best friends in Company D. Ord was away on a hunting trip when Barton arrived but soon returned with two bears and a boatful of grouse.[9]

Unlike his relationship with the battalion commander, Barton and his company commander got along very well. In addition to commanding D Company, Yate's principal duty was post fire marshal. Wooden buildings, fireplaces or wood-burning stoves, and freezing weather were dangerous. The problem, especially on winter evenings, was soldiers smoking in the barracks, often also drinking hard liquor. Everyone on Fort Gibbon remembered what had happened in 1903. One morning that November, in the freezing winter of central Alaska, a fire started in a barracks occupied by D Company, 8th Infantry. No one was sure how the fire started, but the flames rapidly devoured the soldier's clothing, personal effects, and most of the unit's weapons and supplies. The only bright side to the story was the first sergeant saved the unit records that went back to before the Civil War.[10] Although it had occurred ten years earlier, the fire was still a warning to take this environment seriously. Since it needed more attention than he could spare, Yates appointed Barton as his deputy to carry out the almost daily inspections.

As the junior officer on the post, Barton's primary extra responsibility was as a mess officer, which entailed buying provisions, paying bills, and generally supervising the post mess hall. The company hired civilians as cooks, and Barton's first cook was Charlie, from China, who somehow made it to Tanana.[11] The following June Barton had to fire him since he was "too dirty for us," and he managed to get a soldier to do the cooking for a while.[12] In September he hired another cook, Fujá, who seemed to be working out. But unfortunately, as time went on, he kept getting drunk and quitting. Then he would return several days later, begging to be rehired.[13] In August 1913 Barton took leave and went on a long hunt in the Alaskan wilderness. When he returned, his extra duties increased, as one of the other junior officers departed Fort Gibbon for Letterman Hospital in San Francisco. So the new post commander, Captain John L. Bond, who received a direct commission in 1899, appointed him as the post exchange officer, a police officer, and in charge of roads and walks. He also retained his duties as fire marshal and mess officer. Soon he was also running the post library and gymnasium![14]

However, his primary role was as an infantry officer, and the unit trained hard. Then, in September 1913, he and two soldiers went on a week-long mapping expedition to chart Fort Gibbon's area. They carried their canoes, wore snowshoes, and were fully armed. Alaska was a wild country, and one never knew what dangers one might encounter.[15] The following March he wrote his family about a typical tactical exercise. In this instance he took a detachment (a sergeant, two corporals, and eight privates) out on a practice mission. He told his senior noncommissioned officer, "Our company camped last night in Fort Gibbon. It will move out on this road in ten minutes. It is reported that the enemy, consisting of one company of infantry and a detachment of cavalry, camped eight miles out on the road last night.You, Sgt. Rose, with your detachment, will form the advance guard. Move out." From the advanced guard in reconnaissance mode, the detachment changed to establishing a hasty defense in the face of the enemy. It was a good day of small unit training on skis and snowshoes.[16]

Yates liked and trusted Barton and complimented him on his professional abilities, and he thought he would be a great company commander. As a former law instructor, he also felt the young lieutenant had already shown a "peculiar fitness for detail in the Judge Advocate General's Department and on college and military duty."[17] Yates noted his excellent abilities in instructing and drilling enlisted men for the following annual report.[18] He was doing well in his first assignment.

Duty in Alaska was a great experience for a young infantry officer. He often went hunting. Sometimes it was with Yates and his wife, but usually

Barton getting ready to hunt with his childhood friend Orel Busby and future
air force four-star general Delos C. Emmons, Fort Gibbon, 1914. Courtesy
Barton family.

it was with the experienced officers Singleton, Ord, or Emmons. Sometimes he
led his soldiers out into the wilderness. Barton was not ashamed to admit that he
often got lost but had fantastic adventures. He knew he would never have taken
so many exciting trips using boats, mules, and equipment if he did not work for

the government.[19] In September 1913 he had to leave his hunting group early on one expedition. So he returned, over one hundred miles, in a canoe. He had left most of his utensils with the group, so he had to eat with his fingers. His meals on the way home were the wild game and fish he captured and then cooked over his campfire in the evening. "One of the best times I have ever had." And he told his parents that he was healthier than he had ever been. [20]

He was running the gym and still had time to wrestle and box. Unfortunately, in one case he got a black eye in a scuffle with a giant soldier from the Signal Company.[21] And despite the post's isolation, there was a social aspect to it. As one soldier's diary notes, when the troops were not working, the camp life was filled with numerous "Social Club smokers, dances, card parties, picnics, and occasional hunting trips."[22] His letters confirm that young ladies lived in town and others, usually with their parents, could visit during the summer.

Although he enjoyed his assignment, he sought new opportunities like most young officers. Barton contacted his father when the possibility of war with Mexico was looming in 1913. If the nation mobilized, he anticipated each state raising troops as it had during the Civil and Spanish-American Wars. Therefore, if that happened, he wanted his father to visit the governor and lobby on his behalf. He wanted an appointment in the Oklahoma Volunteers. He believed a rank of major or lieutenant colonel would be appropriate.[23]

Meanwhile, the aviation craze attracted Barton's classmates Ed Gorrell and Delos Emmons, who applied for the air service and probably convinced Barton to join them. However, when asked on the application if he had ever suffered from dizzy spells, he said yes. Although they were minor, the comment immediately disqualified him from a flying assignment. He appealed this action, claiming it was his statement that resulted in the disqualification, and requesting a formal medical examination. By January 1917 the War Department agreed that he was qualified to fly. However, his interest in flying waned by then, and he never received orders to report to flight school.[24]

In June 1914 Yates, Barton, and the rest of the 30th Infantry departed Alaska and moved back to the Presidio of San Francisco. It was the first time he had been on this large a post with the assembled regiment. Among the West Point classmates assembled now were Ira Wyche (1911), Charles Sawyer

(1912), Pete Corlett (1913), and Harold Bull (1914). The commander's praise for Barton continued.[25] He spent part of November 1914 at Letterman Hospital due to a sinus infection. He loved being around the nurses and being cared for like he was "just a youngster." Indeed, he enjoyed the food once he could get off his liquid diet. He had hoped to come home for a visit after taking a prisoner detail to Fort Leavenworth, but the hospitalization canceled that. While disappointed, he was excited that he would have the opportunity to sail through the Panama Canal next month on the way to their new assignment in New York.[26]

Plattsburgh and Fort Niagara, 1915–1916

In 1914, after years of building enormous naval and military establishments, the European powers went to war. Prominent Americans argued that the US Army was unprepared to battle a significant military power. They had witnessed an unprecedented scale of mobilization with France alone, the size of Texas, creating a military force of over eight million men. At the same time, the US Army and National Guard combined could muster only 301,500 soldiers, most with no training in modern war. Although few envisioned combat overseas, the prospect of war with a German-supported Mexico, or the defense of the American coast against a determined opponent, was possible. Therefore, many argued that the nation needed to develop an officer corps to lead soldiers in modern battles.[27]

This preparedness movement's most essential demand was for government-supported civilian volunteer officer training in regularly scheduled summer camps. Collectively called Plattsburgh Training Camps because of the original training location, the instruction took place at several locations across the country.[28] In 1915 almost four thousand civilians spent the summer supervised by commissioned regulars learning to be officers. The National Defense Act of 1916 expanded this program, and that year about sixteen thousand young men, mostly college students, learned the basics of leading soldiers. Ultimately, about twenty-seven thousand graduates of this program became commissioned officers and fought with the AEF in Europe.[29]

The 30th Infantry became an integral part of this program. In November 1914 the War Department alerted it for deployment to New York. On December 24 Barton, Corlett, Ord, and the rest of the regiment boarded the USAT *Buford*, a 371-foot passenger steamer that operated as part of the little-known US Army Transport Service. Rather than rail, the army's method of moving troops across the continent was by sea. The *Buford* and the fleet members had a general schedule of transporting service members and their families between New York, the Panama Canal zone, San Francisco, Alaska, Hawaii, and the Philippines. While travel by transcontinental rail would have been faster, loading troops, families, and belongings on these transports was more cost-effective. Interestingly, the *Buford* had returned the regiment from Alaska only several months before.[30]

To those alive in 1915, the Panama Canal construction was nothing short of a miracle, and now Barton would have a chance to see it firsthand. He stayed in a first-class cabin as an officer, rooming with Pete Cortlett. Altogether, twenty lieutenants from the 30th Infantry, a handful of captains, and a few majors sailed from San Francisco down the American and Mexican west coasts. This was a special trip, as the *Buford* was the first army transport through the Panama Canal, arriving at the entrance on January 7. The hot tropical weather was a shock to the Alaskan veterans. It is easy to imagine these young men, who had spent months in Alaska and just left wintery San Francisco Bay, lining *Buford*'s rails—most likely shirtless and all smoking as they did then, admiring the tropical environment as they passed through the canal and continued on to Gatun Lake, where it anchored for the night. The next morning the transport moved to Colon to unload and load several passengers. It remained for a week, and most of the officers took rooms in the relatively cool Washington Hotel. Most of the lieutenants headed to the city to enjoy its cosmopolitan atmosphere of shops and bars. Only two of the lieutenants decided not to join their comrades in the downtown excursion and remained at the hotel. As Pete Corlett noted, "The two who did not see fit to participate in these festivities were Tubby Barton and myself. The unadvertised reason we didn't join the throng was because both Tubby and I were broke."[31]

Then the ship headed across the Caribbean and past Cuba, and rode the Gulf Stream north. On January 17, 1915, their 6,210-mile journey ended as the *Buford* passed the Statue of Liberty and sailed up the Hudson to the docks at Weehawken, New Jersey. They boarded a train and headed north to Plattsburgh, New York. Plattsburgh was a good army town, and soldiers sometimes referred to it as the army's mother-in-law because of all the local ladies who married soldiers. Welcoming the regiment was eighteen inches of snow and temperatures hovering near zero.[32]

Once Barton arrived in New York, he again went on vacation and returned home to Ada to visit his parents.[33] On his way back in February, he visited Chicago, Niagara Falls, Toronto, and Montreal. While in Canada, he saw thousands of soldiers training and preparing to move overseas.[34] Plattsburgh was an old post, dating back to the War of 1812, along the shores of Lake Champlain. Barton did not particularly like it: "It is some[what] nearer to civilization and all of that, but the cold and isolation is about as bad as Alaska but without the compensation of hunting and skiing." He was now rooming with Ira Wyche, and they were getting along famously. He was dating local women, but none appeared interested in a long-term relationship with a soldier.[35]

While army histories and the classic book by J. Garry Clifford, *The Citizen Soldiers: The Plattsburg Training Camp Movement, 1913–1920*, discuss the volunteers who participated in the training camps, few mention who supervised the training in 1915.[36] Using standard army infantry drill regulations, the 30th Infantry Regiment instructed eight companies of 150 trainees each in the fundamentals of military drill. From early in the morning until late at night, they practiced the tasks of the school of the soldier, squad, and company.In addition, they underwent physical training and learned how to march and shoot. They also knew about the officer's role, which separated this course from other military training programs.[37] Among the trainees in that first class was Theodore Roosevelt Jr., son of the former president. Roosevelt most likely witnessed the dapper regular officer directing training, even if he did not know him personally.[38] Barton was doing well professionally, and his superiors recognized his performance.

At Plattsburgh Barton was still working for Yates and with most of the officers he had served with since Alaska. In addition to instructor duties, his other role was similar to what officers would call today an executive officer. The commander's principal assistant, usually the senior lieutenant, managed the organization's equipment and personnel details, and supervised the company's daily report to senior headquarters.[39] He also acquired other additional duties. In August he took on a short assignment as the 3rd Battalion's quartermaster and commissary officer, all essential for a well-run organization. He acted as camp treasurer for the second (August 10–September 6, 1915) and third (September 8–October 6, 1915) camps. Barton also began his career as a machine-gun training officer, a role he would continue for several years. He had a chance to demonstrate his leadership skills when he took temporary command of the company in October.[40]

In November, as the training in northern New York had stopped for the winter, the regiment started to stand down for leave and recovery. Barton, who had already had a vacation before arriving in Plattsburgh, headed to Fort Niagara to supervise one of the oldest military installations in North America, founded by the French in 1687. It is a beautiful location on Lake Ontario at the tip of the Niagara River on the Canadian border. The nearest town is Youngstown, and Buffalo, New York, is about thirty-five miles south. He had few operational duties on the post and was primarily the officer in charge of the post's guard force, responsible to the government for its care and security. His report for January 1916 showed that he was the only line officer assigned, with a medical corps captain acting as both the post surgeon and summary court officer. He had fifteen enlisted soldiers assigned to spend the cold winter of 1915–1916.[41] While beautiful, that region is also frigid, with temperatures often dropping below zero in the winter and the wind chill usually intensified by the lake. One wonders how he spent his time that lonely winter. Finally, just as the weather improved, he said good-bye to Fort Niagara in the middle of May. His regiment was now on orders to move to the Mexican border.[42]

Mexican Border, 1916–1917

In March 1916 a band from one prominent Mexican revolutionary faction, led by Pancho Villa, attacked Columbus, New Mexico, killing fifteen Americans. President Woodrow Wilson ordered Brigadier General John J. Pershing to organize an expedition to destroy this army and capture its leader. Unfortunately, Pershing's expedition of ten thousand or so troops accomplished little besides displaying how poorly prepared the US Army was for a European war and creating animosity among the Mexican population.[43] In May Congress passed the National Defense Act of 1917, which included provisions for a larger army. Once the act passed, Wilson sent most of the remaining regular troops to the border, mobilized another 112,000 National Guard soldiers, and also ordered them to the Rio Grande. By August the War Department's southern department had over 7,500 officers and almost 151,000 soldiers deployed along the border. By American standards this massive show of force ensured that the Mexican troops would not directly interfere with Pershing's operations. Nevertheless, it was a valuable training experience for the US Army and a warning about how unprepared the American Army of 1917 was to fight a major war.[44]

After leaving Fort Niagara in May 1916, Barton joined the 30th Infantry as it headed south to the Mexican border along with most of the regular army. Many of his comrades from the Panama Canal voyage were also on their way to the regiment's new encampment at Eagle Pass, Texas. Also at Eagle Pass that summer was James A. Van Fleet (USMA 1915), assigned to the 3rd Infantry Regiment and serving as a machine-gun platoon leader. Although neither mentioned it, Van Fleet and Barton probably crossed paths on that small post. Also nearby was his old classmate Terry de la Mesa Allen, who, after flunking out of West Point, received his commission from Catholic University and was serving with the 14th Cavalry Regiment.[45] Arriving on May 18, 1916, the 30th Infantry Regiment joined the 3rd and the new 37th Infantry Regiments to form the 1st Provisional Infantry Division.[46]

Now an experienced small-unit leader and trainer, Barton thrived in the field environment. His friend Jim Ord was commanding the machine-gun company and gave him special credit for "being able to lead parties through unknown country without guides." He also "wanted him in any command I might have."[47] Ord would soon become General Hunter Liggett's aide-de-camp. Under Pershing's direction Liggett organized and commanded the first American corps and, later, its first field army in France.[48] Barton had validated his fitness as an infantry officer and became a first lieutenant on July 1, 1916, when a vacancy opened in the 30th Infantry. His regimental commander, who approved the promotion, was Colonel Edwin A. Root, a campaign veteran in Puerto Rico in 1898 who had been commanding the 30th Infantry since July 1915. He was especially impressed by Barton's skill with the machine gun and believed he would be a superb commander of a machine-gun battalion.[49] Barton would remain working with the regiment's machine-gun company, except for a short assignment to Fort Clark, until early May 1917.[50]

The 1st Provisional Infantry Division spent its time on the border training and preparing for a war with Mexico that never came. Barton stayed with the 30th Infantry Regiment, but others, such as Pete Corlett, became advisors to the Kansas and Maryland Brigades from the National Guard. Most officers, both regular and National Guard, believed the mobilization served no strategic purpose and otherwise did little but convince the War Department that the National Guard would be ineffective in a future war.[51]

America and World War I

By April 1917 Wilson decided it was time to intervene and support Britain and France in their war against Germany. He asked Congress to declare war without considering how America could contribute to an Allied victory. Seldom has a military force been less prepared for war than the US Army that spring. Many politicians who approved the declaration had never thought through its consequences. Of course everyone knew the navy would move to the North Atlantic and begin confronting German submarines. But American troops on the European continent were another matter. Soon after the declaration, during army testimony before the Senate Finance Committee, its chairman, Senate Majority Leader Thomas S. Martin from Virginia, asked why the War Department needed so much money to fight the war. The major testifying indicated that it was for rifles, artillery, and other equipment in France. Martin exploded: "Good Lord! You're not going to send soldiers over there, are you?"[52]

Madison Barracks, May–September 1917

To increase the army's size, Congress passed the Selective Service Act on May 18, 1917. While that was an excellent first step to move young men from the civilian world into the military, it was not an appropriate way to find officers.

Immediately after the war declaration, the secretary of war used his authority under the National Defense Act of 1916 and created sixteen officer training camps nationwide. The first session went from May 15 to August 11 and the second from August 27 to November 27. There would be later sessions, but the structure and character would change later as the program progressed.[53]

The source for these future officers was America's colleges and universities. Unlike the plethora of such schools in the twenty-first century, however, less than one thousand such institutions existed in 1915. They awarded less than forty-four thousand bachelor's degrees in all fields. Schools were generally of two categories: public and private. Public universities are usually the flagship institutions of each state today, such as the University of Indiana, the University of Kansas, or the University of Connecticut. Private universities, such as Harvard, Yale, Princeton, or Stanford, are also familiar to the modern reader.[54] From this small body of elite schools, thousands of young men reacted enthusiastically, supporting the new program. The first two training camps alone produced more than forty-four thousand second lieutenants. Considering West Point's graduating class of 1917 had only 139 officers, the value of this training program is evident.[55]

Barton was off the border within days of the War Department's decision to establish this program. His almost five years of service with the 30th Infantry had ended. He stopped in Ada to visit his family and then took the train north to New York.[56] His new post was Madison Barracks, established after the War of 1812 outside Sackets Harbor. During the War of 1812, Sackets Harbor was a principal naval and military base, attacked by the British in 1813. In the postwar years, as border tensions continued and American nationalism intensified, military posts along the border remained to protect against the British and help control smuggling. In 1816 this post, named for President James Madison, was part of America's frontier defenses and the center of its military and naval activity on Lake Ontario.[57]

With the American entry into the war, the War Department began training officers to lead the rapidly expanding army. Lieutenant Colonel William R. Sample, a National Guard officer, commanded the 32nd Provisional Regiment at Madison Barracks. Like the other sixteen training centers across the country, the War Department organized it as a provisional training regiment, with nine infantry companies, two cavalry troops, three field artillery batteries, and one engineer company. Sample had responsibility for 2,500 young men learning how to be officers.[58] Based on the content of the *Plattsburg Manual*, written by two of the training program's instructors, candidates underwent a rigorous and comprehensive program comparable to modern officer candidate schools. Barton found himself supervising his eager cadets in a series of logical programs such as the school of the soldier, the school of the squad, and the company, all requiring a young officer's proficiency. Training included physical exercise, attack and defense fundamentals, running a range, signals, and first aid.[59]

On May 17 Barton took command of Company 7, 1st Training Camp, 32nd Provisional Regiment. Like everyone else Barton was ready to go that morning with his contingent of 130 officer cadets, but it was May in upstate New York. The weather became stormy, and wind and rain blew off Lake Ontario, causing a day's delay in getting the training started. But he got things operating and was an exemplary leader, according to some of his graduates.[60] In July, in the middle of the camp, the War Department promoted Barton to captain in the regular army.[61] Colonel Sample thought the new captain to be ready for battalion command and "a very satisfactory and efficient officer in all respects."[62] Madison would be a short assignment, because in August all of the camp's cadre and equipment moved across the state to Plattsburgh.[63] Most likely, the move was designed to consolidate resources.

Plattsburgh, September–November 1917

At Plattsburgh Camp Barton's new commander was Colonel Paul Wolf (USMA 1890). While not selected for command in the Spanish-American conflict, he had made his mark as a trainer of civilians.[64] He had two provisional regiments, the 17th Provisional Regiment, called the New England Regiment because of the origin of most of its cadets, and the 18th Provisional Regiment, the New York Regiment. Wolf gave Barton the command of the 1st Battalion, 17th Regiment, and designated him as a senior assistant instructor. He got along well with his regimental commander, Major George E. Goodrich, a veteran of the Spanish-American War and the Philippine Insurrection.[65]

Capt. R. O. Barton
1st Bn. 17th P. T. R.
Asst. Senior Instructor.

Captain Barton as a trainer in Plattsburgh, New York, 1917. *Plattsburger*, 1917.

Barton's battalion consisted of two training companies, "The First—in name and fact" and "The Snappy Second." The camp's yearbook for 1917, *The Plattsburger*, was similar to a college yearbook, and with good reason. Like the previous camp, these officer cadets represented the country's best and brightest young men. They attended schools like Dartmouth, Harvard, Yale, and Amherst. The tone and writing quality of the yearbook, peppered with last names such as Parkman, Abbot, Buckley, Fitzgerald, Hutchins, Dinsmore, and Putnam, reflect the solid roots of old New England. These were not typical of officer candidates but the American equivalent to the British Pals who marched to battle and infamy on the Somme in 1916, and reflected the commitment of America's best and most affluent families to the war effort.[66]

One of the reserve officers assigned to the 18th Provisional Brigade was First Lieutenant Edward J. Stackpole, son of a publisher from central Pennsylvania. After the war, where he earned a Distinguished Service Cross, a Silver Star, and three Purple Hearts, Stackpole inherited his father's company and renamed it the Military Service Publishing Company. It published many books targeted at military officers, including the famous *Army Officer's Guide*, which in 2020 was in its fifty-third edition. Stackpole himself wrote several books on the Civil War, such as *Chancellorsville* (1958), *They Met at Gettysburg* (1956), and *Sheridan in the Shenandoah: Jubal Early's Nemesis* (1961). He and Barton remained friends after they left camp.

Barton's enthusiasm for training his troops intensified as he believed he would soon lead some fine young officers in Europe. However, as the camp approached its end, he discovered it was not to be. Instead, the War Department had noted his skill as a trainer of machine-gun officers, and he was now on his way to Fort Sill, Oklahoma.

Fort Sill, November 1917–March 1918

It is difficult in this modern era to understand that the army had no centralized place to train infantry soldiers until it organized the School of Musketry at the Presidio of Monterey, California, in 1907. Lieutenant General Arthur MacArthur Jr., commander of the army's Pacific Division, was personally concerned that his troops could not practice marksmanship skills. Soon the school grew to encompass all aspects of infantry training. In 1908 Captain John H. Parker arrived, and Major George W. McIver, the commandant, instructed him to develop a program of instruction and doctrine for the machine gun. This officer was the same Parker whose Gatling gun battery broke the back of Spanish resistance on San Juan Hill on July 1, 1898.[67] Most considered him the expert on developing these new weapons, and by June 1908 he and his team published the weapon's first firing manual. Experimentation and training in these systems continued until the school closed in 1913.[68] In February 1917 the School of Musketry resumed operation at Fort Sill, a much larger post. Captain Henry E. Eames, a driving force behind the school in San Francisco, became its first commandant. It began its first sixteen-week class for noncommissioned officers, devoted to using the machine gun as part of the reopened course. In August 1917 the school became the Infantry School of Arms.[69]

Like Dwight D. Eisenhower, who would find himself training tank crews during the war, Barton was consigned by the War Department to doing the same for the machine gun. As soon as the Plattsburgh course was over in November, he was going to Fort Sill, Oklahoma. It was still early in the overseas deployment process, and Barton had not yet given up hope of seeing action. He stopped at home on the way, and the local reporter noted, "He is eager to go to France, and the chances are that within a few months, he will be promoted to the rank of major."[70] Forty-three members of the West Point Class of 1912 were on their way to join the AEF, but not him. For example, Walton H. Walker would command the 13th Machine Gun Battalion in the Saint-Mihiel and Meuse-Argonne offensives, where he earned a Silver Star.[71] While many headed to France, the War Department needed experienced instructors, and there were few with Barton's experience on the border and training civilians.

He became an assistant instructor of automatic weapons, working for Captain William B. Loughborough, and later Captain Jesse C. Drain. Drain's comments perhaps foreshadow future relationships: "[He is] considered stubborn by some but in reality is simply firm and honest in his convictions; he has plenty of initiative and ability in the subjects of machine guns and automatic arms." However, he did not particularly impress Colonel Henry E. Eames, the school commandant, who rated him below average in "Judgment and Common Sense." The enthusiastic Barton, who had now been on active duty for only five years, probably irritated the old-school Eames. The school's original commandant had received a direct commission before the Spanish American War in 1897, and the War Department had only promoted the old veteran to permanent major in July 1916.[72]

Barton enjoyed being an instructor and spent much of his time revising the machine-gun training course for the new draftees rolling through the gates of crowded Fort Sill.[73] He spent much off-duty time with his classmate Paddy Flint and his small family.[74] When Drain promoted him to senior instructor, Henry Cheadle (USMA 1913) arrived as his assistant. Cheadle had been Major General Edward Plummer's aide-de-camp while he served as an observer of operations in France. However, Pershing decided the old general (USMA 1877) was unfit for command and sent him back to Fort Sill. The War Department reduced Plummer to brigadier, and Cheadle lost his job and moved to the machine-gun school.[75] Barton's brother, Percy, had also joined the army, and the two spent time together during his assignment.[76]

In February 1918 Barton came home from Fort Sill to attend Percy's wedding. The two young soldiers had a photograph taken together in uniforms. Raymond told everyone he was looking forward to going to France.[77] However, that was not to be. Fort Sill had become crowded as the AEF's staff demanded increasing numbers of trained artillerymen and machine gunners.

Camp Hancock, March 1918–March 1919

On the west side of Augusta, Georgia, near the present location of Daniel Field and the Augusta Municipal Golf Course, the 28th (Keystone) Division, Pennsylvania National Guard, established a post named after one of their favorite sons, Winfield Scott Hancock. After the division deployed to Europe in May 1918, there was an empty facility with space for campsites, training, and firing. As a result, the War Department ordered the machine gun school to cease all training activity at Fort Sill in early June and move to the abandoned facility. By the middle of the month, the school was operating at an intense pace, preparing newly commissioned officers to command machine-gun units in Europe.[78]

Raymond and Percy at home in Ada, 1918. Last known photograph of the two
brothers. Courtesy Barton family.

Barton commanded the 3rd Group and became a temporary major. Soon after, in September 1918, he returned home to Ada to see his family and brother. He was proud of Percy and received a note from the Infantry School secretary at the end of September saying that the younger Barton was doing fine and the army had promoted him to sergeant.[79] A few days after sending an optimistic letter to his family and commenting on his pride in his brother, Percy was dead.

In what sounds like a Wild West showdown, lawyer and former Oklahoma State Senator Reuben M. Roddie shot and killed Percy in the middle of the day on October 3, 1918. The lawyer and Judge Barton had a physical encounter in the city's courtroom earlier, and witnesses indicate that Roddie threw a chair at Conway, injuring him. Another observer testified that the elder Barton found Percy, who was home on leave in his army uniform, and told him, "He [Roddie] tried to beat me up in the courtroom, and if you don't whip him, you are no son of mine." The young Barton encountered his father's assailant and may have thrown the first punch. However, Roddie was expecting the encounter and pulled out his gun, pumping three rounds into the unarmed soldier. So less than a month after his last visit and only nine months after Percy's wedding, Raymond returned for the funeral. The family buried him on October 10, just outside the city at Rosedale Cemetery. In one of the largest funerals in the area's history, over one hundred automobiles filled the procession.[80]

His brother's murder severely affected Raymond since he and Percy were incredibly close. Several months later, Percy's widow, Roby, gave birth to their daughter, Barbara.[81] Raymond took a particular interest in Barbara's upbringing and would ensure she remained a part of the Barton family. Meanwhile, the Infantry School commander sent the major a note expressing his sympathy and asking to send him "all government clothing and equipment in his possession at the time of his death."[82] Roddie's trial was an emotionally charged event that resulted in his conviction and sentencing.[83] He would later appeal his conviction.

Meanwhile, Camp Hancock became a massive training center with thousands of officers and men instructing or taking courses at any time, preparing for the next great offensive in France scheduled for early 1919.

However, the war ended in November 1918 when the German high command requested an armistice.[84] Barton's boss, Colonel Frank D. Wickham, a graduate of the University of Missouri, thought Barton to be an energetic officer who should be back with troops. The camp commander, Brigadier General Oliver Edwards, agreed with Wickham's assessment. Unfortunately, Edwards died in 1921 at 49 after an illness, most likely part of the Spanish Flu pandemic.[85]

When not on duty, Barton fell in love with this part of the country, so different from Oklahoma, Alaska, and upstate New York. He kept running into friends like Paddy Flint and many of his former cadets from Madison and Plattsburgh, who all seemed to be "hitting the ball right along."[86] By November 1918 Barton was the machine gun school's assistant commandant, and the school's commander, Lieutenant Colonel Louis A. Kunzig, noted that he "was one of the best officers I have ever come in contact with."[87] Of course, that was the problem: the leadership would not let him go while the war was on, and the demand was to continue to turn out machine gunners, anticipating the final offensive into Germany in 1919.

Camp Benning

In September 1918 the War Department ordered the various infantry schools at Fort Sill, Camp Perry, and Camp Hancock to move to Columbus, Georgia, home of the new Camp Benning. With all infantry schools now at one location, Colonel Eames continued as the commandant. With advice from the War Department, Eames named the new camp for a local personality, Confederate General Henry Lewis Benning. He wanted to develop the goodwill of the region's citizens and local chamber of commerce, a difficult task as the army confiscated land and moved out local farmers. By the end of October 1918, the contingents from Fort Sill and Camp Perry arrived at Camp Benning. In November 1918 the war ended in Europe, and everything began to change. In April 1919 the cadre from Camp Hancock, including Barton, arrived at the new post and prepared to continue instruction.[88]

Before the move Barton attended a short staff officer's course at the Army War College in November and December. Away from leadership pressures, he had time to reflect on his future. Like many officers in the postwar era, he was unsure about continuing in the army. He was very attached to his parents and concerned about how they were adjusting to Percy's death. He seriously considered resigning and attending law school to return to Ada and join his father.[89] After his course ended, he came home on leave to see his parents in January. This time the newspaper account of his visit said nothing about him wanting to get to France.[90]

Now assigned at Benning, Barton continued to labor away as the senior instructor at the school. His boss, Major Owen R. Meredith, found him "very frank in his expression of opinions as to policy in instructional and other matters. He was equally loyal in the performance of duties whether or not they were in accord with his personal views."[91] For two years he had hoped to join the troops he had trained for that last offensive in 1919, but now the war was over. Still, as one of the premier experts on the employment of machine guns, the Infantry School leadership was not about to release him until they had an acceptable replacement. So he was busy directing 2,600 trainees and 267 officers. Most of the officers were young with no practical experience.[92] He enjoyed working with his fellow officers, some he knew from West Point and others from his previous assignments. His letters home concerned Roby (Percy's widow), Barbara, and his parents. He contemplated leaving the army and returning to Ada when he thought the timing was right.[93] By June he had decided to resign "unless unforeseen things occur to change my plans."[94]

At the same time, he was working with the headquarters to change his situation and get himself to Europe. Friends from West Point were arriving at Benning, and one of them was Lieutenant Colonel Alexander (Sandy) M. Patch (USMA 1913). Patch had gone to France and commanded a machine-gun battalion in combat and then directed the AEF's machine-gun school. Because of his overseas service, he was now the Machine Gun Department's director. With enough field-grade officers at the school, Patch readily approved Barton's request. In his endorsement to the post commander, he noted, "A tour of duty overseas would certainly be of value to Major Barton in that it would afford the opportunity of a closer study of the practical operation of the war."[95]

Now the young major was on his way to join the army in Europe. Since leaving Ada eleven years earlier, the 31-year-old Barton had seen far more of the world than most of his high school classmates. Coming from a relatively warm climate, he probably never considered before leaving home in 1908 that he would spend most of his winters in the frozen environments of Alaska and northern New York. The warm winters and lush green landscape of Georgia were an appealing contrast at all times of the year. He had proven himself able to operate in the field and train soldiers and civilians on complex military tasks. With most of his peers and those from the following classes having seen combat, he feared that his prospects for the future were no longer as bright as they had been only a short time ago. Now he was off to Europe as a field-grade officer, still the place for an aspiring officer and, since the Germans had not yet signed a peace treaty, the possibility remained for him to see some action. It was also the only place in the US Army where units still conducted large-scale training with any sense of purpose. While he was glad to be going, he must have been anxious about this new phase of his life.

Chapter 3

Europe and Battalion Command, 1919–1923

November 28, 1920

Dearest Folx,

I have wonderful news for you. I am finally engaged to be married. She is an American Red Cross girl. Age 24—dark hair and eyes and of course very pretty. She hasn't set a date yet but its going to be just as quick as I can make it. January, I hope. Her name is Clare Elliott Fitz Patrick. She comes from New York.[1]

This book is not the place to refight the First World War. Barton, of course, was not there. But the US Army was, and the effects of the war would define this generation of officers. For the AEF the First World War was a humbling experience regarding preparation, performance, and results. While Pershing's command improved in every regard, the price of this education was high. In approximately six months of combat, German defenders had killed 50,300 and wounded another 198,059 American soldiers in battle—more than 41,300 casualties a month. These numbers do not include deaths from disease, suicides, or other long-term effects.[2] There is no question that professional army officers were horrified by their institutional incompetence and would spend the remainder of their careers ensuring it would not happen again.[3]

For Germany the war did not end as it anticipated. The Hohenzollern Dynasty ended with its armies in retreat, the kaiser seeking sanctuary in the Netherlands, sailors scuttling its high-seas fleet, and the nation in revolution. Almost two million of its soldiers were dead, and more than four million more were wounded, many with crippling wounds. In addition to military casualties, the new government estimated 760,000 civilians perished, primarily because of the Allied blockade. The new German government had to give up its conquests in Belgium, all its Polish territory, and its overseas empire. The defeated nation had to limit the size of its army and pay substantial reparations to the Allies. And its opponents would occupy territory along the Rhine, adding insult to their defeat.

As part of the cease-fire conditions, the German Army in France had to withdraw immediately across the Rhine and remain outside a demilitarized zone eighteen miles away from Mainz, Coblenz, and Cologne, on the east bank. On November 17, less than a week after the Armistice, the Belgian Army, which had tenaciously defended a sliver of its territory, reoccupied its ravished country and moved to the Rhine opposite Düsseldorf and would establish its headquarters in the ancient city of Aachen. At the same time, a newly formed British Army of the Rhine moved across Belgium and into Germany, establishing its center in Cologne. To the south the French Tenth Army, under General Charles Mangin, who had commanded American forces at Soissons, moved through the Rhineland and established its Rhine headquarters at Mainz. From Louis XIV to Napoleon III, French national policy sought to bring this Rhineland area, especially the Mosel Valley, under its domination. For them the Rhine was always its natural boundary. As part of this potential postwar settlement, this goal was within reach.

The original purpose of the US Army's occupation of this zone was to compel the new German government to sign the peace treaty and continue operations into Germany's heart if they refused. However, the occupation's nature changed with the acceptance of the controversial Treaty of Versailles on June 28, 1919. As a result, a smaller American unit would remain to ensure the German government fulfilled its treaty obligations. As part of that transition, the Third Army became the American Forces in Germany, commanded by Major General Henry T. Allen (USMA 1882) a Spanish-American, Philippine Insurrection, and Mexican expedition veteran. When Allen, closely connected to Pershing, arrived in Coblenz on July 8, 1919, his force was down to 110,000. However, only about half of those were combat ready, as the return of the soldiers in the AEF to the United States was well underway. Over the next several years, the general would maintain relations with the Allied force commanders and the regional German politicians. Meanwhile, the War Department continued to bring soldiers home, leaving as small a force as possible in Germany until Congress directed it to end the occupation.[4]

France Service of Supply, November–December 1919

In early July 1919, Major Barton signed out of Camp Benning.[5] We do not know if he returned to Ada to visit his family, but he probably did. After that it was off to Camp Meade, between Baltimore and Washington, DC. Meade was one of the army's "special embarkation facilities," established in 1918 to handle officers and enlisted men traveling overseas as replacements without a specific destination unit. There the troops boarded the train and headed for Hoboken, New Jersey.[6]

Barton boarded the SS *Cap Finisterre* on July 19. When the troops left after the Armistice, one officer noted, "There was no fanfare at the dock, since the excitement of war was over, and our sailing was just another maritime incident."[7] The ship itself has a fascinating history. Launched in 1911 in Hamburg, Germany, it became part of the Hamburg–South American Line. In April 1919 the German government transferred it to the United States, which used it as a troop transport. Since it only made four round-trip voyages, Barton's group may have been the last. In November the US Navy decommissioned it and gave it to the British government. The British never used it and transferred it to the Japanese, as part of the postwar reparation arrangements. Now named the *Taiyō Maru*, it became a regular part of the Japanese merchant fleet traveling the Pacific. In October 1941 it reconnoitered the route the Japanese fleet would use on December 7, ostensibly carrying the last foreign nationals in Japan to Honolulu. On November 5 the

Taiyō Maru quietly slipped out of Pearl Harbor with its spies onboard and returned to Japan.[8] In May 1942 the American submarine USS *Grenadier* sank the old *Finisterre* near Singapore.[9]

For Barton the journey itself was excellent. Unlike other troopships, this one had genuine beds, with two officers in a stateroom. Each room had a washroom with hot and cold water and a toilet. He was traveling in style. During the day he and his fellow officers studied French. His roommate was Major James C. R. Schwenck (USMA 1911), a cavalry officer who also missed the war because of instructor and staff assignments.[10] In his letter home, he described a relaxing and pleasurable voyage.[11]

After his ten-day journey, he arrived at the port of Brest in early August and signed in to Pontanézen Barracks, the primary American replacement camp in France. The command housed Barton and the other majors in the Hotel Continental. Colonel Asa Singleton, his mentor and hunting companion from the 30th Infantry days, was now chief of staff of the Brest Base Section (Section #5) and responsible for American activities from Brest along the coast to Cherbourg in Normandy.[12] Singleton's wife had just arrived from the United States and settled into her new environment. The army had assigned him a big Cadillac for his official duties. Now a senior officer, he thought it was "necessary for him to make a three-day inspection trip," and decided to take his wife and Barton along for the tour. From Brest they traveled along the coast to the resort at Dinard for the evening. The following day they crossed the bay on a ferry and stopped at the fortified harbor town of Saint-Malo, one of the base's secondary ports.[13]

Then the group played tourist and visited Le Mont-Saint-Michel, where Barton had a chance to climb the narrow street and see the abbey. Next they drove south to Rennes, Brittany's capital, where Barton remembered this was the location of Alfred Dreyfus's famous trial only twenty years earlier, and they spent the night in a good hotel. Finally the group headed southwest toward Quimper and back to the base headquarters the following day. Barton reports visiting cathedrals throughout the trip and seeing a wide array of French art. He confessed that he had little appreciation of what was food or not. But he had "seen nearly all of Brittany. It was beautiful. I know now why artists come to the coast." He admired the French peasants and marveled at their markets and hardworking way of life. He wrote extensively about how wonderful a trip it was. Barton's comments about the places he visited indicate a sincere appreciation of French life and a deep understanding of European history.[14]

On August 19 he said goodbye to Singleton and took the train to Tours with a stopover in Le Mans. His slow-traveling train jumped the tracks before arriving, and everyone had to get off and walk to the nearby station. After a few hours, they reboarded and continued to Le Mans. He spent the night at the Hôtel L'Univers in the city's center. While there he visited the cathedral and was impressed with its enormity and history. However, he didn't "care much for these cathedrals. They are all Catholic, and some sort of service is always going on. . . . The result is that I feel like I am a disturbing element and am so uncomfortable I don't see much but get right out." He commented on Roman walls and a garden dating back to Caesar's occupation. He arrived at Tours the next day, remembering that it was here that Charles Martel stopped the Moorish invasion. He also complained to his parents that the French did not drink water but consumed wine when traveling. To him the local water smelled like manure and was undrinkable. Since he could not live on wine alone, he would always carry a canteen in the future.[15]

He wanted to get to Germany and join the occupation army. But not yet, as his first assignment was at the Service of Supply headquarters. This massive organization consisted of six base areas, an intermediate logistic center at Tours, and an advanced section near the French border. In addition to the combat forces, it supported the US Army's European schools, repair organizations, and airfields. When the war ended, it was the source of supply and training for the two-million-man AEF, an unprecedented American logistics effort.[16] While making his case to the adjutant about joining the occupation force, a request came in for a field grade officer to be assigned to the Rents, Requisitions & Claim Service. But he would not remain in Tours long, as the entire Service of Supply headquarters was moving to Paris. So before the move, Tubby and five fellow officers borrowed a government car and took a day trip down to the Loire Valley. He loved the chateaux and was most impressed with the one in Chinon, where Charles VII had a historic conference with Joan of Arc in 1429. His awareness of these events is, frankly, remarkable.[17]

By September 9 he was working in Paris at the headquarters near the Arc de Triomphe on Rue de Tilsit and living at the Hôtel le Mediterranean near the Tuileries in the Twelfth Arrondissement. His duty was to oversee the claims department consisting of about three dozen civilians and a few officers. Its task was to audit and approve all claims submitted by the French against the US government. It was not a job he wanted, and he was always scheming for a way to get back to the army in the field.[18] But he took advantage of his posting and on his first Sunday in Paris, he visited Versailles. As he arrived, all the fountains erupted and remained on for an hour. "It was wonderful." Over the next few weeks, he had the chance to visit many historical places, often with his classmate Bill Wilbur. These included sights like Napoleon's Tomb, Les Invalids, Notre Dame, the top of the Eiffel Tower, and the Pantheon. He loved Paris and wrote long letters home describing his experiences and travels in incredible detail. However, while he did love the city, he was not fond of the Parisians.[19]

That fact became obvious a few weeks before he departed to a new assignment. One morning in mid-November, on the steps of the headquarters, Barton intervened in an altercation between one of his officers and a taxi driver. Unfortunately, the Frenchman made the mistake of punching the former wrestler, who hit him right back, and the driver tumbled down the stairs. He got up, still swinging, and struck a sergeant who had just emerged from the building, apparently by mistake, resulting in a few more blows. Other officers and noncommissioned officers got hold of the driver and ejected him from the headquarters. Barton emphasized that the driver was at fault when he returned with a gendarme. Both quietly departed with little recourse after measuring the American officer's determination and the crowd of soldiers standing by. The Frenchmen filed a police report, and the local American commander ran a quick investigation and buried the whole affair.[20] Soon after the incident, Barton ended his responsibilities supervising claims and prepared to sign out of his assignment. At the end of the year, as scheduled, he was on his way to Germany.[21]

Company Officer, AFG, 1919–1920

Barton's new posting was to the American Forces in Germany (AFG) in Coblenz. Dominating the city was the massive Ehrenbreitstein Fortress, resting on the site of many previous strong points that withstood or fell to sieges by Romans, Gauls, and the French. In 1918 it became the headquarters of the Third US Army and, subsequently, AFG.[22] Barton arrived in Coblenz in December 1919 and reported to Colonel Morris M. Keck, commander of the 8th Infantry Regiment. Keck began his career as an enlisted man in the Pennsylvania National Guard and joined the regular army as a second lieutenant in 1901. Although Barton did not know it then, this assignment began an association with this regiment, and later the 4th Infantry Division, that would last for the rest of his life.

At the end of 1919, the army was in a stage of severe disruption as enlisted soldiers continued to return to the United States for discharge. Officers had options of applying to remain in the service or requesting a discharge. At the same time, the War Department made decisions on the final ranks for those officers who held temporary commissions at higher grades. At this stage Barton had to give up his temporary rank of major and revert to his permanent grade of captain. So when he arrived wearing captain's bars, Keck assigned him to the regimental training school. The possibility existed that Germany would not comply with the armistice terms, and the regiment needed to prepare its soldiers for a potential resumption of combat. With troops rotating in and out of Germany, the school ensured the command remained qualified and proficient in current weapons. Naturally, Barton oversaw the automatic-arms (machine-gun) course. He ran three sessions, one each for the three battalions. Each class consisted of a group of four officers and fifty-six men. Off duty, he had few expenses, was saving money, and was benefiting from the favorable German-American currency exchange rate.[23]

The AFG maintained an aggressive athletic program to keep soldiers fit and busy. The opportunities for soldiers were many, including participation in baseball, football, wrestling, and track, among the many sports sponsored by the Young Men's Christian Association.[24] We have no record of Barton participating in or advising the football and wrestling programs. However, given his background, it is difficult to imagine him being unconcerned, especially when his soldiers competed. We know about his role in developing and maintaining the marksmanship skills of the regiment. In October 1920 Allen, the AFG commander, noted, "Out of the 3600 men of the 8th Regiment of Infantry, only three have failed to qualify in shooting. That record has probably never been surpassed in our service."[25]

The most critical competition was with the British, French, and Belgian soldiers stationed in Germany. But again, Barton's discipline and training skills paid off, and his soldiers swept the competition. He personally won a gold and a silver medal, a platoon from B Company won the platoon competition, and in the automatic rifle event, the regiment's enlisted men won most of the awards.[26] At another match later in the year, the American shooters again dominated, winning two out of three events (one-pounder, automatic, and second place [machine gun]).[27] Allen was pleased: "In the Inter-Allied shooting competition at Cologne today with the machine gun and with the rifle at snap, rapid, and slow fire, the following results were obtained: American team, 510 points; English 400; French 303; Belgian 148. The winning is all the more decisive, since it included every event."[28]

Finally, in February 1920, Keck sent him down to Captain Matthew H. Thomlinson's (USMA 1904) 1st Battalion. His commander was a veteran of combat against the Moros in the Philippines and one of Barton's instructors during his last year at West Point. Thomlinson gave him D Company, the machine-gun company, where he replaced his classmate Wade (Ham) Haislip, who moved up to the regimental staff.[29] D Company occupied the German town of Montabaur, sixteen miles east of the Rhine and on the edge of the American occupation sector. Consisting of six officers and 250 enlisted soldiers, it was the only American military force in the area. Barton and his officers lived in the town's central hotel, and he spent much of his administrative time writing letters home to concerned parents and working with the town's mayor to maintain order. He enjoyed this new assignment and did an excellent job on the large-scale AFG maneuvers near Ransbach, northeast of Montabaur.[30]

When Barton's parents began planning a trip to San Francisco in the summer of 1920, he contacted his friends to help them get around in the city. Most importantly, he told his father to contact his good friend and former commander James G. Ord, now stationed at the Presidio. He assured them when they mentioned they were "Tubby Barton's Folks, he will do the rest." Since he had struggled with money throughout his early years of service, he was proud to report to his father that he was now out of debt. He was still considering leaving the army, so not having any lingering financial obligations was essential to him. He had also received several employment offers, and while wanting to practice law with his father, he was looking into their details. Meanwhile, he continued to enjoy Germany, especially its massive strawberry harvest.[31]

Meanwhile, the 1st Battalion's commander departed, and Barton was now the most senior officer available. He was also eligible for promotion to major in the regular army, so Lieutenant Colonel Alex M. Hall, the regimental commander, assigned him as the battalion's new commander on July 18. This appointment was contingent on a successful physical examination, which Barton took in September. The medical report noted that he was 31 years old, five feet, seven inches tall, and weighed 178 pounds. Unfortunately, the examination report also had an ominous entry indicating a chronic history of hyperacidity in the stomach. Despite this problem the board cleared Barton for promotion.[32] Two months later the promotion board approved his selection, and a few days before Thanksgiving 1920, he took the oath of office as a major, regular army, with his date of rank backdated almost five months to July 1.[33]

Battalion Command, 8th Infantry Regiment, AFG, 1920–1921

Now in command and relocated to Coblenz, Barton encountered old friends and made new ones. He kept running into classmates, such as Ham Haislip, whom he succeeded at D Company, and Paddy Flint, who worked at the AFG headquarters and lived at the same Coblenzer-Hof Hotel. Also in the area was D'Alary Fechét, who seemed to rotate between assignments in Coblenz and Paris. During the war Fechét commanded a battalion of the 23rd Infantry Regiment during the fighting near Soissons in July 1918. Badly wounded during the battle, he was awarded a Distinguished Service Cross for his bravery.[34] Another highly decorated classmate at Coblenz was Gilbert R. (Doc) Cook, serving with the 8th Regiment's headquarters. In the Aisne-Marne and Meuse-Argonne offensives with the 58th Infantry Regiment, Doc's performance earned him two Silver Stars and a Croix de Guerre. Finally, Paul Mueller (USMA 1915) earned a Silver Star during the war while leading an infantry battalion in the 64th Infantry. Now he was the editor of the *AMAROC* (American Army of Occupation) *News*, the newspaper for the American soldiers in Germany.[35]

Several officers in the area would serve with Barton in later assignments. Two, Robert T. Foster (USMA 1918) and Hervey A. Tribolet, would each command the 22nd Infantry Regiment. Richard G. McKee (USMA 1918), recently back from delousing operations in Poland, would be the VII Corps chief of staff on D-Day and later command the 8th Infantry Regiment.[36] Several others in the Coblenz area deserve notice, such as the command's G-3, Colonel Jonathan M. Wainwright, who in 1942 would be forced to surrender his forces at Corregidor in the Philippines to the Japanese. Prominent in the command was Lieutenant Colonel Edmund P. Easterbrook, the chief AFG chaplain and soon to become the army's chief of chaplains. Working for Wainwright was Captain Joseph Lawton Collins (USMA 1917), the brother of James L. Collins, Pershing's former aide-de-camp. In July 1921 J. Lawton, as he preferred to be called, married Easterbrook's daughter Gladys in a ceremony in Coblenz.[37] As VII Corps commander, Collins would be Barton's boss on D-Day.

Barton commanded the 1st Battalion in Coblenz for thirty-two months (July 1920 to February 1923). This regiment looked good, trained hard, and routinely demonstrated its military skills in garrison and field events. It practiced all the time, on ranges and in company and battalion maneuvers. Soon after taking command, his battalion joined the rest of the AFG in another round of large-scale unit maneuvers. By any standard this was an effective military organization.[38] In November 1920 Colonel Walter T. Bates replaced

Hall as the regimental commander. Enlisting in Ohio in 1895, Bates was offered a direct commission in June 1898 by the 17th Infantry commander and had a solid reputation as a military leader.[39] Barton impressed the old soldier, who reported he was "a hardworking, painstaking, studious battalion commander. Can be depended upon to bring his battalion up to the highest state of efficiency. An expert with automatic rifles. Will make an excellent instructor for infantry school."[40] Of course, being an instructor again was the last assignment Barton wanted.

Clare Fitz Patrick

One constant theme in the many letters Raymond Barton wrote to his parents in the dozen years after he left home was about the women in his life. Whether they were among the parade of young ladies searching for husbands at West Point or those living near military bases in Alaska, New York, or Texas, he always had a girlfriend. He seemed pretty serious and determined to start a long relationship in some cases, but none of these lasted more than a few months. His military duties and sensitivity to living on junior officer's pay were most likely the primary reasons for these short love affairs. All of this changed in the fall of 1920. On a Wednesday morning in mid-November, Barton walked into his office near the army headquarters at Ehrenbreitstein Fortress across from Coblenz. Two American Red Cross ladies were waiting for him, seeking permission to solicit his soldiers for funds to sustain their work in Europe. Barton, of course, agreed, and they departed after a short visit. They returned Saturday morning for a more extended office call and attended the headquarters' weekly dance that night. The bachelor major and one of the ladies, Clare, danced many times. She departed the following day, leaving a thoroughly smitten Tubby Barton alone in the fortress.[41]

She was 24-year-old Clare Elliott Fitz Patrick, who grew up on Sixty-Third Street in Manhattan, New York. Her father, James, who died in 1906, had been a steamfitter, installing pipes that carried liquids and gasses in the growing urban environment. He and his wife, Frances (Fannie), were second-generation Irish, with their parents most likely arriving in the era following the Potato Famine of the late 1840s. It was a large family, with one boy (Herald) and five girls (Florence, Marie, Edna, Clare, and Helen).[42] In 1917, after the United States entered World War I, the American Red Cross went overseas with the AEF and looked for men and women to support the soldiers and civilians the war had affected. Although Clare was only 22 and her sister Helen, who everyone called Kiki, was only 17, the enthusiasm of the times prompted them to apply for service overseas. The young women had learned stenography, a critical skill in 1917 and one needed by the Red Cross. After a training program in the late summer, they participated in a grand parade of nurses and Red Cross workers down Fifth Avenue at the beginning of October. The young ladies left New York with their cohort on the French liner *SS Rochambeau* on October 20, headed for Bordeaux.[43] Clare's first assignment was with the tuberculosis bureau, working among the many French and Belgian refugees that fled the German Army. She then moved to different service posts in France and Italy. After the armistice she remained in Italy until 1920, when she returned to Paris. Her focus now was on helping children whose lives the war had so profoundly affected.[44]

After Clare's departure Barton had to see her again and took the night train to Paris Monday night. They had dinner and went to a show Tuesday evening. The following night they had dinner again, where he proposed! Over tea at the Hôtel de Crillon on the Place de la Concorde the next day, they decided to be sensible about the whole thing and not rush the process. So, along with Kiki, they had Thanksgiving dinner at Hôtel Claridge on the Champs-Élysées. After breakfast the following day, she saw him off, returning to Germany. The plan was for Clare to return to the United States and for Raymond to meet her in New York. But he was determined to see this through: "Sensible be dammed. I'm not going to let her get away from me."[45] So they talked each other out of returning to America and spent the next few weeks figuring out the bureaucratic details of getting married in Paris. As of January 23, 1921, they had not yet set a marriage date.[46]

However, Kiki's boyfriend, Doctor Robert Wynn, who worked for the Red Cross, returned from his assignment in Montenegro that evening.

Almost immediately Robert proposed. The two incredibly close sisters started planning. Clare called Raymond the next day long-distance and asked if he was happy about a double wedding on Saturday! He was ecstatic and invited his classmate D'Alary Fechét, still at the French École Supérieur (war college), to be his best man. Tubby arrived in Paris the day before the wedding, and the two couples navigated through the incredible maze of bureaucratic red tape Americans needed to get married in France. And it was expensive, costing hundreds of francs just for the appropriate permissions. Fortunately, Fechét, who spoke French well and was familiar with the system, could resolve all problems by nightfall. Like a typical French wedding, it took place in several stages. First, they went to the arrondissement's *mairie* (city hall) for the civil ceremony at eleven o'clock. Then it was off to lunch at "their favorite haunt," and then the sisters did "a little shopping." Then at five-thirty that afternoon, the two couples exchanged vows at the American Church in Paris, located on the Rue de Berri, near the Champs-Élysées. Then it was off to tea at the Le Meurice hotel, across from the Tuileries, then home to change clothes. Finally, they ended their evening at a wedding dinner at the Ritz hotel. Although Raymond and Clare had planned to travel to Spain on a honeymoon, the two spent the next three weeks getting to know each other in Paris. Then they returned to Coblenz and moved into Barton's downtown hotel room.[47]

By the spring Clare needed to return home to see her mother, who was not in the best health. When Barton's battalion began an intensive summer training program, she sailed home to visit her mother and sister in New York. Her older sister Edna was raising her son alone, so Clare wanted to spend time with her and her son, Marshall. After two months of visiting family, she was ready to return to Germany. Of course the War Department had no intention of sending her back if Major Barton was not going to remain in Germany for another year. General Allen personally sent a cable to the adjutant general in Washington, assuring him that he was keeping Barton in Coblenz and requesting that Clare get on the subsequent transport. On August 18 she boarded the USAT *Cantigny*, a relatively new troop ship, and headed to Antwerp.[48]

Pershing's Escort Battalion, 1921

The most permanent reminders of the First World War's carnage are the many cemeteries covering a swath of countryside in southern Belgium and northern France. Politically and logistically, most governments did not wish to return the massive number of dead. Municipal and regional graveyards could not accommodate the enormous influx of bodies. Commonwealth soldiers generally remained near the battles, hence the many cemeteries maintained by the Imperial (currently Commonwealth) War Graves Commission. The US government repatriated thousands, but about 30 percent remained in eight American Battlefield Monuments Commission–operated cemeteries. Even France sought to maintain their buried soldiers at the front until the deceased's mothers and daughters covertly entered the gravesites, dug up their poilu, and carried him home for regional burial. Many soldiers could not be either found or positively identified, yet their families wanted something to commemorate their loss. In response, and as a common site of remembrance, each nation brought one unidentified soldier home and buried him at a prominent location in its capital. In November 1920 unknown warriors were buried by the British government at Westminster Abby and by the French under the Arc de Triumph. The United States established the Tomb of the Unknown Soldier at Arlington National Cemetery.[49]

Allen temporarily pulled Barton out of his 8th Infantry command during the summer of 1921 and directed him to organize a ceremonial battalion to accompany General John J. Pershing when he awarded the Congressional Medal of Honor to the British and French unknowns in the fall. Allen wanted a composite task force of the best and tallest soldiers in the 5th, 8th, and 50th Infantry regiments, still assigned to AFG. Among those included were Lieutenant McKee from the 5th Infantry and Chaplain Easterbrook, Joe Collins's father-in-law.[50]

Pershing got his first look at Barton's escort battalion when he arrived in Coblenz on September 27. It was a triumphant return for the former AEF commander, and soldiers lined the streets from the rail station to the AFG commander's home. It was an impressive affair with all international commissioners, the commanders of the international forces, selected dignitaries, and the command's senior officers.[51] Although Clare probably did not notice, Barton had observed that some of the officers' ladies did not appreciate his wife's pedigree and history as a working woman. That all changed when Pershing, who had met Clare Fitz Patrick during her service with the Red Cross, encountered her at the event's receiving line. The general "stopped her for several minutes, almost breaking up the receiving line." Then, after dinner, when the dancing began, Pershing left his partner, General Allen's daughter, and headed toward the Bartons on the dance floor. He cut in and danced with her several times and, according to Barton, "would have continued if I hadn't taken her away." This display eliminated "the climbers" ill will toward Mrs. Barton, and now "they break their necks to be nice."[52]

The first award ceremony was in Paris. Early on October 2, 1921, the escort battalion arrived at the Champ de Mars railroad station (across from the Eiffel Tower) and marched down the Champs-Élysées to the École Militaire. Behind them, in sequence, came battalions from the French 6th, 7th, and 10th Infantry Divisions and the 5th Colonial Brigade. Behind the marching troops, artillery battalions from the French 13th and 22nd Regiments and 3rd Horse Group formed with all their equipment. Taking up the column's rear was a logistics train with examples of all the towed and trucked equipment needed to support an early twentieth-century army in the field. By 08:00 the parade was standing at the edge of the Place de la Concorde, the location of the French Revolution's guillotine. At 08:20 the honored guests, including Generals Pershing and Allen, members of parliament, the municipal council, and most of France's senior officers, including Marshals Foch and Petain, arrived at their reserved chairs arrayed on the south side of the Arc de Triomphe. Thanks to D'Alary Fechét, Clare Barton sat with the small contingent from the American Embassy.

At 09:00 several automobiles carrying President of the French Republic Alexandre Millerand, Minister of War Louis Barthou, and other national dignitaries drove slowly up the Champs-Élysées from the Place de la Concord. Behind them came the Republican Guard's band, playing military music and stirring the crowd lining the broad avenue. Behind them marched the assembled soldiers, led by Major Raymond O. Barton. Almost two hours later, the parade encircled the ceremony as Pershing lay the Congressional Medal of Honor on

In Clare's words, "This was taken under the Arc de Triomphe in Paris when General Pershing was decorating the tomb of the 'Inconnu Poilu' with the Congressional Medal of Honor on October 1921."

Officers of Pershing's escort battalion pose on the steps of Duke of York's Royal Military School, October 1921. Author's possession, courtesy of McKee Family.

a cushion placed at the head of the tomb of the unknown soldier on the floor of the Arc de Triomphe. Minister Barthou thanked Pershing and the United States for this gift and spoke of the friendship between the two countries.[53] After the presentation reporters quoted Allen: "Never have I seen a better-looking exhibit of foot-soldiers than this battalion." That evening at the ball, Pershing not only "congratulated Barton for his fine showing but paid special honor to Clare for her service with the Red Cross during the war."[54]

Pershing had hoped to go directly from Paris to London, but by October 8 the British government had not finished their arrangements or agreed on a final ceremony date. Therefore, Barton and the ceremonial battalion returned to Coblenz the next day.[55] But they worked out the details, and on Saturday, October 15, the escort battalion left Coblenz for Ostend and crossed the English Channel to Dover. The battalion spent its first night in Dover at the Duke of York's Royal Military School. The next day at 09:00 the contingent arrived at Victoria Station in London to the music of the Welsh Guards band. The crowd was massive, and Barton led the battalion, carrying weapons at "port arms," wearing dress uniforms and polished helmets with a large *A* for

Army of Occupation stenciled on the front. It marched a mile up a crowded
Ebury Street to a local armory. After dropping their equipment, the soldiers
moved to a drill hall, converted to a dining facility, for a meal hosted by
the Territorial Army Association.[56] Clare came to London and joined Tubby
at the Grosvenor House, where he and the other battalion officers were
billeted.[57] On October 17 the battalion accompanied Pershing to Westminster
Abby, where he placed the Congressional Medal of Honor on the British
Unknown Warrior's tomb.[58] Pershing, Allen, and Bates were happy with both
Barton's performance on this sensitive task and the fine comments the American contingent received in local and international newspapers.[59]

Battalion Command, November 1921–February 1923

After the London trip, Barton was at the top of his game. His battalion made
Allen and the command look good internationally and pleased Pershing,
which was always important. Barton now had three options: assume
command of the machine-gun battalion, retake command of the 1st Battalion,
or become the liaison officer to the Allied headquarters in Aachen. He wanted
his battalion in the 8th Infantry, and Allen gave it back to him. The Bartons
settled down to a year in Coblenz. They still lived in the Koblenzer-Hof
Hotel downtown as the new apartment homes for American soldiers were still
under construction.[60] He applied to the War Department to study Japanese in
California; however, the chief of infantry explained that it was impossible to
approve an application as long as he was overseas.[61] In January Clare made
her mother in New York happy by arranging a formal church wedding with a
Catholic chaplain from Paris. Fechét and his brigade commander, Bates, were
standing with Tubby for the ceremony this time.[62]

Professionally, he was dismayed at the declining strength of the
command and was well aware that many of the soldiers saw their training
and duties as busy work. Although he had three companies in his battalion,
the total strength was only ten officers and 259 soldiers, not enough to do
any challenging battalion-level training. Fortunately, the deutsch mark–
dollar had a favorable exchange rate, so soldiers lived well. However, he
was beginning to explore the possibilities for his next assignment. He wrote

Major Barton and wife, Clare, on a balcony of Fortress Ehrenbreitstein, Coblenz, August 1922. Courtesy Barton family.

one of his comrades from 30th Infantry days, Max Lough, now at the War Department. "I suppose you get a lot of letters like this from everyone who knows you, but that's what a feller gets from being in Washington anyhow." Barton's preferences, in order, were to study Japanese at the University of California, take the infantry course at Fort Benning, "COM [commander] of some good Tin [training] School," or command of troops on a post "(for the love of Mike, not a cantonment!)."[63]

The rumors about when he might be returning to the United States increased, and he thought he might be on the way home as early as April. French troops were starting to arrive, intending to replace the Americans

after they departed. The German citizens were unhappy about the changes
and truly liked Barton's soldiers. Meanwhile, he and Clare were living well,
and he now had a Cadillac and a driver to get him around. Thanks to Clare,
his financial affairs were in order for the first time, and he saved money.
They were also thinking about Percy's daughter and were concerned about
how his widow, Roby, brought her up. She lived near her family, who were at
least part Native American. Clare and Raymond both thought this would hurt
Barbara in the long run. He thought it best for her to live with them "before
her current surroundings make a lasting mark." He asked his parents to help
in making this take place.[64]

Barton had adjusted to his new lifestyle as a married field-grade officer
by the early summer. Allen needed him and canceled a set of orders sending
him home. They moved into the new quarters near the fortress and got a
dog, Beaucoup. Barton was competitively shooting rifles and machine guns
in matches within the American command and the other occupying forces.
Usually he earned one of the top scores. He took up golf, which he enjoyed
immensely, and they traveled. Both he and Clare went to the passion play
at Oberammergau in June. In December he spent several weeks visiting the
previous war's battlefields. Kiki and Bob arrived in Coblenz to spend the
holidays with Raymond and Clare in the fortress overlooking the Rhine. In only
one year, the rough bachelor with no long-term plans had become a married
gentleman living a life of domestic tranquility and professional satisfaction.[65]

General Allen hosted his last annual reception on New Year's Day 1923.
In the old army, this was a mandatory duty, and attendees left their calling
cards on the appropriate silver plate as a reminder they had participated.
Then, dressed up in his military best, each officer, their spouse, or another
escort passed through a receiving line. Finally, the aide or adjutant confirmed
the couple's name and relayed it to the receiving line, including Allen, Bates,
and Chaplain Easterbrook.[66] There was little time for small talk as over four
hundred officers and international guests moved through the line. Finally,
everyone stayed for the designated time and filed into the late morning, or
early afternoon, Rhenish winter.

Five days later the United States Senate voted to end the American
occupation of Germany. On January 10 Allen received a telegram from

President Warren G. Harding to bring his command home.[67] On the morning of January 24, Major Barton formed up the remaining troops of the Coblenz garrison on the grounds of Ehrenbreitstein Fortress. These included two of the 8th Regiment companies (D and M), a color guard, and the band; most of the regiment had departed Coblenz the previous week. The French Army, who would reoccupy the fortress on the American departure, provided two fifty-man detachments, each with a small band. General Allen noticed that many German citizens were crying, probably not because they were sad to see the Americans leave but because the French were replacing them. The good news for the Germans was that the Allies had decided not to destroy the fortress, as they had with others in the Rhineland. Allen argued it was a historical monument that should be left intact. A noncommissioned officer mounted the platform and lowered the flag at the appropriate time while the band played.[68]

With the colors retrieved and replaced by the French tricolor, the American troops departed the garrison. This event symbolized the departure of the last element of the AEF to leave Europe, closing out America's participation in World War I. Clare anticipated this event would become famous in the United States, but it did not. The only indication of its importance after the Americans departed was the prominent display of the flag in the secretary of war's office, opposite the Fort Sumter surrender flag. It remained until 1943, when the office relocated to the newly constructed Pentagon.[69] At the end of the ceremony, the soldiers marched out the fort's gate, returned to their quarters, and packed their belongings. The next day they moved to the train station and caught a train for the port at Bremen. The Bartons boarded the first-class cabin of the USAT *St. Mihiel,* a new ship only in service since 1920, and headed through Antwerp to Savannah, Georgia.[70]

8th Infantry Regiment, Fort Screven, Georgia, 1923

For the next six months, Barton continued to command the 1st Battalion. His assignment to Fort Screven, near Savannah, was a pleasant period professionally as he prepared for his next assignment. However, Clare's situation with her mother, sisters, and domestic support made it a period of personal turmoil.

The return to the United States got off to a bad start. Clare's mother, Francis (Fannie), was severely injured in an auto accident a week before their departure. Since their transport, the *St. Mihiel's*, last stop was in Brooklyn, Barton requested and received permission for her to remain onboard, and the transportation officer was able to adjust Clare's trip to continue to New York. The voyage across the Atlantic was fine as the senior officers and their families, including Colonel Bates and Majors Barton, Doc Cook, and Augustine Hofmann, occupied the first-class apartments. After landing in Savannah, Tubby said good-bye to Clare and moved with the battalion to his new post.[71]

Clare had only planned on staying in New York for a few weeks, but her mother's situation was precarious. For over three months, she struggled to regain her strength. She had bronchial pneumonia and was extremely close to dying. Since Clare was generally exhausted, Edna, her sister, often wrote Raymond and kept him informed on the New York situation. By late April, according to Edna, Fannie's health was improving, and Clare had become a marvelous cook, housekeeper, and the perfect nurse.[72]

The two sisters became quite close during Clare's stay in New York. Edna was her senior by four years and worked as a stenographer at a bank in the Woolworth Building. Sadly, her personal life had suffered a significant blow in 1912, when she had married another Irish New Yorker named Joseph Francis Kelly. The details of what happened next are unclear, but soon he was gone and deserted his young wife. Unfortunately, Edna was also pregnant and gave birth to a son, Marshall Holmes Kelly, in 1913. The sisters started talking about Marshall's future, with Edna working and helping to care for her mother. Growing up without a father and a with a working mother in 1920s Brooklyn was not a good prospect for the 9-year-old. So the sisters decided that Marshall would live in the stable environment Clare and Raymond offered for the near future. He was only supposed to stay for the summer, but this temporary relationship would last over a dozen years.[73]

However, the domestic complications were not over. Almost two years before leaving Coblenz, Raymond had interceded on behalf of a young

German girl, Sophie, who had worked at the casern's Salvation Army office. One of the local soldiers seduced her, promising marriage. He decided not to go through with it and then walked away. But, of course, she was now pregnant and alone. Barton hunted down the soldier's commanding officer, and they confronted him over the affair, making him pay the costs of the child's birth and subsequent medical expenses. Meanwhile, Sophie moved into the military quarters in Coblenz and became Clare's devoted housekeeper.

Once the Bartons moved back to the United States, they worked with immigration to arrange for her and the baby to join them. Finally, the official permission arrived, and Sophie and the baby sailed for the United States. They disembarked at Ellis Island in mid-April while Clare cared for her mother. And, as fate would have it, both immigrants were sick with a bad cold. Before they could be released, the baby developed a case of measles, entailing a longer delay. To make things more complicated, the immigration administrators required that the Bartons post a one-thousand-dollar bond for each new arrival. This requirement caused a flurry of letters between Edna and Raymond, and he scrambled to arrange for the needed funds. Finally, by the middle of May, the immigration officials released both, and they were in Brooklyn living with Clare. By the end of the month, the little group—Clare, Marshall, Sophie, and her baby—were on their way to Georgia.[74]

Throughout Clare's drama, Tubby had been commanding his battalion at Fort Screven on Tybee Island, sharing the post with the 8th Regiment headquarters. The remainder of the regiment, the 2nd and 3rd Battalions, occupied old Fort Moultrie, north of Charleston, South Carolina.[75] Controlling the Savannah River entrance, Fort Screven has been occupied by Spanish, British, French, Confederate, and United States forces since the seventeenth century. By the end of the American Civil War, weapons technology, especially rifled cannons, made traditional stone installations obsolete, such as nearby Fort Pulaski. In 1885 a board chaired by Secretary of War William C. Endicott developed a plan to refurbish and restore America's coastal defenses. The possibility of war with the old colonial powers Spain and Great Britain was becoming a concern to many in Washington. The Corps of Engineers identified the site at Tybee Island as an excellent location to control and protect the entrance to Savannah's port. Construction began in 1897 in a modern style almost impervious to direct naval guns and seaborne assault. Abandoned during the war, this relatively new installation, with family quarters and barracks, became a natural location to station a contingent of regular army troops.[76]

When the *St. Mihiel* docked in Savannah, the city gave the battalion a hero's welcome and threw them all a party. Bates and the other officers from headquarters stayed in the city to continue to enjoy its hospitality as Major Barton and his battalion boarded a train and moved to the abandoned post. Because he was the commander and senior officer on the island, he had a large set of quarters just off the beach. It was ironic that Clare was not there since he had all the space they could require: six rooms, a bath, a kitchen, and a butler's pantry. Besides battalion command, his most important duty was as the "police officer." As he explained to his parents, it had nothing to do with law enforcement but bringing the post up to army beautification standards. He spent much of his time off duty cleaning the home and supervising maintenance and painting crews to get it in shape for Clare's arrival.[77] The lad from Ada loved this assignment. "It is great to live on the seashore. As I sit here, I can hear the breakers roaring not over 400 yards away. This summer we can put on our bathing suits at home, go down to the beach for a swim and come to our own bathroom to wash off the salt. They say we can catch gallons of crabs practically in our front yard. Right now we can buy fresh oysters at $1.00 a gallon. Fishing and hunting are both good."[78]

Barton entered a critical time in his career and needed to find his role in the stateside army. His most important mentor in this regard was Colonel Bates, his boss for the last two years. Having worked with Barton so long, Bates reported, "I consider him the best battalion commander I have ever known."[79] The decorated Spanish-American and First World War veteran continued to work with the National Guard until he retired from the service in 1936. He died in 1956 and lies at rest in Arlington National Cemetery.[80]

Bates turned over command in March and reported to the War Department. While there he learned that West Point wanted Barton to join the faculty as a tactical officer and sent him a note about what was afoot. In many ways that was an appealing assignment. The army's most promising officers passed through the departments at this much-expanded institution. Two years earlier this group had included Courtney Hodges, Oscar Griswold, Charles Bonesteel, Jacob Devers, Wade Haislip, Omar Bradley, Leland Hobbs, Matthew Ridgway, Ernest Harmon, and, of course, J. Lawton Collins.[81] If connections were meaningful, this was the place in the army to be. But Barton wanted none of it. He had been with troops or training troops, except for his short war college course before going to Europe, since his commissioning in 1912. More than anything he wanted to attend the Command and General Staff School (CGSS) at Fort Leavenworth. Warned by Bates, Barton wrote to the chief of infantry requesting they pull him off the West Point assignment and send him to the next class. In Washington, Infantry Branch agreed, and in April it revoked his orders and detailed him to Fort Leavenworth, Kansas, instead. He was ecstatic and began preparing intellectually and physically for the demanding Leavenworth experience.[82] For the last few months, he worked for his classmate and friend Doc Cook, who served as the 8th Regiment's temporary commander. Finally, after serving on a contentious court-martial over embezzlement of government funds, Barton and his group departed Georgia in August.[83]

The three years Barton spent in Germany were essential to his life. The performance of both his 1st Battalion on maneuvers and the ranges and the escort battalion in London and Paris demonstrated that he could train and command troops. At Ehrenbreitstein castle Tubby watched experienced leaders such as Allen, Bates, and Wainwright as senior commanders, interacting with political authorities and foreign officers. His marriage to Clare, an accomplished and experienced partner, gave him the foundation and encouragement he needed to continue growing as a soldier. Family life was also becoming more complex as Raymond welcomed other members, this time Marshall, into the Barton home. He was embarking on over a dozen years as a staff officer, military instructor, and student. It was a new phase of his professional life, but one that even the most aggressive field-grade officers must endure. It was also very much about connections, and he would continue to encounter old friends from West Point, Alaska, and Plattsburgh as he moved through this career phase.

Chapter 4

Leavenworth and Omaha, 1923–1933

Omaha, Nebraska

Dear Folx,

Since April 16, I have been working almost night and day on flood
relief work. We are running on a 24-hour schedule, divided into shifts.
The chief of staff, G-4 and myself bearing the brunt of things. You see
Missouri and Arkansas are in our corps area so we have had plenty to
do and more ahead of us. Thousands of army cots, blankets, tents, etc.,
shipped, line officers, airplanes shifted about. I have had as many as
5 stenographers writing my telegrams at once.[1]

Fort Leavenworth Student, 1923–1924

If the US Military Academy at West Point molded this generation of officers,
Fort Leavenworth educated it for its role as senior commanders and staff
officers. The post was where officers who had excelled in their first decade
in the US Army assembled to meet other promising field-grade officers
and renew friendships from previous assignments. It originated before

World War I, with a small cadre of professional officers, especially J. Franklin Bell and John Morrison. With the German experience as a model, they transformed a tactical school at Fort Leavenworth into a staff college. Two schools, the School of the Line *and the* Staff College, produced a group of officers who supervised all the significant combat operations in France. The graduates who popularized the staff college educational value included George C. Marshall, Fox Connor, and Hugh Drum. In addition, the chiefs of staff of most corps and critical staff positions manned at the army and general headquarters' were all Leavenworth graduates.[2] As Pershing noted, "I declare without hesitation but for the training in General Staff duties given our officers at the Service Schools, at home before the war . . . , our successful handling of great masses of partially trained troops . . . could not have been possible."[3]

By 1921, after extensive study of the recently ended conflict, the War Department had decided to close both old schools and reconfigure them as the CGSS. The reorganized school's objective was to produce field-grade officers in "the combined use of all arms in the division and the army corps, the proper functions of commanders of divisions and army corps [and] the proper functions of general staff officers of divisions and of army corps."[4]

Barton was a member of that first class, with the new course developed by veteran officers of the last war. This new instruction program had a practical tone focusing on combat orders, tactics and techniques, command-staff logistics, troop leading, military history, and the largest of them all, tactical principles. Most important, the new Leavenworth instruction centered on division and corps tactics, two levels of command that did not formally exist in the army a decade earlier. Training methods included conferences, lectures, problems, tactical rides, and map maneuvers at the division and corps levels. The developers also realized that this group of officers would have to train a citizen army; that is why fourteen sessions focused on training methods.[5] Textbooks such as *Troop Leading: An Infantry Division in the Attack* and *Combat Orders* sought to create a shared understanding among this class on how the army, at all levels, should operate in combat.[6] Another difference from the preceding years is that these texts, with few exceptions, were prepared by American officers based on their combat experience, rather than on foreign tactics, techniques, and procedures, to guide development and operations.[7]

This new course was challenging and competitive. The training day started at 08:30 and continued until 17:00. Its intensity ensured that students had little free time during the evening and would spend almost all off-duty hours preparing for class. The means of instruction called the applicatory method had three goals: "Impart to the students the knowledge of large formation operations; provide problem-solving skills; and imbue professional confidence."[8] They were always presenting, collaborating, and studying. After dinner the students repaired to their study den to complete assignments and prepare for the next day's lessons.[9] However, in a memorandum sent to officers en route to Leavenworth, the chief of infantry reminded them, "Don't forget this one fact—IN THE LAST FOUR YEARS, NO STUDENT HAS FAILED TO GRADUATE" (capitalization in original).[10]

Although the new road between Tybee Island and Savannah was near completion, the Bartons did not yet have a car. Therefore, at the end of July 1923, they boarded the commuter train managed by the Central Georgia Railway and rode to its main passenger terminal in downtown Savannah.[11] Changing trains, the family continued to Atlanta. Next they traveled through Nashville, Memphis, and Oklahoma City, changing trains at each stop. Finally, in Oklahoma City they boarded a train run by the Oklahoma City–Ada–Atoka (OCAA) Railway for the last eighty miles to Ada. In 1923 it would have been a several-day journey, and for Clare this was a true adventure. Having grown up in New York City and lived in evergreen and relatively congested Germany and France, Oklahoma's wide-open and sparsely populated terrain must have come as a shock. It was much hotter and dustier than either coastal New York or northern Europe.

They stayed with Conway and Carrie for about two weeks. It was the first time Barton had returned home since Percy's funeral in 1918. It appears most of the trip went well, with Marshall enjoying this different, old-west environment. Clare got along very well with Carrie since the two had been exchanging letters for several years. Raymond and Conway ended the trip on a sour note, however. Toward the end of the visit, the two had an emotional talk about the future. Then, Raymond borrowed his father's car and drove to Rosedale Cemetery to visit Percy's gravesite. By his admission he was an emotional wreck by the time he returned. Conway said something, and the two strong, confident men went at it verbally. Raymond said things he seriously regretted. He truly loved and admired his father, but both men were used to getting their way, and Conway was unaccustomed to being challenged by another family member. Raymond spent the next few weeks writing to his father and mother separately, expressing his regret for arguing with his father.[12]

The Bartons returned to Oklahoma City and caught a train to Kansas City's Union Station.[13] In 1922 Kansas City, Missouri, was at the center of American intercontinental travel, and Union Station, constructed in 1914, was its hub. During World War I more than 260 trains passed through the station daily, moving soldiers from the southern and western United States to ports on the east coast. Recognizing the city's importance in the war effort, General John J. Pershing, Field Marshal Fernand Foch, Vice President Calvin Coolidge, and other international leaders broke ground on the massive Liberty Memorial on the ridge opposite the station in 1921.[14] From Union Station the Bartons traveled to the Santa Fe rail station in Leavenworth, Kansas. Then they boarded the Fort Leavenworth Rapid Transit Railway. This little rail line then carried the couple onto the installation, passing the main gate and down the west side of Grant Avenue to the small depot at the corner of Grant and Pope Avenues, where they arrived on August 23.[15]

It was a short walk to their new quarters at 228-H Doniphan Avenue, just west of the station. To the south of their apartment was Grant Polo Field, the location of several baseball fields today. The post's golf course was a bit farther south, an activity center for students and faculty. Another popular facility for after-duty events, and part of the military culture, was the officer's club. It was closer to the main post area, near the instructional buildings, and did not relocate to the golf course until 1930. Six other families shared the apartment building on Doniphan: the Johnson, Booth, Butcher, Rumbough, Tipton, and Winslow families. There is no evidence that Barton knew any of them before he arrived at the post.[16] These were nice, simple quarters. The family's furniture arrived the next day, August 24. Barton spent the first few days setting up his study den, where he would spend most of the next nine months. Meanwhile, it appeared that Sophie was losing her enthusiasm for being Clare's maid, so they told her to start working harder or pack her bags. The following month she decided Clare was too demanding and quit. Raymond found her in March, working for a family in Kansas City. Barton managed to get a few papers signed, releasing him of any responsibility for her and her child.[17]

According to his accounting, he knew at least ninety-one other classmates from previous assignments, including twelve others from the West Point class of 1912.[18] The group's alumni committee had just published a "Ten Year Book," so everyone had a pretty good picture of their peers' activities over the last decade. For example, Bill Nalle's career resembled Barton's. Although commissioned in the cavalry, he had spent most of the last decade learning about machine guns and arrived in France in early 1918 but was never in combat. Another good friend was Duke Edwards, who had been with Barton in the 30th Infantry and was his roommate in San Francisco before the long voyage through the Panama Canal. Edwards applied for and was selected to law school during the training camp and was the only judge advocate general (lawyer) officer in the course.

Paddy Flint joined Barton at Leavenworth, as did his fellow cavalry-man Henry "Huck" Flynn. Flynn spent his time in France directing traffic in Paris and escorting German prisoners before participating in the Rhineland occupation. John Kelly started with the cavalry, got assigned to the Quarter-master Corps, and then moved back to the cavalry. He never saw service in Europe. Russ Maxwell began his career with the field artillery but in 1915 was recruited to join the Ordnance Corps and had run into Barton several times in Germany. Max Sullivan spent time in the Philippines and then ended up in New York, helping to ship soldiers overseas. Bill Hobson also spent most of his last decade in the Philippines and returned to the United States in 1918, spending the last few years in South Carolina and Washington, DC. John S. "P" Wood had fought with the 3rd Division at Château-Thierry and the Saint-Mihiel offensive. Frank "Schnitz" Schneider saw combat with the 6th Infantry and the 5th Division, and T. J. Hayes saw combat with the 5th Division. As this snapshot indicates, most of his peers also missed the action, and only a few had received combat decorations. Considering his classmates' diverse records, Barton's professional fear that not getting into battle during the last war had ruined his career appeared unfounded. Jim Ord had left the Presidio of San Francisco and was now one of Tubby's classmates. He also knew two faculty members from his assignment at Coblenz: Majors Eugene Santschi Jr. (USMA 1907) and his former battalion commander, Matthew Thomlinson, now the assistant school secretary.[19]

Several future World War II senior commanders attended Fort Leavenworth as students that year. Troy H. Middleton would command the VIII Corps in France and Germany, and John P. Lucas (USMA 1911) would lead the VI Corps at Anzio Beach. George S. Patton Jr. (USMA 1909) was also a fellow student and a member of the informal association of officers connected to General Pershing.[20] When the course was over, Patton would lend his CGSS notes to another group member, Major Dwight D. Eisenhower, who later attended the 1925–26 class. Eisenhower had commanded the tank training organization in Pennsylvania and spent the war years in the United States. He was part of this group partially because of his relationship with his mentor Major General Fox Connor, who had been Pershing's G-4, or logistician. Connor was an essential leader of this association of officers in contact with Pershing and his current aide, George C. Marshall. Eisenhower worked for Connor in Panama from 1921 to 1924. James L. Collins, Joe's brother, was one of Eisenhower's Leavenworth classmates.[21] Pershing's men, especially James Collins, Fox Connor, and George Marshall, substantially influenced the army's assignments and professional development in the post–World War I era.

Barton worked hard in the course and enjoyed the challenge. His letters are full of comments about studying and attending this or that demonstration. Clare commented on it often and noted that Tubby and Marshall shared a study that was the only room in the house with natural sunshine.[22] It was the age of Henry Ford and his affordable automobiles. The officers on post embraced the new machine enthusiastically, which appeared on base almost overnight. Barton bought his first automobile: a Ford Touring Car. It had been a demonstration model, so he got a significant discount. "I have never got so much pleasure out of anything in my life."[23] In addition to the courses, it was a busy year for the Bartons. Marshall had settled in, attended school, and joined the local Boy Scout troop. His mother, Edna, came out for the

Christmas holiday and was happy with how her son had taken to living with his aunt and uncle.[24]

Reuben Roddie, Percy's killer, had appealed his conviction, with his retrial scheduled for January 1924. Tubby had secondhand evidence concerning the event and received a subpoena to appear at the trial. He wrote his dad in early January about his fears about the prosecution and that Roddie would get off. A little while later, Barton headed to Tecumseh, Oklahoma, the trial's new location. And, as he expected, the jury overturned the conviction and let Roddie go. Now free, he moved away from Ada, continued practicing law in Norman, and died in September 1943.[25] Raymond was disgusted by the verdict. He wrote his father a few days later, "Even with the obvious rottenness of that court, I was unprepared for the outcome."[26]

By the spring he was feeling better and invested in camping equipment. The family tested it at a Missouri campsite at the beginning of April and had a great time. Clare and Marshall, who were new to this, enjoyed it immensely. They drove south the last week of April and met Conway and Carrie at a campsite near Mannford, Oklahoma, west of Tulsa. In addition to spending time with his parents, Raymond had a chance to see his niece Barbara, who he loved as if she was his daughter. They did some more camping and got rained out on the way back. Taking back roads in 1924, often without good road maps, was dangerous. With over two hundred miles to go to Leavenworth, the road ran out and turned into a dirt path. With the heavy rains, it was a treacherous journey back. Nevertheless, they returned to Fort Leavenworth the night before school commenced. One element of good news was Clare and Marshall enjoyed the whole journey immensely and began planning almost immediately for another road trip.[27]

But Barton's courses kept him busy, and these distractions were on the margins of his routine of study and class. When the registrar compiled the grades, he rated 95 out of the 248 graduating officers. His school report also noted that he was qualified and recommended to command a regiment, and, not surprisingly, it suggested he would be an excellent instructor of "Machine Gun Tactics."[28] The chief of infantry was correct: all students, except two who had to withdraw because of illness, graduated from the course.[29]

Before Barton graduated, several organizations, such as Syracuse University and Staunton Military Academy, contacted the War Department and requested it assign Barton as its next professor of military science. In addition, the 8th Infantry Brigade at Fort McPherson wanted the new graduate to replace his old friend Doc Cook, the current operations officer.[30] However, nothing could happen until the War Department waited for the school commandant to publish the General Staff Eligible list. This essential qualification opened many assignments at the War Department's highest levels.[31] Somewhere in his career, probably in Germany, Barton-had met Major General George B. Duncan, the 82nd Infantry Division commander during the war's latter stages. He was now commanding the 7th Corps Area in Omaha, Nebraska. Barton was afraid West Point would try to grab him again, and he had been communicating with Duncan to get assigned to one of the universities in his region.[32] As late as June 20, graduation day, Barton had no idea what his next assignment would be, and the adjutant general in Washington told him to remain on the post, along with twenty others, until July 1. That day he got word that he was heading to Omaha to work for Duncan in his headquarters.[33]

Omaha and 7th Corps Area, 1924–1928

Once Raymond received his orders, he and Clare began the process of moving to another post. These steps included moving out and cleaning their quarters on Doniphan Avenue at Fort Leavenworth. Then the post-housing officer inspected them, ensuring they were clean enough for the following class members to move in. They also had to arrange with the post quartermaster to ship their household goods to Omaha. While this took time, Barton was impatient and ready to get to work and learn the details of being the corps' operations officer. Within two weeks he was at work and very busy. On July 31, 1924, he reported to his parents that he had already been to Missouri, Kansas, and Iowa and was leaving that night to spend four days in Des Moines. He told them he was "Well, happy & busy."[34] Clare and Marshall moved into the post's temporary housing and began looking for somewhere permanent. With the increased number of senior officers assigned to the headquarters,

Barton found no housing available, and they ultimately moved to an apartment four miles northwest of the old city.

Fort Omaha was less than sixty years old and established to support the Indian Wars campaigns of the 1860s and 1870s. During World War I it was the center for army balloon training.[35] After the war several units used it as headquarters, including the 14th Infantry Brigade, the 134th Infantry Regiment (Nebraska National Guard), and the 355th Infantry Regiment (Organized Reserve, Nebraska). When the 134th relocated to Falls City, the space was open to moving the 7th Corps Area headquarters from Fort Crook in 1922.[36] The fort is a classic nineteenth-century army post, with no walls, an extensive parade ground, officer's quarters on the rise to the west of the ground, a hospital on the north side, and an administrative building and the corps headquarters to the south. On the northern side of the officer's row is the General George Crook House, explicitly built for the Civil War and frontier general in 1879, and later used by various post commanders.[37]

The corps area was a new, large army organization. Responding to the National Defense Act of 1920, the War Department created nine of these commands. Each integrated the responsibilities of two previous agencies: the old territorial departments and the more recent World War–era zones of the interior. This headquarters had the task of planning and executing the organization, training, mobilizing, and inspecting the hundreds of regular army, National Guard, and regular army reserve units stationed within its area of responsibility. In addition, it planned and directed unit maneuvers and command-post exercises. As required by the 1920 legislation, each area corps organized and operated the summer training encampments of reserve officer training corps detachments and citizen military training units. Finally, in the era of manual records, it had administrative responsibility for maintaining all participants' personnel records. In the reorganizing peacetime army of the 1920s, these were critical command positions, second in prestige only to the army chief of staff. Each had a major general as its senior officer, who, upon mobilization, could expect to take command of a mobile army corps or field army. As expected, these organizations had large staffs, two to three hundred officers, enlisted men, and civilians, with sections tailored to the area's unique requirements.[38]

Duncan was glad to get Barton, who had a great deal of administrative experience and was a recent Leavenworth graduate, on his staff. It was an expansive command, supervising all War Department activities in North and South Dakota, Nebraska, Kansas, Minnesota, Iowa, Missouri, and Arkansas. Among his responsibilities was mobilizing all units for the Third and Sixth Armies. These included the VII Corps (7th, 34th, and 35th Divisions) and the XVII Corps (88th, 89th, and 102nd Divisions). In addition, it operated its training area for small units, ROTC cadets, and civilian training at Fort Snelling outside Minneapolis. Other ground units trained at Fort Leavenworth and Fort Riley, while the air units went to Marshall Field near Junction City, Kansas. Specific training assignments changed over the years, but the area headquarters assigned each army installation within this large region its tasks and responsibilities. These installations included twelve active army, eleven National Guard, and four organized reserve posts of various sizes.[39] Barton, the assistant chief of staff for operations (G-3 in army jargon), was Duncan's principal staff officer for planning and supervising all the organization's training and support operations.[40]

Because he was one of the few infantrymen on the post, he did not know many other officers when he arrived. But two of his Leavenworth classmates joined him on the corps area staff. De Witt C. T. Grubbs (USMA 1905), a veteran of the Moro War, was one of his class's oldest graduates and became the assistant adjutant general, and Max Murray (USA 1911) was with the 17th Infantry but working at Fort Omaha. Barton knew Murray from West Point as he did Charles Andrew King, who was nearby at Fort Crook. Also in the Omaha area was his classmate Bill Weaver. Bill had left the active army but joined the National Guard and was on the 89th Infantry Division's staff.[41]

Soon after his arrival, Barton moved into his role as operations officer for a large peacetime organization. Summer had arrived, and the command's priority was setting up and operating the Citizen Military Training Camps and ROTC summer camps scattered around the seven-state area. While the peace movement was strong in America, the military still drew the attention and participation of the region's young men. Activities involving military preparedness, the National Guard and Reserve, and veterans' affairs were popular with the local citizens. The annual civilian training camps were a

Barton family, Omaha, Nebraska, July 1924. *Clockwise from left,* Marshall
Kelly, Raymond, Clare Conway, Clare Fitzpatrick. Courtesy Barton family.

particular draw for the region. At government expense young men between
17 and 31 years old could get away and spend a month hiking, camping, exer-
cising, shooting, and practicing other skills that had declined in urbanizing
America. A month before they opened, young men had signed up for all of the
4,700 training positions available in Barton's region.[42]

In October 1924 Clare gave birth to a daughter, who they also named
Clare, with a middle name Conway, in honor of Barton's dad.[43] Her sister,
Edna, came out to help her with the baby and spend some time with her son,
Marshall. While she missed her son terribly, it was apparent the Bartons were
giving him the guidance and education she could not. She and other members
of the Fitz Patrick family were helping to defray the cost of the Bartons

hosting a teenage boy. Tubby and Clare were highly fond of the young man, who pulled his weight around the house regarding chores, so everyone was happy. Meanwhile, Edna continued to care for their mother, Francis, who worsened back in New York.[44]

In Omaha during the holidays that year, things almost got out of hand a few days before Christmas when wires on an electric lamp in the bedroom crossed and started a fire. Home electricity was still relatively new, and most modern safety standards were nonexistent. Clare briefly walked out of the room to check on her daughter and returned to find it in flames. Reme mbering her Red Cross training, she wrapped a wet towel around her head for protection and started battling the fire. By the time the fire department arrived, it was under control. The fire singed her hair, but she suffered no burns. The fire chief commended her in the Omaha paper for the "pluck and perseverance she displayed in fighting the fire."[45]

The War Department was now requiring its officers to take an annual physical. The medical officers sent the examination report directly to the post or senior commander so he could review it when it was time to write the yearly efficiency report. At the beginning of January 1925, 35-year-old Major Barton arrived at the Fort Omaha Dispensary. The report indicates he was twelve pounds overweight, having gained two pounds from the previous year. The weight standards were extremely severe, as he was just under five feet, eight inches and only 169 pounds! More concerning was his ulcer, referred to in this report as chronic gastritis. Before leaving for Europe in 1919, he had noticed these symptoms, but by 1925 he had more frequent attacks of what twenty-first-century doctors call gastroesophageal reflux disease or GERD.[46] This problem would follow him for the remainder of his career. Then, toward the end of January, his older sister, Ann, passed away in Detroit. She was only 43 years old but had not been well, having a form of epilepsy. Raymond was not close to his half-sister but had been helping her financially for several years.

Beyond the family and health issues, the Bartons enjoyed Omaha's social scene. One exciting evening in 1925 was a dinner at the Omaha Country Club. General Pershing was the guest of honor. Pershing, who had been a professor of military science and earned a law degree at the

University of Nebraska–Lincoln, was well-known to many in the Omaha area. The Bartons joined various military and civilian guests, including the governor and former governor. Most likely the Bartons had a pleasant discussion in the receiving line.[47]

Colonel Harry Eaton, Barton's outgoing chief of staff, reported that in his first year, Barton "has been very successful in coordinating the training of all components of the Army." Duncan watched him closely and noted that Barton, without previous staff experience, "has steadily developed. . . . for his age and length of service he is the most efficient officer of my acquaintance."[48] In September 1925 Barton picked up a significant additional duty as the corps area's G-1, or personnel officer, while retaining his responsibilities as G-3. It was an important event in early October when President Calvin Coolidge visited Omaha. Even in those years, a presidential visit required high security. Barton had the role of coordinating all the visit's military support. The performance and appearance of the soldiers were noted by many, including the president's official party. Duncan commended Barton for his detailed plans and staff supervision,[49] and his new chief of staff, Colonel Tenney Ross, remarked that Barton "is able to accomplish an enormous amount of staff work most efficiently." Ross was, however, concerned about his tendency to be excessively blunt with seniors and subordinates and his health, especially his problems with his digestive system.[50]

Early in 1926 Barton's new commander, Major General Benjamin A. Poore (USMA 1886), found himself on a round of dinners and meetings explaining the purpose of civilian training and ROTC programs. The anti-war and isolationist movements continued to grow, and the military officers often found themselves explaining these programs' value. As the operations officer, Barton provided the general details and statistics for his high-visibility presentations.[51]

He also found himself as a member of a court-martial that summer. It was the time of Prohibition, and drinking, even on a military reservation, was not allowed. Two captains, James Arnold and William Allen, and two women were driving on post at Fort Crook (now Offutt Air Base) on May 18 when a federal agent pulled them over. Inside he found three pints of liquor and arrested them. It became a little more complicated since the lady with Arnold was not his wife, and now divorce proceedings added to the drama. It gained much attention in the local papers because of its trifecta of military misconduct, infidelity, and illicit liquor. Once the court began its work and modified the proceedings into separate trials for each defendant, the community's prurient interests waned. The editors buried the trial's results in the back of later papers. Although the formal picture of Barton and the court looks serious, the paper reported the officers laughing behind the scenes.[52] One suspects they were not excited about enforcing this set of laws.

Meanwhile, the regular training cycle continued, and Barton was everywhere, coordinating and checking preparations for the student camps and training for active and National Guard units. He often flew by army aircraft, logging almost fifteen hours in the air as the operations officer. Aviation was still relatively primitive then, so this was an essential entry in his record.[53] But he must have enjoyed it. In July 1926 he and his pilot visited Ada on their way back from an inspection at Fort Sill. The local newspaper noted they landed perfectly in a wheat field, spent the night with his family, and headed off the following day to continue inspecting training near Fort Leavenworth.[54] We don't know what kind of aircraft he arrived in, but air corps and civil aviation regulations would eventually catch up to make such drop-in visits much more difficult.

While Tubby was at work, Clare immersed herself in the local social scene and received several flattering articles in the local newspaper. "Mrs. Barton Attractive Member of Army Circles," one article header proclaimed in the spring of 1926. Clare's spring project was working with the Women's Overseas League's national conference held in Omaha that June. This organization was one of the first to recognize and publicize the contribution of those American women who served their country overseas during the Great War.[55] Behind the scenes, however, she was often sick. Her letters often complained of colds, fevers, and fatigue.[56]

The most dramatic event of Barton's tenure as operations chief at the 7th Corps Area was the Mississippi Flood of 1927, then the most disastrous flood in American history. Heavy rains that began in August 1926 continued all winter. Water was high on the Mississippi levees by March, and more water flowed from the Missouri, Cumberland, and Ohio Rivers. The river began breaking through its saturated levees in Missouri, Mississippi, Arkansas, and Louisiana in April. At least 145 breaks occurred, flooding over twenty-six thousand square miles of land in seven states. No national organization existed to coordinate the federal response, and President Calvin Coolidge sought to do as little as possible. So he placed Herbert Hoover, his secretary of commerce, in charge of a commission. It was an apt choice since Hoover was a veteran of humanitarian operations in Europe during and after the war. The burden fell on the American Red Cross and the Army Corps of Engineers. The scale of the relief effort was massive, with over 640,000 Americans displaced.[57]

Barton supervised and coordinated day-to-day events as the operations officer for one of the five corps areas affected by the flood. By April 23, 1927, he had been working around the clock to dispatch hundreds of cooking ranges, soldiers to operate them, and twenty-five thousand tents, twenty thousand blankets, and fifteen thousand cots by fast rail to serve fifteen thousand refugees taking shelter in Arkansas. While the Red Cross did much of the groundwork, it needed the US Army to deliver tents, trucks, and food. The soldiers also erected refugee camps, established latrines, and provided power. For all of this, within his sector Barton supervised the operation.[58] Colonel Ross noted Barton's performance when it was over: "During the recent Mississippi River flood this officer worked day and night with marked efficiency, loyalty, and disregard of self. The prompt relief of refugees by these Headquarters was due in no small part to the work of this officer."[59]

In March 1927 Clare gave birth to Raymond Jr. This was a complicated birth, and she did not recover well. In addition, her mother Fannie passed away only two weeks later, removing some of the joy from this happy event. It would be a challenging year for her as her husband's constant travels and the stress of raising two babies affected her physical health. In November 1927 Tubby took time off to spend a few days in the hospital at Fort Leavenworth, having his tonsils out and receiving treatment for his GERD, which continued to plague him when he was stressed. Edna visited often, but her health was rapidly deteriorating. Again West Point asked him to join its faculty, but he turned them down and hoped to return to a troop unit.[60]

After the challenge of responding to the great flood, Barton's last year as the command's combined G-3 and G-1 was smooth sailing. They never bothered to get a replacement as a personnel officer while he was there. He was often on the move, usually flying to regional training events. In one incident he was returning from a training event at Fort Robinson in northwest Nebraska when the pilot came down with an attack of appendicitis. As sick as the pilot was, he landed the aircraft at Fort Crook, then headed home, where he collapsed and his wife had him evacuated to the hospital. Barton had no idea how sick he was and was surprised to learn the details.[61]

As the end of his tour approached, Barton continued to arrange for the annual ROTC and civilian training encampments, planning to host six camps across the region in 1928.[62] When she was well, he and Clare enjoyed the post's social life, such as the West Point Founder's Day dinner in March and a farewell dinner for departing ladies in April.[63] At another event in early June, Bill Weaver's wife hosted a bridge club luncheon.[64]

But before we move on, we should note where Barton was in his career. He had spent eight years either as a small unit leader or as an instructor of civilians and military officers in tactical military skills. He had thirty-two months of battalion command and had done it, by all accounts, exceptionally well, producing well-trained and competent soldiers. Barton had just finished thirty-six months as the operations officer for one of the most significant standing commands in the US Army. Twice he turned down assignments to West Point, where many army officers made connections useful in their later career. However, he was happy with his career so far. Now on his way back to Fort Leavenworth as an instructor, his commander, Major General Harry A. Smith, the former CGSS commandant remarked that he was "one of the best young officers I have come in contact with."[65]

CGSS Instructor, 1928–1932

In the middle of August 1928, after a short camping vacation in Minnesota, the Barton family returned through the main gate at Fort Leavenworth. They drove again down Grant Avenue to their new quarters. With the possibility of Pennsylvania Avenue in Washington, DC, no street in America has witnessed more American military officers' passage than Grant Avenue. Since 1900, almost every regular officer who attained the rank of major drove down this two-mile street that begins at the fort's main entrance. It terminates at an intersection dominated by the statue of Ulysses S. Grant, the commander in chief of the US Army at the end of the Civil War. While he may have had problems as the American president, most professional soldiers in 1898 considered him the nation's greatest general. On the way to the statue, residents and travelers had to pass Sedgwick, Reynolds, Buford, Meade, Augur, and Pope Avenues, all reminders of Union commanders who led soldiers in that bloody conflict. The academic buildings, where students and faculty worked, were an additional monument to those who ended the war. They consisted of three connected buildings on the bluffs of the Missouri River. In the center, with its large clock tower, Grant Hall is flanked east by Sherman Hall and west by Sheridan Hall.[66]

Barton, now a field-grade instructor, received much larger quarters. Their new home at 217 Meade Avenue was a brick, two-story duplex with a basement, screened porch, large kitchen and pantry, and two servant rooms. The quarters were large enough for the two young children (Clare and Raymond Jr) and a young live-in maid named Olive Meas. At army expense they had a janitor who cared for the home's heating and yard. He also polished boots and helped with the cleaning. Tubby converted one of the servant's rooms into his home office. He furnished it with a large desk and a small bed for "his loafing." Still an avid hunter, he had his guns and hunting equipment arranged just as he liked them. "That room is my joy. It has only my personal things and no one is even allowed in it without my permission." Sixteen-year-old Marshall was back in New York with his mother, Edna. She had stopped sending money to help defray her son's expenses. Living on the limited pay of an army officer compared to those living in the economic boom of the Roaring Twenties, Barton needed Edna's help defraying expenses. They resolved the problem, and Marshall returned later in the year.[67]

Like his time at West Point, the four years Barton spent as an instructor at Fort Leavenworth were among the most important of his career. As an instructor he encountered hundreds of students, many who would go on to the highest levels in America's military establishment. More important were the relationships he formed with his fellow instructors. Many, and he served with over 120 fellow majors and lieutenant colonels, he would serve with in Europe during the next war. About fifty officers, mostly majors, provided the instruction at the CGSS. When Major Barton joined the faculty in the summer of 1928, he reconnected with some of his friends, former bosses, and acquaintances on the faculty. Most important was his old comrade and a future division and corps commander, Charles "Pete" Corlett, from the 30th Infantry in Alaska, Plattsburgh, and Camp Eagle Pass. Corlett had done well during the war, working on expanding the Signal Corps and becoming its first commander in Europe. By 1918 he was a brevet lieutenant colonel and the recipient of the Distinguished Service Medal. After the war his rank reverted to major. He went to CGSS after Barton and then to the Army War College.[68] Other friends included his USMA classmate Walter "Robby" Robertson, and his old boss from Fort Sill, Jessie Drain. Those he had known in passing included Alden Strong, who had been with the AFG G-4 in Coblenz, and John Burleigh, who had been at Eagle Pass simultaneously but with the 3rd Infantry.[69]

In 1932, Barton's final year teaching, twenty-two instructors were infantry officers and a dozen were West Point graduates, with class year groups ranging between 1907 and 1917.[70] These mainly were first-class soldiers who sought out this duty at one of the best places in a peacetime army to hone their military skills. As a result, the War Department considered instructor duty at Leavenworth a critical requirement, and it is no wonder that almost half of the army's World War II corps commanders had served a tour at the school.[71] Instructors rotated in and out, about one-third each year. Corlett and Robinson would leave before Barton, but other reliable officers took their place. A significant addition was Clarence Huebner, who had risen from private to sergeant in the 18th Infantry Regiment and received a direct commission in 1916. He fought with the 1st Infantry Division at Cantigny, Soissons, Saint-Mihiel, and the Meuse-Argonne. As a result, the army awarded him two Distinguished Service Crosses, a Distinguished Service Medal, and a Silver Star.[72]

The CGSS's academic program continued to develop during Barton's three-year absence. It would be the last year of the course that Barton took and the first for the reinstatement of the two-year educational program that was in place before 1922. From a practical perspective, the faculty taught two different but related courses. The focus of both programs that year was the infantry division, which had replaced the regiment as the army's primary tactical unit. The War Department revised the AEF infantry division in 1921, making it somewhat smaller but still structured with two brigades, each with two infantry regiments and a field artillery brigade with two artillery regiments. In addition, engineers, medical service, a quartermaster, and a division air service supported these combat arms. Altogether, it contained just under twenty thousand officers and enlisted soldiers.[73]

Veterans of the last war developed the program to teach midgrade officers to manage this complex organization. Over four hundred lectures and conferences, each one-hour long, examined various topics, including tactics and techniques, command and staff, logistics, training, writing combat orders, and military history. The students practiced what they discussed in class with hands-on map maneuvers, map problems, and terrain walks, usually lasting a half or full day. When possible, the faculty pooled resources on more extensive projects by conducting them with the second-year students. History courses included lectures and historical research, most emphasizing the American Civil War. The final one-year course was intense, with schedules allowing little time for recovery or reflection. It was a challenge for not only the students but also the instructors.[74]

In his annual report, Major General Edward L. King explained that the one-year program had been too short, resulting in "some important matters had to be lightly touched upon, others omitted."[75] Now Leavenworth had returned to a two-year program. The second-year instruction program resembled the first, except its focus was on the corps and army. The 1921 reorganization created a table of organization for a corps headquarters that controlled three divisions and assigned artillery, engineers, air service, medical service, quartermaster, and special troops. This commander had about eighty thousand soldiers of all ranks. Eighteen of these headquarters existed across the country. Also, based on the army's wartime experience, the War Department created six field army headquarters, each designed to command three infantry corps and two cavalry divisions. Veterans of the early years of the previous war knew officers needed to practice, on paper and in exercises, the control and direction of these large units.[76]

Additions to this course included classes in tactical and strategical principles, logistics in a theater of operations, and military geography. The second-year instructors also introduced students to the growing role of air forces and mechanized units.[77] Research and writing were essential parts of the course. J. Lawton Collins, who passed through the second-year portion in 1932–1933, wrote at least two papers. One was pure military history: "Did the German Enveloping Maneuver through Belgium in 1914 Surprise the French General Staff?" The other was a practical application of doctrine and tactics: "The Conduct of the Secondary Attack."[78]

This course produced an impressive collection of general officers. While Barton was an instructor, Edward Almond, Jonathan Wainwright, George Stratemeyer, Charles L. Bolte, Lewis B. Hershey, and Collins, as mentioned earlier, graduated from the course. Overall, 133 of the 424 officers attending from 1930 to 1933, fully one-third, became general officers, an amazingly high percentage.[79]

In one case it was critical to Barton's career as Major J. Lawton Collins, mentioned above, who he last encountered in Coblenz, reported to Leavenworth at the beginning of Barton's final term as an instructor.[80] After Germany, from August 1921 until June 1925, Collins taught chemistry at the military academy with an elite group of instructors. Next, he attended the Infantry Company Officer's course at Fort Benning the following academic year. Then, from June to September 1926, Collins experienced the artillery captain's course at Fort Sill. Finally, in July 1927 he returned to the Infantry School and commenced teaching machine-gun tactics and techniques under the assistant commandants George C. Marshall and Joseph Stillwell.[81] Collins had a more significant relationship with Marshall than most since his brother, James, preceded him as Pershing's aide.[82]

For the previous ten years, he served only as a student, a classroom teacher on a nonmilitary topic, and a small unit instructor. He had not been in combat, had never commanded a battalion, and had never been a principal member of a large staff. Then, in August 1931, Collins arrived at the CGSS and felt qualified to criticize the school as too "cut and dried.

In many respects, they didn't have the same attitude that General Marshall had toward originality." For the rest of his career, he slighted those who taught at CGSS.[83] In one example, describing the firing of his G-3 in 1944, Collins noted, "He was so damn stereotype that you couldn't get it through his head. . . . that I was going to fight that corps in a certain way . . . no matter what Leavenworth was teaching."[84] Among the instructors for Collins's class were Barton and Huebner, who would each lead divisions under his command in 1944.

Fort Leavenworth was, and is, one of the best posts on which to live and work. While the students might have had little time to enjoy the area, the instructors had much more flexibility. Golf became one of Barton's passions, and he played with the Saint Joseph, Missouri, American Legion team in its competition with the Kansas City Legion's club. These events often included post-tournament banquets, where Barton was one of the sought-after speakers, especially toward the end of his tour.[85] Because of his Omaha experience, he was adept at speaking to regional gatherings of Army Reserve and National Guard officers, as he did in Kansas City on October 21, 1931, discussing "The Mechanics of Solving Problems."[86]

Gatherings at the officer's club and golf club were regular events for faculty members, especially when significant visitors arrived, such as West Point's superintendent, Major General William R. Smith, in January 1930.[87] And, of course, because Kansas City is relatively close to Oklahoma City, there were numerous family visits, as he and Clare did in mid-July 1929 for a small family reunion.[88] Marshall returned in the fall of 1928 and was doing well in school. Edna moved to California after Fannie's death, but her health declined. Finally, in October 1929, she asked Marshall to leave school and spend time with her. Raymond noted that he would permanently take the young lad back after her impending death. "He had become quite attached to him and missed him a lot." Edna died in November, not yet 40 years old, and Marshall accompanied her body back to New York City, where her sisters took care of her funeral. He would return to the Barton household at the end of the month.[89] He was an integral part of the family and took part in all of its outings and activities. Raymond inquired about getting him into West Point as he approached high school graduation.[90]

Barton family riding, Fort Leavenworth, Kansas, November 1932. *Left to right,*
Marshall, Raymond Jr., Clare Fitzpatrick, Clare Conway, Raymond. Courtesy
Barton family.

But it was also early in the Great Depression, and military officers faced
financial challenges like most others. Not only did their pay receive a 15
percent reduction, but they also had to endure one unpaid month a year.[91] But
in 1930 Barton somehow managed to get enough money to buy a Hupmobile
Eight. This five-passenger, eight-cylinder sedan was a classy and elegant automobile. However, the purchase disgusted Clare, who sensed they had more
critical financial obligations. She was correct; he could barely afford the fifty
dollars per month car payment, and they had to put off visiting the family in
Ada that Thanksgiving.[92]

Although he had first arrived at Fort Leavenworth in 1923 qualified as
a field-grade officer, Barton had almost none of the skills needed to operate at that level. His year as a student gave him an overview of division

activities and operations, something he had little understanding of before. His tour as a large unit assistant chief of staff, G-3, grounded him in planning and operating significant events, such as those ROTC and civilian training encampments. Responding to the flood of 1927 was his introduction to the complexity of planning where the enemy, this time the Mississippi River, has a say in the operation's outcome. His four years as an instructor at Fort Leavenworth, teaching complicated topics to some of the US Army's brightest minds, if not the nation's, was a personal education. No one in a school learns more than the teacher. He also encountered most of the US Army's most promising officers. Therefore, Tubby's almost ten years in the Midwest had transformed him from a small-unit tactical officer to someone capable of planning and directing activities at the division, corps, and army levels. Finally, he evolved as a family man, with two children and his nephew, participating in the interwar army's rhythm. He had come a long way since the company barracks at Fort Gibson and his home in Ada.

Chapter 5

Washington, Fort Benning, and Fort Screven, 1932–1940

Ever since Czechoslovakia, I have foreseen events. The march of Germany toward world domination has been a clear picture. Never have I been able to understand why the American people couldn't see that we should have gone in at the beginning. We may go in before it is too late, but I am afraid not. About 5 years hence—I at 56 and R. O. at 18 will have to do a job which I wish I could do now. Germany, if she wins, will digest the rest of Europe, regenerate their resources and manpower and will be invincible. We must go in now—but we won't, not until England and France are on the brink of defeat and that will be too late.[1]

Army War College, 1932–1933

Barton had done well enough for the War Department to select him to attend the Army War College and join the eighty-seven officers, including four Marines and six naval officers, in the class of 1933. Conducted at Washington Barracks, today's Fort McNair, it was then, as now, the highest level of professional military education.[2]

One theme of this book is that the interwar officer corps was relatively small and connected. Sometimes the common link was their shared experiences at West Point, while others stemmed from previous garrison and training assignments. Historians often ignore these noncombat connections in military biographies. However, they are crucial, as working with the same group of officers over many months or even years creates impressions that do not necessarily pass. By the end of each army school or military assignment, the officer added a new cohort of acquaintances, increasing each officer's entire circle of contacts. As officers ascended the ranks, especially in this small interwar army, these connections became more critical and reacquaintance more common. These relationships were especially true at the war college, as the War Department selected this cohort with the intent of using them as strategic war planners during their academic year and, after graduation, placing them in the most senior staff and command billets.[3]

The nation the Barton family traveled across that summer of 1932 showed the effect of two years of the Depression. It was apparent that the stock market crash of 1929 was not a normal business cycle. Most American banks were failing and shutting their doors. Millions of formerly middle-class citizens were out of work and searching for employment. In the cities homeless men and their families lived on the street. The United States had never before witnessed such an economic catastrophe of this scale, and the government had little idea of how to improve conditions. Moreover, the financial crisis had spread to Europe, especially in Germany, as the National Socialist Party and its leader, Adolf Hitler, began their ascent to national power.[4] At the personal level, living on military posts generally isolated army officers and their families from most Americans' daily struggles. But the officers were not unaffected, as they took a 15 percent pay cut and suffered one month without pay as part of President Franklin Roosevelt's cost-cutting measures. But compared to the average American, they were in good financial condition.[5]

World War I veterans were among those suffering the most. The thousands of AEF veterans camped out that June and July on the Anacostia Flats in southeast Washington, DC, reflected their plight. Out of work and hungry, they petitioned for and demanded the early payment of the bonus promised by Congress in 1924. In June 1932 the House of Representatives passed a bill allowing these advanced disbursements, which the Senate rejected. On July 28 President Herbert Hoover ordered the army to disperse the protesters. General Douglas MacArthur, the army chief of staff, took personal charge of the operation, with Major Dwight D. Eisenhower, his aide, nearby. Tanks from the 3rd Cavalry Regiment, led by Major George S. Patton Jr., helped the 12th and 16th Infantry Regiments disperse the marchers and destroy their campground. The callous performance soured many Americans' opinion of the army and, along with the Great Depression's effects, contributed to Franklin D. Roosevelt's presidential victory in November.[6] When the Barton family pulled into Washington, the Bonus March suppression results were still fresh in everyone's mind.[7]

The Barton family moved into a nice neighborhood on Twenty-Ninth Street, NW, Washington, DC. These homes were recently constructed near Woodley Park on Connecticut Avenue, just north of Rock Creek. Secretary of State Henry Stimson had an estate about a block away. The Barton's was an upscale, quiet home built in the French classical tradition on a beautiful tree-lined street. It had four bedrooms, and Tubby was overjoyed to have his own bathroom and used the large sunroom for his study. Clare, recovering from an operation earlier in the spring, was also excited to have the luxury of a General Electric refrigerator in the kitchen.[8]

Understanding the personalities attending each war college class is as important as their studies. Each cohort was a collection of old acquaintances and new introductions. They all understood they had passed through career obstacles, from the first assignment to senior field-grade challenges. Now these classmates realized that they would lead the nation's armed forces in the case of war.[9] More than likely they would serve with or under or command many in this class. As much as the class activities, the social interaction made that year important.[10]

When Barton arrived at Washington Barracks, he knew many war college classmates. Twenty-nine of the attendees were West Point graduates, six from the class of 1911, who he probably encountered over the three years they shared at the academy. In addition, as many as 150 of his classmates and acquaintances worked in Washington. His USMA roommate Sid Bingham lived only a few blocks away. His mentors from 30th Infantry days, Jim Ord and Asa Singleton, were nearby, and by the end of September, the three had already gone deep-sea fishing.[11] His war college academic work required him to visit the War Department regularly to research various topics. He told his parents, "It is mighty comfortable for me to go from office to office down there and in each one to find some old friend, usually several, who is in high position there. It's 'Tubby' and 'Bill' or 'Mucker' or 'Doc.' Not only do I get what I want easily, but it makes my contacts with the few I don't know easy."[12] The Bartons and Ords traveled to Philadelphia to watch the Army-Navy game, Barton's first since leaving West Point.[13]

From the West Point class of 1912, Ed Rose, Bird S. Dubois, and Steve Chamberlin joined him in the course. Another good friend from his early career was Harold Bull, who served with him in the 30th Infantry from 1914 to 1917.[14] Francis Brennan was one of Barton's captains in Coblenz and had traveled back to Savannah on the *St. Mihiel* in 1923. Also from AFG headquarters was Campbell Hodges, who had just completed a tour as President Herbert Hoover's military aide. Hodges would retire at the beginning of the war in 1941 and become president of Louisiana State University. Also from the Rhineland was a member of the quartermaster section, William F. Campbell, and Frank Andrews, an aviator. Andrews was an interesting character. Before the war he had married Jeannette Allen, daughter of the AFG commander Henry T. Allen. After the armistice Allen transferred the couple to Coblenz, where Andrews ran the aviation section and worked with Barton, who commanded the headquarters. Partially because of his relationship with Allen, Andrews was one of the Marshall Men and would become part of that special group.[15]

Finally, eight of Barton's fellow CGSS instructors joined him in this course: Thoburn K. Brown, Stuart Godfrey, Earl Landreth, Harold F. Nichols, Vergil Peterson, Wallace C. Philoon, Donald Robinson, and Alden G. Strong. Before class even started, Barton had interacted with about 50 percent of the majors and lieutenant colonels attending that year.[16]

Barton crossed paths with several officers that year who would contribute to the American World War II experience. One of the more senior officers in the course was Jacob L. Devers (USMA 1909). Before arriving at the school, his assignment was at the War Department on the chief of field artillery's staff. He was one of the branch's influential thinkers and helped develop the artillery doctrine for fire direction centers and centralized fire control.[17] Devers had a wide range of significant commands, ending World War II as commander of the Sixth Army Group, which landed on the French Riviera and advanced north, across the Rhine, and into Bavaria.

Another was George Kenney, who worked closely with Frank Andrews and Henry H "Hap" Arnold to develop the future Air Force framework. Kenney led the Fifth Air Force during the war, supporting Douglas MacArthur's southwest Pacific area. By coincidence, another class member was Richard K. Sutherland, who became MacArthur's chief of staff in the same period. Finally, Truman Smith was one of the more controversial class members. After several years of teaching at the Infantry School for George Marshall, he joined the war college class. After graduation Smith became an attaché in Berlin and, in 1936, accompanied the famous aviator Charles Lindbergh to Germany to inspect Luftwaffe (German Air Force) facilities. The Nazi aviators impressed Lindbergh, who later argued against the American war against Germany. As a result, many in the United States considered him anti-American and a Nazi sympathizer. Smith's relationship with Lindbergh also caused many within the service and the administration to question his dedication to the war and loyalty to the United States. Nevertheless, Marshall protected him from enemies and retained him as one of his advisors throughout the war.[18]

If the CGSS was an intensive course, the Army War College was more relaxed.[19] Some have claimed that the course was not particularly challenging or interesting and even a waste of time.[20] These were professional officers at a pivotal point in their careers. While the nation may have ignored the global dangers, these army, navy, and marine officers knew they would take the lead in a future war. It is no coincidence that fifty-three of these students later became flag officers (generals or admirals)—more than 60 percent of the class. That high rate of general officer selection would continue until the beginning of the war.[21]

The CGSS was about training majors to provide a standard way of solving problems and issuing orders across the army. In contrast, the war college focused on educating a select group, all potential general officers, to think creatively. Each class served as a research agency for the War Department, and students worked on actual war plans in a joint (in this case) army and navy environment. As historian Mark Calhoun describes in his biography of Lesley McNair, the student and faculty interaction's scale and scope made grading, in the Leavenworth model, irrelevant to these professionals involved in intense and practical discussions. They realized that the nation might call on them one day to implement the products they produced.[22]

From September until December, the class studied issues concerning the preparation for war, topics often assigned by the War Department staff. The faculty divided the students into several committees, each with a different problem. Before Christmas each group presented a staff study briefing to the entire college. Students and faculty challenged their findings and forced each committee to defend their solution. While faculty criticized and evaluated, there were no standardized solutions, as had been the case at CGSS. After the Christmas break, students returned and organized into seven staff groups. Six groups attacked one of three prewar scenarios, one taking the American perspective and the other the potential enemies'. The seventh group joined their peers at the Naval War College to continue joint war planning. In February the class transitioned into studying the conduct of war. Based on the earlier student war plans, they conducted map maneuvers, command post exercises, and professional staff rides. Students also wrote individual papers of interest to the War Department. History was a vital component of the course, and students were well-versed in the conduct of the American Civil War, the Russo-Japanese War, and the First World War.[23]

After three years as a staff officer, and three subsequent years as an instructor, Barton appears to have enjoyed his year as a student. He did well in the course, receiving positive comments for his "force, aggressiveness, self-confidence and tenacity."[24] He did not have far to go at the end of the year, as his next assignment was across town at Georgetown University as its new professor of military science.

Lieutenant Colonel Barton and his staff, Georgetown University, Reserve
Officer Training Corps detachment, 1936. James McD. Gallagher, ed.,
Ye Domesday Booke (Washington, DC: Georgetown University, 1936).

Georgetown University, 1933–1936

It was an easy transition to Georgetown since he did not need to move the
family. However, before school started, he and Clare repainted and fixed their
quarters since they would be there for several years. He also had his parents
send many of the things he had stored with them since he had anticipated
deploying somewhere after his war college course.

Many friends were still in the Washington area. Just before school started,
he joined Jim "Sonny" Ord, some of his old friends, and new acquaintances
on a week-long journey down the Chesapeake. He was part of a small flotilla
of three boats and had other friends on each. It was a great time, and he
reported to his mother that he did nothing but cruise and swim. He did not
tell her they were probably doing their share of drinking, as the Prohibition
era was coming to an end. The Bartons and Ords, who had known each other
for over twenty years, spent much time together. The two infantrymen went
hunting and fishing whenever they could get time off from work.[25]

It was an excellent time for the family. They rediscovered camping, and Raymond, Clare, and the kids would travel to many campgrounds in the Appalachian Mountains when school was out. The Civilian Conservation Corps had started repairing and improving these sites, so they were a joy for those who liked camping.[26] By 1935 Clare had recovered from the health problems plaguing her since Fort Leavenworth. Just when everything seemed fine, she fell, breaking her leg on New Year's Day 1936. She had to wear a cast for the next few months, limiting some of Barton's family travel.[27] While he enjoyed the company of his friends, friendship also had obligations. His Leavenworth classmate and fellow instructor, Oliver Allen, died from cancer. He arranged his funeral and helped his wife and family adjust to his loss.[28]

Georgetown University is one of America's oldest and most prestigious higher learning institutions, with its first term of instruction beginning in January 1792. President James Madison issued the school the nation's first federal academic charter in 1815, authorizing it to award academic degrees.[29] Its ROTC program began in 1919 before Congress approved the National Defense Act of 1920. Besides the military academy at West Point, the ROTC program was one of the few ways a young man could earn an officer's commission. In addition, Congress authorized the War Department to detail regular military personnel as instructors to support the program. With few professional advancement opportunities in the small Depression-era regular army, it was a logical place for officers and noncommissioned officers to hone their leadership and training skills. These training programs included classroom instruction, local off-site training events, and encampments operated by each Army Corps Area Command. The program proved its worth, and by the beginning of the next war, over 106,000 ROTC-trained officers from schools across the country were ready to join the active army.[30] By 1934 Georgetown was one of America's premier private universities. Barton joined the Georgetown faculty that year, replacing his USMA classmate Bill Hobson.[31]

During the academic year 1936–37, about one hundred students participated in the course. First-year students learned the basics of close-order drill and the manual of arms and ended the year learning about rifle marksmanship. During their sophomore year, the cadets began learning about tactical activities such as patrolling and scouting and began taking on squad and small-unit leader duties. The faculty offered the best of this group, about twenty students, permission to enroll in the junior class, indicating their commitment to continue this activity as part of their university experience. These juniors now assumed the role of noncommissioned officers, and their classwork was much more intensive. They studied the employment of crew-served weapons, such as machine guns, mortars, and light cannons.[32]

The cadets headed toward a six-week camp at the end of their junior year. When they returned as seniors, now acting as student officers, they commanded the detachment, supervising all drills and training activities. They studied American military history, military law, and more courses in strategy and tactics in class. Being in Washington, DC, the Georgetown ROTC detachment participated in several national-level parades and activities, such as the March 1933 inaugural parade of President Franklin D. Roosevelt, before Barton joined the faculty, and the Memorial Day parade in Baltimore in May 1934.[33]

Each year the detachment participated in a corps area military day with ceremonies for the corps area ROTC detachments and the presentation of academic and service awards. The Georgetown detachment generally did very well, such as in 1934 when Cadet Robert W. Hall distinguished himself in all aspects of the competition. Hall would later serve with the air force, command the 1st Air Commando Group in Southeast Asia, and end his career as a brigadier general, commanding the Air Photographic and Charting Service.[34] In September 1936, during Barton's tenure, the War Department listed the Georgetown detachment as a nationally distinguished program.[35] Twenty-three seniors became commissioned officers in 1936.[36]

The annual summer camp was one of the year's highlights for the faculty and the students. Before the army centralized the ROTC program in the 1980s, each corps area supervised the camp that sought to transform college students into army officers during their junior summer. The advanced camp was an experience common to ROTC students across the country. Schools within the 3rd Corps Area sent cadets to the designated training installation. During Barton's tenure, Fort Meade and Fort Washington, Maryland, alternated as training locations. The corps area commander selected one of its regimental commanders as the supervisor for the training, and each school provided the cadre to organize, plan, and conduct the training.[37]

Since so many officers served as professors of military science, the summer camp was an excellent opportunity to reconnect. The 1935 session, held at Fort Washington, was a typical experience. Barton served as assistant director of training, executive officer, and camp inspector. Major Ed Bertram, from Gettysburg College, ran the training battalion and rated all assigned officers. Unfortunately, Bertram passed away in 1942 without participating in the upcoming war. Sandy Patch, who graduated from West Point a year after Tubby, commanded the ROTC detachment at Virginia Military Institute. They were good friends; it was Patch who approved Barton's assignment to Europe in 1919. They would remain close in the 1930s and 1940s.

Greg Hoisington graduated from the academy a year before Barton. They had served together briefly at Plattsburgh Barracks, and, like Barton, he had spent the war in Georgia. He was now a professor of military science at John Hopkins. Early in the next war, he developed heart problems while at Camp Roberts, California, and was never deployed to a combat zone.[38] Carroll (Jake) Bagby, also in Hoisington's class and one of Barton's classmates at the Army War College, was the battalion executive officer.[39] By coincidence Jim Ord was now commanding the 12th Infantry Regiment and responsible for the training camp. When he had the chance, Ord took the opportunity to praise his long-time protegee's performance: "A resolute officer of great loyalty whose initiative acts as a spark plug to any detailed group of which he may be a part."[40] The camp experience highlights that this was a close army, and regular officers would encounter each other often in the years between the world wars.

As a military faculty member, Barton regularly spoke at events, such as when he accompanied Major General John L. DeWitt, the US Army's quartermaster general, to an assembly of Gold Star mothers at Arlington National Cemetery on September 24, 1933. Eight years later, following the Japanese attack on Pearl Harbor, DeWitt would recommend and supervise the relocation of over one hundred thousand Japanese Americans into relocation camps in the American West.[41]

In August 1935 the War Department promoted Barton to lieutenant colonel in the regular army.[42] He knew he could not stay in Washington longer than four years, and he began to sound out his friends in the area, such as his classmate Duke Edwards, who worked in the secretary of war's office, about his future assignment. By the following March, he was able to write his parents, "I am almost certain, although I have no orders yet, that I shall go to Fort Benning, Ga., for a two-year tour of duty when I leave here. Ft. Benning is perhaps the finest post in the Army, so we are all looking forward to a fine tour of duty there. Of course, I don't care much for leaving this job here."[43] He loved his time in Washington and always had fond memories of his time at Georgetown.

Civilian Conservation Corps, 1936–1938

In August 1936 he was back at Fort Benning, Georgia. As the most extensive military installation in the United States, Fort Benning was a hub of activity as the post expanded to accommodate the growing army and support the massive Civilian Conservation Corps (CCC). The camp had changed a great deal since Barton left in 1919. Instead of the temporary buildings and mud-caked construction sites, an enormous construction program had produced the military post familiar to most officers who passed through that facility since the beginning of World War II. While temporary buildings from the First World War remained, now most soldiers lived in solidly constructed barracks. Unlike the small, compact posts of the old regular army, such as Forts Omaha, Screven, and McPherson in Atlanta, Fort Benning was a massive, sprawling installation. It housed two entire infantry regiments, an artillery regiment, all Infantry School–related training, and, after 1932, the tank school. It was one of the best possible assignments for a senior infantry officer.[44]

The post now possessed a first-class football stadium, gymnasium, movie theater, headquarters buildings, and a school for the soldier's children. Most importantly, from Clare's perspective, it had brand-new, state-of-the-art officer's houses. The small officer's club, the hub of commissioned activity in the prewar army, was still in a small building among classroom buildings.

The new one, a much larger and more elegant facility, was almost finished and scheduled to open the following summer, becoming one the most impressive in the nation.[45]

A little more than three weeks after assuming office, on March 21, 1933, President Franklin D. Roosevelt sent a message to the US Congress asking it to authorize the CCC. Improving America's wilderness sites and trails was a secondary task but something the government could do without treading on the prerogatives of American unions. Its purpose was to, first, get the nation's idle young men back to work. Money needed to start flowing into the homes of the unemployed. Secondly, and as necessary, was to improve many American young men's physical, educational, and mental attitudes. This generation suffered psychological and physical anguish as they cowered in homes or searched far and wide for employment. Most were unfit for physical labor, and many questioned their masculinity. Getting them back into society, among groups of young men working together, could improve all aspects of their lives.[46]

Ultimately, it was one of the New Deal's most successful programs. By its end in 1942, as the Roosevelt administration changed its priorities to fighting the Germans and Japanese, over two million young men had been part of this program. This cohort of young men learned many practical skills, improved their overall health and fitness, and was mentally prepared for America's entry into the war. Many of these enrollees became noncommissioned officers in the expanding US Army.[47]

While this corps was called "civilian" and jointly managed with the Departments of Labor, Interior, and Agriculture, the War Department provided its structure and organization. The participants worked in national parks and forests, along rivers and streams, and in open fields after May 1934, when a combination of dry soil, heat, and high winds created a Dust Bowl across the central United States. They lived in camps, each containing about two hundred enrollees, the size of an infantry company. At the beginning of the program, a regular army officer commanded each camp. He had only a deputy, a first sergeant, a supply sergeant, and a cook to run each. Later, given the participants' conditions and hazardous work, they added a doctor to the organization. Also, they included an educational advisor because few could read and write. The army provided tents, organized transportation, prepared meals, and even supervised the wearing of CCC uniforms. The demand for regular officers to oversee this program in the field was beyond the 1930s army's capability, even after it closed many of its schools and nonessential programs.[48] To alleviate this shortage, the War Department initially mobilized fifteen hundred Organized Reserve Corp officers for assignment to the camps for the first time. By 1937 over 6,600 of these part-time leaders were operating camps nationwide. Since most members of this organization had little or no military experience, it had practical value in developing their leadership skills. Later, most of the regulars departed the camps, and Organized Reserves officers assumed most of these duties, supervising approximately two thousand work camps.[49]

The War Department assigned the supervision of this massive program to the corps area commanders. For example, in the southeast the 4th Corps Area based in Atlanta had responsibility for 169 camps covering most of the old Confederacy. For the corps commander, the program became more complicated when considering that he had to coordinate with eight state governors, hundreds of counties and communities, and three federal departments and their agencies, such as the Park Service and the Forest Service. Therefore, each corps area had a civilian liaison officer tasked with acting as the intermediary between the commander and the complex web of civilian bureaucracies and personalities involved in the program.[50]

As in the case of Fort Leavenworth and the Washington, DC, area, many of the officers that Barton had known during his almost twenty-eight years of service or would meet during his next decade on active duty were based at Fort Benning. One of the best sources of who was on the post is skimming the society pages of the two local papers: the *Columbus Enquirer* and the *Columbus Ledger*. These chatty articles identify local events detailing the purpose, who hosted them, and who attended.[51]

His West Point classmates assigned to Fort Benning included Ham Haislip, who gave Raymond Jr. a hunting outfit consisting of a fleece jacket, high boots, and knitted socks. Also from the class of 1912 were Frank Sibert and Albert Brown. Jim Weaver and John Lucas were friends from the 1911 class. Sandy Patch (USMA 1913) had left Virginia Military Institute and was

now on the infantry board, as was Jim Ord, who left his command with the 12th
Infantry. In addition, Barton's other mentor from the 30th Infantry in Alaska
and Brest Harbor in 1919, Colonel Asa L. Singleton, was commanding Fort
Benning's 29th Infantry Regiment. Within a few weeks of Barton's arrival,
the War Department selected Singleton for promotion and assignment as the
Infantry School's commander. By November 1936 Barton was working hard
for someone he deeply respected.[52] So far we have no evidence that the three
visited the Georgia backcountry to replicate their Alaskan hunting and fishing
exploits, but they most likely did. Other officers on post included his fellow
Leavenworth instructor Charles A. Willoughby, who would later become
Douglas MacArthur's intelligence officer.

When Barton arrived, his initial assignment was with the 24th Infantry
Regiment, essentially the command for the officers and men assigned to the
Infantry School. On November 25, 1936, the *Columbus Ledger* announced
"Barton Named to Post Staff" on its first page and lauded the return of one
of the Infantry School's "old timers."[53] In addition to acting as Singleton's
deputy and advisor, he supervised three CCC companies responsible for
road construction, bridge and dam building, and reforestation, mostly on and
around the Fort Benning installation.[54] Barton was effective and managed to
get Singleton and the army good publicity, such as when they opened a bridge
across the Upatoi Creek, making travel in the post's maneuver area much
faster.[55] His experience at the Plattsburgh Camps and the 7th Corps Area paid
off, as he now had to be the area commander's political fireman. However, the
problems were continuous as state governors fought for resources, challenged
military policies, and attempted to maintain some control over what was
happening in their territory. Moreover, since Singleton's primary role was
operating the post's training establishment, he had little time to devote to the
complex relationships that resulted from the War Department's involvement
in the CCC. Nevertheless, Singleton was pleased with Barton's performance
as he consistently rated him as a superior officer.[56]

The Bartons and Singletons were good friends and socialized often.
Singleton remained in command until August 1940. However, before he
reached his mandatory retirement, his wife, Elizabeth, passed away; she was
only 60 years old. After retirement the veteran infantry officer served as

president of a military school in New York and remarried. He did not appreciate New York and returned to Warm Springs, Georgia. However, Singleton did not last long, as he had a heart attack and died in June 1943. The old soldier and Barton's mentor from his earliest days as a young lieutenant is buried at Arlington National Cemetery.[57]

Fort Benning was a family-centered installation, and the Bartons took advantage of living in this environment. Both children were in local scout troops and enjoyed living on post. Raymond finally got Barbara, his late brother's daughter, away from her mother and out for an extended visit. She was almost 20 years old, and the family treated her like royalty. The children loved her, and his wife immersed her in the post's social scene. The children took her swimming at the local pool, and Raymond had her out riding and hunting. On one of the hunts, done in automobiles, the object was to hunt wildcats. After bagging one, the master of ceremonies presented the dead cat to the ride's guest of honor, "Miss Barbara Barton." More impressive, from Barbara's perspective, was her participation in West Point Week in early August 1937. The academy's seniors arrived for a week of tactical activities with troops in the field. In the evening there were social events, including formal teas, culminating in a dance at the officer's club. By the end of the month, she was back in Oklahoma. The family wanted her to move to Georgia permanently and attend school there, but she was hesitant. However, during West Point Week, she had met a cadet named John H. (Jack) Chambers and began corresponding. Over the next few months, the two continued to communicate, and they married after his graduation in 1938.[58]

On a more humorous note, one event that reflects the nature of the army's bureaucracy and the frugality of the period took place in November 1936. Clare was driving the family's Oldsmobile on the post behind a truck from the 29th Infantry Regiment. The army vehicle stopped at a crossing, and Clare waited. Suddenly, the driver, Private Joe McFarlin, backed up and hit Clare, not once but twice, forcing the car several feet back. When she testified to what happened after the truck pushed her back, she said she was "too frighted to do anything but stand fast and scream." Barton filed a claim against the government for twelve dollars to repair the damage caused by "a careless and negligently driven government vehicle." Rather than a simple investigation and approval or denial of payment, the post adjutant initiated a full-scale investigation with multiple officers and testimony. The board did not prepare some of the reports correctly and was ordered to rewrite them. The adjutant ordered several enlisted men present at the scene to return, at government expense, to Benning for deposition. It is difficult to determine if the Bartons ever got their reimbursement. But when considering all the effort expended on this investigation, it appears that the government wasted time and money to ensure its paperwork was in order.[59]

By June 1938 Barton may have been beginning to sour on this training experience. He was ready for a new opportunity, which most likely originated while serving at Georgetown. The military publisher, Edward Stackpole, whom Tubby knew from Plattsburgh days, approached him to see if he would like to retire from the service and join his firm as its executive editor. He took three months' leave and spent it with the company. Making only $7,200 a year as an army officer, he expected triple that amount if he resigned and went with the publisher. After careful consideration he asked the War Department to grant him one year's leave of absence to work as its military editor. Unfortunately for him, but great for the army, the adjutant general turned him down.[60] The War Department had other plans.

Fort Screven and the 8th Infantry Regiment, 1938–1940

At the end of September 1938, the War Department announced that Lieutenant Colonel Raymond O. Barton would leave Fort Benning and report to Fort Screven to command the 8th Infantry Regiment. Local newspapers, such as the *Atlanta Constitution*, extracted this information from War Department press releases and published it in its October 1 edition. Somehow in the twenty-first century, it seems quaint that newspapers took an interest in the comings and goings of relatively junior officers.

Before he left the Infantry School, he attended a four-week refresher course for senior officers. Many officers approaching the colonel's rank, such as Barton, had been away from soldiers for years. His last troop command was in 1923, fifteen years earlier, and organizations, policies, tactics, and weapons had changed during this period. This course would help shift their focus from administrative and policy issues to the nuts-and-bolts requirements of leading soldiers.[61] Among those in that group were his war college classmates Wallace Philoon and John Lucas. For the first time, he worked with Lloyd R. Fredendall, Manton S. Eddy, and Robert Eichelberger, all future corps commanders.[62]

The Bartons returned to Fort Screven on December 15, sixteen years after their last tour, and he assumed command of the installation and the regiment that day. They moved into Quarters 38 on Officer's Row. These fourteen homes overlooked the Atlantic Ocean and must have seemed like paradise to any officers who remembered duty on the plains, in Alaska, or on the Canadian border. The bachelor officers' quarters and the post officers' club were at the southern end of this street. The commander's house was near the south end of this complex. It was a two-story framed structure with a spacious hall, four bedrooms, and five baths, designed to provide adequate ventilation during the summer. These were, and are, beautiful homes with large front porches on two levels that families could enjoy for most of the year. The regimental headquarters building was at the northern end of this street. Behind this strip was the standard parade field for training and reviewing troops. Locals credit much of the fort's beauty to George C. Marshall's short tour as commander in 1933. According to the historic register nomination, "Many of the landscape additions to the fort made under Marshall's command remain. The colonel liked crepe myrtle and, as a result, it appears throughout the fort and surrounds the commandant's quarters on Officers Row."[63] Not far from Savannah, on the warm Atlantic Ocean, it was one of the best places for soldiers to serve in the interwar army.[64]

Joining the Bartons on Christmas Eve were Percy's daughter, Barbara, and her husband, Lieutenant Jack Chambers. After graduating from West Point, Jack attempted flight training. Unfortunately, he washed out of the program like many others because of his "dangerous flying tendencies." Anticipating that event, Barton pulled a few strings to get him assigned to Fort Screven and put him in A Company, where he could keep an eye on him. With a baby due in late May, the Chambers' priority was to find a place to live, which they did not far from the post's front gate.[65]

However, not all was well with the new regimental commander. Barton struggled with two persistent medical conditions during his career, a propensity to gain more weight than the army allowed and a peptic ulcer. From the army's perspective, his weight was always an issue. However, at five feet, seven inches tall with a stocky build, his physique allowed him to play football and be a first-class wrestler in college.[66] However, it was also the build that, if not monitored, could absorb extra fat. There is no evidence of weight problems in Alaska or on the Mexican border. In 1920 the physicians reported that he was "well proportioned and muscular," weighing 166, but noted that he had lost about 20 pounds the year before. In 1925 doctors considered him 12 pounds overweight. However, by 1939, when he was forty-nine, his weight was 181 pounds, displaying some results of four years of good living in downtown Washington without heavy physical activity. By 1941 his weight improved after several years of watching his diet, working outdoors with the CCC, and being around other officers all seeking to stay fit. When he was 52, his examination that year recorded him as weighing 168, only 2 pounds heavier than he was over twenty years earlier. Compared to twenty-first-century American men, there was never any indication that Tubby was ever actually "tubby."[67]

More concerning for Barton and the army was the ulcer that had bothered him in varying degrees since 1919. He had been hospitalized in Coblenz for a few days in 1920 and again in 1925 at Fort Leavenworth; both groups of physicians agreed that he had a duodenal ulcer at the top of his small intestine. It caused a burning pain, especially at night, a few hours after eating. He generally treated it by drinking large quantities of milk, hence some of his weight gain problems. Based on the first examination, he routinely took a "sippy powder" preparation consisting of powdered sodium bicarbonate and calcium carbonate, two ingredients in modern antacids such as Tums. While there are many causes for these painful intestinal sores, excessive smoking and heavy drinking significantly contribute to their intensity. Barton, like many of his contemporaries, did both. In February 1939 the doctors at Fort Screven ordered him to Walter Reed General Hospital, Washington, DC, for a detailed medical examination. He arrived at the hospital on February 20, leaving Clare and the children on Tybee Island.[68]

He stayed in the hospital for almost six full weeks on a strict diet, limited his alcohol consumption, and generally curtailed his after-hours lifestyle. At Walter Reed one of his West Point classmates and several old friends were there, so he was not feeling alone. He wrote his mother a week later, telling her he was fine and under excellent care. He also reassured her that Barbara and Jack were doing well and that he was "a splendid young officer."[69] He also wrote to both his parents, admonishing them for "dwelling too much on the nearness of death and if you don't look out you will develop a frame of mind which can but hasten the day." While they were getting older, they should get out and enjoy many more happy years.[70] Not surprisingly, his condition rapidly improved. The board returned him to duty with no restrictions.[71]

At the end of May, he was back at Screven and getting control of his command. He reported to his parents that all of his symptoms had disappeared. He was thankful that the doctors had not discovered any cancer in his system, something he greatly feared. Clare and the children were fine and enjoying life on the island. He also reported that Barbara and the new baby, Barton Patrick Chambers, were doing well, although she had had a difficult childbirth. The army doctors on post took good care of her, and she was recovering. Barton had a relatively normal command experience for the first six months of his tenure with the 8th Infantry. Operating the post, small unit training, inspecting the part of his unit still at Fort Moultrie outside Charleston, and small unit maneuvers were typical of regimental duty in the prewar army. Among the officers who would work for him in the future included Capt. Charles T. Lanham and his battalion commander, Robert H. Chance.[72]

This bucolic military existence ended on September 1, 1939, when 1.25 million German soldiers, organized into sixty divisions, attacked Poland. The Wehrmacht, the well-trained and reasonably equipped German armed forces, slashed through the poorly deployed and armed Polish Army. Two days later France and the United Kingdom declared war on Germany. Two weeks later, the Soviet Red Army attacked Poland from the east, ending this state's existence after only twenty years. In contrast, the regular US Army had less than 12,000 commissioned officers, not including doctors, chaplains, and full-time USMA professors, and 167,000 enlisted soldiers. Less than 60,000 of these officers and soldiers were infantrymen, and slightly more than 22,000 were in the Air Corps.[73]

George C. Marshall formally took charge of the US Army on the same day as the German invasion. However, he was not the most senior officer on active duty. But President Franklin Roosevelt wanted him in that post, so he promoted Marshall from brigadier general to major general in the regular army. Then the president advanced him two grades, which he could, to general in the US Army. Now that Marshall was at the proper grade, Roosevelt appointed him chief of staff, US Army. Of course, Marshall did not get this post by accident but partially accomplished it with General Pershing's active support. Pershing, the victor of World War I and one of America's greatest commanders, still influenced the public and its politicians. His support was crucial and helped disqualify other contenders, especially the more political Lieutenant General Hugh A. Drum, who commanded the First Army.[74] As Marshall ascended to the War Department's top military position, he combined the AEF's commander's robust network of former soldiers and senior officers with his coterie of Marshall's Men. That September, as historian Geoffrey Perret noted, "It was his Army now."[75]

Among the US Army officers, there was no illusion about their future. Senior officers in the grade of major and higher had seen this movie before, as noted by Barton's letter to his family at the beginning of this chapter: the Europeans would go to war, and American politicians and the public would pretend they could ignore the conflict. However, several years would go by, and the nation's unprepared and underfunded military forces would be forced to fight a veteran enemy army before they were ready. From now on, with war a real possibility, everything soldiers would do had a specific purpose: to prepare for the coming conflict.

Like others of his age and experience, Marshall, and Lesley McNair, now the chief of staff for US Army General Headquarters (GHQ), would test Barton in increasingly challenging and responsible positions. At 51 Barton was older than many the War Department leaders were considering for senior command. Omar Bradley, by comparison was 47, and much younger was James M. Gavin (USMA 1929), who was only 33. If Barton gave any indication that he was not physically capable or professionally aggressive, he knew he would be moved to staff or rear-echelon assignment. However, Barton would succeed at each station, rising from regimental commander as a lieutenant colonel in 1939 to major general and division command by the middle of 1942, only three years later. His letters home reflected the whirlwind pace he was working and this new sense of urgency in daily activity.[76]

The Polish invasion alarmed President Roosevelt, and his experience in the previous war gave him no illusions about how unprepared the American Army was. His first step toward improving the nation's military posture was declaring a national emergency on September 8, 1939. Unfortunately, this action did not include increases in weapons and soldiers. Not generally informed about world events, the American public did not yet support activities to improve the army's readiness and training. With memories of the last war still fresh in many minds, they saw no value in sending their young men to another foreign conflict. However, the army had to begin getting ready.[77]

The US Army was still a regiment-based force in 1939, and the its initial focus was to bring these units up to standard. For the remainder of the year, urged on by the 4th Corps Area and Third Army Commander Lieutenant General Stanley D. Embick, one of Marshall's close confidants, the 8th Regiment continued training.[78] Meanwhile, the War Department was activating and organizing infantry divisions, each consisting of three regiments. It also activated or reorganized corps headquarters, which could command any number of divisions and subordinate units. By early 1940 Embick decided it was time to move beyond the regiment and get some of these new corps and divisions into the field to evaluate their progress. His staff, working with the War Department, selected an area near the Sabine River in Texas and Louisiana. In late April 1940, two corps moved to the area and prepared for activities to begin on May 9.[79]

Meanwhile, the 8th Regiment was moving from Fort Screven to the Harmony Church area of Fort Benning to become part of the reactivated 4th Infantry Division, commanded by Brigadier General Walter E. Prosser.[80] Since his regiment was not participating in the exercises as it relocated, Barton was available for a supporting leadership assignment. He headed

Barton as Camp Beauregard, Louisiana, headquarters commandant,
Third Army Louisiana Maneuvers, May 1940. Courtesy Barton family.

for Camp Beauregard, Louisiana, to work for Embick as his headquarters
commandant, one of an officer's most thankless yet essential duties. Everything
inside the camp's boundaries, besides the discipline and training of the housed
units, was his responsibility. This included managing local security, operating
the main mess halls, supervising the headquarters motor pool, and coordinating camp cleanliness and sanitation. Everyone would notice if he were not
an effective operator of this vast camp. If the peace-time army was proficient

at any task, it was conducting unit inspections, which every visitor automatically did. Barton's role in receiving visitors, arranging to house, and ensuring escorts to their destination was most visible to everyone. Given the importance of these maneuvers as America edged closer to war, dignitaries from Marshall and Secretary of War Henry L. Stimson, many congress members, and well-known journalists visited the camp almost daily.[81]

Embick, not one to give praise lightly, was impressed with his commandant and awarded him many superior ratings on his efficiency report that ended in the middle of June 1940. "His performance of duty at Camp Beauregard was of an outstanding nature, eliciting the favorable comments of all, both officers and civilians, with whom he came in contact."[82] The local CCC commander was also impressed. His enrollees did much of the camp's construction and maintenance work. Major N. G. Bush wrote in his letter to Embick, "The relationship between this activity, a civilian organization having no connection with the Third Army, and the units of the Third Army at Camp Beauregard were exceptional. This pleasant relationship was due in a large measure to Lieut. Colonel Barton. His friendly understanding of our problems, his consideration, tact, and good humor made it a genuine pleasure to this headquarters to have the Headquarters of the Third Army at this station."[83] Once he relinquished control of the camp to his successor, Barton returned to Fort Benning, took two weeks of vacation, and turned over his regimental command to Colonel Carlin C. Stokely (USMA 1909).

Chapter 6

Increasing Responsibilities, 1940-1942

War Department: This is Walker, Executive Officer in G-1 at the War Department. We want to ask you if you can get away from down there (Camp Beauregard, LA) and come up to G.H.Q. for a conference tomorrow morning. Just a moment, Colonel, I'll read you here— this is a confidential announcement—"Colonel Raymond O. Barton, Infantry, designated as Assistant Division Commander, 85th Infantry Division," that's one of those new divisions to be activated, and Commanding General of that division, together with his Assistant Division Commander and the Artillery Commander, and Chief of Staff, in conference with General McNair, commencing tomorrow morning at 08:30 at G. H. Q. . . . . If there is any way that you can get up—fly up—for the conference, we'd certainly like to have you do it.

Barton: I'll be there.[1]

4th Division Chief of Staff, 1940-1941

During the May 1940 maneuvers, units across the country moved to Fort Benning to join the reactivating 4th Infantry Division. Barton's role would be as the new unit's first chief of staff, working for its commander, Brigadier General Walter E. Prosser (USMA 1905) and assistant division commander Brigadier General Oscar W. Griswold (USMA 1910). The three formed a strong team and worked with a purpose to get the Ivy Division up and running. This book's remaining chapters will revolve around infantry divisions, so this is a logical place to explain their background, development, and organization.

The massive national conscription and subsequent deployment of American soldiers to France during World War I forced the War Department, for the first time, to design a standard divisional organizational structure (called a table of organization and equipment, or TOE). With this organization, personnel managers could integrate draftees, regular army, and national guard soldiers into one standard organization and develop standard protocols for training and equipping them. In 1917 the War Department created thirty-two divisions and activated sixteen others from the National Guard to accommodate the influx of troops. Historians refer to it as the "square" divisional organization, built around two brigades of two regiments each. By design it was a considerable force, with over twenty-seven thousand soldiers.[2] Among these units organized following President Wilson's war message was the 4th Infantry Division. Its original headquarters was at Camp Greene, near Charlotte, North Carolina, with the 39th, 47th, 58th, and 59th Regiments as its principal combat forces. It began arriving at Brest at the beginning of May 1918 and entered combat in the middle of July as part of the Aisne-Marne operation. Soldiers called it the Ivy Division, corresponding to the Roman numeral for four, IV. Its patch consisted of four green ivy leaves arranged in a cross issuing from a small open circle (one leaf in each angle of the square), all within a light khaki border. Its motto was "Steadfast and Loyal."[3]

Under Major General George H. Cameron, and later Major General Mark L. Hersey, the division fought in the Saint-Mihiel and Meuse-Argonne offensives. After the war it participated in the postwar advance into Germany and remained as part of the occupation army until July 1919, when it returned to the United States. The War Department retired its colors at Camp Lewis, Washington, on September 21, 1921. Now, nineteen years later, on June 1, 1940, the nation called it back into service, this time at Fort Benning.[4]

Even before the Germans began their march across Europe, senior officers at the War Department realized that the previous war's square division was too large and cumbersome. It was simply not flexible enough for their vision of modern combat. In late 1937 US Army Chief of Staff General Malin Craig created a panel of three of the most experienced officers in the service—Fox Connor, Lesley J. McNair, and George C. Marshall—to recommend a new divisional organization. With flexibility as the guiding principle, they settled for an organization with a triangular framework. From platoon through the division, all tactical levels of command had three primary maneuver units and one or more supporting battalions or companies. The new infantry division had three infantry regiments as its main combat commands. Adding to this organization was an array of other units, including the division artillery, a headquarters company, and signal, quartermaster, and medical battalions. It had little organic combat support, logistical, or transportation resources, relying on superior headquarters for this augmentation. Without the customary reinforcing units, such as tanks, tank destroyers, trucks, or additional engineers or artillery, its assigned strength was slightly more than fourteen thousand officers and men. After a series of tests in 1937 and 1938, Marshall ordered that all infantry divisions convert to the new organization.[5]

Barton's 8th Infantry, from Forts Screven and Moultrie, became one of the reactivated 4th Infantry Division's initial regiments and began moving to Fort Benning in April 1940. Other units assigned to the new division included the 4th Signal Company, 20th Field Artillery, 4th Engineer Battalion, 4th Quartermaster Battalion, and the 4th Medical Battalion. The division headquarters moved near the Harmony Church Cemetery into a CCC camp headquarters, with the 4th Reconnaissance Troop and 4th Military Police Company nearby. The division had two other infantry regiments: the 29th Infantry, which was already stationed at Fort Benning, and the 22nd Infantry, stationed at Fort McClellan, Alabama.[6]

As was the case during this period, many officers Barton would work with in Europe were senior leaders at Fort Benning. Brigadier General Courtney H. Hodges had been the Infantry School's deputy commandant since 1938,

and in October 1940 he became post commandant. In this role he influenced
the early 4th Division's organization. He departed in March 1941 to become
chief of infantry, and Marshall replaced him with Brigadier General Omar
N. Bradley.[7] George S. Patton, his fellow student from CGSS in 1923, was
commanding the new 2nd Armored Brigade.[8] Other officers who would later
work closely with Barton, and whom he knew from previous assignments,
included James Van Fleet, commanding the 29th Infantry Regiment's
1st Battalion, and Richard G. McKee, Hodges's operations officer
responsible for supervising the expansion of the school's training facilities.
Later, McKee would command the school's regiment (300th Infantry) and
follow Hodges to the Third Army in 1943.[9]

Personalities aside, Barton and Prosser's tasks became more complicated
than just organizing a standard infantry unit. By the middle of 1940, German
tanks had run amok across Western Europe. Analysts studying these events
noticed that the panzer divisions had motorized divisions supporting their
advance. These units had the same general configuration and support structure
as armored units, except their primary combat units were two specially trained
truck or half-track mounted infantry regiments rather than tank regiments.[10]
Given that the US Army's organization in 1939 was primitive at best, it made
sense to consider other formations that appeared to be successful. From the
early days of the war until 1942, the War Department experimented with
several armored, infantry, airborne, and cavalry divisions. One of these
modified infantry units was the motorized division.[11] On August 1, 1940,
the War Department ordered Prosser to convert his command to a motorized
division, the first in the army.[12]

The ninety days following the division's activation were a whirlwind
of activity as new units, officers, and individual replacements arrived on the
post. Calling it *motorized* was interesting, as it would not have most of its
trucks and other weapons until nearly the end of 1941, so it used borrowed and
modified equipment to conduct its training. In addition, the War Department
was constantly adjusting its organization, adding and subtracting units, or
changing equipment. Unlike infantry and artillery, the idea of motorized
infantry was an experiment.[13] Based on War Department guidance, Prosser
and Barton designed individual and unit training programs and organized

the reception of units and replacements into the division.[14] But turmoil was standard within the service in 1940, and General Marshall ordered Prosser to move to the Panama Canal Zone in October.[15] The departing commander was grateful for what Barton had done and noted, "This officer is a natural military leader. He possesses to a marked degree unusual qualities for high command. . . . [and] should be promoted to the grade of Brigadier General at an early date."[16]

With Prosser's departure one of Marshall's favorites, Major General Lloyd R. Fredendall became the new division commander.[17] Around the same time, on February 14, 1941, the War Department promoted Barton to full colonel, giving him the rank his position required.[18] In February the division was finally at full strength and began training in earnest. From then until the middle of June, it exercised with the new Third Air Force, developing close air support techniques. The training was rough, and the results indicated gaps between what the army wanted and what its air corps could deliver.[19]

In early June the Barton family took time off and returned to Ada to visit Raymond's parents. His father had been sick, and he thought he needed a visit. While there he gave a speech to the chamber of commerce. He reminisced about his childhood, but most of his speech was about leadership and how the army was changing to stay ahead of the enemy. "We must look ahead and get ahead—get ahead of any potential enemy and not conform to him, but have them conform to us."[20]

Soon after he returned to the division headquarters, Brigadier General James I. Muir (USMA 1910) from the 26th Infantry Regiment took over from Griswold. This change of leadership increased the strain on Barton, who wrote to his parents at the end of June, "Terribly busy. Working nights. Am very anxious to hear how you both are doing."[21] Two weeks later, on July 13, Conway passed away at 85. His life spanned from the end of the Civil War to the beginning of the Second World War. His attack of the flu, which had prompted the earlier visit, had returned, and he never recovered. As this story has revealed, he and Raymond were very close, and it pained him much to return home to bury his father next to his brother, Percy, in the cemetery on the edge of town.[22]

The army and its expansion were not waiting, and two weeks after returning to Fort Benning, the War Department ordered Fredendall back to Washington to begin working on various plans to invade North Africa.[23] The departing commander praised Barton as "fitted to perform either staff or command duties and should be promoted to the grade of brigadier general."[24] The division's artillery commander, Brigadier General Fred. C. Wallace, temporarily replaced him for the forthcoming maneuvers. With Wallace in charge, the division continued practicing its skills. It was no longer a ramshackle collection of novice units with broken or improvised equipment. As it moved into the next phase of large-scale maneuvers in the summer of 1941, it demonstrated that it was a powerful, highly mobile force with over 2,600 vehicles and 14,000 soldiers. With the additional tank battalions it often trained with, it resembled the German light armored division in fighting power.[25]

With Wallace in charge, the division joined the other elements of the IV Corps, commanded by Major General Jay L. Benedict, in the Third Army Maneuvers near Dry Prong, Louisiana. This was part of the army's preparation for the War Department's General Headquarters (GHQ) maneuvers that would take place in mid-September. Conducted between August 11 and 23, the event began with a command post exercise. These events take place within unit headquarters and train commanders and staffs in corps policies, command procedures, and the fundamental techniques of processing and reacting to orders. This event has no troops and only exercises a unit's headquarters. Barton supervised his command post as it interacted with the corps staff, adjacent divisions, and subordinate regiments and other units.

After a short break to attend briefings and commander courses, Oscar Griswold returned as division commander. Except for the few months he was away before his promotion, Griswold and Barton had worked closely together since the 4th Motorized Division's reactivation.[26] He arrived to assume his new post as the Ivy Division finished its maneuvers and observed his unit as Wallace and Barton returned it to Fort Benning.[27] Barton was glad to see him return.

The family was still a big part of Barton's life but was also in turmoil. Since he had entered West Point, Barton could confide in his father about almost anything. However, with Conway entombed in Rosedale Cemetery, he needed someone other than his wife to correspond with, and his daughter, Clare, became the recipient of his many letters. The two Clares, the 15-year-old daughter and 46-year-old mother, apparently were continually clashing—nothing unusual in the 1940s as it is in the twenty-first century. During the summer of 1941, he convinced Clare Conway to get away for a while to maintain some sense of harmony during this busy period. She traveled to Colorado to visit her grandmother's family in Colorado Springs and stay with Carrie's younger brother Jesse and his sister-in-law Lillian, a teacher.[28] Tubby's daughter became one of his principal correspondents. Using a Dictaphone as he traveled between division training events and meetings in all parts of the region, he dictated letter after letter that one of his clerks typed during the night. He wrote easily readable letters on weekends or when the clerk had more critical tasks. He was very concerned with how his daughter was doing and pointedly wrote, "Now listen, Sis, you just write your old Daddy all about how you feel. Don't hold out on me either. I can take it. If things are not right, if you are blue, if you are unhappy—about anything just tell me. If you are all Ok and truly so, let me know that too."[29] He signed all his letters, "De De."

Meanwhile, Raymond Jr., now referred to as R. O., enjoyed playing tennis, which he apparently was quite good at, and looked forward to registering for high school and joining the football team. However, at the last minute he had a change of heart and almost backed out of the sport when he registered for school. He continued, but Barton was concerned since R. O. wanted to take music lessons. In a sign of the times, the colonel remarked, "Since there is no danger of him ever showing any sissy proclivities, I am just as well pleased." But he had no reason to be concerned. Soon he would be the football team captain and scored two touchdowns during one game in November.[30] His wife's sister Kiki was living with them, and they enjoyed participating in the games of bridge that cropped up in the officer's housing area.[31]

And, when he was away on maneuvers, he kept his wife appraised of what was taking place. In the middle of the exercise on August 17, he sent her a long, detailed letter about the upcoming changes. "Things are moving. I go to Lake Charles (175 miles away) to meet Griswold at Third Army Headquarters at 5:00 AM tomorrow. We have orders to send representatives to Augusta, Georgia, to meet War Department and Corps Area representatives with reference to construction of a new cantonment for the 4th Motorized Division at that place."[32] This post, of course, would become Fort Gordon and, later in the twenty-first century, Fort Eisenhower. For several pages he describes the hectic world they were entering. They needed a plan on where they should settle as they entered this period of uncertainty. No decision yet, as they could talk about the details when he got home at the end of the month. But he was definitely in the chief of staff mode when he ended the letter to his wife with, "P.S. – Make a decision and go into action, or leave the decision up to me and be prepared to go into action as soon as I get home."[33]

Because of the changing situation, they did not make any moving plans in September but looked forward to the division moving to Augusta. In a letter to his mother after returning to Benning, he noted, "That makes a cycle for me, because almost 23 years ago, I left the Infantry School at Fort Sill for duty in a large war camp at Augusta, Georgia. This time, however, thank goodness, I am with a combat division, instead of what amounted to then a replacement center."[34] For the last six months, the 4th Motorized Division was in constant turmoil as soldiers brought into the service by the Selective Service Act of 1940 arrived in Fort Benning. In July Brigadier General Harold R. Bull, Barton's old friend from 30th Infantry days in Alaska, San Francisco, and Plattsburgh, became the assistant division commander. The War Department moved the 29th Infantry Regiment to Fort Jackson, and the 12th Infantry Regiment moved to Fort Benning from Fort Dix.[35]

The turmoil would continue. When Third Army commander Lieutenant General Walter Kreuger and his chief of staff, Brigadier General Eisenhower, reviewed the evaluator's comments from the Dry Prong Maneuvers, they were not impressed with Benedict's handling of the IV Corps. The list indicated that the unit was not prepared for combat, never mind the next set of maneuvers scheduled for November. From a fundamental perspective, the corps did a poor job of selecting command post locations, exhibited poor light discipline, maintained unsatisfactory communications, and did a poor job of employing its liaison officers. From a command perspective, it deployed its units on too wide a front and displayed poor march discipline.[36]

Kreuger wanted Benedict gone, and Marshall moved Griswold on October 6, after only thirty-six days with the 4th Motorized Division. His short tenure allowed him to write a report on his chief of staff, with whom he had worked closely for more than a year. Griswold noted: "One of the most loyal officers I know. Careful, forceful, very energetic, and thorough with a rather gruff exterior which might be misunderstood on slight acquaintance. A fine leader who gets superior results from officers and men under him. Should make a splendid general officer." He also added, "Recommend for early promotion to Brigadier General."[37]

The day Griswold left, Raymond wrote his daughter describing the day's events. He did not believe that Wallace would stay in command long and lamented, "Thus, I have the prospect of having to break the division in to the idiosyncrasies and peculiarities of a sixth division commander since we organized a year ago in June." He also reported that his days with the Rolling Fourth were probably numbered with all the changes taking place in the army.[38] The next day he learned that his prediction was perhaps correct, and he would be following Griswold to Jacksonville, Florida, home of the IV Corps, shortly.[39]

IV Corps Chief of Staff and the Carolina Maneuvers, October–November 1941

Griswold had no time to ease into his role as the IV Corps commander, with only two months until the large-scale maneuvers in the Carolinas. Marshall and McNair, now commander of Army Ground Forces (AGF), were preparing the US Army for war and had no tolerance for general officers who did not produce the results they demanded. Griswold knew he was on the hot seat, immediately realized the chief of staff he inherited was part of the problem, and relieved him almost immediately.[40] He wanted Barton, whom he knew he could depend on and was comfortable working with. On October 9 Barton's orders arrived as predicted. He, Clare, and her sister Kiki, who had been living with them, jumped into their car on Friday and headed for Jacksonville, arriving at 3:00 a.m. on Saturday, October 11. Barton had a room, but Clare and Kiki had to stay with friends in the area until she found somewhere to live. R. O. was able to stay with friends at Fort Benning. While not in the command position he wanted, Barton knew Griswold needed his help. It was an excellent opportunity to participate in one of the most critical events in the prewar army.[41]

The new commander had a big task, as his so-called corps was almost a field army, with over one hundred thousand soldiers and the largest concentration of mechanized forces to that point in army history. Never having commanded at this level, he admitted feeling "like a gawky high school boy who suddenly finds himself on a college campus."[42] Under McNair's critical eyes, he had to direct three cavalry regiments (3rd and 107th, both horse-mounted, and the 6th mechanized), the 4th Motorized Division, and the I Armored Corps with the 1st and 2nd Armored Divisions. His infantry support came from two "square" infantry divisions (31st and 43rd) and the new 502nd Parachute Infantry Battalion. The 75th Field Artillery Brigade was his corps artillery headquarters. For air support, a vital training objective for these maneuvers, was the 3rd Air Support command, consisting of the 2nd Bomber and 10th Pursuit Wings.[43]

While Griswold provided the directions, Barton's task was to translate the commander's directives into operational and logistics orders and ensure that all the subordinate units received them on time and understood the commander's intent. For several weeks units across the region moved into their assembly areas. The corps staff and its equipment were on the way soon after. Barton had approximately eighty officers and warrant officers assigned to the headquarters as primary or secondary staff officers and another 150 soldiers performing as clerks, drivers, and other essential duties. Additionally, supporting his staff was a headquarters company that fulfilled all its regular responsibilities, such as mess, maintenance, security, and supply functions.[44]

This expanding army headquarters had to be mobile and capable of moving about the battlefield, not traditional tasks of the interwar army's senior headquarters. It is no wonder Griswold brought Barton in to shake up the staff and get it moving, and he enjoyed the challenge. On the eve of the exercises, Barton wrote his wife and confessed,

> It has been fun to take the lead out of the pants of this headquarters, and I am just beginning to get action when I call for it instead of next week sometime. Late yesterday afternoon, I asked why certain steps into the trailers hadn't been painted, and they told me that they had requisitioned the paint about a week ago, but hadn't gotten it. I raised unshirted hell because they hadn't followed up on their requisition. To my surprise and satisfaction, I found green painted steps when I got out of bed yesterday morning. Then I found the youngster responsible and praised him for his efficiency, and told him that was the way I liked it to go.[45]

In these maneuvers Griswold's IV Corps was to act as the opposing force to Lieutenant General Hugh A. Drum's blue First Army. Drum's command was, according to historian Christopher Gabel, "a traditional infantry-oriented force with a traditionally-minded commander."[46] His eight infantry divisions and six regimental-sized antitank groups contained 195,000 soldiers organized in three corps (I, II, VI).[47] The maneuvers, taking place east of Charlotte along the Pee Dee River in North and South Carolina, were to last for two weeks, from November 16–30, 1941. McNair was the exercise supervisor, and supporting him was the Third Army Commander, Kreuger. Barton and Kreuger had locked horns back in Omaha when the senior was a National Guard officer and the junior the area corps G-3. Barton was happy that the prominent general held no grudges and was quite friendly, although with the reputation as being the army's most exacting commander.[48]

Before Raymond headed to South Carolina, he took care of a few details. The family found a house in Jacksonville, smaller than Benning's field-grade quarters but lovely just the same. Finding places to live in the rapidly growing area became problematic as soldiers and sailors poured into the Jacksonville and Saint John's Bay area. The family would not move in until after the maneuvers, as Clare needed to return to Fort Benning to have her wisdom teeth removed. While they were house hunting, one of Kiki's friends, who had a cottage on the waterfront, invited them to a fish fry, where they had the opportunity to sit on the dock and do some fishing. In a letter to his mother, Barton noted that this was "right down my alley."[49] On October 28 he arrived in the maneuver area and began getting the staff in shape. Several days later he and Griswold visited General Drum at his headquarters, exchanging greetings and coordinating various issues that could arise once the exercise began. Finally, they called on their former boss Lloyd Fredendall, who was now commanding the opposing II Armored Corps.[50]

Complicating things, both Barton and Griswold were fighting colds, and he was concerned since "a sick or half-sick commander and chief of staff is the least desirable thing for this critical period in both of our careers, much less being hard on the troops."[51] He thought he was getting better, but instead he began to worsen and developed a sharp pain in his neck. Griswold sent him to the corps' field hospital, located at Camp Croft near Spartanburg, South Carolina. Doctors discovered he had a wryneck, a condition where neck muscles twist beyond their normal range. In addition, the doctors noted he had a swollen lymph gland and possibly pneumonia. The doctors gave him one of the new sulfa (Sulfonamide) drugs and ordered sleep and rest.[52]

Of course, he was on the edge of the most critical training event in his career, and he was eager to "break out" of the hospital as soon as possible.[53] But he appreciated the rest and admitted that he needed it before jumping into the maneuvers. In a letter to his entire family on November 6, he was in good spirits and reported on his hospital stay. One of his acquaintances during the previous war, Colonel Walter Denison, commanded the hospital and personally kept his eye on Tubby's progress. Sandy Patch was in North Carolina training troops, and he, his wife, Julia, and daughter, Sandy, lived on the new post. The two women came over daily to bring Barton flowers, treats, and good company.[54]

By November 7 he returned to work, exchanging "a warm hospital for a cold tent."[55] Reflecting on his experience just before the maneuvers began, he wrote to his wife about his boss: "Gris treats me like a son, not only having sent me to the hospital but having taken steps to keep me there a couple of

Major General Oscar Griswold, commander, IV Corps, and Brigadier General Raymond O. Barton during Carolina Maneuvers, October 1941. US Army photograph, courtesy Barton family.

days after I was recovered. Night before last he made me leave camp and sleep in his room at the hotel, where I had a grand warm rest with a hot tub bath. He is the kindest most considerate and fatherly chief I have ever had. His quietness is but an outward evidence of his complete modesty and

unassuming character. Behind it however is plenty of fine steel."[56] He felt
good and was ready for the contest to begin.

For two weeks two massive units, by American 1941 standards, fought
against each other along the North and South Carolina borders. Rather than
using real bullets, the units were evaluated by umpires and awarded or denied
tactical success. During the first phase from November 16 to 22, McNair
gave both commanders offensive missions designed to create a head-on
clash. Historian Christopher Gable described this operation as the Battle of
the Pee Dee River. General Drum intended to win at all costs and started
moving before the exercise began, including laying telephone lines across the
river in advance, violating McNair's directives. This violation was serious
business, and the exercise director, and General Marshall, did not appreciate
cheating by one of the senior commanders.[57]

The following six days were wild as these two units, red and blue,
punched and counterpunched. When one of the red team (Griswold)
reconnaissance units captured General Drum, who was too far forward
observing operations at the front, morale went up at Barton's command
post. However, the soldiers let him go and Barton wanted to know why
he was not brought back to the corps headquarters. As one could expect,
he was also dissatisfied with some of the umpire decisions that affected the
corps' maneuver. However, that is a common complaint, mainly since the
army was relatively new to training events on this scale. He also noted that
many visitors showed up, and he had the secretary of war on his schedule on
November 17. The next day the assistant secretary would arrive with about
twenty-five members of Congress. He was feeling well, not sleeping much,
and enjoying the entire event, although he lamented the headquarters' mess
trailer getting stuck in a ditch. When the maneuver phase ended, the blue
forces defeated Griswold's red army. But McNair was content as they had
maneuvered well in the face of overwhelming odds. He and his observers
had learned much about reorganizing the armored force and about other
essential changes to make in the ground forces before they faced either the
Japanese or German Armies.[58]

After a hasty Thanksgiving dinner, the troops repositioned. Griswold now
had a mission to defend a nation's border from an impending enemy attack.

Gable named this operation the Battle of Camden.[59] General Drum sought to impose his will on the smaller but more agile IV Corps for five more days. Barton continued to work behind the scenes to translate Griswold's operational directives into orders that made sense and to get them down to the units. In the early stages of the operation, Lieutenant General Courtney Hodges, the former Infantry School assistant commandant and current chief of infantry, visited the corps headquarters. Needing division commanders for the rapidly growing army, Hodges was visiting partially to check how ·Barton and other commanders were performing in the field. With him was. his deputy, Lieutenant Colonel Charles "Buck" Lanham. A year earlier Captain Lanham had been one of Barton's company commanders, both at Fort Screven and during the Third Army's Louisiana Maneuvers in May 1940. Since leaving the 8th Infantry in January, he had worked for Hodges, who was then chief of infantry and ensured his rapid promotion to lieutenant colonel. Lanham told Barton that he was under consideration for advancement since Griswold and his previous commanders had written letters to the War Department recommending his promotion to general officer. It was welcome news.[60]

Between stressful activities, the maneuvers were "regular old home week" as Tubby—no record of anyone calling him Ray or Raymond—continued to run into many of his old friends. These included classmates Archie Arnold and Frank Sibert. Also showing up were Jim Muir, Ed Stackpole, and his mentor Jim Ord, who had just returned from the Philippines and was now the 1st Infantry Division's deputy commander.[61]

Despite working incredible hours, as expected of any staff chief, he had enjoyed everything about the exercise.[62] When McNair terminated the maneuvers on November 30, Griswold's force had stopped the blue army and accomplished its mission to defend Camden.[63] The corps commander was also happy with the results and the help he received from his deputy. In December, when Griswold knew the nation was looking for leaders to command the new divisions, he wrote to the War Department: "Since August 9, 1941, Colonel Barton has been under my immediate command as Chief of Staff, 4th Division, and Chief of Staff, IV Army Corps. As Chief of Staff of an independent Army Corps in the Carolina Maneuvers, he had to weld together, in a minimum of time, a new Staff, with few exceptions, and train it to assume numerous Army functions. His achievement along these lines was noteworthy. His outstanding attributes are, first, an intense devotion to duty and, second, unquestioned loyalty to his chief." Griswold concluded, "This letter was written entirely without the knowledge of Colonel Barton and is in inspired in no way by him. It is my honest belief that in this emergency, he is the type of officer who can and should be charged with high command responsibilities."[64]

IV Corps Chief of Staff after Pearl Harbor, December 1941–February 1942

Only days after Barton returned to Jacksonville, the world he and other military officers predicted arrived. Events moved quickly after the Japanese attack against the US Pacific Fleet at Pearl Harbor on December 7 and against American and British forces across the Pacific the following week. Following the Hawaii attack, Congress agreed to Roosevelt's request to declare war against Japan. Germany and Italy made it a world war on December 11, when they joined Japan to fight the United States. The War Department put units across the army on alert. Commands of all sizes and capabilities began preparing for deployment to defend the American coast from an anticipated Japanese or German attack. Eisenhower, the Third Army chief of staff, canceled all training programs to prepare for combat contingencies. He passed orders to all mobile units to look for surprises along the gulf and southern coasts. In addition, he began responding to wartime requests from Washington and individual state governors.[65] Barton was on the other end of many of those calls with Eisenhower and his staff, often talking with other staff officers across the southeast twenty-four hours a day for the first week. Where are your units now? What is the status of their weapons, equipment, supply, and soldiers? How long will it take to move from the home station to this or that assembly point? The IV Corps was one of the army's most proficient and mobile forces, so it would have been one of the first headquarters reinforcing either coast in the event of the invasion.

Meanwhile, like most married officers, Barton had to also address family affairs. First, he managed to move his wife and son into their new apartment at 2978 Riverside Avenue in Jacksonville, to the city's south side. Next he wrote the family, advising them to ignore the hysteria that seemed to be gripping the nation. While there might be some incidents along the Florida coast, it was doubtful anything would directly affect them. Finally, like most American soldiers and sailors, he and Clare had to cancel all their best-laid holiday plans.[66]

As a part of a process that would go on for more than two years, he watched as former colleagues and friends entered the war. The initial actions were not comforting. One of the first casualties was his fellow Leavenworth instructor Walter Short, who Marshall replaced as commander of the Hawaiian Department because of his role in the Japanese success on December 7. Jonathan Wainwright, from Coblenz days, was now trapped on Luzon by the Imperial Army. His CGSS classmates Albert Jones and Brad Chynoweth commanded the 51st Philippine Division and the 61st Philippine Division, respectively. James Weaver, a year ahead of him at the academy, supervised the Philippines command's tank force. His fellow Leavenworth instructor Edward P. King commanded the Luzon Task Force. His war college classmate Richard K. Sutherland and his Eagle Pass comrade and fellow CGSS instructor Allan McBride were on MacArthur's staff. Like soldiers across the country, Barton watched in horror as the Japanese onslaught continued without letup. Their struggle was never far from his mind.[67]

A week after the Japanese attack, Barton was still sleeping in his office. His position as a corps chief of staff gave him a better appreciation of what would happen over the next few years. "I can see from the events and increasing tempo that each day from now on out will make it less possible for me to get away from the telephone night or day," he wrote to his daughter on December 17. Visits and travel were out for the near term, and there was no way he and her mother could travel to Colorado Springs for a family wedding. He told his daughter to send his regrets to Uncle Jesse and Aunt Rossa and noted, "I am sure that they can all realize that the Chief of Staff of an Army Corps must remain at his post of duty, particularly at the beginning of a war with three major nations. Personal affairs must go by the board, not only for this Christmas but for probably three or four years to come."[68]

His boss, Griswold, deputized him to give speeches to reassure the local citizens. On December 19 he gave one at the Jacksonville Women's Club, describing what the army had done before December 7 to prepare for the future. He pointed out that the idealists who thought this conflict was England's had not done the military any favors by not allowing them to rearm and prepare for the war everyone knew was coming. "It takes two years for a peaceful nation to get on a wartime basis." Finally, he concluded, "To keep America out of war is an unhelpful slogan, but to keep war out of America is a sound historic fact." The citizens liked it, and Griswold sent him out the following week to give it again to a different group.[69]

The army's professional soldiers were constantly attempting to balance personal responsibilities with the service's increasing demands. Barton's family had little genuine appreciation for the importance of what he was doing and continued to generate their issues. By December 23 Clare had the house up and running, but without R. O., who was staying with friends at Fort Benning. Clare Conway was still in Colorado, and her father wanted to know where she intended to go to school. He suggested the University of Oklahoma near Ada or the University of Florida near Jacksonville. He preferred Florida since he wanted her near her mother, especially if he did not return from the war. The College of William and Mary had been a possibility, but that seemed to be falling through. Meanwhile, his daughter was experiencing high blood pressure and had an auto accident, so her life had its own set of challenges. His wife worried about having enough money for everything that might happen, but Raymond knew they were doing fine and could hire a maid to help with the cleaning. On New Year's Eve, he sent a short note to his daughter, noting how tired he was and working so many hours at the end of a telephone line. Barton could get home each day to see her mother now but was usually pretty tired with little to do other than sleep and get back to work.[70] It is doubtful that either of his children had any idea of the stress he was experiencing.

He expected the War Department to move him from the IV Corps to a new division at some point, although he had no clue when that might be happening.[71] Meanwhile, Fred Wallace and Hal Bull were relocating the 4th Motorized Division to the post he had helped design, Camp Gordon near Augusta. In January Ham Haislip replaced Bull, who moved on to a War Department staff job. Barton noted that Wallace had his command concentrating on driver training and testing. Readers should remember this was early in the twentieth century, and relatively few young men had learned to drive automobiles during the Great Depression. Most recruits had never before operated a car or truck; since it was a motorized unit, everyone needed to know how to drive. With most starting from scratch, this training on large vehicles with manual transmissions was no trivial task. By the end of the month, sufficient soldiers had licenses, so the Rolling Fourth could hold its first full review of all division units.[72]

Jacksonville was a good location, even if speeches and meetings with local citizens diverted him from his military tasks. Then, in the second week of February, the War Department ordered the corps headquarters out of its plush surroundings. Its new destination was Camp Beauregard, where Barton had been camp commander two years earlier. He left his wife and now R. O., who had returned home to Jacksonville since he had no idea how long he would be in Louisiana. His journey took him to the camp through Mobile, Biloxi, Gulfport, and Baton Rouge. When he arrived, Barton moved back into the same building with the same desk he had occupied in 1940. This time he had a dog, Ches, whom he had picked up several months earlier and who became quite the celebrity about camp.[73] He was sharing a duplex with Harry Collins, the corps G-2, whom he had met at Eagle Pass years before. Barton had to manage seventy-eight separate commanders and five divisions, including Omar Bradley's 28th Infantry Division, for the IV Corps' forthcoming maneuvers.[74]

Campbell B. Hodges, his Army War College classmate, had retired from the US Army a year earlier and was now the president of Louisiana State University. He sent Barton a letter on February 26 welcoming him to Louisiana and asking him to stop by for a visit. He began to consider this another option for Clare Conway's college future.[75] He liked working for Griswold, whom he considered his mentor, but he was depressed by his current situation. The War Department published a new promotion schedule every month, and he was not on the February general officer list. He wrote his daughter on February 15, "The last list of generals got me down. It is apparent that I am to be passed over. No use to inflict on you the utter depths of my disappointment and the seas of the injustice of it all."[76] He was also quite lonely, other than Ches, who was somewhat out of control in the exciting, for him, swampland of Louisiana.[77]

His complicated life continued into February. On the one hand, the family issues continued. Clare Conway was doing well in her senior year of high school in Colorado and was the girls' basketball team captain. Mother Clare missed her and felt terrible for the tension between the two. She wanted her home for the summer after graduation. The daughter wanted nothing of the sort and had no intention of spending all summer in Jacksonville with her. Raymond was trying to make everyone happy and balance all the unknowns facing him and the family. R. O. was at home, doing well in school, and considering following in his father's footsteps to attend the military academy.[78]

On the other hand, Barton was quite frustrated being stuck as the corps chief of staff, a position that could preclude him from ever becoming a division commander. Griswold sensed his despair and decided to get personally involved. He could not assume the War Department was aware of Barton's potential for senior command. About the time the promotion list came out, the general went to San Antonio to meet with Lieutenant General Walter Kreuger, the Third Army Commander. While there Griswold presented his deputy's qualifications and argued for his promotion. He handed Kreuger, whom he had known since their assignment in the 84th Division during World War I, a formal letter summarizing his argument for Barton's early promotion. In it he noted, "This officer's background, experience, and efficiency are such that in my opinion the service needs men of his caliber for higher command in the emergency which now confronts the country." It was a powerful letter, and Griswold admitted losing his chief with maneuvers on the horizon would cause him many personal problems. But "I feel it would not be just either to this officer or to the service if I did not recommend him for early promotion."

Furthermore, he told Kreuger that Barton knew nothing about the letter and had not suggested its writing.[79] Later, after he returned, he gave Barton a copy of the letter.

On Friday morning February 27, Barton was out in the field checking on the arriving units when he received a call from GHQ, telling him to report to McNair's headquarters in Washington, DC.[80] Although it was 1942, when transportation was relatively slow, and he was in the middle of a swamp, he said he could get to Washington the next day. Within two hours he packed a fresh uniform, boarded an army airplane at Camp Beauregard airfield, and flew to New Orleans. On short notice but with military priority, he boarded a commercial aircraft and traveled all night to Washington. He arrived at 07:00 and went directly to the meeting room at the Army War College. His small group consisted of two new division commanders, two new assistant division commanders, two new artillery commanders, and two new staff chiefs. Major General Wayne (Mark) Clark, deputy chief of the War Department General Headquarters staff, started the briefing. Then McNair, commander of AGF, took over and talked to them about their new assignments. Suddenly George Marshall arrived, listened to Clark and McNair complete their remarks, and then took the floor. He spoke "informally but most earnestly and inspiringly for quite a while. It was history in the making."[81] Barton was no longer depressed and wrote his daughter that evening, telling her he would get promoted to brigadier general in a few weeks and take over as assistant division commander of a new division. His new boss, the 85th Infantry Division commander, would be his classmate and great friend Ham Haislip. He ended this letter by mentioning Griswold's generous and continuous support. His intervention was essential to all that would follow.[82]

Assistant Division Commander, 85th Division, March–June 1942

Although he told his family about his promotion, he wanted them to say nothing about it. His first posting would be back to Fort Benning for an officer's course. Only recently he had felt the sting of possibly being passed over, and he did not want to get ahead of events. He knew that a board of officers had to meet and confirm that he was qualified. But he was looking forward to the new job that would "take me off the swivel chair and put me in the open. By summer, I will be hard and fit."[83] Thankfully, before he arrived at Benning, the War Department announced his promotion, and cards, telegrams, and letters poured in from his friends and colleagues sending their congratulations. In a letter to his wife, he reflected on his promotion and some who had gone before. Not mentioning any names, he noted, "At least we can know that I got mine on merit, and it took a lot to overcome what appeared to be considerable obstacles." He added that he had not gone on this journey alone and was happy that she was as excited about this advancement as he was. He told her, "You share with me the result of long and hard effort on your part for my success, and with all humility and appreciation, I express my gratitude."[84]

Tubby Barton and Ham Haislip needed no introduction and quickly got to work. The new division commander was well-connected within the army's informal hierarchy, having introduced Eisenhower to his wife, Mamie, while stationed in Texas in 1914. Haislip had attended the French Ecole Superieure de Guerre (war college) and taught at Leavenworth after Barton's departure. He had spent significant time in the War Department and was there when he was selected to organize the new 85th Infantry Division. He did not have as much experience with a tactical staff as his classmate, but with his knowledge of the leaders and procedures running Washington, the two would be a good fit.[85] The new field artillery commander was Brigadier General Jay W. MacKelvie, who entered the army as an enlisted man in 1914, was commissioned in 1917, and remained in the artillery during the interwar period. His previous assignment was in the War Department's Plans Division with Eisenhower and Leonard G. Gerow, so he was also connected to the Marshall clique. He and Barton had met when he attended Fort Leavenworth in 1931–32.[86] The division's G-4, most important during the reactivation phase, was Lieutenant Colonel Thomas J. Sands (USMA 1929), an artillery officer who had been a member of the 1936 American Olympic Fencing Team.

After more than two years of experience, the AGF had developed procedures for creating new divisions. The first step was to ensure the leadership knew what it was doing. The staff and ninety of the division's new officers first met at the division officer's course at Fort Benning from March 10 to April 11. For Barton, returning to Benning meant he could socialize almost every evening. The post's officer's club, which opened in 1934, was one of the most beautiful and functional in the army. Members and all commissioned officers could take their meals there during the day, meet friends in the infantry bar in the evening, get a haircut, and socialize at events in the various ballrooms or outside on the manicured lawn.[87]

Most significant commands assigned to Fort Benning had their own officer's mess. For example, Barbara and Jack Chambers were still at Fort Benning, where he was a member of the 2nd Armored Division. On Sunday, March 15, they took Tubby to dinner at the division's club. George Patton, still in command, and his wife were there and congratulated Barton on his promotion. Then, in the middle of the dining room, with a swagger only the Pattons could muster, they each publicly kissed him on the cheek. Next, Patton told Tubby he would give him a set of his stars. Also at the mess that night was his good friend Paddy Flint, now commanding the 56th Armored Regiment, and many other friends and acquaintances. Patton made good on his promise the following week when Barton dropped by his home after work. He gave him a pair of general officer stars engraved with GSP on the back. Raymond wrote his wife, "I have a foolish sentiment about them. . . . I'll wear them into my very first battle." Patton also promised he would be a major general in a few months, although Barton was not sure.[88]

The social pace was a strain of its own, as Barbara and Jack were always inviting him to dinner, and he kept running into old friends and acquaintances, all colonels and generals now. These included the post commander, Major General Leven C. Allen, one of his students at Fort Leavenworth, and Willis Crittenberger, who graduated a year behind him at West Point and would go on to command IV Corps in Italy. His war college classmate John Wogan worked for Patton and soon took command of the 13th Armored Division. Ira Wyche, one of his pals from the 30th Infantry whom the War Department had just promoted, was commanding the 79th Infantry Division. He felt like he had arrived and told Clare it was a different world now: "School and faculty going out of the way to please me . . . can have anything I want." On Sunday, March 29, the new division's officers visited Fort Jackson and Robert L. Eichelberger's 77th Infantry Division. Like the 85th it was a new unit, and this visit provided an excellent opportunity to understand how they conducted training and what they had learned. Eichelberger went out of his way to entertain and assist Barton, who could not say enough about his kindness and generosity.[89]

His wife, Clare, came to visit him at Benning the first week of April. After she left he spent a few days at Camp Wheeler near Macon, Georgia, with 150 officers from the 82nd and 93rd Divisions studying the training methods the center was using. It immediately took draftees from the induction centers and gave them thirteen weeks of military training. It turned out Barton's new division was going to get its soldiers directly from the induction centers; there were not enough training facilities in the country to process them. As a result, the new divisions often had to serve as primary training centers. His small group of officers had to bring sixteen thousand civilians into the division, teach them the basics of soldiering, and turn them "into a fighting team." His letters home from this time are gossipy and cheery. This commentary is especially true as he mentions the friends and colleagues from years past that he continues to encounter, such as Harry L. Collins, his IV Corps G-2 during the Carolina Maneuvers and future 42nd Infantry Division commander. Harry was concerned that his daughter's husband was on Bataan, and they had heard nothing about his condition. It was a sense of helplessness felt by many at this stage of the war.[90]

Barton was also paying attention to his family and the many issues still consuming some of his thoughts. He wanted Clare Conway to decide on a college. Partially because of his friendship with the Louisiana State University president, he was trying to get her and possibly Raymond Jr. to go there. In his letters Barton continued to advise his daughter. He warned her of hanging around the USO too much, and he was glad she would visit her grandmother in Ada.[91] Not all was well with R. O., as he had gotten into trouble at school, which sent him home for not applying himself. Barton was

Brigadier General Barton and Clare Conway, graduation, June 1942. Courtesy Barton family.

not upset since he believed his son was a good kid and just needed to learn that "the world disciplines the laggards and rewards the efficient." He was also glad Clare's sister Kiki was happy. She had been staying a great deal in their home in Jacksonville. Tubby noted, "She belongs to the innermost circle of this family whether she realizes it or not." He finished his letter home by telling Clare he was on his way to downtown Columbus with the officers of the 85th Division. He signed his letter, as he usually did, "All love always, Tubby."[92] He and his wife had been arguing over many things the last few years, but things were going well. He had confided in his daughter in his many letters, so he told Clare Conway to rip up any that mentioned troubles with her mother. "Believe everything is in good order, and some of my letters would hurt her."[93]

On May 16 he wrote to his daughter about his coming to visit. Somehow, he arranged for AGF to send him on an inspection trip to Camp Carson to study the post's use of training aids. It is doubtful that this was simply a coincidence since Carson is outside Colorado Springs, where his daughter lived with his mother's family. And the visit would take place at the same time as Clare Conway's high school graduation. He would go on inspection, stay with the family, and attend graduation. Then father and daughter would hop on a train and travel to Atlanta, where they would meet up with Clare and R. O., stay on post at Fort McPherson, and all "have a grand reunion in Atlanta." He wrote to her a week later and told her how much he looked forward to the visit. Again, he reminded her to get rid of any of his letters venting about her mother. He also told her to gather everyone in the family and schedule a meeting. He wanted to take everyone to dinner, partially as a graduation party but also to thank them all for taking such good care of his daughter.[94] Because they were all together, we have no letters describing the events. But clippings from the Colorado Springs newspapers confirm that Brigadier General Barton came to Camp Carson to inspect the camp and its training facilities. In addition, the family was there for Clare's graduation from Colorado Springs High School on June 5.[95]

The 85th Division began its organization at Camp Shelby under the direction of the IV Corps. Barton stopped by Camp Beauregard to gather his belongings that he had left when joining the division, among them his dog, Ches, who had been staying with friends while he was away. The corps chaplain tried to get the dog shot since he was not always on the leash and running a bit amok during Barton's absence. Fortunately, the IV Corps staff jumped into action and took care of Ches. Barton does not say who did it, but he notes that the "chaplain [was] properly instructed." While he was there, Barton and Griswold spent several evenings discussing personal and military affairs.

Griswold, who was instrumental in propelling Barton to division command, remained with the IV Corps until April 1943. Then the War Department sent him overseas to replace Sandy Patch with the XIV Corps in the Pacific for Operation CARTWHEEL and continue through the liberation of the Philippines and capture of Manila in 1945. Like most of the US Army's excellent corps and division commanders in the Pacific, he is generally known to only professional historians and students of the

Pacific War. But, like Singleton and Ord, "Gris" significantly influenced Tubby's development and remained one of his best friends until his death in 1959.[96]

Barton enjoyed working with Haislip, whom he had known for thirty-four years. There was nothing on the post other than a few members of the division's advance party. He thought it was desolate: "A tent camp without the tents." He now had a small personal staff. His commissioned aide was Captain Parks Huntt.[97] He had two enlisted aides, whom the army called strikers. One, Private Jason K. Richards, whom he used as his driver, was especially promising. Richards kept his car clean, kept his clothes always pressed and ready to wear, and woke him up each morning with a cup of coffee at his bedside. Barton was enjoying the life of a general.[98]

Assisted by his stenographer, he usually wrote one letter and then sent it to his wife, daughter, and mother. He would then annotate a personal note to each. In mid-May he told everyone about his typical day. At 06:30 Richards woke him up and brought him a cup of coffee and, if available, fresh orange juice. Then to the officer's mess for breakfast. Then into the jeep to visit every unit commander and watch some of the training they were conducting. Around 11:00 he was back at headquarters for Haislip's daily staff conference. With all the issues requiring coordination, this was an important event that invariably resulted in taskers for the chief of staff. When it was over, he was back in the jeep. Lunch could be at the headquarters mess or with one of the units in training. In the evening he was at the headquarters, discussed events with the chief of staff or commander, and then he had time for the necessary paperwork. One stop was often the hospital, where they treated him for problems with his nose and throat—probably caused by an allergy. He also had an eye exam and a new set of glasses for the first time at government expense.[99]

Since it would be a motorized army, division leaders had to know something about automotive basics. From April 20 to 24, the division's leaders traveled to Holabird Quartermaster Depot, near Baltimore, to attend the Motor Transport Special School for general officers of new divisions. Haislip, Barton, McKelvie, and Sands all participated in the course. While a special class for senior officers, it most likely summarized what the enlisted

Motor Transport Special Service School, Holabird Quartermaster Motor Base, April 20–24, 1942. C-2 refresher course for general officers of new divisions. *From left to right*, Raymond O. Barton, Wade H. Haislip, Jay W. MacKelvie, and Thomas J. Sands. US Army photograph, courtesy Barton family.

soldiers were studying in the formal "F" course. Officers learned about the various kinds of automotive engines, how to perform operator and crew maintenance, and the procedures for diagnosing automotive problems and repairing vehicles. Each officer took six pamphlets on how to inspect vehicles before, during, and after operations. Most important were lessons on how to supervise operators and maintenance personnel. The intent was not to teach the senior leaders how to do the work but to manage those who did.[100] Tubby put his new training into use almost immediately. Writing to Clare, he reminded his wife to take care of the car and get it serviced. He even had the nerve to send her copies of the army's "system of checking vehicles." Unfortunately, we have no record of how she received this gift, but one can only imagine what she did with this packet.[101]

He continued to write to his friends, especially those still serving with the 4th Motorized Division at Camp Gordon. Most notable was James S. Rodwell, who had been his G-3 when he was the chief of staff. He liked Rodwell, a cavalryman who had gone to the infantry advanced course and was one of his original staff members. On May 8 Barton wrote his wife, "Nice letter [of congratulations] from Rodwell. He means it. Whatever his shortcomings, he dishes out what he thinks—good and bad." Clare had mentioned that he was still showing up in reports as part of the IV Corps and not getting credit for being the assistant commander. Tubby explained that he was still technically assigned to IV Corps, since the new division did not exist as the War Department had not formally activated it. His big news in this chatty letter was about the dog, Ches, who was doing well and living the life of a pampered general's pet. Haislip liked the dog, who was always welcome in the commanding general's headquarters. Barton had a jeep and a sedan but seldom used the car. He made his impressive driver and assistant, Richards, a sergeant.[102]

Also on his mind was the drama taking place in the Philippines. In late April the Japanese captured Luzon, on May 5 they landed on Corregidor, and the next day Wainwright surrendered the fortress. Soon they would begin the horrendous death march on Bataan. The Japanese sent Wainwright, McBride, Chynoweth, Jones, Weaver, and King to prisoner-of-war camps in Formosa. They later evacuated Wainwright and others to camps in Manchuria to keep them away from the advancing Americans. All but McBride, who died in May 1944, made it home at the war's end. Sutherland avoided the Bataan march since he accompanied Douglas MacArthur when, on President Roosevelt's orders, he fled from Corregidor in Manila Bay to Australia before the capitulation. Harry Collins's son-in-law, Captain M. Griffith Berg, survived the death march to Bataan. In September 1944 the Japanese loaded 750 American captives on the ship *Shinyo Maru* for transport to another camp near Manilla. The American submarine USS *Paddle* intercepted the vessel, not knowing of its cargo. According to Japanese records, 668 Americans, including Berg, perished in this attack.[103] The fall of the Philippines was a personal and emotional event for army officers still in America.

Barton took some time off to visit Jacksonville and was back at Shelby on June 10, when he took temporary command of the 85th Division to give Haislip some time for his leave and rest.[104] Meanwhile, on Monday, June 15, the G-1 for AGF began considering impending personnel changes. McNair was replacing Fred Wallace as commander of the 4th Motorized Division and moving him to command a corps support area. The change implied Wallace was a reliable manager but not the kind of leader needed for combat command. The army command centered their discussion on Barton, who knew the division well and was an active, hands-on leader. On June 16 McNair recommended the 53-year-old brigadier for promotion and assignment to Camp Gordon to replace Wallace. Marshall concurred the next day.[105]

Meanwhile, Barton continued his inspection regime and worked with the individual units. Most likely Ham Haislip told him about the promotion the following Monday. On Thursday, June 25, the War Department's formal orders arrived, sending him to the 4th Motorized Division. There was a minor protocol issue since the old seniority rules were still War Department policy. The two other brigadiers in the division were senior to him. Therefore, to bypass this restriction, his orders stated, "by Command of the President." On July 1, 1942, Barton returned to the division he helped reactivate as its wartime commander.[106]

Chapter 7

Training and Deployment, July 1942–December 1943

The 4th Division did not magically appear on Utah Beach in June 1944. Before that it had received extensive training in the American southeast, much of which Barton had planned or supervised. Now he would continue that preparation process as its commander. The *Augusta Chronicle* said good-bye to General Wallace and welcomed the new commander in a front-page article on Sunday, July 5, 1942. It noted Barton's association with Augusta in the previous war and that he had been a member of the 4th Division longer than any other officer when he left the previous October.[1]

4th Motorized Division Commander, Camp Gordon, July 1942–April 1943

When Barton arrived at Camp Gordon, he had two brigadier generals, the assistant commander Maxwell A. O'Brien and Fay B. Prickett (USMA 1916). Prickett, the division artillery commander, had been one of his students at Leavenworth, and Barton was happy to work with him. He did not know O'Brien, who had replaced Ham Haislip as assistant commander in February. While well liked by all, Barton, who was probably biased because of O'Brien's National Guard background, did not consider him

Major Garlan R. Bryant, 4th Infantry Division G-1, administering oath of office to Major General Barton at Camp Gordon, Georgia, August 18, 1942. US Army photograph, Dwight David Eisenhower Presidential Library.

professionally qualified. Therefore, at the end of January 1943, he recommended replacing him and sending him to another division.[2] As a replacement, Brigadier General Henry A. Barber Jr. (USMA 1917), a decorated veteran from the First World War, moved from the 45th Infantry Division to become Barton's new deputy.[3]

When Barton took command in July 1942, his former G-3, James S. Rodwell, was now his chief of staff. Major Orlando C. Troxel Jr. (USMA 1931) was his G-3. Lieutenant Colonel Richard S. Marr was his G-4, and his G-2 was a bright young officer, Major Richard C. Hopkins, (USMA 1935). Unfortunately, in February 1943 Hopkins died after being sick for only a week. Only 31 years old and very athletic, his loss was a shock to the headquarters that had not yet been in combat. Major Harry F. Hanson took over his duties.[4] The G-1 was Lieutenant Colonel R. Williams, who would soon be replaced by Major Garlan R. Bryant. Barton's trusted assistants, Jason Richards and

Parks Huntt, followed him to his new assignment. His promotion caught up with him and Bryant administered his oath of office as a major general, army of the United States, on August 18.

Like all infantry divisions in the new US Army, the 4th Motorized had three infantry regiments, the 8th, 12th, and 22nd. We already met the 8th Infantry, Barton's former unit from Fort Screven, commanded since July 1941 by Colonel James Van Fleet. A member of the USMA class of 1915, he was with Barton at Eagle Pass in 1916 and later commanded a machine-gun battalion in the 6th Infantry Division in the Meuse-Argonne campaign. After the war he became an ROTC professor at three successive universities: Kansas State University, South Dakota State University, and the University of Florida. While at Gainesville and still on active duty, he became its head football coach. His Florida Gators in 1923 and 1924 had an overall winning record of 12–3–4. He later coached the US Army's enlisted football team and then served another ROTC and assistant coach tour at the University of Florida. Unlike his peers, especially Eisenhower and Bradley, he never attended either the CGSS course or the Army War College. As a result, when Marshall began selecting officers to command his expanding number of divisions, Van Fleet was not on his list. [5] Another rumor for Van Fleet's lack of advancement had to do with Marshall confusing him with another officer he remembered from Fort Benning. Captain George Mabry, then in the 8th Infantry Regiment's 2nd Battalion, confirmed this story in his memoirs. Before deploying overseas Mabry heard Marshall ask Barton, "Tubby, Van is still a colonel? Haven't you recommended him for promotion?" Barton's response was he had "recommended Van on three separate occasions, but every time I recommend him for promotion, I get the word back it has been disapproved." According to Mabry, Marshall admitted confusing Van Fleet with Colonel John H. Van Vliet, an officer he did not particularly like. Marshall was prepared to push though Van Fleet's promotion immediately, but Barton convinced the army chief of staff that he needed him as a regimental commander and to wait until after the invasion.[6] But Van Fleet's failure to attend the senior service courses was probably the main reason for his nonselection to brigadier general. Without a large-scale war, it is doubtful that he would have ever progressed beyond regimental command.

The 22nd Infantry had spent the 1920s and 1930s split among Fort McClellan (Alabama), Fort Oglethorpe (North Georgia), and McPherson (Atlanta). Colonel Albert S. Peake moved the regiment to Fort Benning in June 1940. An old soldier who started his career in the Philippine Constabulary in 1908, Peake had difficulty adapting to the new motorized division concept and turned over command to George H. Weams in November 1941. In February 1942, after less than six months in command, Weams became Fort Benning's assistant commandant, replaced by Colonel Herve A. Tribolet. A graduate of Denison University, he served, like Barton, in the United States during World War I but did get to the Rhineland and served briefly in Coblenz with the 5th Infantry Regiment. A solid and well-liked commander, he would lead the regiment into Normandy.[7]

The 12th Infantry experienced more turmoil among its commanders than the other two regiments. It spent the interwar years at Fort Meade, Maryland, and Arlington Cantonment, Virginia. Its primary role was ceremonial, serving as the US Capitol Guard, the Arlington Cemetery Guard of Honor, and the Guard at the Tomb of the Unknown Soldier. Colonel Carroll A. (Jake) Bagby, who graduated from West Point a year before Barton and was his classmate at the Army War College, had commanded the regiment since June 1941 when he moved most of the unit to Fort Dix, New Jersey. After several months of expansion and reorganization, the War Department ordered it to move to Georgia and join the reactivated 4th Motorized Division in October. Having watched Bagby while he was 4th Division and IV Corps chief of staff, Barton was not impressed and replaced him. Colonel James Sutherland succeeded Bagby, but he lasted only until the middle of September, when Barton replaced him with Colonel Jerome K. Harris. Harris departed the division to become the III Corps G-3 in February, and Colonel Harry Henderson, a World War I veteran, took command and took the regiment to England.[8]

Officers moved in and out of commands at a dizzying pace at that stage of the war. In some instances they had impressed senior leaders, who wanted to give them more challenging assignments. In other cases they were incompetent and relieved for cause. Finally, in the division commander's judgment, some competent officers did not possess the aggressiveness sufficient to lead a regiment in combat. No matter the cause, the replaced officer moved to another duty, contributing but not part of a deploying combat unit. Seldom a paper trail remains indicating the transfer's reason. In Bagby's case, he took command of the 29th Infantry, the Benning school's regiment, and moved it to Iceland in 1943.[9]

Most students of the US Army in the Second World War are aware of the extensive training exercises that took place in the United States before America entered the war. However, the AGF maneuvers that continued at its five maneuver areas in the Carolinas, Tennessee, Louisiana, California, Arizona, and Oregon are not as familiar.[10] Even less well-known are the many training events run by stateside-based corps commanders. From July 12 to 25, 1942, Major General John P. Lucas, commander of III Corps, and Major General Ernest J. Dawley's VI Corps conducted force-on-force maneuvers in the Carolina maneuver area where Barton and Griswold had fought the previous November. Barton's division was the red army, and he fought against Major General Alvin C. Gillem's blue army. The weather was hot and muggy, registering almost ninety-eight degrees without considering the effects of humidity. By all accounts Barton's force did well, outmaneuvering his opponent. The locals noted that these soldiers were unlike those who came through a year earlier, undisciplined, looking ragged, and often using wooden sticks instead of actual weapons. These soldiers had the best available tanks, trucks, artillery, and aircraft. They also noticed a sense of seriousness and intensity not apparent in the pre–Pearl Harbor days.[11] Barton's sense of pride was evident as he noted they returned from the maneuver area, 150 miles away, with fifteen thousand soldiers and 2,300 vehicles without an accident. "At the conclusion of the march, the entire division was ready to march or fight the next day; the mark of a well-trained and coordinated outfit."[12]

However, Barton inherited a division that the army did not know how to use. It had already demonstrated proficiency in moving long distances and working with armored divisions. As in the army's armored divisions, the 4th Motorized Division was waiting for a chance to go into action. In July, soon after Barton took command, President Roosevelt told Marshall and his military advisors that he wanted the United States to be engaged in a land war in the European theater of operations (ETO) before the end of 1942. By August

Roosevelt and Prime Minister Churchill had agreed to drive Germany and
Italy from North Africa. Operation TORCH was the code name for that
task. In theory the Rolling Fourth would have been an excellent unit for
America's first assault against the Axis. It was the best-trained motorized unit
in the United States and the only one with its full complement of equipment.
Its experienced commanders and staff had practiced mobile operations with
both Patton and Fredendall, two of TORCH's senior American commanders.
Army planners assumed that it would be part of the invasion. However, the
problem was that it was in the United States, and shipping units overseas
was a significant problem. When they finished their projections, only the 2nd
Armored Division and the 3rd and 9th Infantry Divisions, both nonmotorized,
would make the journey from America to North Africa.[13]

Now, like other units in the United States, it was in reserve for some
future operation. However, the world situation was moving on. On August 7,
1942, US Marines landed on Guadalcanal, beginning the American ground
effort against Japan. The next day Churchill and Roosevelt agreed on the
details of Operation TORCH. A week later they selected General Eisenhower,
a plebe when Barton was a firstie, as its commander. On November 8
American and British troops landed in North Africa, commencing ground
operations in the ETO. Barton was now an observer as the leaders he knew
went into battle across the globe. His old boss Lloyd Fredendall led Task
Force Center into Algeria, and George Patton led his troops against the
Vichy French in Morocco. A month later, Sandy Patch's Americal Division
relieved the 1st Marine Division and entered combat on Guadalcanal. A few
days later, on December 16, Bob Eichelberger, who had been so kind to him
the previous March, took command of the 32nd Infantry Division in New
Guinea. For the remainder of the year, Barton continued to develop his
motorized division. But the wait was frustrating and far from the battle line.
For example, in December the division newspaper, the *Ivy Leaf*, reported
on dances, intramural sports, and holiday events. The paper gave little indication that the Rolling Fourth was doing anything other than small-unit
training and biding its time.[14]

Barton broke away in the third week of January to visit some supporting organizations at Fort Sill. When done, he stopped in Ada to spend time

with his mother. He called on his high school friend Orel Busby, who had become a respected Oklahoma lawyer and had recently finished a term on the state supreme court. After Ada he traveled to Camp Hood to examine training there. When he got to Texas, he sent Clare Conway a short note, remarking that his 83-year-old mother was very frail. But she was in good spirits and had a nice lady taking care of her.[15] He warned his daughter that the next few months would be intensive training periods, so letters might not be coming as regularly as before.[16] At the end of the month, he was back at Camp Gordon, happy that they cleaned and painted his office while he was gone. He felt good.[17]

But while the 4th Division remained at Camp Gordon in early 1943, Barton watched those he knew well begin engaging the Germans and Japanese, with mixed results. In the Pacific Sandy Patch now commanded the XIV Corps on Guadalcanal, and one of his units, the 25th Infantry Division, had J. Lawton Collins in command. Barton watched from a distance in mid-February as German General Erwin Rommel humiliated Fredendall's II Corps at Kasserine Pass. Then, at the beginning of March, Patton arrived to replace his old boss and restore the troop's fighting ability. From Barton's perspective these historical events all had personal meaning. In early March Marshall sent all division commanders a summary of Eisenhower's report on his visit to the American troops outside Kasserine Pass. The letter's main thrust: take training seriously, and do it regularly, even when in a combat zone.[18]

And practice they did. Most of it was small-unit and individual skills, such as squad drills and marksmanship. It was intense, and one incident received national attention. In mid-January an infantry company conducted an assault drill under live machine gunfire. They had to crawl under barbed wire about a hundred yards until they reached the enemy position. While there was no real danger, it was scary for those involved. Two soldiers refused to go through the course. Barton was out watching that day and decided it was time to lead. According to the newspaper accounts, "He [Barton] didn't reprimand them, nor did he order them to get down and crawl. He changed speedily into coveralls and personally led the doubtful doughboys through the fire."[19] But all this was training, and the War Department had not yet scheduled the division for deployment.

This well-trained unit was not deploying to North Africa and Italy due to its organization and the problem of the motorized division. In theory there would be one of these for every two armored divisions, essentially replicating how the Germans had developed their panzer grenadiers to support their panzer divisions. McNair never liked the concept and considered it wasteful for the American Army. From his perspective every infantry division was mobile as soon as the army headquarters sent them six quartermaster truck companies. The inability of the War Department to ship the Rolling Fourth overseas, despite its high level of training, was evidence of the problem with this organization. It had over one thousand more vehicles than a standard division and, as a result, required almost twice as much shipping tonnage, about sixty thousand tons. In March 1943 McNair argued for reconverting all motorized divisions to standard infantry divisions. The War Department agreed to eliminate all motorized divisions except for Barton's, which would remain the only motorized unit in the army for the time being.[20] With that in mind, Barton led his command back to the Carolina training area for two weeks of maneuvers, beginning on March 14.[21]

Fort Dix, April–August 1943

While Barton's soldiers were out training, Eisenhower's forces were in their last phase of destroying the German and Italian armies in Tunisia. Churchill and Roosevelt decided at the Casablanca Conference in January that the follow-on Allied tasks were to clear Sicily, invade Italy, and knock the junior Axis power out of the war. The War Department was determined to get its best-trained unit in the United States into the next phase of combat. Since it would require more transport than any other infantry division, the planners decided to move it to a location where they could take advantage of America's most developed harbor system. As the 4th Division returned to Camp Gordon, Barton received orders to move the division to Fort Dix, New Jersey. By the second week of April 1943, the division was on the move, this time by train, hauling its equipment. The War Department had used Dix to process and ship troops to and from Europe during the last war. Facilities were in good shape, and the troops had easy access to recreation in Philadelphia, New York, and Atlantic City.[22]

After arriving at Fort Dix, most soldiers got a week of rest, with many heading to the Jersey shore. The troops continued to train in garrison with more weapons firing, small-unit attacks on fortified positions, and air-ground operations. Mortar crews received special training attention since they gave the infantry battalion commander his best fire support for close-in combat. However, training in these areas was often interrupted by events in the local communities, and in one case the division assisted during a labor shortage in unloading tomatoes in danger of rotting at a nearby Campbell Soup plant.[23]

Barton arrived from Camp Gordon in a B-18 Bolo bomber reconfigured as a transport. He traveled with his new aide, Phillip Hart, as Parks Huntt received a promotion and took the post as the division's headquarters commandant. The post commander greeted him with a small honor guard and held a ceremony officially welcoming the division. However, since this was a more urban and developed portion of the country, Barton was not particularly happy with the restrictions on his troop training.[24] With little space for large unit maneuvers, he was often involved in less military pursuits, such as when he helped to persuade the J. P. Morgan family to help refurbish the unit's officers' club, which opened on May 17. During the division's assignment, it was part of XIII Corps, headquartered at Fort DuPont, Delaware, with Major General Emil F. Reinhardt, a colleague from Camp Hancock days, as its commander. He submitted a glowing report at the end of June, concluding with, "General Barton is aggressive, energetic, and a steady leader. The snap and precision of his officers and enlisted men, the organization and execution of training indicated a high degree of leadership on the part of the division commander. He is firm but eminently fair in his dealing with subordinates and has won their wholehearted respect and confidence."[25] But Barton was not in a combat zone and spent much time on events like politicking with the Morgan family or entertaining visiting groups, such as models from the Conover Modeling Agency in July. He wanted to get his division into the war.

Meanwhile, Barton's family was never far from his mind. Since his wife and daughter were not on good terms, he tried to act as the intermediary and get them to reconcile. He was uncomfortable with his two ladies being so far apart, one in Florida, the other in Colorado. He was also

Major General Barton entertains the Conover models from New York City at Soldiers Island, Fort Dix, New Jersey, July 24, 1943. US Army photograph, Dwight David Eisenhower Presidential Library.

concerned with his daughter's transition into adult life and urged her to reduce her smoking and refrain from drinking. At Colorado College, where she was taking courses, she had an incident and got into trouble over a girls' drinking experiment. He was also working to get his son, R. O., into West Point.[26] But most troubling was the passing of his beloved mother, Carrie, on August 5, 1943. He returned to Ada to bury her alongside her husband and Percy.[27] Barton had been incredibly close to his parents, and now that connection had passed. Her passing also marked the end of his close association with Ada, and he adopted the southeast United States as his new regional base. When Barton returned from his mother's funeral, he found orders waiting to begin moving again.

Behind the scenes, the War Department's Operations Division and AGF wrestled with the problem of how to get the 4th Infantry into combat. McNair wanted it converted immediately into an infantry division and shipped to

Europe. On the other hand, planners at the Operations Division wanted to keep it configured as was. As a compromise, on May 4 they agreed to begin reconfiguring the 4th as an infantry division but kept it intact in the event European planners wanted a motorized division for the forthcoming invasion. By August the European staff confirmed they had no plans to use such a unit during Operation NEPTUNE. At the end of June, the division's soldiers began cleaning, inspecting, inventorying, and repairing the equipment and vehicles that the War Department did not authorize for a standard infantry division. On August 4, the day after Barton's mother's death, it was final, and the Ivy Division was officially, again, the 4th Infantry Division.[28] On August 24 AGF scheduled the unit for amphibious training at the amphibious training center on the Florida coast.[29]

Camp Gordon Johnston, September–December 1943

In 1943 the army had two relatively well-known special training centers: the desert training center at Camp Young, California, for armored units, and the mountain training center at Camp Hale, Colorado, for preparing the 10th Mountain Division for combat. Less well-known is the amphibious training center at Camp Gordon Johnston, located near the beach town of Carrabelle, Florida, about sixty miles southwest of Tallahassee. However, by the time the 4th Infantry Division arrived in September 1943, the center had been in operation for more than a year. Moreover, it had changed from a purely army endeavor to a joint army-navy operation.[30] Moving the entire command from Fort Dix to Carrabelle took several weeks. It began by turning in its large assortment of trucks and self-propelled weapons. Then the troops headed south; each one-way trip took three days in Pullman cars. In Florida the soldiers moved into barracks, each with between thirty and fifty men. It took several weeks to move into the encampments and acclimate to the environment. Once they were in place, the soldiers could take leave, visit nearby towns, such as Tallahassee and Panama City, and fish.

Before the formal training began, Lloyd Fredendall, recently relieved from II Corps command after his defeat in Tunisia, came to visit. After his relief one of the great disgraceful and celebrated incidents of the war,

Lieutenant General Lloyd Fredendall meets with Barton and selected officers upon his arrival at Camp Gordon Johnston, Florida, October 1943. Eisenhower had relived him in March, following his defeat at Kasserine Pass in North Africa. He now commanded the Second Army, based in Memphis, Tennessee. US Army photograph, Dwight David Eisenhower Presidential Library.

Eisenhower sent him back to the United States. Rather than waste his good friend's years of experience, Marshall appointed him commander of the Second Army, based in Memphis, Tennessee. Visiting the amphibious training center was one of his first official duties. Barton and Fredendall had worked closely together during the division's early training, and Fredendall was again his rater. One suspects the private conversations were interesting and informative.[31]

In August War Department planners privately let Barton know the 4th Division would be part of the assault on France, code name OVERLORD. In September he flew to England for a general briefing on his role and to examine potential training and bivouac areas.[32] Therefore, he knew the general outlines of the division's role over the next year, and in a training memorandum he published on October 14, he spelled out the division's training plan for the next nine months. He identified three training phases, beginning at Gordon Johnston between October 18 and December 31. Next was general training in January and February 1944, and phase three, beginning in March, would be determined once they had more definite guidance on the division's mission.

For phase one amphibious operations were the most crucial task, followed by other essential skills such as mine laying, sanitation, patrolling, and night operations. During assault training he wanted units to use live ammunition and to emphasize bayonet use. In addition to regular exercises, officers and noncommissioned officers would attend schools on leadership and tactical subjects. Physical fitness was essential, and he expected officers and men to conduct long-distance cross-country runs at least once weekly. They would practice marching, with full gear, from distances of fifteen to twenty-five miles. This training memorandum leaves little doubt that, in the commander's mind, the unit was now preparing for a specific mission. While not on the prescribed training plan, the division ran a modified Ranger training program for select members of each regiment. Captain Oscar Joyner Jr., a former amphibious training center staff member, who had previously been with the 8th Infantry and was now with division G-3, ran this program. Its essence was on fundamental individual skills such as map reading, land navigation, use of explosives, detecting mines and booby traps, and scaling defensive walls.[33]

The amphibious training center organized the division into five "groupments," lettered A through E. Groupment A was for the division staff and commanders or selected staff members from each subordinate command. Its objective was to develop teamwork in the organization. The division had many separate battalions and companies (such as engineers, medical, quartermaster, ordnance, etc.). Working together was an essential component of a successful landing. Groupments B, C, and D consisted of an infantry regiment, an artillery battalion, attached engineers, medics, and other elements assigned to each combat team. The intent was to develop "regimental combat teams and special units that are physically hard, well-coordinated, fast-moving, and efficient in all phases of amphibious operations, including combat that is likely to take place on a defended shoreline." E, the final group, consisted of all other division elements not trained in one of the other groups. These included the military police; signal, ordnance, and quartermaster companies; reconnaissance troop, medical battalion, and artillery headquarters.[34]

The detail for much of the training was a 271-page syllabus titled "Shore to Shore Amphibious Training." It covered nearly everything a unit could expect to experience, from loading the vessels and landing on the far shore to communicating during the passage to the coast and the beach organization after landing. It also had a series of tutorials for commanders and staff on how to write an amphibious order. Finally, this program ended with a series of exercises designed to put everything the soldiers and their leaders learned into practice. Historians and D-Day students have often wondered about the cross-pollination of amphibious techniques between the European and Pacific theaters of war. Beyond what individual leaders might have brought from one theater to another, there is no question that the assaulting divisions everywhere used the amphibious training center's fundamental techniques.[35]

The training program was challenging and demanding. Working with the 4th Engineer Special Brigade, soldiers got seasick for the first time as they spent hours offshore bobbing in their landing craft. They landed at night on beaches on local islands and the Florida coast. They hiked at night to build their physical fitness while avoiding the day's heat. They went swimming every afternoon to learn how to escape a sinking ship and reach the shore. Combat teams practiced, for the first time, as units: infantry, engineers, medics, and artillery. As the historian for the 22nd Infantry noted, "Probably no phase of the regiment's training was more useful or more thoroughly detested than the time spent at Camp Gordon Johnston, Florida." By the end of November, these young men were in the best physical condition of their lives, lean from the exercise and tan from hours in the sun. Among them was the 54-year-old division commander, who was now lean and fit, as he had promised his daughter months before.[36]

Before moving to Florida, Brigadier General Prickett had departed to take command of the 75th Infantry Division.[37] Replacing him was Brigadier General Harold W. Blakeley, a graduate of Boston University. Since the army began its expansion in 1940, he had progressed through the ranks, commanding the 6th Field Artillery and 5th Armored Division and training with it in the Mojave Desert maneuver area in 1942. He led the 5th Armored Division's artillery to England and then took command of Combat Command A. After a

4th Infantry Division commanders and staff, Camp Gordon Johnston, Florida, August 1943. US Army photograph, Dwight David Eisenhower Presidential Library.

short time, the War Department moved him from this command and sent him to the 4th Infantry Division to replace Prickett.[38]

Headlines for the November 13, 1943, edition of the *Ivy Leaf* were, "Three generals, staff officers swim their fifty yards." Everyone in the division had to pass the fifty-yard swim test, and Barton was determined to lead the way. The photograph at the bottom of the paper shows a picture of Barton diving headfirst off the twenty-eight-foot tower into the "cold, cold water." The caption assures us that the remainder of the staff and commanders followed. The newspaper's top has a photograph of the commanders and staff, shirtless in swimming trunks, gathered after their swim. Barton sits in the center next to Blakeley, Marr, and Rodwell, who would be his closest friends and advisors for the following year. Maxwell O'Brien is there but will not travel to Europe with the division. Behind them are two regimental commanders, Van Fleet and Henderson, and most division headquarters officers. This is a unique and classic photograph, capturing a "band of brothers," to quote Shakespeare's Henry IV. It displayed the core of the division leadership that planned and directed the unit's landing six months later Utah Beach. After more than a year together, it was a close-knit group.[39]

The Movement to the UK, December 1943–January 1944

The 4th Division began its journey to Europe by leaving Camp Gordon Johnston on December 1. Wheeled vehicles moved by convoy the 450 miles from the coast to Fort Jackson, just east of Columbia, South Carolina. While on an administrative road march, the unit moved in serials by individual combat teams (a regiment and its supporting units). Barton had no intention of breaking up the cohesion these groups had developed over the preceding months. On the way north, Tubby certainly stopped in Jacksonville to see Clare. These had been a busy few months, and he, correctly, anticipated this might be the last time he saw her for a long time. The purpose of assembling at Fort Jackson was to get the troops and equipment back to serviceable condition. They had been operating in Florida's saltwater and jungle-like environment for the last several months. Trucks, jeeps, weapons of all kinds, and clothing needed repair or replacement. Troops lose equipment when they operate, and it was time to replace everything missing. Supply sergeants accompanied company commanders as they inspected every soldier in the unit. Commanders and staff officers reviewed the status of every company. Nothing was too mundane to check on, from a soldier's immunizations to his weapon qualification. The supply system replaced damaged uniforms and individual load-carrying equipment. Finally, it was also time to grant some soldiers, especially those who lived in the southeast and could get home quickly, one last furlough. Of course, commanders ordered the men not to disclose what they were doing, but they all knew this would be their final Christmas home for a long time, and perhaps forever.[40]

The division started moving again at the end of December to Camp Kilmer, New Jersey, where they would spend several weeks preparing to travel. Located northeast of New Brunswick, the facility had been developed by the War Department into the largest staging area for units deploying to Europe. With barracks, chapels, five theaters, nine post exchanges, three libraries, and four telephone exchanges, soldiers had plenty to keep them occupied in the evening. War Department inspectors and officers from various agencies moved soldiers through one last series of redeployment checks during the day. Soldiers received physical examinations and lectures on security and removed all their unit patches and insignia. The men filled in the change of address cards and sent them home, along with any items they were not permitted to take with them. Soldiers had their shipment number written in chalk on their helmets. The 12th Infantry, for example, was now referred to as Shipment 1589-G. Those who had accomplished all their preparation tasks had some last-minute time to visit the local cities, such as New Brunswick, Trenton, and New York. The War Department alerted the division for deployment at the end of December, and its advanced party, led by Jim Rodwell, departed New York harbor on December 27. All soldiers returned to camp, said good-byes to family members in the area, and prepared to get on the trains headed to the piers.[41]

The shipping units moved to the camp's railroad yard and traveled over a special track to the mainline and then to the Jersey City rail terminal. The troops then boarded sealed ferries and traveled to the Brooklyn Army Terminal. As they debarked from the ferry, local American Red Cross ladies met them with hot coffee, doughnuts, and candy bars no matter what time of day. At the foot of each gangplank, a company officer, watched by the regimental S-1, began calling roll. Soldiers grabbed their gear and boarded the ship carrying them to England. Soldiers probably knew that this would be the port where they would return to the United States, either dead or alive. The ship boarding continued all night until everyone and all the equipment was in the right place on the ship.

Van Fleet's 8th Infantry was first, leaving on January 10, 1944, on the RMS *Franconia*, a Cunard Liner. Henderson's 12th Infantry loaded onto the USAT *George Washington* on January 18, the same ship young Lieutenant Henderson sailed on when he traveled to France in 1917. Herve Tribolet's 22nd Infantry joined Barton and the 4th Division Headquarters on the British transport the *Cape Town Castle* on January 16. Some units, such as the 4th Medical Battalion, traveled with the teams they supported. By January 19 the entire division was at sea. Barton and his senior officers lived well, having "comfortable staterooms and were served excellent meals in the dining salon." The 22nd Infantry historian continues, "Quarters and rations for the enlisted men were inadequate."[42] Chaplains were popular and held services each night in the dining hall; in the face of the unknown world the soldiers faced, attendance was excellent. Movies were plentiful, and the army's special services had stocked the library with hundreds of books for reading. Leaders circulated among the troops, informing them what to expect when they arrived in England. There was time for sleeping, time for troops' orientation, and much time for wondering what was ahead. It took thirteen days to cross the icy Atlantic Ocean. By the end of January, the entire division had arrived at Liverpool, and the debarkation process began.[43]

The division's soldiers boarded trains from Liverpool and moved to encampment areas in the large peninsula in southwest England called Devon (or sometimes Devonshire). This assignment highlights an aspect of military operations that historians seldom discuss: military terrain management. This task, usually performed by the operations (G-3) staff, determines where units will locate on the ground, which commander is responsible for all activities within this space, what routes he is authorized to use and control, and what services and support he provides to other military units. This task becomes more complicated when considering the aspects of the British civilian society with which they shared the space. With over 1.6 million Americans and hundreds of thousands of vehicles moving into the United Kingdom by June 1944, and the construction and operation of dozens of airfields and training areas in a relatively small space, this management process needed dedicated attention. Finally, these soldiers and airmen were not in the United Kingdom on vacation and needed to prepare for combat. Most importantly, they required access to ports and training areas.

Arriving American forces were part of Operation BOLERO, the US Army and Air Force's deployment to England. Determining American units' general location became the responsibility of the BOLERO Combined Committee, working for the Combined Chiefs of Staff in Washington. In England the BOLERO Combined Committee (London) supervised the "reception, accommodation, and maintenance of US forces in the

United Kingdom." This latter group coordinated with all British national and local government elements to ensure the process was as smooth as possible. This group supervised the terrain and facilities for American troops and designated billeting areas. It sent the 4th Infantry Division to Devon, which would facilitate amphibious training, both in the English and Bristol Channels, relatively easily. It was also close to the embarkation ports and the ultimate landing areas in western Normandy.[44]

When the troops arrived in Liverpool, they traveled by train to Exeter. From there trucks carried the soldiers to their new encampments. Unlike their experience in the United States, the regimental headquarters, individual battalions, and sometimes companies found themselves in various facilities of varying standards. Mix-ups in billeting occurred, which was inevitable. However, "with the cordial cooperation of the British townspeople and the rapid adjustment of the troops to the circumstances," as the division's historian noted, "the solution was inevitably forthcoming. Certainly, there were beds for all and no one was hungry."[45]

The division headquarters and several smaller supporting units moved into Tiverton, a market town dating back to 650 in the mid-Devon district. The headquarters was at a lovely mansion from the early eighteenth century called Collipriest House. It was the northernmost of the division headquarters complexes, on the A38 motorway and equidistant between Bristol Channel and Exeter near Lyme Bay. This location allowed Barton and his staff to maintain contact with his units no matter where they were training. Blakeley's division artillery headquarters moved into an elegant home called Hillersdon House, in the nearby village of Cullompton, with the battalions scattered near their supported regiments.[46] In addition to the staff and commanders coming and going was 25-year-old J. D. Salinger. Once the government drafted the future author, they sent him to a unique training program for those relatively fluent in German and, often, of Jewish origin. Working for the division's counterintelligence unit, he would interrogate enemy prisoners of war and gather information that analysts could convert to intelligence the commander could use for immediate plans. Once units moved out for the coast, Salinger joined the 12th Infantry for the campaign's duration.[47]

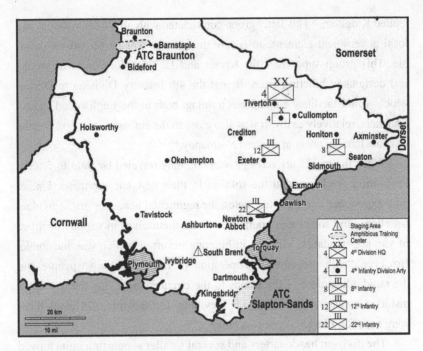

4th Infantry Division in Devon, March–May 1944

Henderson's 12th Infantry Regiment moved into the Higher Barracks in Exeter. The city began as a Roman encampment and legion headquarters around 55 AD. As in the case of many cities in southern England, it had a long and interesting history. The regiment's new home was a defensive facility leftover from the French Revolution era and remained useable despite age. Unfortunately, the Luftwaffe destroyed much of the historical city before the regiment arrived. As the headquarters and medical detachment moved into the barracks, the battalions and supporting units moved into other villages, such as Burleigh-Salterton and Exmouth, on the English Channel.[48] Van Fleet's 8th Infantry occupied the ancient town of Honiton on the old Roman road linking Exeter to Lincoln. This area was to the east of the A38 Motorway. Most of the regiment found space in Heathfield Camp, a training center built southwest of the town at the beginning of the war.[49] Like the 12th Infantry, Tribolet's 22nd Infantry was scattered in various villages, with the headquarters and 2nd Battalion moving into a newly constructed camp near Denbury. Probably the worst facility, "ancient and forbidding buildings" housed the 1st Battalion in Newton Abbott. Stationed several miles to the west was the 3rd Battalion, and the cannon and antitank companies moved into Quonset huts at South Brent.[50] The distance from division headquarters to Newton Abbott was over forty-five miles, making it a challenge for Barton and his staff to interact with his commanders, who now were pretty much on their own when not on training exercises.[51]

Chapter 8

England, February– May 1944

May 14, 1944
Tiverton, United Kingdom

Dear Mrs. Barton,

I thought perhaps you might like to have a report on Tubby.

To begin with, he's in good physical shape in spite of the very hard and responsible work he's been doing. The only trouble in this way that he's had is that conferences and planning have kept him from getting the exercise he'd like.

The Division which is really his work from beginning to end is recognized as one of the best in the Army. It would do your heart good to see the way both the officers and men look up to him and the affection they have for him. These are not empty words on my part for I have been working every day for the last six weeks with the rank and file.

Personally I have a great admiration for him also. He is so splendidly honest. When he acts he always shapes his course on what he believed to be right without thought of himself. Of course this is no news to you, but I've found mighty few (in the army) who really did this. It's been a joy serving with him.

. . .

We stand on the brink of the greatest adventure in history and you
can look forward with confidence and pride to the part your husband
will play in it.

Yours truly,
Theodore Roosevelt.[1]

Training for an Invasion, February–March 1944

On February 1, two days after the division arrived in Liverpool, Barton
headed for a meeting in London with General Omar Bradley, currently the
US Army commander of the ETO. While the two had previously met at
Fort Leavenworth in 1928 and probably during the Louisiana Maneuvers,
it is doubtful that they had much contact in the intervening years. However,
Bradley had worked closely with Marshall at Fort Leavenworth and was
one of his most trusted disciples. Unlike Eisenhower, who had no front-line
experience, by 1944 Bradley had a distinguished combat record, commanding
II Corps in North Africa and Sicily. Soon after this meeting, he would take
command of the US First Army. Accompanying Barton was his G-2, Harry
Hanson, G-3, Orlando Troxel, and G-4, Richard Marr. The reason for the
meeting was a change to Operation NEPTUNE.[2]

Only a week earlier, on January 23, Eisenhower notified the Combined
Chiefs of Staff that he had approved a significant modification in the
invasion concept. Because the Allies' posture for men and material had
improved since the original invasion plan's development, they could now
assault another beach, Utah, on the Cotentin Peninsula. Bradley assigned
this mission to the 4th Infantry as part of the VII Corps. The division had the
task of seizing that beach, linking up with two divisions of airborne forces
dropped inland, and turning north to lead the effort to capture the port at
Cherbourg. That evening Barton and his staff returned to Tiverton. The next
day he convened a meeting of all staff principles, led by his deputy, Hal
Barber, and his chief of staff, Jim Rodwell. Barton outlined the parameters
he received to develop their initial estimates for the focused training and the
division's assault order. It was a planning process that would continue until
the end of May.[3]

Not present at this early February meeting was the outgoing VII Corps commander, and Barton's colleague from teaching days at Fort Leavenworth, Roscoe B. Woodruff. He was the first captain at West Point the year Bradley and Eisenhower graduated. The official story is that both commanders were concerned that Woodruff had no combat experience as a division commander. However, neither did Gerow, Eisenhower's Leavenworth study mate, who retained command of V Corps. There was probably some friction between Woodruff and his classmates, which may have contributed to Eisenhower's decision to let him go. But the main reason was to make room for a more politically connected commander who needed a corps command, Marshall's most beloved protégé, J. Lawton Collins.[4]

Collins, whom Barton encountered in Coblenz and Leavenworth, had arrived in England with some professional baggage. In 1940 he worked for Marshall in Washington, and the following year he served as VII Corps chief of staff during the Louisiana Maneuvers. After the Japanese attack on Pearl Harbor, Marshall sent him to Hawaii to take over as the department's chief of staff and then commander of the 25th Infantry Division on Guadalcanal and New Georgia. However, here his meteoric career stumbled.

Alexander Patch was now commanding XIV Corps, the 25th Infantry Division's senior headquarters. Patch was not particularly impressed by the young division commander and on his April 1943 efficiency report rated him as "average" of all the general officers he knew, and commented, "An exceptionally energetic, industrious and aggressive officer, technically well informed and persistent in execution of any assigned mission. He is opinionated to a pronounced degree and a strong tendency to tell everyone not only what to do but how to do it. He does not encourage his juniors to feel free to voice their opinions."[5] Barton's mentor Oscar W. Griswold succeeded Alexander Patch and was initially impressed, rating him "superior" and his best division commander, although he did remark, "Impulsive, talkative, inclined to tell other how to do their job . . . can pay more attention with profit to administrative and disciplinary matters."[6] However, after six months working with Collins, Griswold had soured on his subordinate. At the end of November, McNair asked the XIV Corps commander to evaluate his division commanders' corps command potential. On Collins Griswold replied,

Collins is brave, brilliant, aggressive, and has many fine qualities, but he definitely does not have a happy command. He is unduly professionally ambitious, professionally selfish as toward of subordinates, and without doubt the most egotistical officer I have ever come in contact with. I have been very much surprised in Joe Collins, for I had always heard of him as tops. I definitely do not consider him big enough caliber for a Corps Commander, though having learned and being able to discount his personality, I do like him as a good fighting man and as a Division Commander. One, however, who must be kept in hand.[7]

In his final efficiency report, which covered the period that ended at the beginning of November, Griswold credited Collins as being a superior division commander, but rated him as second best out of his four. In his remarks, the corps commander noted, "Although possessed of many fine qualities he impresses me as being somewhat unduly ambitious, professionally selfish, and very egotistical. . . . Not recommended for Corps Command."[8] More than Marshall's mysterious black book of officer's names, the steady stream of efficiency reports crossing his desk kept him informed of the progress of his generals. Griswold's letter indicated there was little prospect of his protégé ever getting a corps command in the Pacific.

The army chief of staff had no problem helping favorites, and the young Collins, brother of Pershing's aide, was at the top of his list. He ordered the 25th Division commander to return to the United States and report to his office.[9] Collins is disingenuous in his autobiography about how and why he returned to the United States in early December. But he describes in some detail how he was greeted back in Washington. Few division commanders could return from the front lines thousands of miles away and walk into the army chief of staff's office, but he did. Marshall sent Collins and his wife on vacation to the Greenbrier Hotel in White Sulphur Springs, West Virginia. On his first night, he had dinner with General Eisenhower, who had just returned from North Africa, and his wife. According to Collins, Eisenhower told him, "I understand you are coming over to join us."[10] Therefore, Eisenhower and Bradley had to relieve Woodruff to make room for Collins, and he took command of the VII Corps on February 14.[11]

Collins, who had been the VII Corps chief of staff during the Louisiana Maneuvers, picked his team. However, Griswold ended his report with the remark, "must be kept in hand." It is probably because of that remark that Bradley and Courtney Hodges, the army's current deputy commander, decided to select Collins's chief of staff for him. They appointed Colonel Richard G. McKee, Hodges's trusted deputy from Fort Benning and Third Army, to the VII Corps as its chief of staff. Hodges and McKee were very close, and McKee could be a direct line to the chain of command if things went awry.[12] Collins was not happy with the appointment, but there was little he could do about it for now. And he was now Barton's boss and undoubtedly aware of his subordinate's strong connection to both Patch and Griswold. Internal politics and personal conflict are common themes of the US Army's senior leaders in World War II.

Meanwhile, for Operation NEPTUNE, the army planners attached units to the 4th Infantry to improve its combat capability. The term *attached* indicates a temporary assignment that would change once the operation ended. Direct fire support units included the 6th Armored Group (70th Tank Battalion, equipped with duplex drive tanks, and the 746th Tank Battalion) and the 801st and part of the 899th Tank Destroyer Battalions. In addition, the 65th Armored Field Artillery Battalion, a self-propelled unit and veteran of operations in North Africa and Sicily, augmented its fire support. For clearing obstacles and improving routes off the beach and cross-country, the planners attached the 1106th Engineer Group. It consisted of four battalions of combat engineers and several specialized companies providing bridge and truck support. It also received the 87th Chemical Battalion (Motorized), which could use its 4.2-inch mortars for immediate fire support during the assault. Finally, if the German Air Force attempted to attack the beaches, Barton had the 377th Anti-Aircraft Artillery (automatic weapons) Battalion. As the Germans had demonstrated throughout the war, this unit could also use its guns in direct fire mode against ground troops.[13]

The division had crossed the ocean with only the soldiers' equipment. Now its quartermaster and ordnance staff had to find the weapons and vehicles they should have. These included fifty-seven antitank guns, sixty-seven howitzers, five half-tracks, thirteen armored cars, 1,370 trucks and Jeeps of various sizes, and ten liaison airplanes.[14] The army had scattered supply dumps across the United Kingdom in response to practical transportation and installation concerns and as protection against air attacks. Because it was one of the assault divisions, the 4th Infantry Division received equipment that other units did not. For example, three field artillery battalions (29th, 42nd, and 44th) drew M-7 self-propelled howitzers (Priest) instead of towed howitzers. M-2 half-tracks replaced trucks as prime movers for the 57 mm antitank guns. The tracked M-29 cargo carrier (Weasel) became a substitute for many of the trucks in infantry and artillery battalions, allowing them to cross the water-inundated ground beyond Utah Beach. Soon after signing for their vehicles, division truck companies began traveling to and from dozens of installations, moving equipment, training ammunition, and vehicles to the individual units. Instructors with amphibious landing experience taught soldiers how to waterproof their new gear since a waterproof paste was needed to cover every crack. They had to protect wiring, engine batteries, and spark plugs from the elements. Vehicles landing on the beach had to have extension tubes added to their exhaust pipes. By April 10 the division had acquired most of its essential items and had made them serviceable for amphibious combat.[15]

As soon as the regiments were in place, they began training. But the nature of their billeting locations made it difficult. In addition to disbursement problems, the British had deployed many searchlights, antiaircraft guns, logistics, and signal installations, occupying key terrain that limited the training space. Other restrictions, such as land devoted to farming or historic sites, also sometimes prevented units larger than battalions from using the ground for maneuvers.[16] But this was only a hindrance and soon after arrival they got to work. Eisenhower visited the division's units in their training locations on February 5. As was his custom, he gave informal talks and bantered with the troops. At the 8th Infantry's camp at Heathfield, he said he would see them all "east of the Rhine" and personally make sure they had champagne, "even if I have to buy it myself." Later his aide, Harry C. Butcher, remarked that he was running up quite a bill that he might have to pay up. Eisenhower replied that he was sure "there would be plenty [of money] in the contingent fund to buy champagne and that nothing would please him more."[17]

The problem of restricted training did not last long. The American theater command arranged for the division to practice at an area they called the US Army Assault Training Center, located on the north Devon coast between Braunton and Barnstaple. Here the division's troops could maneuver with infantry weapons, tanks, artillery, and air support, all using the same ammunition they would use in combat. The camp had 505 Nissan Huts designed to hold 4,250 soldiers, virtually a regimental combat team. At Braunton soldiers learned or refreshed their memories on organizing boat teams, leading assault groups, and overcoming "hedgehogs" and other obstacles enemy defenders could use to stop the division's assault.[18] Barton decided to lead the invasion with the 8th Infantry regiment, supported by the 3rd Battalion, 22nd Infantry. Therefore, he sent these units immediately to Braunton to begin specialized training. These included assault amphibious techniques, reduction of beach defenses, and assault against fortified locations. The division historian noted, "The training at Braunton was well organized, intensive, interesting, and of immense practical value to its recipients."[19] The remainder of the division spent February practicing with its new equipment at the company and battalion levels. This training included live-fire exercises and shooting direct and indirect fire over the assaulting troops. "Discretion and diligent prosecution of safety measures reduced training casualties to a minimum."[20]

After a month of gathering equipment, assigning it to the proper units, preparing it, and training soldiers to use it, Barton began conducting unit training during the last half of March. The amphibious practice occurred at a British training area in Scotland, the Assault Training Center at Braunton, and the better-known Assault Training Center at Slapton Sands on the south Devon coast. The entire division and the 1st Engineer Special Brigade, which had the task of facilitating the landings and improving the beach after the lead elements moved inland, trained in a series of seven exercises between March 13 and 30. Barton and the corps staff designed four exercises to test battalion landing teams in the assault. Two more activities tested the performance of regimental combat teams. Finally, two regiments and their supporting units conducted a major joint exercise at Slapton Sands.[21] Also, as serious training commenced, Barton's senior aide, Phillip Hart, received his promotion to major and moved to another assignment on the division staff. His replacement, Captain William B. York, began keeping a diary of the division commander's daily events. This valuable document provides historians with a fascinating insight into Barton's activities for the remainder of 1944.[22]

Since the 4th Infantry Division was his priority for the forthcoming landings, Collins spent much time observing unit training and visiting Barton and his commanders. On March 1 Collins dropped into the division headquarters, and he and Barton discussed some of the problems and shortages his unit was experiencing. They also talked about discipline problems between white and Black troops. They were both men of their time, so modern readers should not be surprised by a strain of racism common to many officers with southern backgrounds. They also discussed a political problem facing Eisenhower and Bradley: Brigadier General Theodore Roosevelt Jr.[23]

Fifty-six years old and the son of the famous president Ted Roosevelt, he had already had a distinguished civilian and military career before he arrived. After graduating from Harvard in 1909, he married Eleanor Butler Alexander, from a well-connected family active in New York's social circles. He joined the Citizen's Military Training Camp program at the beginning of the First World War and accepted a commission as a major. He fought with the 1st Infantry Division in France at Cantigny and was gassed and wounded at Soissons. As a result he had a limp, used a cane, and had far more medical problems than mere arthritis. The war's end found him a lieutenant colonel commanding the 26th Infantry. Before leaving France he was one of the original and most influential founders of the American Legion. He maintained his reserve military career during the interwar period, completing the Infantry Officer's Advanced Course and CGSS. Among his interwar jobs were assistant secretary of the navy, governor of Puerto Rico, and governor-general of the Philippines. In 1933 he left public service and became a vice president with Doubleday Doran publishers.[24]

When the war began, he rejoined the active forces and found himself a brigadier general.[25] He had been the 1st Infantry Division's deputy commander, serving with Major General Terry Allen, Barton's nongraduate USMA classmate, in North Africa and Sicily. While the 1st was an aggressive unit on the battlefield, Eisenhower and Bradley believed it was an ill-disciplined mob behind the front lines. They replaced the division's chain of command once the Sicilian fighting ended.[26] After his relief Roosevelt traveled to England, where doctors forced him to check into a hospital to treat his pneumonia. But Roosevelt was not happy on the sidelines and lobbied with everyone he knew in Washington to get back into the field. As one of the most experienced and decorated combat leaders in the US Army, it made no sense to ignore that experience, so Bradley and Eisenhower decided to send him to the 4th Infantry Division. Barton was not excited to get a pretentious and presumably arrogant president's son as one of his subordinates but had little choice. After three weeks Ted got his clearance and assignment to the 4th Division headquarters as an extra general officer. On March 25 he and his aide, Lieutenant Marcus O. Stevenson, arrived for duty. Surprisingly, Barton and Roosevelt hit it off quite nicely within a short period.[27]

Harry Henderson's 12th Infantry called its two training exercises MUSKRAT. On March 12 the regiment's soldiers, with all their gear, boarded trains for the short trip to Plymouth. Three assault transport ships awaited them: the USS *Dickman*, the USS *Barnett*, and the USS *Bayfield*, which would be the corps and division command post during the invasion. They headed north to the Firth of Clyde, southwest of Glasgow, Scotland. There they dropped anchor, and for the first week (MUSKRAT I), the battalion practiced various drills, such as reaching boat stations under blackout conditions and debarking over the sides of the ships while wearing full gear and with ladders, nets, and ropes. Throughout the week, soldiers experienced cold rain and the expected seasickness of bouncing around in the late winter coastal waters. For the following week's exercise (MUSKRAT II), a detachment from the 1st Engineer Special Brigade boarded the three ships. Now the soldiers put their training to use as they organized into boat teams and scurried down the transports' sides into their assigned landing craft, vehicle and personnel (LCVP), generally referred to as the Higgins boat. The individual vessels formed up into assault waves and approached the hostile shore. On order the soldiers jumped into the icy water, often up to their armpits, and waded to shore. It was a harrowing experience with the constant danger of injury or drowning; everyone was always wet and cold.[28]

Barton had watched the final exercise from a high point overlooking the beach until thirty minutes after the troops landed. He then went down to the beach. He was displeased by what he found, as the soldiers seemed listless and unmotivated. In most cases they were going through the motions, not using the terrain for cover and hiding from direct enemy fire. More importantly, from his perspective, leaders were not taking charge and making corrections. He found Henderson and took him up and down the beach, pointing out what he saw. After his talk with Henderson, the naval commander, Rear Admiral Don P. Moon, came ashore with some of his staff and discussed things that both services needed to improve. That night Barton returned to Tiverton and found his West Point classmate Henry Flynn waiting for him. Flynn was a cavalryman and was serving as president of the cavalry board. This group was supervising the army's transition from horses to mechanization.[29] Meanwhile, back off the coast of Scotland, the 12th Infantry reboarded their three ships, headed back to Plymouth, and took a few days to recover, discussing what they had learned and thoroughly warming up.[30]

The 22nd and 8th Regiments went through similar exercises. Herve Tribolet called his training series MINK, which took place at Slapton Sands. Unlike the 12th Infantry, he only had to qualify two battalions since the 3rd Battalion would train with the 8th Infantry. The first series was from March 15 to 18 for the 1st Battalion, and the 2nd practiced the same drills as the MINK exercise from March 19 to 22. The 8th Infantry plus the 3rd Battalion of the 22nd moved to Dartmouth and conducted its assault training (Exercise OTTER) during the same period. Since the 8th would be the lead regiment, the first to face the fire, its practice was more in-depth and took on a little more urgency.[31]

The following exercise would begin on March 27, a VII Corps–directed rehearsal of the invasion called Exercise BEAVER. From then on the 4th Division's regiments took on the role of a combined arms organization called regimental combat teams and no longer operated as pure infantry regiments. Some units, such as platoons from the 4th Signal Company and companies from the 4th Medical Battalion, would remain with their assigned regiments for the war's duration. Others unit attachments changed as a result of different combat requirements. For this exercise and the invasion, the 1st Engineer Special Brigade and the 1106th Engineer Group joined the 4th Division. Since this was a VII Corps–directed activity, Collins and his headquarters also controlled the 101st Airborne Division's 502nd Parachute Infantry and received support from the Ninth Air Force.[32]

The next few days were a whirlwind of planning meetings, inspections, and troop visits. They are worth describing in detail since it illustrates the scrutiny and pressures the lead division commanders experienced in the weeks before the invasion. When not in meetings, Barton was on the road visiting the companies and battalions that Collins had recently attached to the division. BEAVER would be the first combined exercise for these newly arrived units, such as the 377th Anti-Aircraft (AW) Battalion with its 90 mm guns. When Barton visited the air defenders to welcome them to the 4th Infantry, his walk through the motor pool left him less than impressed, considering them "very mediocre."[33] He called Rodwell at headquarters to ask him to get the VII Corps antiaircraft officer to come down and inspect the unit thoroughly. Things were better when he dropped in on Lieutenant Colonel Elmer B. Horsfall's 801st Tank Destroyer Battalion, with its towed 3 in. guns. As he walked around the motor pool, watching the troops unpack equipment and tools, he was impressed with their morale and efficiency. He then visited his fellow Leavenworth instructor Clarence Huebner, who would simultaneously lead his 1st Infantry Division ashore on Omaha Beach as the 4th landed on Utah.

On Thursday, March 23, Barton drove to corps headquarters in Breamore, south of Salisbury in Hampshire, and linked up with Henry Barber. Together they went to another conference to discuss Exercise BEAVER with Collins. Also present was Collins's new chief of staff, McKee, and his G-3, Colonel Peter Bullard, a classmate at Fort Leavenworth. When the meeting ended, Bullard handed Barton a formal alert order to prepare for the exercise.[34]

Bullard would not be with the corps much longer. The 1914 USMA graduate was an engineer who taught at the CGSS just before the war.

Although he had no combat experience, he continued to argue with the newly arrived Collins, a former combat division commander with little respect for Leavenworth instructors, on how to array corps units on the battlefield. Collins was not generally impressed with Leavenworth's instructors and had little tolerance for those who argued with him. He would soon banish Bullard to Eisenhower's headquarters, and Bradley replaced him with Colonel Richard C. Partridge.[35]

While his staff prepared for BEAVER, Barton met with other senior commanders and critical leaders, such as Major General Lunsford Oliver, commander of the 5th Armored Division, who visited Tiverton. Oliver graduated a year behind Barton at West Point and had been one of his students at Leavenworth. The 5th's current task was operating the marshaling yards, freeing the training units from administrative and housekeeping operations. Brigadier General Maxwell Taylor, commander of the 101st, joined Barton and Roosevelt for dinner on March 25. The three worked into the evening on how the 8th Infantry and 502nd Parachute Infantry would coordinate after the landing.[36] The addition of Taylor's command, with a simulated airborne drop related to an amphibious operation, was a new wrinkle to the landing exercise program.

These were the first amphibious exercises for VII Corps and the 4th Infantry Division. However, the V Corps, scheduled to land on Omaha Beach, had already conducted several of these, including Exercises DUCK, FOX, and FABIUS. Most of these took place in the Slapton Sands Assault Training Center, located south of Dartmouth. The Allied planners had selected it as a training area because it was not too far from the American troop concentrations, was isolated, and would not excessively bother civilians. It was rugged terrain, with ten- to fourteen-foot tides, and with the hills in the background, it resembled Omaha Beach. It also had a six- to nine-foot deep water body called Lower Ley that resembled some of the flooded areas behind Utah Beach. However, it was also dangerously close to the German naval base in Cherbourg.[37]

As the 8th and 22nd regimental combat teams moved toward Plymouth on March 27, Barton, Roosevelt, Rodwell, and Troxel headed for one of the temporary camps at Saltram, east of Plymouth. Here Barton had several meetings with Colonel Jake Bagby, whom Barton had removed from the 12th

Infantry soon after he took command. Bagby now commanded the marshaling area responsible for moving the 4th Infantry from the cantonments to the appropriate transports on the coast.

In his daily travels through the division's area, he often encountered officers from corps and army headquarters, prompting informal meetings. For example, while driving near South Brent, east of Plymouth, he encountered Roosevelt, and they had an impromptu discussion about problems with the division's camouflage and security. Collins and McKee drove by and joined the discussion. With them was Bill Weaver, Service of Supply, and Colonel Mason Young, the VII Corps engineer and BEAVER exercise director. He was a 1930 graduate at CGSS, when Barton was an instructor. Collins had just visited the 8th Infantry and was impressed by the unit and Van Fleet. So on the edge of the road, the group had an unplanned conference on exercise problems. Barton's diary mentions many such impromptu meetings on the narrow Devon roads as leaders moved about checking unit training and equipment.[38]

Barton headed to Plymouth on the afternoon of March 28 and took a motor launch to the USS *Bayfield*, his designated transport and command ship for the invasion. Admiral Moon and his chief of staff, Captain Rutledge Tompkins, met Barton and escorted him to a fine navy meal and discussed the forthcoming exercise. Early the next morning, Roosevelt, Barber, Blakeley, and the staff came on board and continued planning, and that afternoon the *Bayfield* headed out of Plymouth Harbor and moved out to sea, anchoring south of the exercise area. During a foggy morning on March 30, they watched Van Fleet's regimental combat team land as planned, with no major problems. The next morning the exercise continued as the logistics units began landing on the shore. That evening the units began to return to their camps in Devon.[39]

Barton did not stay to watch but headed to the Grand Hotel in Plymouth by way of Kingsbridge and Modbury. Waiting for him were Henry Barber and Peter C. Bullard, still with the corps staff. Then they all went to Admiral Moon's headquarters and joined Collins in discussing the recent events. As a training exercise of this scale would, it exposed numerous flaws in unit training and army-navy cooperation. Many participants remembered it as a too confusing event. One element of the discussion probably included Barton's unhappiness with Harry Henderson's command of the 12th Infantry and his intention to relieve him. There is some indication that Henderson was in bad health, but his performance on the recent exercise had not shown the vigor and attention to detail that Barton required. Since the army commander had a voice in regimental commanders' appointments, Collins most likely approved and told him to bring it up when he saw Bradley in the next few days. When the conference was over in the late afternoon, Barton returned to Tiverton.[40]

Barton's schedule for the next few days centered on gathering all the results and observations concerning Exercise BEAVER and preparing for Exercise TIGER, which would be the invasion's grand rehearsal. On Saturday, April 1, he boarded the 07:30 train from Exeter to London, arriving at Waterloo Station at 11:45. A British officer met him at the rail station and took him to the Dorchester Hotel, east of Hyde Park, where he freshened up and dressed for the day's events. Then he went to lunch at the Grosvenor House, a regular dining location for senior American officers, where he encountered many old friends and acquaintances, including Major General Milton S. Reckord, the theater's provost marshal. Barton had met him when he was stationed in Washington and Reckord was Maryland's adjutant general and 29th Infantry Division commander. After lunch and a few meetings, Barton spent an hour with Bradley and his chief of staff, Brigadier General William B. Kean. Barton discussed his concerns about Henderson and the 12th Infantry. Bradley told him he was in luck since Colonel Russell P. Reeder Jr., one of Marshall's young protégés, had just arrived in the theater. Reeder had extensive combat experience in the Pacific and would be an asset for the still-green 4th Infantry Division. Bradley had not yet decided where to assign him, but Barton and Bradley both agreed that Reeder was the right choice.[41]

Barton arrived in Plymouth at 09:30 the next morning, and one of Admiral Moon's aides met him at the station and took him to the headquarters. They had a fine breakfast with Collins and other VII Corps staff members. They discussed various aspects of training and the division for the remainder of the morning. After lunch Collins and Barton attended a critique of the naval phase of Exercise BEAVER at the Hamoaze House in Plymouth.

Barton reported his conversation with Bradley and his intent to replace Henderson with Reeder. Before he departed Barton called his headquarters at Tiverton and asked for the commander of the 12th Infantry to meet him at his office. He relieved the colonel of his command that evening.[42]

The following Monday, April 3, Barton had Lieutenant Colonel James S. Luckett, the regimental executive officer, report to his office. The general gave Luckett, who had been the regiment's backbone for over a year, some background to his decision to relieve Henderson and to assign the new colonel, but seasoned combat leader, as commander. Back at headquarters his series of planned and impromptu visits continued. Colonel John C. Whitcomb, one of his fellow Leavenworth instructors, commanded the army components of Plymouth and came by to coordinate activities. As Whitcomb departed, chemical warfare training inspectors from First Army visited Barton to discuss what they had observed with the division's chemical readiness. Students of the period often forget that the threat of Hitler authorizing his troops to use chemical weapons on the beach was a significant planning concern. That evening Colonel Paul W. Thompson, commander of the 6th Engineer Special Brigade, came by for dinner. Thompson's command would be supporting Clarence Huebner's 1st Infantry Division on Omaha Beach.[43]

Training for OVERLORD, April–May 1944

Barton and Bill York left Tiverton by train for London at 06:50 on April 6. Upon arrival they checked into the Grosvenor House. Henry Barber was already there, and they talked about various division issues for a while. Barton then went to see Collins, who was at the Dorchester Hotel. That night he went to dinner at Prunier's Restaurant in the Saint James District with his old friend Pete Corlett. The two friends had much to discuss. Corlett had just finished leading the 7th Infantry Division in brilliant amphibious operations at Kiska in the Aleutian Islands and Kwajalein in the Marshall Islands. General Marshall was thoroughly pleased with his performance and had just sent him to London to work for Eisenhower and share some of his hard-learned lessons of amphibious operations ahead of Operation NEPTUNE.

The Supreme Headquarters Allied Expeditionary Force (SHAEF) staff was not interested. As Corlett wrote in his short autobiography, "Not a single American general or staff officer in England—Bradley, Lee, Patton, Smith [Lieut. Gen. Walter B. Smith, Eisenhower's chief of staff], Hodges or anyone else ever mentioned my experience in the Pacific or asked my opinion on anything, although our contacts were frequent." When he persisted and challenged some of NEPTUNE's aspects, the pushback was intense. At one point Bedell Smith "pounded the table (with his fist) and said. 'Do I have to defend the plan to you?'"[44] Eisenhower, Smith, and Bradley had no interest in learning lessons from the Pacific. Neither Corlett nor Joe Collins ever had the opportunity to affect the overall plan. Eisenhower assigned Pete the command of the XIX Corps, which would land four days after the main assault. So on the evening of April 6, Cowboy Pete and Tubby enjoyed a fine evening of premier caviar and seafood in one of the best restaurants in London. What they talked about is anyone's guess.[45]

At 08:00 the following day, Barton and Pete left the hotel and walked over to General Bernard Law Montgomery's headquarters at Saint Paul's School. This gathering of senior officers was the first Thunderclap conference. On a massive map, the width of a city street, Montgomery, commanding the Twenty-First Army Group and the overall ground force commander; Admiral Bertrand Ramsay, commanding the Allied Naval Expeditionary Force; and Air Marshall Trevor Leigh-Mallory, commander, Allied Expeditionary Air Force, spent the morning presenting an overview of Operation NEPTUNE to senior commanders and their staffs. That afternoon, all five corps commanders came forward and outlined how they intended to fight their part of the operation. The briefing at Saint Paul's School was an important milestone. For the first time, all of the tactical commanders understood how their battle contributed to the overall process. The meeting lasted all day, and Barton returned to the hotel at 17:30.[46]

Barton started the next day by joining Collins at a meeting with other commanders and staff officers to discuss the previous day's events. That afternoon his classmate and best man at his wedding, d'Alary Fechét, came by the hotel "for tea." He had medically retired in 1932 and began teaching military science at the University of California–Los Angeles.

With war on the horizon, he returned to service in 1940. Joining the 1st Infantry Division, he commanded the 16th Infantry at Kasserine and was, again, wounded in action, and was now working for Eisenhower. That afternoon "Fetchit" saw Tubby off on a late afternoon train to Exeter, arriving back at his headquarters around midnight.[47]

Barton settled into a routine of inspection visits, conferences, and social events. On Tuesday, April 11, two of Eisenhower's influential subordinates, Major General Everett Hughes and Major General Leonard T. Gerow, visited his headquarters. Hughes had the title of special assistant to the commander in chief, ETO, and everyone knew he was the supreme commander's personal troubleshooter. Gerow, the V Corps commander and one of Eisenhower's best friends, was probably accompanying Hughes because of his expertise as an infantryman. Everyone knew that whatever information Hughes discovered or believed would end up on Eisenhower's desk in the morning. That afternoon the theater of operations inspector general, Brigadier General Oliver L. Haines, and his assistant arrived and spent the afternoon and evening looking around the area. While Barton does not report these inspections' purpose, most likely Eisenhower was checking out the division in preparation for the high-level visit the next day.[48]

Around 08:00 on April 12, the distinguished party arrived, led by Bradley and Lieutenant General John C. H. Lee, commanding the Service of Supply. With them was Assistant Secretary of War John J. McCloy and Lieutenant General Joseph McNarney, the deputy chief of staff. McNarney also happened to be a USMA classmate of Eisenhower and Bradley. Starting at 09:00 they visited the 29th Field Artillery Battalion and watched batteries perform camouflage drills and occupation of firing positions. The next stop was the 2nd Battalion, 8th Infantry, where they observed soldiers firing, assaulting over walls, and assaulting with a base of fire and a movement onto the objective. They drove over to an observation point and watched the 3rd Battalion conduct a cross-country march. Next, they gathered at Heathfield Camp and ate lunch with the 8th Infantry's battalion and company commanders. The training inspection continued in the afternoon as the War Department visitors observed the 42nd Field Artillery conduct security drills, the 8th Infantry's 1st Battalion conduct squad and platoon training, and then again the 3rd Battalion, which had been marching all morning, now firing on the rifle range. Then it was off to the 20th Field Artillery to observe gun drills and occupation of firing areas. Finally, they all moved at 18:45 to Topsham Barracks in Exeter, where Bradley and McCloy gave a speech to the officers who had put on the show for them that morning. The next day, April 13, the show continued as the group observed training activities by almost every division element. Bradley and McCloy left about 17:00 that evening, with Barton seeing them off at Exeter Station. He then went to the nearby 12th Infantry headquarters and visited its new commander, Red Reeder. After two demanding days, he was back in Tiverton around 21:00 hours.[49]

The inspection regimen continued as almost every commander and senior staff officer in England wanted to visit the division. While it may have satisfied the egos of senior officers, they were severe diversions from the training that Barton, his commanders, and their troops were seeking to accomplish. General Montgomery wanted a similar series of ceremonies the day after Bradley and McCloy's departure. Barton drove forty miles south to Newton Abbot, where he met Montgomery and took him to Denbury Camp, where Barber had assembled approximately one-third of the division. Montgomery reviewed the troops and gave them one of his classic motivational speeches. They then drove north to Exeter, about twenty miles, where Roosevelt commanded a similarly arranged group of about six thousand soldiers. Montgomery again made a speech and reviewed the troops. Red Reeder, who had been in command for only a few days, hosted lunch at his headquarters. Then, Barton and Montgomery drove east for twenty miles, where Blakeley had the 8th Infantry and its supporting troops waiting for a similar speech and inspection. Then everyone went back to Tiverton, where Montgomery and his aides departed. For three full days the division was unable to do any practical training.[50]

The diversions continued on Saturday, April 15, when Harvey Gibson, a successful and prestigious American banker, and his wife joined Barton at his headquarters. Gibson left his business interests and dedicated his war years to serving as the American Red Cross commissioner to Great Britain. After lunch they headed to the 4th Signal Company motor pool in Tiverton, where he presented the eight Red Cross "clubmobiles" and their female crews,

Major General Raymond O. Barton addresses members of the American Red Cross Clubmobile crews, Tiverton, Devon, England, April 22, 1944. US Army photograph, Dwight David Eisenhower Presidential Library.

led by Elizabeth Schuler, to the division. General Barton gave a short speech to the Red Cross Girls, welcoming them to their new home, and certainly pointing out that his wife served with the organization in the previous war. On Sunday McCloy, McNary, Lee, and Collins returned to spend another day with the division. The day's agenda was for the commission to observe soldiers "in normal activity." But, of course, it was Sunday, so "normal" activity would have focused on church services, rest, and preparing for the upcoming exercises. It is doubtful that the 20th Field Artillery, 42nd Field Artillery, or the 8th and 12th Infantry commanders would have allowed their soldiers to lie around when the inspecting committee arrived. Fortunately, by noon the brass had departed, and the troops could, indeed, resume their "normal" activities.[51]

On Monday Barton welcomed Lieutenant Colonel James H. Batte's 87th Chemical Mortar Battalion, recently attached to the 4th Division.

The battalion had as its primary weapon the 4.2 in. (107 mm) heavy mortar. It had forty-eight of these powerful weapons that could shoot high-explosive and smoke shells at targets more than two miles away. The latter munitions were critical in protecting infantrymen from enemy observation during offensive and defensive operations. Barton liked what he saw, especially the unit's noncommissioned officers.[52]

He spent Wednesday with his staff putting the finishing touches on Operation TIGER's plan. Thursday was another day of travel with he and Hal Barber starting at Woolacombe, near Braunton on the north Devon coast, for one set of meetings, and then they drove two hours south to Plymouth for another with the VII Corps staff. That evening they had dinner with Admiral Moon before returning to Tiverton.[53]

On Thursday inspectors from Supreme Allied Headquarters showed up at division headquarters. Of course, these were old friends. Eisenhower's G-3, Harold Bull, had spent years with Barton during their lieutenant days together, and Bull had succeeded Tubby as the 4th Infantry chief of staff in Georgia. David M. (P. D.) Crawford, a USMA classmate and now assigned to the Combined Chiefs of Staff, coordinated army and navy communications before the invasion. Barton's aide, Bill York, reports the visit was an inspection, but one suspects it was more of a friendly tour of the headquarters.[54]

Despite the host of inspections, visits, and other diversions, Barton, Rodwell, and Troxel managed to get FO #1 (field order) TIGER out to the unit commanders on April 18. As this was a dress rehearsal, the task organization was the same as the division would employ on Utah Beach in June. Van Fleet's Combat Team 8, reinforced by the 3rd Battalion, 22nd Infantry, led the way and would advance to the south side of the area to practice securing a causeway. Tribolet's Combat Team 22, minus the battalion under Van Fleet's control, would be the next wave. Its mission was to land on the beach, secure another causeway, take command of its 3rd Battalion from the 8th Infantry, and then continue to attack along its assigned avenue of advance. Reeder's Combat Team 12 landed next with the task to secure a river crossing. Finally, Colonel Clarke C. Fales 359th Infantry, from Jay MacKelvie's 90th Infantry Division, would follow the 4th Infantry Division ashore as the corps' reserve.

The exercise was a practice combined arms assault, so mixed in with each infantry combat team were its supporting weapons. These included tanks, artillery tubes, air defense guns, tank destroyers, engineers, medics, and signal troops. Mixed in among the division was the 1st Engineer Special Brigade, supporting the landing and improving the beach for follow-on forces and supplies. This training event was as close to the invasion as the VII Corps staff could plan and execute.[55]

Collins got everyone focused on this next task with an exercise conference on Friday, April 21, in Plymouth at the Royal Marine Barracks, where they worked through many of TIGER's details. When he returned to headquarters, Barton adjusted the plan and met with his commanders and staff at South Brent two days later. On Tuesday, April 25, Collins and Barton visited some marshaling areas and then drove to Dartmouth, where they inspected the "loading hards." These were concrete mats arrayed on the beach to allow vehicles to move over the soggy sand to their assigned landing vessel. Then they traveled to Torquay and met up with Maxwell Taylor and Mason Young to discuss the use of air power in the exercise and the handing off of units of the 1st Tank Destroyer Group to the 101st Airborne. On Wednesday night, after another day of conferences, Barton was back on board the *Bayfield* and sailing toward the exercise area.[56]

Over thirty thousand soldiers moved that night from their harbors to assembly areas off Devon's south coast. Thursday, April 27, was a beautiful day for a practice invasion and the live-fire bombardment was ready to go. However, for various reasons, Admiral Moon decided to postpone the assault from 07:30 to 08:30, never something to try at the last minute. The venerated military theorist Carl von Clausewitz called the problems Moon was having "friction." "Countless, minor incidents—the kind you can never really foresee—combine to lower the general level of performance, so that one always falls far short of the intended goal."[57] For many more reasons, not all the ships heading for the beach got the word, so several landing craft stuck to their originally scheduled times and the naval bombardment got close to some of them.[58]

The division had many problems, among them that Van Fleet and Tribolet were both in one LST (landing ship, tank). The concept was that it was a "free boat" and could land anywhere, thus placing the regimental commanders where needed. The British skipper had other ideas and he did not get them onto the beach until much later. According to Barton it was the only time he ever heard Van Fleet swear. Despite the mix-up, the troops continued, just like they would have to do in actual combat. The division came ashore, and the engineers began to improve the beaches. Barton landed at 10:45 and watched the final waves of the division land. Senior officer supervision was not lacking on the beach as he encountered Montgomery, Admiral Bertrand Ramsay, and Courtney Hodges as he moved among his troops. The British commander, not knowing the background to the problem, confronted Barton. "Where the devil are regimental commanders, now General, they must be with the troops during the landing." Barton knew the comments were unfounded and, like most Americans officers, disliked being addressed angrily by a foreign officer; he replied, "Now listen to me, General, you better tell that to your British skipper, my commanders would be in here but for his inefficiency." Montgomery turned to Ramsay who was with him on the beach and passed on Barton's complaint and a few other comments.[59] There were few casualties, but Ramsay, the overall naval commander, was not impressed and criticized Moon for the delay. Late in the afternoon, Barton went to Collins's forward headquarters in Slapton and reported his status. That night he found his forward command post in a cluster of houses a few miles from the beach called Merrifield, gave his staff instructions, and turned in for the night.[60]

While Barton was sleeping, disaster struck. Early in the evening, a convoy of eight LSTs had departed Plymouth and headed for an assembly area in Lymé Bay, east of the exercise landing area. These large vessels, each four hundred feet long and capable of carrying twenty tanks and more than two hundred soldiers, were the backbone of the Allied invasion force. Onboard this convoy was the follow-up force for the landing, including soldiers and equipment providing engineer, logistics, medical, and communications support. Many of these were from the 1st Engineer Brigade. It is somewhat astounding, examining the situation more than seventy-five years later, that the Allies conducted these operations on the coast of southern England, just across the English Channel from Cherbourg and Brest, two large French

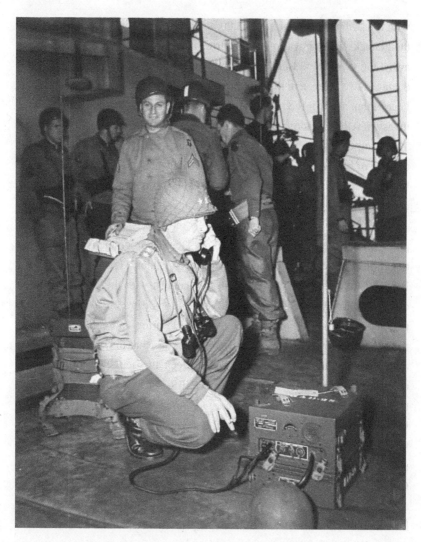

Major General Raymond O. Barton, CG of 4th Infantry Division, transmits radio instructions while on the USS *Bayfield* off the coast of England during Exercise TIGER, April 27, 1944. US Army photograph.

ports occupied by the German Navy. In addition to faulty communications and command and control procedures, the convoy had only one Royal Navy corvette providing protection. Shortly after midnight on April 28, nine German torpedo boats left Cherbourg harbor to investigate. Making contact with the Allied vessels around 02:00, they encountered the LSTs and began their attack. When it was over, and British patrol ships arrived to chase them away, the German vessels had sunk two landing craft (LST 507 and 531), damaged two more, and killed approximately 750 Allied soldiers and sailors. Fearful that news of their success could tip off the Germans to the impending invasion, Allied headquarters slapped a security quarantine around the area. They warned medics and those aware of the disaster to say nothing. Senior officers of both nations and services pointed fingers at each other, assigning blame for the disaster. Taking place at sea, it did not affect Barton and his command, and they carried on with their training.[61]

Like many such instances, however, most considered it the price of preparing for the invasion and moved on. Don Moon graciously sent a note to Collins to "express my deepest sympathy for their [1st Engineer Special Brigade] losses suffered on our first joint contact with the enemy."[62] In his diary Barton says nothing about the attack, reporting on his visits to the regiments and supporting artillery battalions. Barton and Collins discussed the operation the next day, certainly focusing on what they had to do rather than engaging in the finger-pointing between the senior army and navy commanders. Around 13:30 Exercise TIGER ended, and Barton returned to Tiverton for a good night's sleep. One good news element was the 4th Division's capture of its first prisoner, a German pilot who parachuted from his damaged aircraft. A Private Cole from the 4th Military Police Company made the capture. On April 30 Barton talked to the captured aviator, named Gopp, and then visited the 8th and 12th Infantry soldiers in their marshaling areas, preparing to return to their home stations. That afternoon he gathered his commanders and staff at the command post near Slapton for an after-action review. While brief, it appears comprehensive:

1. CG: Outline of Critique - 10 min.
2. CO, CT 8: Description of action - 5 min.
3. CO, CT 12: Description of action - 5 min.
4. CO, CT 22: Description of action - 5 min.
5. CG: Div Arty- Artillery in Exercise - 10 min.
6. Div Engr: Analysis of Engineer Problems and Plans - 10 min.

7. Open Forum: Criticism of Division Staff - 20 min.

8. CG: Conclusions - 10 min.

Total -1 hr. 15 min.

It is worth noting that the topic that allocated the most time was discussing his and his staff's performance. That night he ended this busy month back in his headquarters in Tiverton.[63]

With the end of Exercise TIGER, the 4th Infantry Division's soldiers returned to their camps and began preparing for departure. They cleaned and prepared their equipment for the sea voyage, landing, and subsequent operations. They inventoried everything, and sergeants and officers at all levels came down to spot-check the results. Companies spent days on weapons ranges, practicing with their personal and crew-served weapons. While company officers and noncommissioned officers spent their days with the soldiers, commanders and staff went to endless meetings and conferences. For the next two weeks, Barton met with commanders and staffs daily. When free, he and Roosevelt drove through the unit camps, engaging the soldiers and keeping an eye on their attitude and morale. Ted slowed down on May 14 to send Clare the letter presented at the beginning of this chapter. Despite Barton's hesitation, the two were getting along very well. The next day Barton held his last command and staff conference in Tiverton.[64]

On Wednesday, May 17, Barton said good-bye to the British friends and hosts who had made the stay at Collipriest House in Tiverton so pleasant and headed to the marshaling area. He motored to Torquay to have lunch with Van Fleet. The two then traveled south to Stoke Fleming, southwest of Dartmouth, to observe rocket firing practice against targets on Slapton Sands. He then returned to South Brent Camp, northeast of Plymouth, his new headquarters. Almost every evening, battalion and regimental commanders from nearby units not assigned to the division would drop by to introduce themselves. Given how the US Army operated, any of them could find themselves attached to Barton's command for a short task or a more extended mission.[65]

Now in South Brent, the meetings and visits continued. Some meetings were small, just two generals reviewing plans or issues that needed

Barton's staff at Brent Camp, UK, May 1944. *Front row, left to right,* Roosevelt, Barton, Blakeley, Barber. *Second row,* Rodwell, Bryant, Hansen, Troxel, Marr. *Third row,* generals' aides-de-camp, names not confirmed. US Army photograph, Dwight David Eisenhower Presidential Library.

resolution. Sometimes they were much larger, such as on May 26 when all ground commanders met with General Montgomery in Plymouth. Barton's schedule in May was a whirlwind of personal meetings, visits, and planning conferences. This interaction among officers at all levels receives little historical attention. The big ones, such as the grand meeting at St. Paul's on April 7, are in most invasion accounts. However, as this chapter indicates, discussions with peers, senior officers, and staff occupied a significant portion of a division commander's time. It is instructive that Barton met with Collins or Major General Eugene M. Landrum, his deputy commander, almost every day, and meetings with Omar Bradley appear in his war diary nearly every week. This constant commander interaction resulted in an organization where army and corps leaders became acutely aware of their subordinate's strengths and foibles. Junior commanders also knew their senior leaders well. This interaction ensured that the chain of command was as ready as any could be on the eve of battle. Of course, there was little time for reflection and contemplation for a division commander on the eve of battle.[66]

As historian Peter Caddick-Adams pointed out in his introduction to *Sand & Steel*, "When compared with the Germans, most servicemen who assaulted northern France had experienced an incredible degree of rugged and realistic training that put them at the peak of physical fitness, acclimatized them to battle, and equipped them mentally and physically well enough to win."[67] This was especially true for the 4th Infantry Division, and Barton could be proud of his accomplishments. Helping to reactivate the Ivy Division in 1940 and commanding it since the summer of 1942 meant the division was indeed his product. It had trained as hard as any infantry unit for over two years, and its proficiency was evident to all. But he knew he did not do it alone and had lots of help. Although most of his letters home have not survived, we know his thoughts were also with his late parents, who had done so much to urge him on, and, of course, his wife, Clare, and his children, Clare and Raymond. Tubby was a family man, but as June arrived, he focused on his professional family and the tremendous tasks ahead. Blakeley, Barber, Rodwell, Van Fleet, Tribolet, and Troxel had been with him since before the Florida training. Roosevelt and Reeder were valuable additions to the team. It was his command group and was as smooth an organization as any in the US Army. He had prepared for this moment all of his life, and now it had arrived.

Chapter 9

Utah Beach, June 1–9

I [Barton], Bill York (Aide), and Jas. K. Richards (Driver) landed, dry footed, by "Snowbuggy" from LCT. Some artillery fire (hostile), one half-track burning, and Co. A, 1st Amphibious Engineers digging in against sea wall instead of doing their job of helping my troops across the beach. I rooted them out and onto the job with my poison and cusswords. I learned later from York and Richards who returned to the beach, that they went right back under the seawall as soon as I left.[1]

Combat Command

The role of a World War II American infantry division commander married the ability of personal leadership with the physical taste of battle. Barton often met with other general officers, including the most senior commanders, such as Bradley, Eisenhower, Montgomery, and Collins. Therefore, he understood what was taking place across the Allied battlefield and how his command played a part. He was the force behind preparing for combat and focusing his division on accomplishing his battle tasks by giving instructions to four colonels (Van Fleet, Tribolet, Reeder, and Rodwell) and three brigadier generals

(Barber, Blakeley, and Roosevelt). All of them had different tasks to perform, and it was Barton that gave this group its character and direction. Unlike Civil War division commanders, who their soldiers usually saw on the battlefield, the division commander was generally out of sight during combat. As a result, these leaders, especially those that remained on the job for more than a few weeks, spent most of their days in close contact with troops and junior leaders, traveling on roads and trails in their Jeeps. As a result of this close contact, these leaders had a unique perspective on morale and combat capabilities. When they sensed the need, they would step out of their semidetached leadership role, such as Barton's attempt to motivate the engineers, as noted above. The death or wounding of trusted officers and noncommissioned officers also took an emotional toll on these leaders. Therefore, division combat command was one of the most physically and mentally exhausting duties an officer could perform, with an average time leading a division of about ten months.[2] The following two weeks would introduce Barton to this unique and exhausting nature of division combat command.

Most division commanders were in a whirlwind of activity and danger. Unsurprisingly, few had the time to publish accounts of their experiences, as did senior commanders such as Eisenhower, Bradley, and Collins. Fortunately, historians have always had detailed division after-action reports to provide a relatively accurate and complete narrative of the 4th Infantry Division's actions. Each evening Rodwell and his staff summarized what took place in their zone of operations and forwarded this report to the VII Corps headquarters. McKee and his team prepared a corps-wide summary for Collins, extracted appropriate portions, and sent it to First Army headquarters. At the end of each month, the division staff complied its reports, including information on personnel, intelligence, logistics, and operations, and sent it through the corps headquarters to the adjutant general in Washington. Historians also have copies of Barton's orders and instructions to his subordinates. When writing *The Longest Day*, Cornelius Ryan captured many of Barton's actions in interviews and extended correspondence.[3] Finally, Barton's recently discovered war diary, maintained by his aide, Captain William B. York, and other personal letters and documents augment and elaborate on the information that has been available since the 1950s. As a result, we now have a relatively accurate picture of how he spent this historic day and the months until he departed command in December.[4]

Since Raymond O. Barton is the subject of this book, it cannot be a history of the 4th Infantry Division during the Second World War. The story of this command's combative journey from Utah Beach to the war's end outside of Munich is far too extensive to describe in detail. So using Barton's command posts as an organizing theme, we will follow him across France and into Germany. Sometimes these locations were temporary halts during a rapid advance. In other instances he spent several days working with his regimental commanders. From these locations Barton made decisions that sent his division into battle. As the division's record shows, these were usually good ones. But as it also shows they were often costly. The same men he had trained over the preceding two years would suffer immensely as the Ivy Division fought against innumerable German units. The casualty lists were extensive, especially among his officers and noncommissioned officers. He was a sensitive man, and each loss pained him dearly.

One element of conventional wisdom we should address now: Darryl F. Zanuck's movie *The Longest Day* distorted what little the post–World War II generation knew about Raymond O. Barton and events surrounding Ted Roosevelt Jr. going ashore with the first wave on D-Day. For weeks after the VII Corps released its plan, Roosevelt pleaded with Barton to land on Utah Beach with the advanced wave. Finally, on May 26, not on the USS *Bayfield* as the movie depicts, he wrote Barton a formal request after Montgomery's commanders conference in Portsmouth. In his letter Roosevelt, a veteran of previous landings, laid out five reasons for going in with the first landing craft. He concluded, "I believe I can contribute materially to all of the above by going with the assault companies. Furthermore, I know personally both officers and men of these advance units and believe that it will steady them to know I am with them."[5]

Barton had good reasons, none of them mentioned in the movie, not to allow Rough Rider, as he was often called and had stenciled on his Jeep, to land at the beginning of the assault. From a practical standpoint, Colonel Van Fleet was his most experienced and competent regimental commander and would be in charge during the assault. Van Fleet did not require a general standing next to him when he needed to make decisions and give his battalion and company commanders clear orders. Roosevelt was not the assistant division commander; Hal Barber was, complicating the chain of command even more. Generals did not land with the first wave for an important reason: they had to allow their subordinates to do their jobs.

Additionally, Barton also depended on Roosevelt's experience. While he was an experienced division commander, Barton had never been in battle and worried about freezing up.[6] When he reported to the Ivy Division, Roosevelt already had a Distinguished Service Cross, a Silver Star with three Bronze Oak Leaf Clusters, a Distinguished Service Medal for World War I courage, a Legion of Merit, and a Purple Heart. He was one of the most experienced and decorated combat leaders in the US Army.[7] Barton's hesitation to let him go ashore had nothing to do with Roosevelt being a president's son and his prospect of being killed in battle. He had been living on the edge of danger in both world wars, and Barton needed that experience when he faced his first fight. He also knew that Ted's son Quentin was landing at the same time on Omaha Beach and did not relish the prospect of the father and son perishing during the invasion on the same day. It had nothing to do with *The Longest Day's* insinuation that Barton wanted to keep him from harm because he was President Teddy Roosevelt's son. He had passed that danger threshold much earlier.[8] The letter went nowhere other than into Barton's file, and he gave in to the request. As he watched Roosevelt and Stevenson get into the landing craft a few days later, Barton "never thought he would see him again alive."[9]

June 1–5, USS *Bayfield*

The division began loading equipment as soon as it arrived in the port area, and Barton spent as much time as possible over the next few days visiting his units and watching them prepare their transports and landing craft. On the evening of June 2, he hosted a special briefing at his South Brent command post for the war correspondents who were traveling with the division to France. It allowed him to personally interact with Fourth Estate members who would connect his soldiers with their families

4th Infantry Division commanders at Brent Camp, UK. *First row, from left to right,* Blakeley (4th Division Artillery), Barton, James Rodwell (chief of staff). *Back row,* Van Fleet (8th Infantry), Tribolet (22nd Infantry), Reeder (12th Infantry), and Wharton (1st Special Engineer Brigade). US Army photograph, Dwight David Eisenhower Presidential Library.

back home. Henry T. Gorrell, the distinguished war correspondent for the United Press, would file the first report on Normandy's invasion and send home detailed accounts of the division's progress across France.[10] Larry LeSueur, from CBS and one of the original Murrow Boys, would be with Barton for most of the war and would be made an honorary member of the division.[11] Kenneth Crawford, from *Newsweek,* would come ashore with Company C, 8th Infantry, and be in the heat of the fight from the beginning.[12] And the Pulitzer Prize-winning journalist Ira Wolfert, reporting for *Reader's Digest,* was with this group and would cross the channel with Barton.[13] Barton's days in Omaha and with the CCC had prepared him well for working with the press. After the gathering he then returned to the *Bayfield* for the evening.[14]

Barton continued visiting the loading areas the following day and talking to the soldiers and their leaders. He started on Plymouth's west side, at
Tamar Quay, and then headed over to Dartmouth, where he spoke to naval
officers about the loading process. From there he motored north to Torquay,
where soldiers from the 3rd Battalion, 8th Infantry, were boarding one of
the transports. Already on board and crowding around the rails were soldiers
from Company I. Riding with Barton and York was the former commander
of that unit. When Barton arrived at the dock, he got out and moved toward
the transport. But when the soldiers on the ship saw their former commander,
they all began booing and hissing. As he later told Cornelius Ryan, he was
"almost sick at this unexpected and bitter greeting. He was so hurt that he did
not know what to say or do." It was not until much later that he learned the
booing was for the captain, whom the soldiers disliked.[15]

After this painful incident, he boarded a motor launch and spent the rest
of the day riding the boat among the ships that carried his soldiers: the USS
Dickman, USS *Barnett*, and HMS *Gauntlet*, the largest. He was now feeling
much better, and at each stop he gave a little speech and wished them all luck.
He then sailed over to Herve Tribolet's transport and spent some time with
him and his staff. Finally, he returned to land and linked up with Sergeant
Richards and his sedan, then drove to Queen Ann's Battery and turned the
car over to his waiting quartermaster. He then walked the short distance to
Victoria Wharf and boarded the *Bayfield* for the last time.[16]

Because of the weather, Eisenhower and his commanders needed to
delay the assault by one day, so the 4th Infantry Division spent the day
onboard their ships.[17] The next day, June 5, the USS *Bayfield* hoisted anchor
at 09:30, moved out of Plymouth, and joined its convoy heading for France.
The scale of this undertaking is difficult to imagine. Each of Barton's regimental combat teams required thirteen landing craft infantry, six landing craft
tank, and five landing ship tanks. Each vessel towed a barrage balloon to
deter air attacks. Cruisers and destroyers protected the flanks of the moving
convoy. Somewhere in the channel, an escorting fighter shot down a German
plane as it approached the convoy. On radio listening silence, the *Bayfield*'s
crew heard the report and used the public address system to let everyone
onboard know the shooting war had begun. The convoy was Task Force 125.

Its crossing was not without incident as the vessel carrying a battery from the 29th Field Artillery Battalion hit a mine as it approached the shore, causing its entire complement of guns and prime movers to sink to the bottom of the channel.[18] It is doubtful that Barton noticed a young gunner's mate on the *Bayfield*, Peter Berra, performing his crew duties. After the war, "Yogi" Berra would become one of the greatest ballplayers of all time and remain a staunch supporter of servicemen for the rest of his life.[19] The *Bayfield* dropped anchor off the coast at 02:00.[20]

The forthcoming events stressed Barton, but his troops were comfortable with their commander, and Ted Roosevelt would know how they received him. In his role as an extra brigadier with the division, Roosevelt's only job was to spend time with the troops, which he continued to do after everyone was afloat. On June 3 he sent a letter to his wife, Eleanor.

> Well Bunny Dear, We are starting out on the great venture of this war, and by the time you get this letter, for better or for worse it will be history. We are attacking in daylight the most heavily fortified shore in history, a shore held by excellent troops. We are throwing against it excellent troops well-armed and backed by superb air and good naval support. We are on transports, buttoned up. Our next stop, Europe.... The men are crowded below [on USS *Barnett*] or lounging on deck. Very few have seen action. They talk of many things, but rarely of the action that lies ahead. If they speak of it at all it is to wise-crack.... Most generals are afraid to battle for what they believe with superiors who hold the power over their advancement. One of the reasons I'm so fond of Tubby Barton is that he is not. He will never, wittingly, let his men down.[21]

Like almost all commanders, there was little Barton could do that night or morning. His unit was well trained, and he had his experienced leaders, Roosevelt and Van Fleet, landing in the initial assault. Barton got little sleep that night and spent most of it in the operations room aboard the USS *Bayfield*, looking at maps and charts. Onboard was the VII Corps staff, but none of the other principals, such as Collins or his chief of staff, McKee, mentioned any discussions or meetings that night. Finally, at about 04:30 the soldiers began loading into their landing boats. Barton walked around the ship and gave the troops a motivational speech when he could. Then he watched as his troops left the *Bayfield*, dropped into their Higgins boats waiting below, and headed for the coast. As dawn broke, Barton observed the Ninth Air Force's bombardment of the beach targets. At 05:50 the battleships *Nevada* and *Enterprise*, five cruisers, and eight destroyers began a bombardment of the Utah Beach defenses.[22] The reporter Ira Wolfert was standing next to the division commander as he watched the action. He asked, "How do you think it will go general?" Barton replied, "It has to go—there's no place for those lads of mine to come back to."[23]

Companies F, E, C, and B (from left to right), 8th Infantry, hit the beach at precisely 06:30 hours. Roosevelt went in with Company B and began coordinating the two 8th Infantry assault battalions: Lieutenant Colonel Conrad C. Simmons's 1st and Carlton O. MacNeely's 2nd Battalions.[24] Barton then observed the 22nd and 12th Infantry regiments forming up and heading to shore. Red Reeder later remembered the radio call before climbing into his landing craft: "Cactus to Cargo, come in." Reeder responded to Barton: "Come in Cactus." Then: "Good luck Red."[25]

Within a few minutes on the beach, the two battalion commanders began telling the brigadier that the actual beach terrain bore little resemblance to the sand tables and maps they had been poring over for months.[26] While the battalion leaders were busy trying to get their troops productively engaged in battle and moving forward, Roosevelt had time to survey the beach area. The veteran of previous assaults realized they were in the wrong place. He got his bearings, located where they should be, and moved from one commander to the other, orienting them on their actual locations. He instructed MacNeely and Simmons to clear the strong points in front of German troops and head toward their original objectives. At 07:20 hours Van Fleet arrived on the beach with the 3rd Battalion, and Roosevelt updated him on the situation and his decisions. The regimental commander concurred; he was the one in command, not the brigadier, and reported the decision back to Barton on the USS *Bayfield*. The follow-on units received instructions to follow the 8th onto the modified landing site.[27] Both Van Fleet and MacNeely emphasized in their reports that Roosevelt was under machine-gun and artillery fire during the entire period he was moving across the beach. They were impressed with his poise under fire and his leadership effectiveness. As the veteran in the group, he was the one that decided on the preferred course of action.[28] Unfortunately, Simmons died in action on June 24, so we have no report from him on what he observed during the landing.

As a lieutenant with the 22nd Infantry, Bob Walk served as a liaison officer between his regiment and division headquarters. He was on the LCT that served as the vessel for the liaison and radio jeeps and other vehicles from the headquarters command group. This cramped boat also served as Barton's command post as the fight began. Bouncing alongside the *Bayfield*, Barton used the hood of Walk's Jeep as the table for his situation map. There he listened to the reports from shore and monitored the action. Walk remembered Van Fleet's reporting that everything was under control. It would have been about now when the commander received word of the adjustment to the landing beach. He checked his map, approved Van Fleet and Roosevelt's adjustment, and passed the information on to Moon and Collins. Then Walk heard Tribolet, his regimental commander, calling in and reporting that everything was going according to plan. After that report, he heard Barton say, "That's enough for me, let's go."[29]

First Command Posts, Utah Beach, June 6, 1944

Although Barton would spend almost 188 days in combat, it was the first one that, in many ways, was the most important. By now he had nearly two full years of training and leading the division. But he had more than that, including his time as chief of staff and 8th Infantry commander. He had supervised its preparation for combat in extensive exercises and amphibious training in Florida and England and knew all of the division's senior officers and most of the company commanders personally. Few American units would be as prepared for their first day of battle as the Ivy Division.[30] Yet this was his first taste of actual combat after thirty-six years in uniform. Barton told Cornelius Ryan, who interviewed him ten years after D-Day, that he constantly fretted that he would become so afraid that he would freeze and fail as a combat leader. On June 6 he would discover which was more robust: his natural human fear or his character, developed in decades of preparing for this day.[31]

As expected, the division's official log of events, and subsequent after-action reports for June 6, do not have the details historians would like. The staff officers were on the move and struggling to establish the first command post on the continent. But thanks to Barton's communications with Ryan and the detailed comments from Bill York's diary, we now have an accurate account of the division commander's actions on June 6.

Henry Barber and the division's advance party had landed around 09:00 and moved beyond the beach as the 8th Infantry cleared the way to the causeways. Around 10:00 Barton, Richards, and York arrived on the shore. Barton later admitted he was terrified as the sounds of the machine-gun, rifle, and artillery fire surrounded him. A German artillery shell exploding nearby only increased his concern. He encountered the engineers behind the seawall, as noted at the beginning of this chapter, and continued moving inland. He did not go far, but around 10:30 found a house with a high brick-walled courtyard on the dunes. The German artillery was increasing its fire rate, and anything on the beach was a potential casualty, so the house gave some protection. Barton is quite open that there was little he could do at this point; his regimental commanders had a plan, and Roosevelt was on the ground making the needed adjustments.[32] While at the beach house, Barton had little idea what was going on. "I was in a semi fog. No contact nor communications with anyone but those present. . . . About a mile off our planned landing point. No idea of where nor how my assault battalions were, except that I did know they had taken their beach and gone on inland."[33] The only influence he had on the battle was when commanders of the attached units found him and asked if he had any instructions. In every case, he said, "No; just go ahead on your job per plan."[34]

Barton was sending his liaison officers and others to find out the situation. Lieutenant Joseph Owen remembered that at about 11:00, Barton sent him toward Sainte-Mère-Église to find the exact location of the 8th Infantry. He remembers running into Roosevelt on the way, who slowed down his Jeep to yell out, "Hey Boy, they're shooting up there," followed by a big "Haw Haw." One constant among 4th Infantry Division soldiers that morning was the ubiquitous Roosevelt. Without fixed command responsibilities, he could range across the beach area, advising, conjoining, and keeping things moving. Owen found Van Fleet, and the colonel instructed one of his officers to mark the battle map for delivery back to Barton.[35]

By noon his battle staff, those who landed to assist during the early hours of the invasion, began to join him. One of the first was Colonel Dee Stone, the G-5 (military government) who had found Major Phil Hart, his former aide and now one of his staff officers, severely wounded at the water's edge.[36] The amphibious engineers present (under the seawall's shelter) refused to help Stone rescue Hart from the advancing tide, but he was able to move the wounded officer to safety.[37] Then Dick Marr, the G-4, and Parks Huntt, his headquarters commandant, arrived, reported, and began moving toward the planned headquarters site. Next reporting in was Colonel James E. Wharton, the 1st Engineer Special Brigade commander and the senior commander for the soldiers Barton encountered at the seawall. As he notes in his letter to Cornelius Ryan ten years later, "The colonel took the trouble to inform me that his men were not the only ones quitting their missions at the seawall but that some of mine had done the same—in the beginning that was true but Ted Roosevelt cured that."[38] One suspects the division commander let him know how he felt.

Around 13:00 Barber's aide found the division commander and guided him to a temporary command post, an impromptu collection of vehicles and staff officers just south of Causeway 2. Orlando Troxel (G-3) and Harry Hansen (G-2) and their small staff were monitoring the combat teams' progress. Dick Marr reported that the infantry had crossed the low ground the Germans had flooded and were making good progress inland. All reports indicated that everything was generally going according to plan. There was little Barton could do; he had to let the commanders do their jobs. However, he noticed that many follow-on units were backing up on the causeways and having trouble moving inland. He saw that the causeway was loaded with vehicles bumper to bumper but not moving. Without intending to, soldiers performing their assigned local duties were making it difficult to get the division's combat power into the fight. Engineers improving the route, antiaircraft guns, and wire teams were all making movement difficult. Finally, Barton and Marr went to the traffic jam, took a look, and ordered everything nonessential off the road.

Brigadier General Roosevelt, Barton, and Lieutenant Colonel Clarence
G. Hupfer, commander, 746th Tank Battalion, Utah Beach, June 6, 1944.
US Army photograph.

Some vehicles had broken down, and Barton had soldiers move stuck
vehicles off the road and into the swamp. Once traffic across the causeway
was flowing, troops would spend the rest of the night pulling the unfortunate
equipment that got in the way out of the mire.[39]

Troxel received reports that the division had captured Causeway
#3 (T7), just to the north, and it was open for use. Nearby, Lieutenant Colonel
Clarence G. Hupfer's 746th Tank Battalion was still near the landing
area, and Barton wanted it off the beach and to its next position near
Audouville-la-Hubert. Because of the congestion in front of him, he began
developing an alternate route for the armor, using the reportedly open
road. In the middle of all that confusion, around 15:00 hours Roosevelt
arrived at the temporary command post. They joyfully embraced each
other. Of course, Ted wanted to talk. Barton later noted, "He was bursting
with information (which I sorely needed). —but wouldn't let him talk."
He was under pressure to get the tank battalion into the fight. He later
noted, "Try some day to keep a Ted Roosevelt from sounding off if he
wants to—but I did."[40]

In the middle of all this, York interrupted the proceedings and notified his boss that some Associated Press photographers wanted pictures of the division commander. "Reluctantly and irritably," he consented. It broke his chain of thought, and then the photographers took their time taking the photos. Barton was "mad as hell" because he only wanted to get the tanks on the road and talk to Ted. Finally, the photographers departed, and Barton later cherished the photographs. Hupfer got his orders and returned to his command, and now Barton and Roosevelt could catch up. Ted had been on the ground for over eight hours and decisively engaged in leading and making decisions the whole time. While talking they noticed more congestion at the nearby crossroads as the 746th Tank Battalion attempted to move through the congested area. So the two generals walked to the crossroads, one on each corner, and began directing traffic, just like military police officers. Barton later remembered how little personal control he had that day. His officers had a plan and knew what to do. All he could do until he could get his command post up and running was monitor what he could see. He also could act as a rallying point for officers needing directions, as noted above, performing tasks that, to paraphrase his comments, any second lieutenant could do. Hal Blakeley's aide-de-camp, Lieutenant Roswell MacGillivray, arrived as the tanks departed to lead Barton to the new command post.[41]

Audouville-La Hubert

It was around 19:00 on June 6 when Barton arrived at Blakeley's division artillery command post. For the first time that day, he had good communications and could contact his regimental commanders. Nearby, Captain Huntt began establishing the division's operations center in the new command post.[42] Not wanting to interfere with his staff, Barton walked over to the road and found Van Fleet, 8th Infantry, watching some troops load a soldier on an ambulance. While the two talked, a tall, distinguished-looking civilian in a coat and knickers came up, waving a marked map and excitedly trying to tell them something. Van Fleet had to leave, and Barton was stuck with the Frenchman, whom he could not understand but who turned out to be a retired army colonel. He tried to convince Barton that a German artillery battery was nearby, but Tubby had recently walked by that location and seen nothing. After politely saying good-bye, he walked over to Rodwell, who had just joined the command post group. Just then, a report arrived confirming the French colonel's warning. He told his chief "to run out to the road, grab the first combat outfit he found and have it go take the hostile battery." Rodwell found an element of an antitank battalion going into a bivouac and grabbed some of its infantrymen. He soon returned with the report, "mission accomplished with ease."[43]

Around 21:00 hours it was still light in this northern part of the world in June, and there was still little Barton and Blakeley could do to influence the battle until the command posts were operational and the staff began processing the unit reports. The infantry was settling into its evening positions, and the artillery batteries were repositioning to best support them. Therefore, the two generals decided to inspect the piece of France that now belonged to the 4th Infantry Division. With Sergeant Richards still driving the M29 Weasel, Barton and York headed out to visit a captured German artillery battery nearby Saint-Martin-de-Varreville. They looked around at some of the other positions, and near Causeway 4 (S9), the farthest north, Barton's vehicle threw a track around 23:30 as it was getting dark. Since they were not able to repair it on the spot and it was located right along the front lines, Barton and York climbed into Blakeley's vehicle. The general assured Richards that they would send help. According to Barton, Richards did not say a word, but after the war he told him, "he never felt so lonely, nor scared."[44]

Barton and Blakeley arrived back at the headquarters in the early hours of June 7, and Rodwell had the staff operating and gave them an overview of his division's status. It was a good report; the landing had gone well. Frankly, it is incorrect to say that no plan survives first contact with the enemy. An operation plan is nothing more than a scripted series of events that provide leaders with the direction for the opening phase of an operation. In this case, the nature of the region's currents and the loss of one of the naval control vessels caused the first wave to land south of the intended landing area. But their understanding of Barton's intent, and training, allowed the assault to progress almost without any disruption. And it turned out to be a brilliant stroke of luck, as the German defenses were weaker than the original sector. Once ashore the leaders went about their business as if on another practice exercise. Everything that happened in those first few hours reflected the division cadre's high level of preparation.[45] Barton was satisfied with how things went that day. He told Rodwell that night, "Things are good, I think we made it." By nightfall D-Day they "were ashore, well inland, an intact operational division—and now proven veterans."[46] Barton's last act before lying down for a few hours' rest was to gather his regimental commanders outside his command post. Someone had liberated a few bottles of champagne, and the commander shared it with his senior leaders and Tribolet, Van Fleet, and Reeder, so they could "drink to the health of the best division in the army."[47]

Audouville-La-Hubert is a small crossroads halfway between Utah Beach and Sainte-Mère-Église. It would become a busy place for the next several days as the 4th Division occupied all portions of the intersection. As Rodwell set up the division command post and established his headquarters' battle rhythm, Richard G. McKee and the VII Corps staff moved into the nearby chateau. The First Army was pleasantly surprised that the Utah landings had gone so well. "The news was quite surprising to some, as it had been generally estimated that Omaha was the easier of the two beaches to conquer."[48]

The situation on the ground at first light on June 7 was beginning to make more sense. However, Barton's major problem was that he had difficulty controlling the battle over such a wide frontage. McNair had not designed American infantry divisions for this kind of deployment. The standard array for a triangular division had two units in contact and the third capable of exploitation or reinforcement.[49] A frontage of over ten thousand yards, about five miles wide, was excessive for a division in the attack; it probably should have been half that.[50]

Two of Barton's regiments, the 12th and 22nd, were online, facing north, with the right flank anchored on the coast. Their task was to attack north to expand the VII Corps' lodgment in Cherbourg's direction. Blocking this advance were concrete emplacements along the coast and two major artillery fortresses at Azeville and Crisbecq. The 8th Infantry, on the division's left side, faced northwest and was in contact with an isolated enemy battalion south of Sainte-Mère-Église, located between

Barton's troops and the 82nd Airborne Division. This battalion, made up of conscripts from Soviet Georgia, was hindering the advance of both divisions. Van Fleet's task was to destroy that German force and solidify the connection with the paratroopers.

One aspect of the operation remains obscure: What was the role of Barton's two brigadier generals? To date historians have not located diaries or reports from either officer. Based on the memoirs of his assigned driver, Barber might not have come ashore on D-Day morning as scheduled, but a division narrative indicates he landed at 09:00.[51] In contrast, we know Roosevelt was busy, traveling in his Jeep with just a driver and his aide, Captain Stevenson. Generally, he assisted in roles beyond what the active regimental commanders could efficiently perform. These included monitoring and intervening on the flanks, helping the staff coordinate with adjacent and supporting units, and giving Barton another set of eyes in that sector. All of this was especially true due to the division's extended frontage. Roosevelt performed these functions on the left portion of the division's sector while Barber acted the same way on the right when he arrived on Utah Beach.[52] Therefore, Barton could remain in the center of the zone, moving about the battlefield where he needed to be.

This arrangement also allowed him to return to headquarters on short notice, such as when Collins arrived at the 4th Infantry Division's command post late on June 7; at this same time, a liaison officer from the 82nd Airborne Division showed up, asking for tank support. According to Collins, Barton was reluctant to release the tanks as he still had a mission into the north. However, the corps commander had control of the entire operation and a better grasp of what he needed. So he told Barton to release the armor, and Company A, 746th Tank Battalion, headed off to support the paratroopers.[53]

Before taking command of the 8th Infantry, James Van Fleet's main claim to fame was as a football player and coach. His aggressiveness and directive leadership certainly contributed to the regiment's operations over the next few weeks. His first task was to break through a German battalion of Georgian descent that held a series of positions south of Sainte-Mère-Église between Fauville and Turqueville, blocking all routes from that direction. By the end of the day, the regiment had seized Écoquenéauville and, with the help of the 746th Tank Battalion, established strong links with the 82nd Airborne Division north of the town.[54]

Red Reeder's 12th Infantry occupied the center of the division's sector and continued to advance north toward its initial objective of the artillery fortress west of Azeville. Like Van Fleet, his prewar claim to fame was as an athlete in football, baseball, and other sports. Interestingly, Reeder played for Van Fleet when he coached the all-army football squad at Fort Benning in 1927.[55] Under Reeder's direction his command had become an aggressive fighting unit, and if it had a problem, it was because its commander was much more comfortable leading the regiment than directing his battalions. Fortunately, Jim Luckett, still the executive officer, filled in all the missing directions and ensured that the unit fought as a team. By the end of the evening, it arrived just south of Azeville.[56]

Herve Tribolet had not coached or played football while at Denison University. But he was a solid trainer and had prepared the 22nd Infantry well for its initial operations.[57] Unfortunately, Barton and Troxel gave him two complex tasks: reduce the fortifications along the coast and capture the German artillery fortified complexes at Azeville and Crisbecq. The regimental frontage was about four miles wide. Multiple disparate objectives made sense if the enemy was on the run. However, in this case the German defenders were going nowhere. Tribolet assigned Major Earl W. Edward's 2nd Battalion, on the left flank, with the task of capturing the Battery Azeville. One of the first Nazi fortified positions built in Normandy, it had four 105 mm French Schneider guns oriented out to sea. The 170 German soldiers protecting the battery occupied machine-gun positions, bunkers, mortar pits, and 37 mm antiaircraft guns. Surrounding all this concrete were rows of barbed wire and mines.[58] Edwards's companies attempted to reach the complex for several hours, only to be driven back by a fierce counterattack. German artillery from Crisbecq and other batteries took a toll on Edward's troops. They spent the night where it started that morning, conceding the day's success to the German defenders.[59]

In the regiment's center, Lieutenant Colonel Sewell M. Brumby's 1st Battalion headed north along a farm road toward Saint-Marcouf, just south of Crisbecq. Unfortunately, this route passed right in front of Azeville's guns, and shelling and machine-gun fire took a toll.[60] It was not a good evening for this battalion. Tribolet's 3rd Battalion, commanded by Lieutenant Colonel Arthur S. Teague, had been the fourth battalion ashore on D-Day. It started D+1 on the coast, south of Causeway 3, and immediately commenced moving north along the dunes, attacking the German positions from the rear. Although focused on the sea, the German military always prepared their fortifications for all-around defense, and they consisted of concrete blockhouses, turreted machine guns, artillery, and mortars. Barbed wire and mines surrounded these weapons and concrete.[61] In anticipation of this defensive array, Teague's command was a special task force and followed the training it had received at Camp Gordon Johnston and the assault training center at Braunton in England. He had an attached naval shore fire control party and could request fire from the navy's high-velocity guns onto resisting positions. German troops fought hard and inflicted heavy casualties on the Americans, but by late afternoon the battalion had reached Widerstandsnest 11 at Hamel de Cruttes.[62]

Operating on an extensive front, Barton sought to influence the action as he could. He visited Van Fleet in the morning and left satisfied that his left flank was well in hand. He returned to the division headquarters and met up with Collins. The corps commander pressed him to move faster, as was his norm. Both generals realized that the Germans had a say in how they would fight the battle. Rather than the fortified positions simply going away, the enemy fought with all they had. Additional Nazi troops continued moving into the Cotentin opposite the still understrength VII Corps. Collins had little choice but to keep up the pressure on his division commanders to move beyond the beachhead. He had to get his corps assembled in Normandy. So, with few options, he ordered Barton to continue the attack. Understanding Collins's directions, the division commander then headed off to Ravenoville to visit Tribolet, who had suffered the worst day in the division so far. Barton directed him to concentrate the regiment by moving Teague's 3rd Battalion, minus Company K and supporting weapons along the coast, to a location opposite Azeville. He also contacted Troxel and told him to prepare Field Order #2, directing the regiments to continue their attacks in their sectors. It was his second day of combat.[63]

Beuzeville-Au-Plain

By the morning of June 8, Collins and the VII Corps were in the unsettling position of having to fight in three directions at once. To the south, Maxwell Taylor's 101st Airborne Division had to satisfy Omar Bradley's main requirement: connecting VII Corps with Gerow's V Corps fighting its way out of the Omaha Beach bridgehead. The army commander was adamant; if Collins needed to, he should reinforce the paratroopers with the arriving 9th and 90th Division's regiments. The focus of that effort was the small port of Carentan, on the Douve River, coincidently defended by German paratroopers.[64]

Therefore, the 4th Infantry Division's attack north was Collins's third priority. Barton's left flank was still occupied by the 82nd Airborne Division, with a unit boundary just east of the Sainte-Mère-Église and Valognes highway and the coast on the right flank. Barton kept his regiments in the same array as the day before, with Van Fleet's 8th on the left, Reeder's 12th center, and Tribolet's 22nd on the right.[65] Some good news arrived with the report that the entire division was finally ashore and moving to its appropriate locations.[66]

Barton's next challenge as a division commander in combat centered on Herve Tribolet's 22nd Infantry. Although he had the most challenging task, his tactical deployment violated the fundamentals of offensive operations. He should have learned on June 7 that attacking with three battalions online would not accomplish his mission. This battle was not a training event; the Germans fought without umpires. While his regiment outnumbered the defending enemy, the addition of their heavy weapons and obstacles ensured that he needed to mass combat power to seize his objectives sequentially rather than simultaneously. As *Field Manual 100-5* noted, "Sound tactical maneuver in the offensive is characterized by a concentration of effort in a direction where success will insure the attainment of the objectives. On the remainder of the front are used only the minimum means necessary to deceive the enemy and to hinder his maneuver to oppose the main attack."[67]

The two strong points' terrain and location required that the regiment capture Azeville first since it covered the avenue of approach to Crisbecq, as evidenced by the previous day's fight. Barton visited Tribolet on the evening of June 7 and the following morning. He believed in giving his subordinate commanders flexibility, so he allowed his commander one more chance to get the 22nd Infantry moving.[68] Unfortunately, the regiment's assault on June 8 was a duplicate of the previous day's fiasco, with two battalions online against the two fortresses and the third battalion pushing north along the coast. Barton had to commit a company from the 359th Infantry, 90th Infantry Division—his reserve force—to support the 2nd Battalion, almost overrun by a German counterattack.[69] In the regiment's center, Major John Dowdy, who had taken over for Brumby (who had been wounded), led his 1st Battalion against the Crisbecq defenders. This time the assault began with a twenty-minute preparatory fire from artillery and mortars. Then it turned into a rolling barrage as Dowdy's infantrymen moved forward. Finally, they arrived at the fortification, exhausting all their explosives and attempting to break into the installation. German Nebelwerfers (rocket artillery) and other guns pounded the battalion. Again, a German counterattack drove it back from the battery and to its original location, this time with excessive losses.[70]

In the division's center, Reeder's 12th Infantry continued to advance north with the 1st and 3rd Battalions online, with the 2nd following in support. At 05:30 hours the naval warships fired a barrage on the German strongpoint at Émondeville, and an hour later the 1st and 3rd Battalions attacked. The regiment encountered the German forward line about seven hundred yards south of the village. The 3rd Battalion on the left broke through the enemy's outposts but was stopped in the orchards and soon ran into trouble from heavy enemy artillery fire and German infantry. Two of the 3rd Battalion's companies were isolated at one point, causing Reeder to commit his reserve to extract them. On the right the 1st Battalion had difficulty moving forward, and as was German doctrine, the enemy counterattacked in the afternoon. The division's reserve, another company from the 359th Infantry, joined the 12th to stop the attack. After a day of heavy casualties but reasonable progress, Reeder's troops spent the night around the captured enemy strongpoint.[71]

Van Fleet's 8th Infantry jumped off from Sainte-Mère-Église and attacked along the eastern side of the highway to Montebourg (N13). The Germans contested the advance by artillery fire, but its first contact with enemy infantry came at Neuville-Au-Plain. The Germans yielded the town again after a sharp skirmish in midafternoon. Beyond these defenses the going was more straightforward as the regiment turned to the northwest and continued its attack on the western side of the highway. As the regiment approached Fresville and Grainville (La Lande), enemy artillery and sniper fire increased and slowed Van Fleet's advance. From here to Crisbecq, the Germans attempted to establish a defensive line to stop the Americans. Late in the day, unsure what waited for him, Van Fleet ordered a halt, sent out patrols, and consolidated to prepare for the next day's advance. The Germans knew the 8th Infantry was there, and it remained under heavy fire all night.[72]

Although Reeder and Van Fleet were moving slowly, they continued to advance, and Barton was happy with their progress. Additionally, the way they deployed their battalions indicated that they were in control of the situation. Unfortunately, he could not say the same about the commander of the 22nd Infantry. While Barton was working through the problems with Tribolet's command, Rodwell and Huntt moved the division headquarters six kilometers north to a farm crossroads named Beuzeville-Au-Plain, closer to the division's center of mass. That night Barton met with Tribolet at the new division command post and gave him specific instructions. He told him to pull Teague's 3rd Battalion, minus a reinforced company blocking the coastal road, to an area allowing it to attack Azeville in the morning. Dowdy's badly depleted 1st Battalion became the regimental reserve while he reorganized it. Barton also directed air and artillery fire to suppress Crisbecq and allow the regiment to concentrate on one task, just as doctrine dictated. It had been a costly day, with a reported 418 killed, wounded, or missing.[73]

On June 9 Collins ordered Jay MacKelvie's 90th Infantry Division into the fight. MacKelvie, as readers will remember, joined Barton and Haislip in organizing the 85th Infantry Division back in 1943. Bradley appointed him to command the 90th Infantry Division in January 1944 after he and Collins determined its commander Major General Henry Terrell Jr. was a poor trainer, and the unit was unprepared for combat. Now MacKelvie had a chance. Soon after that Manton A. Eddy's 9th Infantry Division began arriving in Normandy, and Collins directed it west to link up with the 82nd

Airborne Division and continue the attack. He moved MacKelvie's division to the north, where it soon became the command on Barton's left flank.[74]

Van Fleet's 8th Infantry spent the night entrenched under fire near Fresville. At 06:30 on June 9, the 1st and 3rd Battalions, 8th Infantry, and the 2nd Battalion, 325th Glider Infantry, executed a coordinated attack against the German line between the highway and the Merderet River. A half-hour concentration by at least three battalions of artillery preceded their attack. It started poorly as German fire across the small river ripped into the advancing soldiers before they left their attack positions. Barton and Collins came by, and both commanders got caught in some of the artillery fire. After several hours of firing back and forth, Van Fleet launched MacNeely's 2nd Battalion into the fight. However, Écausseville, a strong point anchoring the enemy's first thoroughly prepared line, had held out all day. But outflanked by the 1st Battalion's drive on the right, supported by Shermans from the 70th Tank Battalion and by the 3rd Battalion's attack on the left, the defenders abandoned the town after Van Fleet called off the attack about 21:00 hours, not prepared to withstand another assault during the night or the next day.[75]

Red Reeder's 12th Infantry provided the day's most impressive performance in achieving objectives. At the same time as Van Fleet's troops, they attacked the enemy strongpoint at the Château Daudinville, northwest of Joganville. Like many of the Norman structures, it was a sizeable walled-in stone building, which the Germans knew how to defend. Reeder sent a platoon of Shermans from Company B, 746th Tank Battalion, to attack from the west while the 1st and 2nd Battalions attacked it, at the cost of heavy casualties, from the south. Barton came by late in the morning but missed Reeder, who was leading from the front. Again, Barton came under a German artillery attack. But he was happy; the regimental commander was giving his division a lesson in the art of small unit tactics: tanks with a base of the fire and two battalions in the assault, while the third remained in reserve. Not content with this objective, Reeder committed Lieutenant Colonel Thaddeus R. Dulin's relatively fresh 3rd Battalion into the mix. It broke through, and Dulin led the regiment in a rewarding advance forward and reached positions northeast of Montebourg, on the edge of its objective.[76]

While the other two regimental commanders drove their troops as hard as possible, Tribolet gave his superiors the impression that he no longer had the motivation to command the regiment. At 11:00, many hours after it was supposed to attack at sunrise, Arthur Teague's 3rd Battalion, which had moved over the previous evening, attacked the Azeville fortress alone. The 44th Field Artillery fired over 1,500 rounds in support while the other two battalions remained in position. By early afternoon Teague's troops managed to use a flamethrower to blast open one of the pillboxes, and the entire complex surrendered. At least six hours of daylight were left available to exploit this success. However, Tribolet gave no indication that he would move his command forward. This lack of initiative was unacceptable to Barton and Collins.[77] When Barton, around lunchtime, realized what was going on, he was furious. Collins, who had brutal fights on his two other fronts, was upset about the lack of progress on the coast, and the two discussed the situation and agreed the division needed an aggressive officer to replace the ineffective regimental commander. After Collins departed Barton grabbed Generals Blakeley and Barber and Colonel Clarke Fales, the commander of the 359th Infantry, which was serving as the 4th Infantry Division's reserve, and drove to the 22nd Infantry's command post at Ravenoville.

Once there he took control of the sector's fight away from Tribolet and gave it to his deputy commander. He told Hal Barber to leave a company along the coast to prevent activity and consolidate the entire regimental combat team, including most of the 746th Tank Battalion and the M10-equipped 899th Tank Destroyer Battalion. Fale's infantry would surround Crisbecq, keep it under fire, and prevent it from interfering with the unit's advance. Task Force Barber now had priority over all division artillery fires. Barton ordered Barber to resume the advance not later than 16:30 hours, along the axis Fontenay to Ozeville, and then attack northwest to seize the high ground at Quinéville. The task force moved out at 16:30, but it was stopped by fire from strong enemy positions at the crossroads west of Ferme du Château de Fontenay, just northwest of Crisbecq, and dug in for the night.[78]

It had been another costly day, with over four hundred soldiers killed, wounded, or missing. Barton was happy with the performance of his two football coaches but deeply concerned with Tribolet's conduct and was probably also worried that Hal Barber had not been more active in keeping the regiment moving. When Barton and his commanders drank their champagne toast that first evening, it is doubtful they appreciated the difficulty in their immediate future. The German Army had not given up but, in their sector, was fighting a determined delay back to Cherbourg. It would make the Ivy Division, and the rest of the VII Corps, pay for every mile on the way.

Chapter 10

Montebourg to Cherbourg, June 9–30

We no longer have the division we brought ashore.
—Barton, after the capture of Cherbourg

Fresville (Le Bisson)

As the reports came in during the night on June 9–10, it was evident that Tribolet had to go. He was a good trainer but could no longer handle the regiment in battle. Because he needed Collins's concurrence, Barton contacted him early in the morning and received approval to make the change and suggest a replacement. Colonel Robert T. Foster (USMA 1918), one of Barton's lieutenants in Coblenz and Fort Screven, had arrived in England in May. Collins sent word to him to come over and report to Barton.[1] A little after 06:00, Barton pulled Tribolet aside, told him he was done, and sent him on his way to corps headquarters.[2] Tribolet, loved by his soldiers, remained in Europe and spent the remainder of the war working for the 12th Army Group.

Roosevelt joined Barton and Barber at the 22nd Infantry's command post and discussed how to change the plan. The main issue was to get Barber's task force, including Tribolet's old unit, temporarily commanded by the executive officer Major John Ruggles, back into the fight. The regiment's

229

attack that day began before Tribolet's relief and continued to reflect bad tactics and went nowhere. The division's after-action report describes it best: the "task force attacked at 06:30, 3rd Battalion attacking in the north, direction of Ozeville, 2nd Battalion attacking west in the direction of Château de Fontenay, 1st Battalion in reserve."[3] Even as augmented, the regiment did not have the combat power to simultaneously attack two sets of German defenses.[4] After the fight the regiment pulled back to where it had started to reorganize for the night. The unit's only bright spot was its Team K, which continued to capture the enemy's strong points along the coast. Meanwhile, Collins had attached the 359th Infantry from the 90th Infantry Division, to the 4th Infantry Division as a reserve. That night Barton attached its 3rd Battalion to Barber's force for the next day's attack.[5] That afternoon after he pulled into his new command post at Le Bisson near Fresville, Barton had a chance to reflect on the day. From his perspective it had not been a good one.

By Sunday, June 11 (D+5), Barton seemed to be getting control of his division in combat. He now had a high-performing staff, two hot-shot regimental commanders, and a promising replacement commander on the way. However, Barber, now leading the 22nd Infantry until Foster showed up, made little progress toward his objective at Ozeville.[6] Meanwhile, the 8th and 12th Infantries continued to consolidate and improve their positions. Ammunition, food, water, and replacement soldiers helped to improve unit resolve for the next attack. Then Barton received another sad disruption to his team.

At about 14:00 Reeder was out checking his battalion's positions on the objective. He had just visited some new soldiers who were replacements and was on his way back to his command post to talk to Barton. Unfortunately, a German 88 mm shell blew up near him, and he fell to the ground. Badly wounded, he was evacuated by his troops to the rear. Barton came to the command post shaking his head. "I am so sorry Red."[7] Major James S. Luckett, his executive officer, took command of the 12th Infantry. Thirty minutes later the 2nd Battalion suffered a significant loss as its commander, Lieutenant Colonel Dominick P. Montelbano, died trying to move his battalion forward. Major Richard J. O'Malley took command and continued the attack.[8] Reeder's wounding affected everyone who knew him. Collins

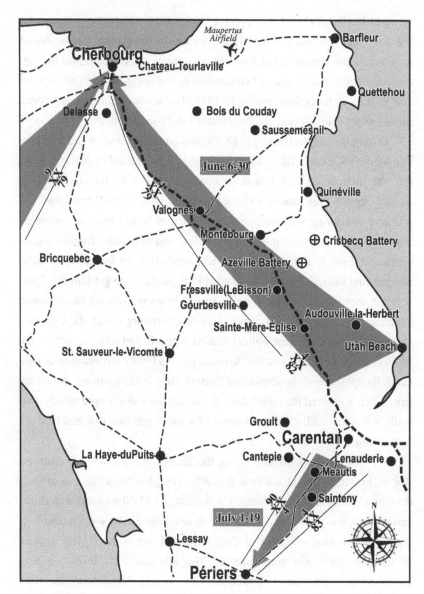

4th Infantry Division attacks toward Cherbourg (June 6–30) and Périers (July 1–19)

came to his hospital tent that evening and pinned, on Bradley's authority, the first Distinguished Service Medal awarded in Normandy. Reeder hoped to return to the regiment, but it would not happen as he would lose his leg. Nevertheless, Reeder remained on active duty and spent the remainder of the war at West Point before retiring in 1946. The school immediately rehired him as its athletic director, and he remained there until 1967.[9]

During the night of June 11–12, Collins contacted Barton and told him that Manton S. Eddy's 9th Infantry Division had just landed its first regiment, the 39th Infantry, on Utah Beach. He attached it to the 4th Infantry Division to clear up the area around Crisbecq fortress, now in the 22nd Infantry's rear and interfering with its operations.[10] Barton would have no problems working with this regiment since Paddy Flint, one of his best friends, was in command. Flint had already established a reputation for living on the edge and pushing his unit hard, so he needed little prodding to get into the fight. It began moving toward the fortress area right away. Sensing the hopeless situation, the German naval commander in Cherbourg called the Crisbecq commander, Oberleutenant Walter Ohmsen, who still had about seventy-eight soldiers and sailors, and told him to break out. As Flint's reconnaissance unit carefully approached the abandoned fortress early in the morning, it took no fire. When it entered the installation, the recon force discovered twenty-one badly wounded soldiers, the remnants of a small garrison that had held up Barton and Collin's advance for six days.[11]

Freed from problems in his rear, the 22nd Infantry's new commander, Robert Foster, executed the plan that John Ruggles, his executive officer, developed with Barber and Barton's assistance. At 12:50 it attacked Ozeville and cleared the village at 15:50. Four hours later Foster's command had seized the division objective at Quinéville and began the typical actions of reorganization and consolidation. The 8th and 12th Infantries also improved their positions in anticipation of clearing Montebourg the next day.[12] Once Barton was satisfied that Foster and the 22nd Infantry would achieve their objective, he felt free to pay a visit to corps headquarters, still at Audouville-la-Hubert. He talked to Collins and the staff and caught up on the corps' overall situation. Other than that, more and more units were coming ashore; the big news was that the 101st Airborne Division had captured Carentan, the hinge between the VII and V Corps. Now Collins was free to push his other divisions across the Cotentin peninsula and advance north to Cherbourg. Barton then drove over to visit Flint, located just north of Crisbecq, to talk about the operation and catch up on personal issues.[13]

Patrols from the 8th and 12th Infantries on June 12 discovered that Montebourg, still a division objective, was essentially undefended. Therefore, Barton told Van Fleet that the town was now in his zone and should be seized and occupied that day if it could do so with minimal losses. Unfortunately, that was not to be, as the Germans moved a battalion of about five hundred soldiers into the city. When a small task force led by the 8th Infantry's executive officer, Lieutenant Colonel Fred Steiner, arrived before midnight, it discovered the enemy strong enough to wait for daylight before trying to enter. At 07:00 the task force tried again but found the town reasonably well defended, and Barton decided to hold in place and not risk more soldiers yet. Nevertheless, he ordered the 8th and 12th Infantries to increase their patrols in Montebourg and toward Valognes behind the German main defense line.[14] Meanwhile, the two regiments continued to improve their positions by securing nearby high ground along the Quinéville Ridge. Barton visited each regiment commander during the day, including Flint, who was still commanding his reserve behind the three regiments. His orders to the commanders were to continue improving their positions, complete the capture of objectives not yet entirely under control, especially near Quinéville, and begin active patrolling.[15]

On June 14 the 4th Infantry Division became the corps reserve as Collins continued to fight across the Cotentin peninsula, essentially separating Generalleutnant Karl-Wilhelm von Schlieben, commanding Cherbourg, from the rest of the German Army in Normandy.[16] Collins's situation had greatly improved with the 4th Infantry Division on its objectives opposite Montebourg and the 101st Airborne and 2nd Armored Divisions capturing Carentan and linking the two corps.[17]

Meanwhile, Collins continued to remove commanders who failed to show enough energy and determination in combat command. One example was Barton's comrade from the 85th Infantry Division a year ago. After only four days of confronting German forces, MacKelvie's leadership in the 90th

Division was not satisfactory to Collins. In combat, he had no time to develop MacKelvie as a division commander, so Collins contacted Bradley and got concurrence to replace him with his deputy Gene Landrum. He also decided to relieve two of the 90th Infantry Division's regimental commanders.[18] Relief from command was not, in 1944, generally a ticket home. These officers had made it to the senior level typically by doing things right. So Collins sent MacKelvie back to Bradley and recommended he remain with the artillery. Later, he took command of the 80th Infantry Division's Artillery and led it to the war's end.[19] Never far from Barton's mind was the knowledge that Collins and Bradley would move another officer into his place if he failed. And the fighting ahead would prove he would have none of that.

One corps-directed change had an immediate effect on Barton's command. Collins decided to send his G-3, Richard Partridge, down to command one of the 90th Infantry Division regiments, the 358th Infantry, replacing the commander he fired. Then the corps chief of staff, Richard McKee, selected the best division G-3 to replace him and take over corps operations. That, of course, was Barton's operations officer, Orlando Troxel, who had been with him since he took command in 1942. Partridge, however, did not last long as a commander and was soon wounded at the head of his regiment. Collins visited him before he was evacuated and promised to make him his chief of staff when he recovered.[20]

Between June 13 and 19, Barton and his commanders prepared to carry the offensive into Cherbourg. Barton would miss Troxel but knew he had a supporter on the corps staff. This transfer had the potential to shake up his well-oiled team. But Major David B. Goodwin, soon to be promoted to lieutenant colonel, seamlessly moved up to replace Troxel. With over a year on Troxel's staff and under Rodwell's supervision, Goodwin continued to operate the division headquarters with little difficulty. Moreover, Goodwin had the opportunity to gain control of his section since the 4th Infantry settled down to almost a week of essentially defensive operations. For the first time since landing, Barton had time to visit his soldiers and mentor his leaders, two of whom were brand-new regimental commanders. The command's significant losses suffered so far in the campaign pained him; he knew most of the officers. That Wednesday evening, June 14, he accompanied his G-1,

Garlan Bryant, to the reception point to greet a large group of men sent to replace his losses from the first eight days of combat. In the crowd stood 116 officers and 1,357 enlisted soldiers. Not all were heading to the 4th Division, but it was a sobering reminder of the battle cost.[21]

Over the next few days, he visited every battalion in the division along the front lines. These visits included Flint's 39th Infantry, which was returning to the 9th Division. Tubby dropped in on Paddy several times during those middle days of June and probably knew he was in line for a division command when the next one opened up. Barton also checked in with corps headquarters and spent some time with Collins and his staff on Thursday (June 15), discussing the next operation. While there he had lunch with Collins, Bradley, and Montgomery, who were also making the rounds of their headquarters.[22] On returning to his headquarters, Barton drove through the battlefield at Crisbecq and Ozeville. He and York inspected the fortifications that had delayed his division and the 22nd Infantry in particular.[23]

The afternoon of June 16 found his leaders assembled in Le Bisson for the first command and staff meeting since landing in France. We are not sure of this meeting's details since few notes have survived, but he told his commanders to take care of their soldiers and get their recommendations for valor awards submitted as soon as possible.[24] Over the next few days, he continued to visit his units and give his soldiers a chance to see the boss up close. He knew how to provide a short, inspirational speech, and there were plenty of those. He was also a good listener and wanted to hear what his men had to say.[25]

Early on June 17 it became apparent that the 47th Infantry, 9th Infantry Division, would cut the peninsula, isolating the Cherbourg defenders.[26] Collins then issued warning orders to his commanders, and Barton did the same for his command.[27] With General Bradley attending, Collins called a meeting for his division commanders early the next day to confirm his orders and prepare for action. Joining Barton's 4th Infantry Division, Collins had the 9th Infantry Division, still commanded by Eddy, and the 90th Infantry Division, now with Landrum in charge. Newly arrived at the corps was the 79th Infantry Division, commanded by Tubby's friend from West Point (class of 1911) and 30th Infantry days, Ira T. Wyche.

Once the meeting broke up, Barton returned to the division command post and passed on his information to Goodwin and Rodwell. Shortly after noon he received a call from Van Fleet, who was back at his command post after being slightly wounded. As planned, Barton called Collins, who called Bradley and gave him the news. Collins then came to Barton's headquarters and met the army commander outside the 8th Infantry's command post. The three then marched inside, surprising everyone as Bradley demanded to know why the colonel had left the hospital without being formally discharged. Perhaps he needed a court-martial to encourage the others? Then the mood changed as Bradley broke into a smile and presented Van Fleet with the Distinguished Service Cross, the US Army's second highest decoration for valor, before his command post staff. Since Barton took over the division, Van Fleet had been his best commander. Everyone knew he was due for a promotion after this operation.[28]

By nightfall on June 18, the American situation in Normandy was about to transition from defending and expanding the lodgment on the beaches to striking out and gaining Operation NEPTUNE's primary objective, Cherbourg. Bradley now had all or part of four corps, directing nine divisions, in contact. The human price had been heavy for the last two weeks, as American forces had suffered 16,513 soldiers killed, wounded, and missing. But replacements continued to arrive, and units remained at fighting strength.[29] No longer fighting in multiple directions, Collins could now concentrate his forces and employ all of his combat power. Eddy's 9th Infantry Division, including Flint's 39th Infantry, attacked on the left flank and approached Cherbourg from the west. In the center Wyche's 79th Infantry Division advanced straight at the fortified city. Barton's division remained on the right flank and would approach the port from the east. Collins also attached the 24th Reconnaissance Squadron from Joe Tully's 4th Cavalry Group to guard the 4th Infantry Division's right flank along the coast, eliminating one more distraction to the offensive. To match this powerful force, German General von Schlieben had only the remnants of the four German divisions and scattered navy and air force units to hold the city.[30]

Although Barton said nothing about it in his diary, it is apparent he was not happy with the situation in the 22nd Infantry, as reflected in the detailed order. Foster had only been on the job for a few days, and Barton had only limited time to observe him in command. More important, he was becoming concerned with his assistant division commander Hal Barber. Barber had apparently not arrived on D-Day as scheduled and had not performed particularly well when leading his task force a few days earlier. Barton was having difficulty relying on his veteran deputy. Back at his headquarters at night on June 18, Barton found General Ray Barker, Eisenhower's G-1, who was there to watch the attack that would kick off at 03:00 the following morning. Barker was one of the principal members of the COSSAC staff that planned Operation OVERLORD and an integral part of Eisenhower's inner group. He was there only to observe the attack and, certainly, report back to his boss on what he saw at the front.[31]

Barton's combat order for this phase reflected his years of experience in command of the division and his days as a tactics instructor at Fort Leavenworth. His scheme of maneuver for this first phase of the offensive was two regiments forward with a third in reserve and for secondary tasks. On the left Van Fleet's 8th Infantry and on the right Luckett's 12th Infantry would begin their assault at the same time and drive northeast. Both regiments were to make their main effort along the regimental boundary, so there would be no dispersion of the attack. Then the two units were to continue the attack north on Barton's order. Foster's 22nd Infantry, under Barton's watchful eye, would follow as the division reserve.[32]

On June 19 Barton rose at 02:30 hours and moved to his command post. Along with Rodwell and Goodwin, he monitored the early stages of the morning's attack. The 8th and 12th Infantries' attacks went off as planned at 03:00. Van Fleet and Luckett met the expected German resistance, but Barton was comfortable with their progress and determination to succeed. However, he lost another key leader, and future regimental commander, as Fred A. Steiner, the 8th Infantry's executive officer, died in the assault. Apparently brave under fire, he had already been recommended for, and received posthumously, a Distinguished Service cross and a Silver Star. Lieutenant Colonel Oma R. Bates took his place.[33]

After breakfast, around 06:00, Barton headed over to the 22nd Infantry's command post. Because of the slow pace of the attack, Foster's command had not yet moved toward Montebourg, and Barton wanted to ensure that the new regimental commander had everything in order.[34] It appears Foster was not an improvement over Tribolet and needed more supervision. Unlike Reeder or Van Fleet, the new commander was not making a mark on his soldiers.[35] But by 10:00 hours the two attacking regiments had broken the German line, and the 22nd Infantry moved forward. Now Barton headed over to the 12th Infantry's command post. Jim Luckett had replaced Reeder without any apparent loss of regimental aggressiveness. In contrast to Foster, Luckett was "displaying his fighting qualities" and motivating his soldiers. Since the new commander had the situation under control, Barton encouraged him and moved on.[36]

But the enemy was fighting back, and the 12th Infantry was under heavy mortar and artillery fire. Luckett's soldiers faced the well-defended V-1 compound at Mesnil au Val west of the Bois du Coudray. That afternoon, a battery of Nebelwerfers, German multiple rocket launchers, fired oil-filled munitions at the Americans and hit the 1st Battalion command post. Its commander, Lieutenant Colonel Charles Jackson, received severe burns on the hand and face. This artillery essentially wiped out the battalion staff, killing or wounding almost all its members. An exception was the executive officer, Major Gerden Johnson, who somehow avoided getting hurt and took charge of the battalion. He contacted Luckett's command post, who dispatched O'Malley's 2nd Battalion to replace the disorganized unit at the front. At the same time, Johnson led the survivors to the rear, where it became the regimental reserve. That afternoon, 34-year-old Lieutenant Colonel John Merrill (USMA 1934) took command of the 1st Battalion, 12th Infantry.[37]

Meanwhile, Barber continued to contribute less each day to his operations, and Barton gave Roosevelt more of the official deputy commander duties. In his memoirs Collins implies that he was just worn out and evacuated back to the States. John Greenwood, who edited Hodges's diary, notes that he "was removed from his post" on July 2 without any indication of why.[38] After returning to the United States and recovering, he served until retirement as an attaché at several posts in Latin America. He died before his 60th birthday in 1956.[39]

Because the 8th and 12th Infantries had moved past Montebourg late that afternoon, June 19, the 22nd Infantry's 3rd Battalion moved in at 18:00. Repeatedly shelled, the town was a wreck. Caught in the crossfire, its civilians had cowered in caves and other underground shelters for an entire week while the two sides exchanged artillery and machine-gun fire. Over three hundred haggard and hungry citizens emerged from hiding as Arthur Teague's infantrymen moved through. At least forty townspeople perished during the week of fighting.[40] That night Barton and Goodwin decided to commit the entire 22nd Infantry to the fight the next day, June 20. The 8th Infantry's objective was the village of Tamerville, northeast of Valognes; Van Fleet was directed to bypass it and leave a detachment to contain it. Foster's regiment would assume responsibility for the 12th Infantry's objective at Hameau Malherbé, northeast of Valognes. Meanwhile, Barton ordered Luckett's regiment to become his reserve force.[41] He returned to his command post that night, sure that his command was ready and they would smash through the weak German defenders in the morning.

After two weeks of battle, Barton's fears of failing in combat had not materialized.[42] He had adjusted his peacetime leadership and pace of activity to combat needs. He learned how to circulate the battlefield, visit his troops, and make regular contact with the corps staff. He had replaced an ineffective regimental commander and was on the verge of sending his assistant division commander home. The loss of key leaders such as Steiner, Montelbano, his G-3, and another regimental commander introduced him more than ever before to the revolving chain of command, which would become a hallmark of his tenure as a commander. In addition, he had experienced the determination and skill of the enemy firsthand and no longer feared them. And finally, he and Collins were working through their command relationship, and Barton was learning what he needed to do to keep his boss satisfied with his role as a division commander.[43] His division's high casualty rate bothered him, and he was only two weeks into the fight. As a result of these losses, the stress of combat, and his intense personal tempo of activity, his ulcer was again causing him pain. Unfortunately, it would only get worse.

Bois de Montebourg, La Tardiverie

Barton and Harry Hansen, his G-2, did not know that von Schlieben had decided to disengage and pull his forces back to Cherbourg during the early morning hours of June 20. The remnants of his four divisions did not have the mobility or combat power to stop Collins's three aggressive divisions, so he ordered his units to break contact and fall back to the defensive line outside the city. Once in the city, Hitler made him commander of Festung (Fortress) Cherbourg, which consisted of probably twenty thousand soldiers and sailors. His line of defense was on the high ground, along a semicircle about five to six miles west, south, and east of the city. While formidable, the line was extremely shallow. Once American forces penetrated it, the infantry had a downhill march into the city's center, with little the Germans could do to stop the advance.[44]

At 05:30 all three 4th Infantry Division regiments launched their attacks, encountering little resistance and few German defenders. By 06:00 Barton was at the front with the 22nd Infantry, joining Dowdy's 1st and then Teague's 3rd Battalions, both of whom were on the front lines and moving. He then drove through the wreckage of Montebourg and linked up with Luckett, whose regiment had just reverted to division reserve.[45] While at Luckett's headquarters, he checked the maps and decided that Foster was not pushing his regiment hard enough and called him to tell him to move faster or else "somebody else will beat the 4th to Cherbourg."[46]

At 11:00 Barton was with the 8th Infantry. While he was having lunch with Van Fleet, Collins arrived and joined them. Barton and Collins then headed back to the 22nd Infantry's command post and met with John Ruggles. Ruggles was one of the regiment's old hands, and Barton depended on him to provide this troubled regiment some stability. After the corps commander departed, Barton moved back up to the front where the 22nd Infantry was in contact. He likely had another talk with Foster, urging him to be more aggressive. Somehow, in the middle of all these visits, he and his command group managed to capture three Germans and turn them over to the men of H Company.[47]

The next day, June 21, would be a day of limited probing attacks to determine the enemy's strength and prepare for a heavier assault the next day. The 4th Infantry Division was arrayed that morning with Foster's 22nd Infantry in the north near Gonneville, near the airport in the north, Luckett's 12th Infantry in the center, and Van Fleet's 8th Infantry in the south on the left flank of the division line south of Rufosses.[48] The new division command post was at a farm called La Tardiverie, located northwest of Saussemesnil and just behind the 8th Infantry's line.[49]

Since Foster's headquarters was the farthest away, that was Barton's first stop, arriving around 08:00. He had ordered the 22nd Infantry to capture a hill called 158, which dominated the countryside and the heavily defended Maupertus Airport to the east.[50] Then Barton was off to Luckett's command post to discuss his attack plan. He wanted the 12th Infantry to break through the enemy's outpost line and determine its main line of resistance. The enemy masked its positions with a large wood mass called the Bois du Coudray, located at the confluence of two small rivers. The general does not mention visiting Van Fleet's headquarters, but Roosevelt had been there twice by noon. He needed little supervision and only simple coordination and support. Van Fleet's primary job was to seize the crossroads, called 148, at the village of La Bourdonnerie just to the north. With that in hand, the road to Cherbourg would be open.[51]

By 10:00 the division's troops were all advancing. The infantrymen faced defenders in fixed concrete positions liberally supplied with artillery and automatic weapons, so movement was slow and deadly. Moreover, many of the defenses in the area were part of a belt of V-1 rocket sites, each protected by large amounts of concrete and wire.[52] Van Fleet's objective, for example, was one of those concrete mazes equipped with 88 mm and other antiaircraft guns. By nightfall the Americans were at the crossroads, but German troops remained in the area and harassed them all night. While Foster's battalions had taken Hill 158, groups of enemy forces had infiltrated the regiment's rear area. These German bands would interrupt supply and communications for the next few days, and all convoys needed a tank escort. But his regiment had cut the Cherbourg–St. Pierre Road from the west.[53]

Leaving Roosevelt and Rodwell to manage division activities, Barton went to Wyche's 79th Infantry Division's command post at Hameau de Haut near the town of Délasse late that afternoon. Because it was a central location, Collins thought it was an excellent place to convene a meeting of his senior commanders to coordinate the plans for the city's capture over the next few days. As the group broke up, Collins sent an ultimatum to von Schlieben by several different means, pointing out the hopelessness of his situation. He had until 09:00 on June 22 to surrender the city. Loudspeakers and radios also broadcast the message in German, Polish, Russian, and French, in the hopes of peeling off noncommitted members of the defending force.[54] Collins's guidance, reflected in Field Order #3, specified the division's task: "VII Corps will attack from present positions at H-Hour, D-Day to seize Cherbourg. The attack will be preceded by an intensive air bombardment of the defenses south and west of Cherbourg by the IX Tactical Air Force. . . . 4th Division will attack within its zone of action and seize the area in the vicinity of Tourlaville in order to isolate Cherbourg from the east."[55]

Early the following day, June 22, the battalions moved to their assigned attack positions. They did not want to get too close since Major General Elwood R. "Pete" Quesada's reinforced IX Tactical Air Command had planned an eighty-minute aerial assault consisting of fighters, fighter-bombers, and medium bombers. The division's leaders knew that Allied aircraft were not precise weapons. Moreover, this attack depended upon the weather, so no one was sure exactly when H-hour would be.[56]

Barton was up early that morning and driving his Jeep, Barton's Buggy, and visiting the soldiers on the front lines. The Jeep (US Army Truck, quarter-ton, 4 × 4, command reconnaissance) was the perfect vehicle for commanders making their rounds on the muddy Norman roads. Because it was relatively light, if (and when) a driver was stuck in the mud or in a difficult location, it was easy enough for soldiers to dig it out or tow it back onto the road. Barton usually traveled with Bill York and Richards, although the general enjoyed driving, and photographs often show him behind the wheel. Roosevelt was also out and about, visiting his troops in "Rough Rider," covering many miles daily.[57] By 09:00, as Collins's ultimatum to von Schlieben expired, Barton had checked on all the 12th and 22nd Infantries' battalions.[58] An hour later he was at Van Fleet's headquarters when Collins drove up to visit his favorite regimental commander. Both generals then returned to the 22nd Infantry and watched its soldiers move to their attack positions. Foster was getting a great deal of attention from his chain of command.[59]

Collins departed and headed over to Wyche's division to observe the air bombardment, along with Quesada and Brigadier General Richard E. Nugent, the Ninth Air Force's G-3. The attack began at exactly 12:40. More than one hundred British Mustangs and rocket-equipped Typhoons swept across Cherbourg, firing rockets and machine guns and dropping bombs. At 13:00 more than 560 American fighter-bombers bombed and strafed the city's fortifications. As usual, sadly these attacks were not accurate, with bombs hitting near the forward lines of the 47th, 60th, and 22nd Infantries. Collins, who had to take cover, was glad he had the two air force generals experience the plight of the ground soldier under friendly air attack.[60] When the fighters departed around 14:00 hours, almost four hundred medium bombers arrived over Cherbourg, attacking eleven specific targets. It was a massive display of air power. Yet other than the Americans losing twenty-seven aircraft in the assault from intense German antiaircraft fire, it accomplished little.[61]

As the bombers departed, the infantrymen from all three regiments moved forward.[62] They did not get far, as besides some shell shock, the defenders were ready in their concrete bunkers. Luckett's troops could not break through the defenses north and northeast of the Bois du Coudray. The fighting was intense, and the 3rd Battalion, seeking to flank one of the enemy positions, was caught in a kill zone of enfilading fires and preregistered artillery. After Thaddeus R. Dulin reformed his command, he led it to occupy the better ground. Finding Germans on the position, he led an attack with fixed bayonets to clear the enemy from the wooded terrain. Dulin died in the assault, and Captain Kenneth R. Lindner, the K Company commander, took command. Luckett was impressed with Lindner, who remained at the battalion's head and was a lieutenant colonel by December. However, Dulin's loss stung both him and Barton.[63] It was the same with the other two regiments. While the battalions were fighting hard to reduce the enemy defenders, it was not going quickly, as the small unit actions continued all day and into the night. While aircraft helped with operations, gains could only be made by infantrymen on the ground, reducing one strong point at a time. Also killed that day was Captain Oscar Joyner, who had helped train the division in ranger operations back at Camp Gordon Johnston. His remains lie in the American Military Cemetery at Colleville.[64]

Barton returned to his command post around 17:00. As he discussed the situation with Rodwell and the staff, Collins called him and urged him to keep the momentum going. By 19:00 he was back at the wheel of Barton's Buggy on the Norman trails, again visiting each of his commanders and urging them to keep up as much pressure as possible. He ended the night at Luckett's command post, where he promoted Lindner to major and talked to him about his new command. By midnight Barton could report to Collins that the division had a small penetration in the enemy defensive line.[65] Readers should note that corps and division commanders did not lead from the rear. Instead, at all levels, from the company through the corps, American commanders were at the front while their executive officers and staff coordinated and took care of the details.

The 4th Infantry Division resumed its attack at 07:00, June 23. While a relatively late time to begin an attack, there was no need for surprise since the Germans knew the Americans were coming. Moreover, the delay gave them time to sort out some communications issues and ensure the troops had enough ammunition and supplies. Foster's infantry seized the dominant terrain at Gonneville, giving the Americans a view of Cherbourg Harbor. Behind (east) of the 22nd Infantry, the 24th Cavalry Reconnaissance Squadron, with the attached Company B, 801st Tank Destroyer Battalion, and the 4th Reconnaissance troop located the enemy positions near the airfield and tested its defenses. Luckett's troops continued to work through the Bois du Cordray and the maze of fortifications surrounding a V-1 rocket base. It was slow going and was made worse by the woody terrain and Germans who seemed everywhere. A barrier blocked one bridge over a street, and Luckett came forward with a monkey wrench to remove it. Van Fleet's battalions continued fighting at the La Bourdonnerie crossroads and the western portion of the V-1 complex.[66]

After lunch with Collins and Bradley at the VII Corps command post, General Hodges went looking for the 4th Infantry Division's command post. Unfortunately, the military police he ran into had no idea where it was. But Hodges persevered and discovered it "stuck off a dusty side road six miles north of Valognes." He discussed the tactical situation with Barton, Rodwell, and Roosevelt, who had been forward with Foster's troops. Barton also complained that the American press had made it seem that Clarence Huebner's 1st Infantry Division had been cited as the "first to land" in Normandy. He asked Hodges to help him get some publicity for the division.[67]

After Hodges left Barton headed over to see Van Fleet, who was far forward and under an artillery attack. The 8th Infantry was in the middle of a tough fight. In one case, Simmons's 1st Battalion mortar platoon lost its tubes during a German attack, fortunately recovering their weapons later. In another, a tank-infantry team from the 3rd Battalion was about to attack a strong point and encountered a company of enemy infantry lying in ditches along some hedgerows. According to one report, "A wild shooting melee ensued and most of the Germans were routed with heavy losses from the combined infantry and tank fire." Lieutenant Colonel Erasmus Strickland, its commander, sent a company back to clean out the bunkers at the V-1 site with bangalore torpedoes, satchel charges, and flamethrowers. Before it was over, 228 German defenders surrendered. But the Germans continued aggressively trying to stop the Americans. Finally, outside the airport at 22:00 hours, a large enemy force attacked Troop A, 24th Cavalry. The cavalry troopers used their mobility to regain their positioning, discovering fifty dead Germans around the position.[68] Barton returned to his command post that night, confident of breaking into the city the next day.

Bois du Coudray (Gallis)

The staff improved Barton's living conditions on Saturday, June 24, when they presented him with a small, modified house trailer, making his existence more tolerable.[69] However, he would have little time to enjoy it as the 4th Infantry Division got closer to Cherbourg's harbor. Foster's 22nd Infantry spent the day fighting to secure the northern flank by clearing out pockets of resistance and keeping the main supply route open. Small but well-led groups of well-armed German infantry still made travel by unescorted convoys or individual vehicles impossible. These enemy units had the support from a strongpoint armed with artillery and several 88 mm antiaircraft guns. The infantry and guns isolated John Dowdy's 1st Battalion on a small hill near the airport at Maupertus. The only way to resupply it was by a small dirt road under well-aimed artillery and small-arms fire. The Germans, masters of the defense, also used antiaircraft guns to fire point detonation ammunition on the trees and hedges growing parallel with this route. Tanks had to be used to bring up supplies.

Barton intended to get that sorted out, but until he could, he was concerned that his young officers and soldiers, many of whom were new replacements, might need some support. Dowdy's position was critical to the eastern drive, and they had to hold it. Over the protests of the 22nd Infantry's command group, he drove down the road and joined the battalion on the hill. Under fire, with casualties growing, he moved from position to position and reassured his junior leaders that the situation was in hand and help would be on the way. Observers noted his "coolness and disregard for personal safety." While he may not have thought much about it, others did. In a ceremony a few weeks later, Collins would pin a Silver Star on his battle-worn jacket in recognition for his coolness in solidifying this battalion's defense.[70]

The 12th Infantry began its attack at 07:30 hours. As the troops moved forward toward their initial strong point, dive bombers from the Ninth Air Force attacked the enemy targets. The infantry was too close, and the airstrike killed and wounded some soldiers and disorganized the attack. But the lead battalion moved forward, and the fighting continued all day. By 20:00 it had reached its primary objective, the high ground overlooking the Tourlaville-Cherbourg highway, giving the soldiers a view of enemy vehicles scurrying along the coast to get into the city. As the 1st Battalion continued to move, supporting tanks from B Company, 70th Armor, mistakenly fired on the American battalion. The accurate, close-range fire killed many of the command group members, including John Merrill, who had been in charge of the battalion for less than a week. The executive officer, Major Gerden Johnson, took command until Charles Jackson, still recovering from his wounds from several days earlier, could resume command on June 27.[71]

Barton needed to restore the situation and capture Tourlaville by dark. Barton and Luckett huddled and decided to mount troops from the 3rd Battalion on the back of B Company's Shermans and storm into town. It worked, and by nightfall the battalion was in control of the town and waiting for a counterattack that never materialized.[72]

On the left flank, the morning attack against the heavily armed La Glacerie strong point kicked off. At 11:00 P-47 Thunderbolts arrived over the target. The regiment's cannon company fired violet smoke on the defenses. Van Fleet wanted them neutralized, and the pilots obliged with a series of precise hits, twenty-three one-thousand-pound bombs on target. German defenders jumped out of the bunkers and started to run. Mortars opened up, killing those not fast enough to get away. Now convinced that the word would spread among defenders, dropping colored smoke on enemy defenders would become a standard procedure, even if the attack did not involve air support.[73]

Although they took the strong point, the Germans still fought back and launched a counterattack around 18:00 hours. The fighting was fierce, as the enemy knew there was nothing between this position and the city. Conrad Simmons, the 1st Battalion commander, died from a direct hit on his foxhole and was replaced by his executive officer Major John H. Meyer. Frustrated by the German resistance and the loss of another key leader, Van Fleet brought up all his tanks and supporting weapons to defeat the counterattack. Barton was with the regimental commander and, sensing difficulty in getting support from his artillery, grabbed the hand mike and barked back to the supporting artillery battalion, "This is Barton. I want all the artillery I've got to fire on [this target]!"[74] Barton's words went up the fire-support channel. Within a few minutes the concentrated fire of five battalions of 105 mm and 155 mm howitzers stopped the enemy in its tracks, and the German effort was over. It is an excellent example of how a division commander can influence the battle. However, it was a costly fight; in addition to Simmons, the regiment lost thirty-seven soldiers killed that day. However, the 8th Infantry Regiment's battle on the Cotentin was essentially over. For the next few days, it would consolidate its positions and clean out the isolated pockets of German soldiers that remained hidden in trenches and the woods.

Back at his command post, Barton found a German general officer among the prisoners and invited him to dinner. We have no mention of who he was or what they discussed.[75] However, it had been a tough day for Barton. For him, losing soldiers was always difficult and emotionally draining. Losing three battalion commanders, a regimental commander, and several majors and captains with whom he was close made it much worse.

The original corps order had the 4th Infantry Division stopping outside Cherbourg's city limits. But on Sunday, June 25, Collins modified his plans and told Barton to attack that night with one regiment into the city's eastern portion.[76] As Foster's 22nd Infantry cleared out enemy bunkers and detachments, Luckett's 12th Infantry headed toward the city. At 20:00 hours, with infantrymen riding on the back decks of Sherman tanks, all three battalions moved forward and reached the division's limit of advance within the city. After interviewing an arrogant German officer, Barton returned to his headquarters for the evening.[77] A short while later, Barton and Roosevelt headed to Luckett's command post, which gave them a great view of the city, 420 feet above sea level and looking down on the port. According to the regimental historian, Barton placed his hand on Luckett's shoulder and said, "It's your show, Jim. Run it any way you see fit. I'm back of you one hundred percent."[78] Luckett had earned his command and would continue to lead the regiment.

The corps commander wanted an informal liberation ceremony the next day, June 26. Most of the senior commanders who participated joined in the festivities. These were friends, many such as Ira Wyche and Paddy Flint, whom Tubby had known for over thirty-five years. He had known Collins since the Rhineland days of the early 1920s. Others were relatively new acquaintances, such as Eddy, Ridgway, and Taylor, who had formed a bond since arriving in England several months ago. It had been a challenging three weeks, but the corps' portion of Operation NEPTUNE was coming to an end, and they were justifiably proud. Meanwhile, the fighting continued against die-hard German soldiers, especially in the east, where Foster's 22nd Infantry cleared out defenders near the airfield.[79]

Around 13:00 hours Barton drove through the city's damaged streets and became concerned with the confusion in his assigned sector. He met with

Roosevelt and told him to take charge of the various division forces in the city, which now included more units than just the 12th Infantry. His tasks included coordinating division activities such as clearing out isolated enemy resistance nests, working with and assisting French civilians, and maintaining order among the various American units. As he was organizing Task Force Roosevelt, across town General von Schlieben surrendered to Eddy's 9th Infantry Division and traveled under escort to Collins's headquarters.[80]

After von Schlieben's surrender on Monday, activities around Cherbourg continued for the next few days as isolated pockets of Germans continued to resist the American forces. Barton's schedule on June 27 began with an early morning visit to Foster's headquarters in the northeastern sector. From there he could see the fires burning from Fortress Hamburg near Cape Lévi. Two days before, as the 4th Infantry Division had fought its way into the city, a naval task force consisting of the battleships *Texas* and *Arkansas* and five destroyers fought an intense duel with German sailors operating this powerful battery. This installation was the most potent enemy fortress near Cherbourg, protected by more than a dozen antiaircraft guns and machine-gun infantry. Its four 11 in. naval guns had twice the range (forty thousand versus twenty thousand yards) of the American battleships. It had been an impressive engagement, with the defenders putting a destroyer out of action and damaging several attacking vessels. Fortunately, some German shells failed to explode, reducing the damage to the attacking warships. The naval task force destroyed one of Hamburg's gun emplacements, turning the fortress into a scarred and burning landscape. What was left surrendered to the 22nd Infantry two days later. Barton then headed to the airfield at Maupertus, where Foster's troops were completing its capture, and then back to division headquarters at Bois du Coudray for a commander's conference.[81]

While proud of the division's achievements, he tempered his remarks by reminding his leaders that the division was not the same unit that they had brought to France only three weeks earlier. He pointed out that of the 193 officers and men authorized for each rifle company, about 70 were new arrivals without extensive training or experience. He suggested that the regimental commanders consider cross-leveling and move some of the proven

leaders in the antitank, cannon, heavy weapons, and headquarters companies
over to the rifle companies. In addition, he needed the division's veterans,
who had been with the unit since Florida, to transmit to these new arrivals
the Ivy Division's traditions and discipline standards. They had to enforce
the fundamental tradition of saluting. With the heavy losses of veterans,
battalion and company commanders might need to act as platoon and squad
leaders until they could bring the new arrivals up to standard. Barton then
admonished them to promptly take care of the division's wounded and dead
and treat captured German soldiers with respect. Division soldiers were not
to rob or inflict drastic disciplinary measures on their prisoners or march
them to the rear with their hands up. Finally, he told them that the division
would take control of the city over the next few days and relieve both the 79th
and 9th Infantry Divisions.[82]

Château Tourlaville

Barton was always on the move, visiting soldiers, urging on commanders,
and inserting himself when he could. He did this at Battery Osteck,
which controlled the terrain between Battery Hamburg and the Maupertus
Airport defenses and had not yet surrendered. It was a modern defensive
installation, and it had withstood the 22nd Infantry's assaults for several days.
On June 28, at 03:00 hours, an American lieutenant approached the battery's
main gate under a white flag. He demanded the fort surrender unconditionally.
Major Friedrich Küppers rejected such terms but indicated he was prepared
to negotiate the terms of a fair surrender, the care of the wounded, and the
release of some captured American soldiers. The lieutenant departed and
returned to his lines. Several hours later, several jeeps with flags flying
approached Osteck's entrance. It was Barton who came to negotiate the
surrender in person. Entering the bunker, he learned that Küppers was from
Wiesbaden, and the two enemies started with small talk about living in the
Rhineland, which Barton had loved. This chatter went on for some time until
Bill York reminded the commander that time was running out.

Barton spoke directly to Küppers: "I want to tell you openly what will
happen in the moment that our negotiations fail." Barton pointed out the

22nd Infantry, with an armored battalion, and the positions of division and corps artillery batteries on his map. "What will come from the air and the sea is not indicated on the map, but I think you can imagine. To what extent further resistance? I admire the fighting spirt of your soldiers. The shooting skill of your artillery groups, which we've been fighting since Montebourg, has astonished me. You've been hard on me." Küppers asked to look at the map and realized that Barton knew everything about the fortress area. He also realized that the Americans had captured much of the city already. Therefore, he decided to call it quits, and by 13:30, the surrender was complete.[83]

Meanwhile, the 4th Infantry Division proceeded to take control of the sectors held by the 39th and 47th Infantry and assumed command of the entire city of Cherbourg. Barton dispatched the 24th Cavalry Squadron to search all defenses and strongpoints between Cape Lévi and Quinéville, both inland and along the coast, for enemy troops and to report hourly.[84] He then motored to naval headquarters in Cherbourg and tried to see if some of his artillery or other units could help defeat the fortresses still guarding the entrance to the harbor. Collins, Roosevelt, and Barton tried to develop some means of support, such as using tank destroyers against the forts, but this had little effect. So finally the group decided long-range artillery and air bombardment would be the best way to break this last resistance element.[85]

By 15:00 the division headquarters had relocated to the Château de la Tourlaville, owned by the Jean de Ravalet family. Its most famous claims to fame were its beauty and a story of family disgrace. The scandal involved a sordid, incestuous affair between a brother and his married sister in the early seventeenth century. After a sensational trial in 1603, the Paris court condemned both to a public beheading.[86] We are unsure if Barton learned the history of the scandal that haunted his headquarters' halls, but the chateau is breathtakingly beautiful.

The fighting around the city continued June 29 as the 9th Infantry Division cleared German defenders holding out on Cap de Hague to the west of Cherbourg. This action would take several days. Later that day, Orlando Troxel, now the VII Corps G-3, sent instructions to move units for the next phase. The 4th Infantry Division was to start moving south to an area occupied by the 90th Infantry Division that evening.[87] That morning Roosevelt, still in command of the city, held a meeting with principal organizations' representatives. A port police battalion, commanded by SHAEFs services of supply, would immediately take over the city's security from the 8th and 12th Infantry. At the same time, the 101st Airborne Division occupied Cherbourg's approaches and allowed Barton's command to begin relocating for its subsequent operation.[88]

Barton spent the day celebrating the first major American victory in Europe. He started in the city, laid a plaque in the city center, and watched as the VII Corps' heavy artillery and Ninth Air Force dive bombers attacked the harbor's remaining German forts. Then while the enemy took a beating only about three thousand yards away, Barton arrived at the 8th Infantry's headquarters, where the troops formed up and twenty-three soldiers stood waiting for their awards. The first Silver Star he presented that morning was to Chaplain (Captain) Julian S. Ellenberg for his bravery under fire on Utah Beach, rescuing and administering aid to the dead and dying back on June 6. Wounded, he continued until others arrived to relieve him and take him to an aid station.[89]

Barton next headed over to Luckett's 12th Infantry and presented another eight Silver Stars. Then, as was his habit, he jumped on the hood of his Jeep, Barton's Buggy, and addressed the assembled regiment. While he was talking, around 12:30, the last German forts surrendered, clearing the way for engineers to remove the damage from the port and place it in operation.[90] Barton then motored to Foster's 22nd Infantry east of Cherbourg. Twelve soldiers waited in front of the assembled regiment for their Silver Stars and the pep talk that was soon to come.[91]

That afternoon Barton went to Cherbourg's town square, opposite Napoleon's statue and the ruined harbor. This was a more formal ceremony than a few days earlier and honor platoons from each of the corps' three divisions formed opposite city hall (Hotel de Ville). He joined Generals Eddy and Wyche and the city's mayor, Paul Renault, as British, French, and American flags floated overhead. Collins arrived in his M-8 armored car and gave a speech to the small crowd in French. Ending it with "Vive La France," he presented Monsieur Renault with a handmade flag made from parachute silk. The corps band played the appropriate music, and the ceremony ended as they could still hear fighting from the city's outskirts to the west and at the harbor forts.[92]

Transition and Aftermath

A few days later, Collins sent Barton a letter commenting on his division's performance.

> Dear General Barton:
>
> At the close of the Cherbourg campaign, I wish to express to you and the 4th Infantry Division my admiration and profound appreciation of the outstanding part played by your division during this campaign. . . . The division was in continuous action during the period 6–28 June when the last resistance east of Cherbourg was eliminated. During this period the 4th Infantry Division sustained over 5450 casualties and had over 800 men killed in action. These relatively severe casualties are a mark of the stern resistance that has been overcome and it is a tribute to the devotion of the men of the division that these losses in no way deterred their aggressive action. The division has been faithful to its honored dead. The 4th Infantry Division can be rightly proud of the great part that it played from the beginning to the very end of the Cherbourg campaign. Please express to your officers and men my tremendous admiration of your great division.
>
> Faithfully yours,
> J. Lawton Collins, Major General, U.S. Army, Commanding[93]

At a fundamental level, one puzzling note emerges from this generally triumphant account: the professional relationship between Barton and Collins. Perhaps it stemmed from disputes in Coblenz twenty years earlier. Maybe it continued or intensified during Collins's two years at Leavenworth when Barton was on the faculty. He certainly knew of Barton's relationship with his nemesis, Oscar Griswold. But at the end of June, Collins had to rate his subordinate's performance using one of the standard abbreviated letter formats employed during the war. Coming from Marshall and Eisenhower's favorite commander, this report ensured that Barton would have a diminished chance of ever commanding a corps.

Collins wrote, "A sturdy, faithful division commander. Not brilliant but tenacious and a determined, capable fighter." The report asks the rater, "Of all general officers of his grade personally known to you, what number would you give him on this list, and how many comprise our list?" Astonishingly, Collins reported, "Of about 150 Major Generals I would place him about 60." For his command of the division, Collins rated Barton "Excellent."[94]

Who were these 150 major generals that Collins knew personally? And, after three weeks of heavy combat, who were the fifty-nine that the corps commander believed were superior? While outwardly Barton and Collins seemed to be on cordial terms, this mediocre report, one of the worst Barton would get in his entire career, provides a glimpse into the nature of their relationship and the political nature of the World War II American Army.

By the end of June, Barton's division had been in continuous combat for over three weeks and had a few days to recover and prepare for the next assault. During this intense combat, 5,400 of his soldiers were killed or wounded, almost 40 percent of the division's authorized strength.[95] Only five rifle company commanders who had made the D-Day landing were with the division three weeks later. Though many officers and newly promoted noncommissioned officers remained to steady the 4,400 replacements who partially refilled the division's ranks, Barton lamented, "We no longer have the division we brought ashore."[96] The 4th Infantry Division, on the beach since the beginning, had the highest casualty rate in the corps: 5,452 soldiers killed, wounded, missing, and captured.[97] Many veterans of the Florida training were missing from the festivities at Cherbourg at the end of June. Henry Barber and Herve Tribolet failed the test of battle, and Barton had to relieve both and send them to less challenging assignments. The intense fighting killed four of his battalion commanders: Montelbano, Dulin, Merrill, and Simmons. Brumby and Reeder were evacuated because of their wounds. Orlando Troxel moved to corps headquarters but would remain in contact over the months ahead. Reeder's loss after only a few days of combat was probably the most heartbreaking for Barton. There is little doubt he would have ended the war as a division commander if the injury had not interrupted his career.

Soon after the Cherbourg ceremony on June 29, Collins gathered his commanders and gave them the warning order on the next mission. First, Barton's division would take control of the city, relieving the other two divisions. It would then move to an assembly area and embark on the campaign's next phase of the operation, clearing the Cotentin up to Saint-Lô.[98] This subsequent period of fighting would be even more demanding than the last three weeks. Now they faced a German force that had recovered and was determined to defend its front and, if possible, throw the Americans back into the sea.

Chapter 11

Carentan-Périers Road, July 1–19

This war is still a movie that I am viewing most of the time. Once in a while it gets real personal and quite realistic but generally I have a certain detachment about it that is hard to explain.

—Barton to his daughter, July 19, 1944

Gourbesville

With Cherbourg's capture Omar Bradley's next goal was to expand the terrain he occupied in the west and bring his four corps online in preparation for breaking out of the lodgment area.[1] He now had about twenty divisions organized into four army corps. His next objective was to seize the area around the market town of Saint-Lô, which would set the conditions to conduct the breakout from the Normandy beachhead. Selecting this town as the focus of the army's attack was an operational decision. It required Bradley to employ the principles of operational art, that domain of war between strategy and tactics. Only the most senior commanders have the opportunity to make "the fundamental decisions about when and where to fight and whether to accept or decline battle. Its essence is the identification of the enemy's operational center-of-gravity—his source of strength or balance—and the concentration of superior combat power against that point to achieve decisive success."[2]

Bradley assigned Collins the task of seizing the town of Périers, half-way between Saint-Lô and the coast on highway N800 (modern D900). From this line the army commander anticipated having his four corps online and prepared to continue their attack to the south, toward a line from Coutances to Caumont-l'Éventé. From there he intended to break out from the Normandy enclave. However, it would be a difficult task as the almost impassable terrain the VII Corps needed to cross was essentially a massive swamp, called the Prairies Marecageuses de Gorges, formed by the confluence of the Douve, Vire, and Taute Rivers. It was an extremely constricted avenue of approach, only wide enough for one division at a time.[3]

From an operational art perspective, the best way to seize Périers was not by fighting straight ahead on the enemy's terms but by attacking from the flank. The VII Corps was now a veteran organization capable of operating at a high level of competency. Bradley could have used his large fleet of trucks to move the combat divisions to another part of the battlefield, behind one of the other corps in contact, and then used this overwhelming force on a narrow sector to seize Saint-Lô. Combining mass and maneuver is the hallmark of the accomplished operational artist. Unfortunately, Bradley and his staff did not think at that level. Foreshadowing later operations in rugged terrain, notably the forests along the German border in the fall, the First Army commander lined up his four corps. He inserted the VII Corps in the center and ordered it to conduct a frontal attack, the least sophisticated maneuver, against a defender prepared to fight. There was nothing subtle or innovative about it, and the soldiers in the VII Corps' divisions would pay with their blood for this absence of sophisticated leadership.[4]

This region, dominated by the Prairies Marecageuses de Gorges, was a terrible place for a motorized force. The venerable military historian Martin Blumenson said it best: "The terrain is treacherously moist and soft, crossing the bogs on foot is hazardous, passage by vehicle impossible. In addition to numerous streams and springs that keep the earth soggy, mud holes and stagnant pools, as well as a network of canals and ditches, some intended for drainage and others originally primitive transportation routes, close the marshland to wheeled traffic except over tarred causeways that link settlements together."[5] And, of course, the fields were often framed by overgrown hedgerows, facilitating good defensive fighting positions. Moreover, heavy rain can turn the area into a series of shallow lakes even in the twenty-first century. In the summer of 1944, thanks to the Germans and rainy weather, the marshland was covered with water, limiting vehicle traffic to the main roads.

The only main road in Collins's sector was the Carentan-Périers Road, today D971, passing through the village of Sainteny. From above the area appears as a peninsula, reducing the land available for combat operations to less than four miles wide. It was a defender's paradise and an attacker's nightmare. The Germans in the Périers sector, comprising part of the right (east) wing of the LXXXIV Corps, were under the local operational control of the headquarters of the I7th SS Panzer Grenadier Division, a formidable, well-trained unit. The division had one of its two regiments holding positions south of Carentan. The separate 6th Parachute Regiment was attached to it, a veteran though somewhat depleted unit. The leadership of these forces was solid and experienced. On the defense they had more than enough firepower to defend this narrow sector.[6]

The first problem that Collins faced was using the three infantry divisions available to him to the best advantage in the constricted corps zone. Retaining the 4th and 9th Infantry Divisions, which had participated in the Cherbourg operation, Collins, on July 2, took control of Major General Robert C. Macon's 83rd Infantry Division already fighting in the Carentan sector. The VII Corps plan was simple, given the current troop dispositions and available maneuver space. However, the terrain did not allow the corps commander to employ all of his forces as he would like; he had no opportunity to concentrate his troops or flank any of the enemy positions. Therefore, Macon would continue attacking south through Sainteny toward the Taute River, now supported by the 4th Division's artillery. Barton's division would move behind the 83rd and online to its west when sufficient maneuver space allowed. Eddy's 9th Infantry Division began the operation in reserve behind the 4th.[7]

On June 30 Collins hosted a commander's call at his headquarters near Sainte-Mère-Église. Barton had been working closely with Eddy for over a month. Macon had been one of Barton's CGSS students and later an acquaintance at Fort Benning. Also joining the group was Major General LeRoy Watson, a classmate of Eisenhower and Bradley at West Point. He also had been one of Barton's CGSS students and then remained at Leavenworth until after Barton departed for the war college. Now commanding the 3rd Armored Division, Watson's tanks would be the exploitation force if the infantry divisions had success.[8]

In a format familiar to American staff officers, Richard McKee, still Collins's chief of staff, would have had the wall covered with maps. Next, Colonel Leslie D. Carter, the G-2, discussed the enemy situation and described the nature of the rugged terrain. Then the G-3, Orlando Troxel, would explain the corps objective and the individual tasks, boundaries, and sequence of events. Colonel James G. Anding, the G-4, then described the issues of supply, especially ammunition, as a precious commodity given the limited cross-channel supply situation the US Army still faced in Europe. Collins would close the meeting, ensuring that they knew their tasks. As he departed the conference, Barton had no illusions as to what was next. His casualties for June, over 5,450 killed, wounded, or missing, surpassed any other division in the First Army.[9]

Barton returned to his command post at Château de la Tourlaville, which was tearing down and moving south. While having lunch he discussed what he had learned from the corps meeting with Rodwell and Goodwin. When done, his only other responsibility was to travel to the new command post to the south. So he, Richardson, and York jumped into the Jeep and took a tour of their recent operation. They headed east toward Quettehou near the coast and south to the battlefield at Quinéville. They then traveled to Crisbecq, the fortress that had stopped his division and the scene of several bloody days of combat. Then it was back to the coast to Utah Beach, the location of massive logistics operations as LSTs grounded themselves on the beach and discharged their troops and cargos in exchange for wounded soldiers and prisoners of war. Then they drove to his new command post near Gourbesville, northwest of Sainte-Mère-Église, to organize the next operations phase.[10]

On Saturday, July 1, Collins's VII Corps began moving south toward its attack zone south of Sainte-Mère-Église. The term *moving* does not describe what was happening that week in a space smaller than the American state of Connecticut. Troy Middleton's VIII Corps was sliding its support units to the western side of the Cotentin Peninsula. Collins now had a mature organization, significantly enlarged since the invasion only three weeks earlier. It now had three infantry divisions (4th, 9th, and 83rd) and the 3rd Armored Division. In addition to these four units, the corps had a tank destroyer group, cavalry group, armored group, three artillery groups, ten independent artillery battalions, six antiaircraft battalions, and dozens of other more minor but essential engineers, tank, and other independent battalions. All of these units required road clearance and places to establish assembly areas.

Additionally, these organizations required massive amounts of food, fuel, and other supplies. In addition to each unit's ammunition, the corps needed to create stockpiles for the upcoming offensive. Medical hospitals and prisoner-of-war compounds needed space and access to routes also. Adding to this confusion, the Ninth Air Force was constructing tactical airfields. McKee and his corps staff were hard at work synchronizing these activities.[11]

Barton's staff was hard at work planning just like the other units across the front. The VII Corps Field Order #4 assigned the division the 801st Tank Destroyer Battalion (Towed), the 377th Antiaircraft Automatic Weapons Battalion, the 70th Tank Battalion, two companies of the 87th Chemical Battalion and its 4.2 in. mortars, and the 951st Field Artillery Battalion and its 155 mm howitzers. With his three regiments, the staff had to allocate space for these units, plus the division's troops and supplies. Given the wet and constricted terrain, it was a tight fit![12]

The 4th Division staff was also changing. Bradley had pulled Van Fleet out of the corps, promoted him to brigadier general, and moved him over to Barton's classmate Walt Robertson's 2nd Infantry Division as its assistant division commander. Replacing Van Fleet, Jim Rodwell turned over his duties to Rich Marr, who moved up from the G-4 position. Major Guy De Young took over from Marr.[13]

For the next two days, Barton and the staff continued to plan. This waterlogged environment would need engineer support, and his engineer battalion's commander, Bill Ragland, joined him on July 2. Joining him that morning was the corps' specialist in these operations, Colonel Grady Paules (USMA 1912) from the VII Corps engineers. Paules performed well during World War I, earning a Distinguished Service Cross and Silver Star for command of the 7th Engineer Battalion, 5th Division in the Meuse-Argonne. He left the service after the war but returned to the army in 1942. Then, commanding the 18th Engineer Battalion, he supervised the Alaskan Highway construction in the Yukon Territory/Whitehorse area. Now he was in Europe working on France's roads that had taken a beating this summer.[14]

Barton spent July 3 on the road, familiarizing himself with the area. Then, taking Rodwell along, he drove across the sector. First Barton stopped in to visit Middleton's VIII Corps headquarters. This corps had been in this sector for a while, and he wanted the latest information on the enemy and the terrain. Then it was over to Landrum's 90th Infantry Division for the same purpose, to discover what his troops faced in this new sector. At some point during the day, he told Collins he needed a replacement for the 22nd Infantry's commander. Bob Foster had not done well as a commander, appearing tired and lethargic, and was no improvement over Triboulet.[15]

Meanwhile, the 83rd Infantry Division led off the attack on July 4 with a ten-minute artillery preparation fire at daybreak. The attack immediately failed, and one of Macon's regimental commanders died two hours later. As Hodges watched from the VII Corps forward command post, Collins pressured Macon to move forward. He was constantly on the landline demanding action, and Macon and his commanders were doing what they thought was best. However, it was a new division, and nothing went according to plan during its first combat. The German units guarding this sector, the 6th Parachute Regiment and 17th Panzer Grenadier Regiment, chose their defensive positions well and put up a stiff fight. At one point the German parachute regimental commander, Colonel Friedrich A. Freiherr von der Heydte, returned captured medics to the 83rd Division, noting that he thought the Americans needed them! Barton got word things were not going well and headed over to corps headquarters to get a sense of what was going on up front. He had already ordered the 12th Infantry to begin moving forward.[16]

Groult

On the morning of July 5, Collins decided to commit his veteran 4th Infantry to the fight. But, of course, since it had lost so many soldiers over the last month, its roll of combat-experienced soldiers was thin. Fortunately, it still had a strong contingent of battle-wise officers and sergeants.[17] While Collins was working out the details and trying to determine where Macon's front lines were, General Hodges, still the First Army's deputy commander, dropped into the VII Corps headquarters. Watching the raging corps commander in action, Hodges quickly left and looked for Barton. He could not find the 4th's command post, but Barton found him on the road and escorted him to his temporary headquarters on a farm named Groult, just above the Merderet River. Based on his discussion with the corps commander the previous evening, his troops were on the move. German artillery fire slowed Luckett's regiment at the Baupte bridge, but Ted Roosevelt, always at the point of danger, supervised the crossing and kept the unit moving. He joined Barton and Hodges at the command post just as Collins arrived. They all discussed how to get the 4th Infantry Division into the fight. Hodges departed on the way to visit Macon and the troubled 83rd Infantry Division. Later, his aide noted, "As the General remarked later, the entire [4th Division] gave the impression of being all the way 'in' this war and, so far as conditions allowed, enjoying it—full of vigor, enthusiasm, will to win."[18]

Once his visitors departed, Barton went forward to inspect the bridge himself. Then he crossed over and moved to Macon's command post. The new division commander already had all the supervision he needed. Bradley and Quesada had already visited and given him advice on using more artillery and air. Barton wanted to get more details of what he could expect in the morning. He then visited Jim Luckett's headquarters and discussed the morning assault and sending an advanced party forward to coordinate with the 83rd Division. Collins called him back to corps head-quarters and ordered him to begin the division's attack at 06:30 hours. It would then become the corps' main effort. Barton's troops were to take their time, using their heavy artillery and tactical maneuver to "overcome enemy resistance."[19] Given the operational situation Bradley had put him

in, Collins was doing his best to drive the Germans south. After the meeting
Barton returned to Macon's headquarters and discussed his meeting with
the corps commander to ensure they agreed on what would happen when
the 12th Infantry entered the battle. He ended the evening at his headquarters with Blakeley, Marr, and Goodwin, going over his recent instructions
and preparing for the next day's fight.[20]

Cantepie

Barton's concept was to lead with Luckett's 12th Infantry, passing through
the lines of the 83rd Infantry Division's 330th Infantry. It would then
continue the attack south toward Sainteny. As the terrain opened, Rodwell's
8th Infantry was to move to the right flank, thus putting two regiments
online. After dark he would cross a small stream and flank the enemy position. Foster's 22nd Infantry would follow Luckett's troops "by bounds,"
and be prepared to pass through the forward troops and continue the attack.
It was as complete and careful a plan as one could construct. But, of course,
it had to stand the test of battle. Barton started the morning by moving
across the Baupte bridge to his new command post at an ancient farmhouse
called Cantepie.[21]

At 09:30 Major Richard J. O'Malley, commanding Luckett's 2nd
Battalion, passed through the 330th Infantry but made no progress. As one
of O'Malley's officers noted, "The enemy lurked behind every hedgerow.
German gunners were dug in every few yards. Forward movement brought
certain fire."[22] Barton came forward and worked with Luckett to get more
soldiers and supporting weapons into the fight. At 13:00 German infantry
supported by tanks counterattacked and attempted to throw the 12th Infantry
back from its meager gains, but the 4th Infantry Division Artillery stopped
the enemy in its tracks. Soon after, Barton decided to stop the attack and
find a better way to breach the enemy's defenses.[23] Meanwhile, Rodwell's
flanking effort crossing the stream in the swamp also failed, and only one of
his two battalions made it across. Under heavy fire, he and Barton decided
to pull the regiment back to the line of departure. As this was all transpir-
ing, Colonel Charles T. "Buck" Lanham reported for duty. A 1920 military

academy graduate, Lanham had been one of Barton's company commanders back at Fort Screven in 1939, and Barton knew he would be an aggressive regimental commander. He kept Lanham at his headquarters for the next few days to get him acclimated to the division's routine and the situation with the 22nd Infantry.[24]

The fighting on July 6 exposed the skill of the German army in conducting tactical defense. These defenders were some of the best it had available on the Normandy front: the 6th Parachute Regiment and the 17th SS Panzer Division. Although understrength these were first-class veteran soldiers. The terrain was in their favor, and when the Americans got off the road, it was wet, miserable, and challenging to move. This lack of mobility made them targets for enemy fire. Luckett's regiment had a little more success the following day but was still short of Sainteny. Barton spent the morning circulating among the three regimental commanders. Later in the morning, he returned to the division command post and found Collins waiting for him. Both commanders were frustrated and sought to break the impasse by getting fighter bombers into the attack. Air strikes arrived at 14:00, reinforced by a field artillery barrage. However, the attack went nowhere. As darkness approached, Barton met with both Luckett and Rodwell to discuss the next day and then returned to his command post to figure out what he could do as the divisional commander. The veteran 4th Infantry Division had done no better than the rookie 83rd Division and is a reminder that in combat, the enemy gets a say in the outcome, no matter how sophisticated the plans. The 8th and 12th Infantry Regiment's frontal attacks cost them almost six hundred soldiers, with very little accomplished.[25]

Méautis

To get closer to the front lines and make his travels to the regiments easier, Barton had Marr move the command post forward to a farm village at Méautis on July 8. By 17:30 it was operational, thirty minutes after it departed from Cantepie. It was an excellent location to control the battle, with buildings for the headquarters staff and closer to the main roads. Barton and Roosevelt's aides had their general's vans park in the adjacent courtyard.[26]

The terrain in the battle area was terrible, and Barton could only get one regiment, now Foster's 22nd Infantry, on the primary axis of advance. Rodwell's 8th Infantry continued to battle in the swamp on his right (west) flank. Although Blakeley had all of his division artillery, plus an extra battalion, to support Foster, the soggy ground did not allow him to place all of his batteries into position to mass fires. As Martin Blumenson noted, "The division not only had to fight the soggy crust of the land and the high-water table, it also had to cross innumerable drainage ditches, small streams, and inundated marshes in an area without a single hard-surfaced road. The terrain alone would have been a serious obstacle; defended by Germans it was almost impassable."[27]

While Barton's diary gives us a good picture of where and how he spent his days, we have less information about his deputy, Ted Roosevelt, who had exchanged places with Barber.[28] But we do know he spent most of his time at the front, visiting the battalions in contact. He was also very fond of the 8th Infantry, with whom he had landed on Utah Beach thirty days earlier. He stopped by Rodwell's command post, where the duty clerk noted his arrival and departure times almost every day during the first two weeks of July.[29] But, as we know, Roosevelt suffered from several ailments, especially a bad heart, that he chose to ignore.[30]

Barton started the morning of July 8 with Rodwell, whose regiment was still stuck on the swamp's edge, trying to drive the Germans out of a flanking position. Then he visited the 22nd Infantry, where Barton explained to Foster and his executive officer, John Ruggles, precisely what he expected them to accomplish. Barton remained there for several hours, observing its progress, then returned to the division command post. Now that he had a prospective replacement at headquarters, Foster was on the spot to produce results. Still on the move, Barton headed to his western flank to watch Rodwell's 8th Infantry pick itself through minefields. He moved forward to the lead company and watched their progress. There was little he could do but show the troops he cared and urge them on. Then he was back with the 22nd Infantry, his main effort. He visited the battalion commanders in the forward area and dodged a shell fired at him from a German antitank gun. The regiment continued its slow advance and the 2nd Battalion managed to gain the day's objective and hold the ground in the face of a German tank counterattack. But Barton was not happy, convinced the problem was not with his battalion commanders but with Foster's leadership.[31]

The three regiments were fundamentally different. Rodwell, with the 8th Infantry, had the benefit of inheriting the first-class operation set up by Van Fleet. The troops were motivated, leaders were competent, and morale was high. It was the same in the 12th Infantry, where Jim Luckett had benefited from the dynamic command Red Reeder had in place and had managed to sustain during this challenging fight. But it was not the same with Foster, who had taken over his command from Herve Tribolet after the Crisbecq disasters. Barton had needed to spend extra time with him during the Cherbourg operation. Finally, and most obviously to the division commander who talked to his troops regularly, Foster had not made things better by inspiring and motivating the soldiers. The 47-year-old colonel did not exude the fire and energy Barton felt around Rodwell and Luckett. That night he returned to the division command post and told Lanham to get ready to take command.[32]

Early Sunday morning, July 9, phones in the 22nd Infantry's battalion headquarters rang. The message was the same for each: "I am Colonel Charles T. Lanham. I have just assumed command of this regiment, and I want you to know that if you ever yield one foot of ground without my direct order I will court-martial you."[33] Earlier, Barton had called Foster back to headquarters. This new commander had the same temperament as Red Reeder and began breathing life into the sluggish regiment. After leaving the 8th Infantry, he had served with the Infantry Board and was one of the authors of Fort Benning's *Infantry in Battle* and a protégé of Courtney Hodges.[34]

He arrived ready to fight with a chip on his shoulder. According to Earl Edwards, who became his S-3, "His energy level was high and, being restless and hard driving by nature, patience was not his long suit. He was relentless and, at times, ruthless in his pressure for results from his subordinates, excuses were not often received kindly. He fully expected his battalion and company commanders to lead their troops in battle rather from a command post or foxhole."[35] This aggressive attitude was precisely what Barton expected. At 08:00, following an attack from the Ninth Air Force's fighter bombers, the 8th and 22nd Infantries, supported by companies from the 70th Tank Battalion and 801st Tank Destroyer Battalion, began a coordinated attack. Now Blakeley's division artillery could start moving forward. But as Lanham's infantry attacked, there was confusion about artillery hitting a small town. Lanham, already making his mark as commander, got on the radio and told Blakeley he "didn't give a shit how much [fire] they poured on the town."[36]

Barton was happy, and the 22nd Infantry took the objectives he had assigned by the end of the day. Barton returned to the command post and joined Blakeley and Colonel Young, the corps engineer, in inspecting the captured German fighting positions. While they were there, Collins arrived, and they discussed the enemy and what they needed to do the following day. Later that evening Lanham and Barton examined the same ground and discussed operations for the attack on July 10.[37] From now on Barton would not have to worry about the 22nd Infantry. He now had three solid regimental commanders and could explain what he wanted, and Luckett, Rodwell, and Lanham would do their best to accomplish their tasks and motivate their soldiers.

Barton spent most of Monday, July 10, working with Collins in the division command post. He did not need to oversupervise his commanders directing this small-unit battle. The day's action began with an attack from the Ninth Air Force and division and corps artillery batteries hitting German troop concentrations and headquarters locations. He ordered Luckett's regiment to pass through Lanham's troops and continue the attack south toward Sainteny. Accordingly, the 1st and 2nd Battalions, 12th Infantry, began the assault around 09:30. As the tank-infantry teams moved forward, the Germans withdrew to successive lines of hedgerows, fighting a delaying action.[38]

As the 12th Infantry advanced, Barton finally had enough space to bring another regiment online and ordered Rodwell's 8th Infantry to Luckett's right flank. At the same time, Lanham's troops moved into the division reserve, secured the division's right flank, and took a quick break. The attack's progress was slow, but by early afternoon the division had two regiments online. As Rodwell moved into his sector, the Germans helped to break the stalemate by launching a counterattack into the heart of the division defenders. American artillery and mortars caught the enemy in the open. Rodwell's troops hit the enemy from the flank, killing almost five hundred and capturing another forty-nine, at the loss of only four Americans.[39] As the enemy counterattack halted, the 12th Infantry's riflemen were surprised as German soldiers, trying to escape the artillery fire, ran across its front. There was only one bridge for them to escape and the regiment fired everything they had. As the regimental historian noted, "The carnage was frightful and the enemy dead lay in heaps about their shattered vehicles. The next morning it took three two and one-half ton trucks to remove all the German bodies."[40]

July 11 was a good but costly day for Barton's regiments, thanks to the failed German counterattack. However, he lost another battalion commander when Lieutenant Colonel Carlton O. MacNeely, commanding the 8th Infantry's 2nd Battalion, and who had landed alongside Roosevelt on Utah Beach, was badly wounded in the leg. Evacuated to England and then the United States, he was recommended by Barton for the Distinguished Service Cross. Back in the United States, he lost his fight to keep his leg and retired from the army in 1945. His executive officer, Major Alfred Yarborough, took command.[41] But the battle went on and Barton watched his tank-infantry teams, his Shermans still from the 70th Tank Battalion, grind their way south. By the end of the day, he had all three regiments online, almost three kilometers south of Sainteny.[42]

As usual, Roosevelt had been on the front lines helping to get division support to the battalions in contact.[43] That night during their evening meeting, Barton noted that Ted was sick. He called the medics and told Roosevelt not to leave his trailer the next day. The division surgeon came by and gave him a quick exam. He found nothing wrong other than the general trying to do what a 20-year-old did with a 56-year-old body. Of course, with more sophisticated equipment, he would have discovered more problems and ordered him to rear. And Roosevelt was also not a very cooperative patient and did everything he could to dissuade the surgeon from restricting his movement. Finally, with few options, the doctor gave him a sleeping pill and told him to get some rest.[44]

On July 12 Roosevelt got up and told Barton he felt fine. The commander relented and told him he could go out, but not any farther forward than regimental headquarters. At 11:40 hours Roosevelt was at the 8th Infantry's headquarters, briefing Rodwell on the division's situation.[45] At the same time, Barton was on the road, driving his Jeep while York rode in the passenger seat, handling the .30-caliber machine gun, and Sergeant Richards sat in the back seat, helping to keep an eye on the area around them. Richards was always prepared to take over the driver's duties. He checked on each regiment and ensured he and his commanders were operating as a team. The regiments moved forward, and the German defenders withdrew in good order, making Barton's infantrymen fight and suffer for every foot of the ground.[46]

Back at the headquarters, Hodges came by the division headquarters in the early afternoon and Barton took him down to see Buck Lanham, who had changed the attitude of the 22nd Infantry. Hodges knew Lanham well and considered him one of his oldest friends from his assignment as chief of infantry. Collins and Roosevelt showed up and spent several hours discussing various personal and professional topics.[47] Tubby and Ted returned to the division command post after the meeting broke up. After dinner they were having their nightly talk in Roosevelt's van when his son Quentin suddenly arrived. The young Captain Roosevelt had been fighting with the 1st Infantry Division and had survived all the carnage on Omaha. Ted had only recently found out that his son was all right and on his way for a visit. Barton excused himself, and the two Roosevelts had a pleasant reunion talking about all kinds of family events. Finally, Ted disclosed how unwell he was to his son. In a letter to his mother two days later, Quentin wrote, "He told me for the first time that night that he had been having heart attacks, and I naturally asked him a lot of things about it and told him to lay low. . . . Apparently after 2 years of steady combat under terrible conditions and after a serious illness, he had begun to get 'very tired,' as he put it to me that night."[48] About an hour after his son left, the general had another heart attack. Barton rushed back to Roosevelt's truck, holding his hand as he passed away. He was only 56 years old.[49] At the time of his death, Eisenhower and Bradley were about to promote Roosevelt to major general and give him command of the 90th Infantry Division, replacing Gene Landrum. Supposedly, the appointment was to take place the morning after he died.[50]

As usual, Barton began his rounds the next day by visiting his combat teams. Indeed, he must have personally passed the news of Roosevelt's death to as many key leaders as possible while maintaining some sense of operational security and not giving the enemy any indication of the loss of this influential leader. The division's attack that morning was a half-hearted affair, beginning at 09:30 when the 12th Infantry, supported by the 8th Infantry, was in a position to shoot into the German flanks. The defenders had prepared their ground well, and the attacking battalions encountered some of the "best organized defensive fires" they had experienced. But unlike the previous days, Barton did not coordinate the operation to the intensity he had previously and did not push Luckett's command. The division had done what Collins asked, and its days of combat in the hell of the Carentan-Périers Road ended.[51] As a first step, Barton pulled the 22nd Infantry out of line to an assembly area. Lanham's command had proven itself as a first-class fighting unit, but at a very high price. In less than one week of combat, the 22nd Infantry had suffered 1,379 casualties.[52]

Roosevelt's passing crushed Barton. After he returned to his van at Méautis, he sat down and wrote a letter to Ted's wife, Eleanor Butler Roosevelt:

My Dear Eleanor,

I address you as Eleanor because in daily conversations with Ted and getting extracts of your letters through him, you have become Eleanor to me, also.

I wish it were possible for me to pour out my heart to you and express to you all of the things that I feel so completely and deeply. That I cannot do, for I am in the midst of a battle, must soon go up to the front where Ted used to go so I could calmly solve my problems, but now I must both solve my problems and go to the front. I have lost more than my right arm, as a Division Commander, and I have lost even more than that as an individual. Thus, I share with you in no small measure our own loss. It is not possible for me to love Ted as you and your children loved him but I assure you that I approach with the depth of my affection very closely to yours.

After a discussion of family and other matters, Barton concludes:

> At 11:50 last night, July 12, I sat helpless and saw the most gallant
> soldier and finest gentleman I have ever known expire. I feel that
> my greatest tribute to him can only be to carry on the work at hand,
> inspired by his gallantry and soul. I know that you and his own
> will have the same inspiration and valiance and therefore I do not
> write you a letter of condolence, just one trying in a humble and
> inadequate way to describe a love and appreciation and a loss we
> mutually share.
>   The show goes on. He would have it so and we shall make it so.
> I should like to end and shall sign this letter.
>
>   Yours with reflected and deepest affection,
>
>   R. O. Barton
>   Major General, U.S. Army[53]

It was not unusual for American general officers and admirals to perish
during World War II; more than forty died from several causes ranging
from enemy snipers, a rare event, to airplane crashes, relatively common.
Before July 14 on the Normandy front, two brigadier generals, both deputy
division commanders, had already died. Don Pratt from the 101st Airborne
from a glider crash on D-Day, and Nelson M. Walker, 8th Infantry Division and one of Barton's Leavenworth students, died from small-arms fire
attempting to organize an assault not far from the 4th Infantry Division's
location. What was unusual was that an entire chain of command—army,
corps, and division commanders—participated in the deceased's funeral.

Roosevelt's son Quentin and his aide, Marcus Stevenson, led the
procession into the temporary Jayhawk Cemetery near Sainte-Mère-Église.
Behind them marched the colors, two buglers, two chaplains, and the half-
track containing Roosevelt's casket. The next group, eight senior officers
serving as honorary pallbearers, marched in. This group consisted of Bradley,
soon to assume control of the 12th Army Group; Hodges, soon to take
Bradley's place at First Army; Collins, commanding VII Corps; and Barton,
Blakeley, and Rodwell from the 4th Infantry Division. Clarence Huebner,
commanding the 1st Infantry Division, where Roosevelt had carved out a
distinguished record, also joined the official party; George S. Patton Jr., who

did not yet have a job but would soon command the Third Army and had been Roosevelt's corps commander in Sicily, rounded out the group of eight.[54]

Following the official party came the VII Corps band and an honor guard made up of one soldier from each company, battery, and troop in the 4th Infantry Division and a contingent from the 1st Infantry Division, with which he had served in North Africa and Sicily. Observing the ceremony were members of the French Forces of the Interior and a few dozen civilians. Eight soldiers unloaded the casket from the half-track and placed it on wooden slats covering the grave. Then, as the bugler played taps and the honor guard fired salutes, the soldiers lowered the casket into the grave.[55] One wonders about the behind-the-scenes discussions preceding this impromptu but impressive and unique ceremony. The Roosevelts were among America's most potent political powers, and we should assume that consideration influenced the nature of the day's events.

Many accounts of Roosevelt's passing often mention that he died soon after D-Day. That, as readers of this book know, is not the case. Ted was an essential division leader and Barton's advisor from Utah through Montebourg to the outskirts of Cherbourg. He was the military mayor of the city for several days, restoring order and essential services. Roosevelt then fought with the division for almost two weeks before expiring. He was a crucial element of Barton's command team and very popular among the Ivy Division's rank and file.

A few days after the funeral, Barton wrote to his daughter Clare:

> I took a terrific loss when Ted Roosevelt cashed in. He was a wonderful man, the most gallant soldier I have ever known, and a friend irreplaceable. You know, as you grow older you form a few intimate warm friendships. Ted was the first one I have made since Father Murphy of Georgetown days. I miss him terribly, both personally and officially. His funeral was impressive. The pallbearers consisted of three lieutenant generals, two major generals and odds and ends, such as brigadiers and colonels. . . . An incident happened at the funeral which I cannot describe but which pertained to a matter concerning which Ted and I had vast mutual understanding and laughing uplift. As I was riding back to my C.P. many miles away, thinking of the matter, I said to myself: "When I get home I must tell Ted about this because he will

get the same kick out of it as I did." It is too damn bad that he wasn't at the other end for me to tell for he, too, would have gotten a belly-laugh out of the incident.[56]

Two weeks before Roosevelt's death, on June 27, Barton had recommended him for the Congressional Medal of Honor. He and Collins discussed it in early July, and he told Barton to withdraw his recommendation, which he did.[57] After Roosevelt's funeral Barton resubmitted it on August 1, and insisted it go through the appropriate chain of command. Collins agreed and processed an endorsement to higher headquarters rejecting the recommendation: "Despite my great admiration and affection for General Roosevelt, I do not feel that his actions on D-Day warrant the award of the Medal of Honor. I recommend that he be awarded posthumously another Oak Leaf Cluster to his Distinguished Service Cross."[58] Hodges and Bradley agreed with Collins's recommendation, and on August 2 the First Army formally announced the award.[59] Most likely Eisenhower learned about the recommendation unofficially; Roosevelt was too political for him to ignore. One also suspects the chain of command believed the entire matter was closed.

However, while the award was moving though the personnel system, events were taking place in the United States. Secretary of War Henry L. Stimson was a good friend of the Roosevelt family, having been appointed by President Theodore Roosevelt as US attorney for the Southern District of New York as one of T. R.'s key "trustbusters." He was also a protégé and longtime family friend of Roosevelt's secretary of war, Elihu Root.[60] He was in Europe in mid-July, after Roosevelt's death, on a tour of the American units and hospitals in Europe. He visited VII Corps headquarters on July 17 and may have spoken briefly with Barton. No one, apparently, mentioned anything about an award.[61] However, after Roosevelt's death Barton sent his widow a copy of the award packet. Stimson arrived back in New York from Europe during the third week of July. Before returning to Washington he stopped by Oyster Bay, the Roosevelt home, to pay his respects to his friend Eleanor. There she shared Barton's letter and the award recommendation.[62]

Somewhat surprised, Stimson confronted Marshall on his return to Washington. The chief of staff, who knew nothing, in turn sent a cable off to Eisenhower.[63] The SHAEF commander replied on August 15 that Bradley had recommended a Distinguished Service Medal (third award) for Roosevelt, and he agreed. However, he did forward the original recommendation to the War Department.[64] A week later an award board met in Washington and recommended supporting Barton and awarding Roosevelt the Congressional Medal of Honor.[65] On September 21, 1944, Henry Stimson presented the medal to Eleanor Butler Roosevelt at her home in Oyster Bay. Standing with the secretary of war in her living room were Marshall, General Henry H. Arnold, commanding the US Army Air Forces, and Field Marshal Sir John Dill, the British Representative to the Combined Chiefs of Staff in Washington.[66] Collins, who never forgot a slight, probably blamed Barton for bypassing the chain of command. This public embarrassment only added to the tension behind the public veneer of professional cordiality.

By July 15 Barton's troops were well south of Sainteny and only four miles from Périers. Collins told him to hold his position and be prepared to redeploy to another sector. That afternoon Barton headed to corps headquarters for a briefing on the next operation. In addition to Collins, McKee, Troxel, Williston Palmer, the corps artillery commander, and other principal corps staff members, Barton encountered an enlarged assembly of division commanders. Over the last few weeks, he had worked with Eddy (9th Infantry Division) and Macon (83rd Infantry Division). Now Clarence Huebner (1st Infantry Division), whom he had seen a few days earlier at Roosevelt's funeral, and LeRoy Watson (3rd Armored Division) were joining the team. Barton was well acquainted with both officers from their assignment at Fort Leavenworth in the early 1930s. Also in the meeting was Leland Hobbs (30th Infantry Division), whom he had met in Washington when at Georgetown and then in England in the spring before deployment, as was Edward H. Brooks (2nd Armored Division), whom he knew while assigned as the IV Corps chief of staff. Six division commanders, twice as many as usual, indicated the scale of their next operation. It was code-named COBRA.[67]

The next day, July 16, the division continued to move out of the line. The last unit out was Luckett's 12th Infantry, which was pulling out in good order, with Richard J. O'Malley's 2nd Battalion as the last unit off the line and needing to hold in place until a battalion from the 329th Infantry arrived the following day. Unfortunately, a German sniper killed him while checking positions and talking to his soldiers. O'Malley was a well-loved leader, and it was a severe blow to the unit. Barton was also fond of O'Malley and ordered the division's artillery and mortars to fire three volleys into the German lines in tribute to this fine officer.[68] Major Gerden F. Johnson, who after the war became the regiment's historian and wrote its excellent history, took command. O'Malley's demise was a final blow that ended a horrible week for the division that suffered over 2,427 killed, wounded, and missing soldiers. Its overall casualty rate since landing was almost 80 percent of its original strength. More important from the leadership perspective was the loss of nine company commanders. Five battalion commanders had perished leading their soldiers in combat since D-Day.[69] Barton was close to his officers and men, whose loss was a terrible burden. He stayed at his headquarters in the morning and visited Troy Middleton's VIII Corps headquarters in the afternoon. Middleton would be his superior for the next few days as Barton's troops took a much-needed rest.[70]

Lenauderie

The following day, July 17, Barton woke up, had a good breakfast, and went to the command post where his West Point classmate John "P" Wood was waiting for him. He had earned the nickname "P" for the professor, and his classmates considered him one of the brightest and most learned in the class.[71] Originally in the artillery, he moved to the tank corps in 1941. The two had seen each other often during the Carolina Maneuvers when Wood was chief of staff of the 1st Armored Corps, which was part of Griswold's IV Corps. He took command of the 4th Armored Division in May 1942, and he and Barton would have met again in England during the buildup. One of the 4th Armor's regiments, the 329th Infantry, was replacing the 8th Infantry. After a lengthy discussion, Wood headed down to visit Rodwell at his command post with some of his staff to finish arrangements for the relief. Barton spent all morning in the command post while all around him its crew and his team began tearing down the operation at Méautis. While he headed down to visit Rodwell and check on the relief, which would be complete

Major General Barton stands on Barton's Buggy and presents awards to members of the 8th Infantry Regiment, Carentan, July 17, 1944. Brigadier General Taylor is behind the formation on the left side. US Army photograph, Dwight David Eisenhower Presidential Library.

that evening, he transferred the command of the sector to Blakeley, operating out of his division command post. After a short visit, he drove over the Périers road to Carentan, crossed the Taute River, and then southeast to the village of Lenauderie, where Parks Huntt had established the new command post in the courtyard of a large stone house.[72] The 4th Division moved to an assembly area east of Carentan, departed VII Corps for the time being, and became part of Middleton's command. The real purpose of the division's move was rest and reorganization, and by nightfall, almost all of it was in the new assembly area.[73]

For the next two days, Barton visited each of his regiments and thanked them for their outstanding work over the last several weeks. Pictures from the time show him standing on army trucks or the hood of his Jeep with soldiers gathered around. He praised some of the bravest leaders at each stop, standing near his podium and awarding them Silver Stars. Among them was his great friend Jim Rodwell, for his leadership with the 8th Infantry in the swamp near Sainteny. He also pinned the brigadier general star on his new deputy commander, George Taylor. Taylor had distinguished himself while commanding the 16th Infantry on Omaha Beach several weeks earlier.[74] When not visiting his soldiers, he was hard at work preparing for the next operation, either in his headquarters or at Collins's command post.

On July 19, he had a chance to write his family. In a letter to his daughter, he reflected:

> This is the first time in the forty-two days since D-day that I have been 'way back like this. I am getting the G.I.s all bathed, shaved, clean underwear, good hot chow, lots of drill, target practice, pep talks and all those things that add up to make the best outfit in the world (and we have certainly proven that.) . . . I am getting along in good order, am well and pleased with myself as normal, under your own definitions; have lost considerable weight which I didn't know until I tried on a belt that fit General Blakeley and to my surprise found that it fit me. Must do something about that. I sort of like a little round belly, having been accustomed to it for so long.

He was covering up his true feelings. The fighting took a physical and mental toll on this gruff but sensitive man. He had lost much more than a few pounds over the past few weeks.[75]

Chapter 12

COBRA to Mortain, July 20–August 17

During the months that the 4th Infantry Division was part of the
VII Corps, it had over two thousand men killed in action and suffered
a total of over ten thousand casualties—the heaviest casualty list of
any American division thus far in France.
—Collins to Barton, August 28, 1944

Eisenhower and Bradley had been searching for a way to break out of Normandy since Cherbourg fell. Barton's meeting with Collins on June 29 was the preliminary briefing for Operation COBRA. By July 11 SHAEF had sketched out the general outlines of the attack, which would take place two days after the British launched a similar offensive (GOOD-WOOD) outside of Caen. This operation, the sequencing of several coordinated battles toward a specific objective, was the last time in the ETO that the entire American army would fight with one purpose: the breakout from the lodgment area and maneuver toward Germany. From July 25 to the war's end, Eisenhower specified different operational objectives for each army group and army. Ultimately, they would all contribute to the strategic goal of conducting "operations aimed at the heart of Germany and the destruction of her armed forces."[1] This single purpose allowed massing all its infantry, armor, and supporting arms on one unified axis of advance. Moreover, it facilitated the employment of the entire US Army Air Force on one concentrated target. In general, two corps (VIII and XIX) would secure the penetration's flanks while Collins's VII Corps conducted a penetration on a narrow portion of the Allied front.[2]

The centerpiece of the assault was a reinforced VII Corps. Bradley had hoped to keep the 4th Infantry Division as his army reserve. However, Eddy's 9th and Hobbs's 30th Infantry Divisions had not yet recovered from the recent battles in the swampy Bocage, and Collins argued he needed Barton. The army commander agreed, and the 4th received orders to move to its new staging area. While the plan's outline came from SHAEF and First Army, the detailed planning took place at VII Corps headquarters. Historians write about generals and decision-making as though they do all the work. Collins was certainly an active participant in COBRA's planning. But his staff, led by his chief of staff, Richard G. McKee, turned his ideas into workable plans and orders. The G-2, Leslie D. Carter, identified the enemy's capabilities and the nature of the terrain. Barton's former operations officer and now the corps G-3, Orlando C. Troxel Jr., laid out the specific objectives, assembly areas, and march routes for all six divisions, the artillery, and the massive corps logistics operation. Finally, his G-4, James G. Anding, developed the details for providing food, fuel, water, and ammunition to keep this enormous corps moving. The result was one of the most audacious operations in US Army history. It was a model of precise synchronization, operational art, and flexibility.[3]

By the middle of July, the plan had evolved so that Collins now controlled the combat power of two corps. Along the line of contact, he arrayed three infantry divisions (the 9th, 4th, and 30th), supported by almost forty battalions of field artillery, north of a narrow portion of the Périers–Saint-Lô Road. In this area the road was straight and easy to locate from the air. On a map Collins, Troxel, and Carter marked a small rectangle extending south of the highway. This symbol, which corresponded a section of German defenders, indicated where they wanted the air force to attack. Ultimately, almost three thousand aircraft of all kinds would strike this target box. Once the attacking

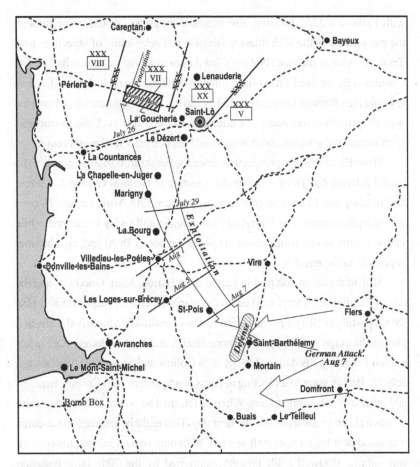

COBRA, July 20–August 17

aircraft departed, the lead infantry divisions would attack to penetrate the, hopefully, neutralized German defenses.

When Collins believed his troops had passed through the Germans' main line of resistance, he would exploit the penetration with three mobile divisions. He now had Huebner's 1st Infantry Division, augmented by Combat Command B from the 3rd Armored Division, configured as a motorized division. It would "drive through the gap" created by Eddy's 9th Infantry Division and seize Coutances, a major intersection near the coast, isolating German forces opposite the VIII Corps to the north. Brooks's 2nd Armored Division, augmented with Lanham's 22nd Infantry, also mounted on trucks, would move through the gap created by the 30th Infantry Division and seize a line of objectives near Tessy-sur-Vire in the east. Watson's 3rd Armored Division, minus its Combat Command B, received a motorized infantry battalion from Huebner's division. It would pass through the gaps created by Barton's two regiments and then head west toward objectives south of Coutances. At the corps level, the instructions were intentionally vague about what would happen after the breakthrough.[4]

From Eisenhower's perspective, once the breakthrough was complete, he would activate the Third Army under Lieutenant General George S. Patton, and Bradley would assume command of the new 12th Army Group. Hodges would replace Bradley as First Army commander and swing to the east, while Patton's army would continue south toward the port at Brest and, on a broader approach, to the east.[5]

Still, at the command post in Lenauderie, Barton, Marr, Goodwin, and the rest of the division's staff worked on the plan's scheme of maneuver and plan for supporting artillery fire and logistics. They continued to modify the division plan as the corps staff announced more details, and Barton shared more information following his daily meetings with Collins and Troxel. On Wednesday, July 19, Barton went to a meeting at corps headquarters with Collins, Bradley, and other division commanders. When he returned he ordered his headquarters to move closer to the front line the next day. That night he returned to the corps command post for another staff session. With only two regiments, his concept was simple. Rodwell's 8th Infantry, supported by the 70th Tank Battalion and companies of engineers, chemical mortars, and tank destroyers, led the attack. Luckett's 12th Infantry followed as his reserve. Barton still had three battalions of artillery and the remainder of the 801st Tank Destroyer Battalion, 388th Anti-Aircraft Artillery Battalion, and the 4th Engineers and 4th Recon Troop. His division's mission was simple in concept: penetrate the German defenses in the zone and secure the gap between Marigny and St. Gilles.[6]

Charlemagnerie

On July 20 Barton started the morning by leaving his headquarters at Lenauderie and visiting Eddy's 9th Infantry Division command post, on his western flank. Paddy Flint's 39th Infantry held the sector that the 4th Infantry Division would attack through, and since Flint would be working for Barton, he wanted to ensure all the details were in place. Then he drove to the VII Corps headquarters, located at the village of La Goucherie, and discussed the division's plan with McKee and Troxel. Then he visited the 8th Infantry, still at its assembly area near Carentan, for a regimental formation, addressing the troops and awarding medals, including a Silver Star for Jim Rodwell, who had performed superbly in the fight near Sainteny. Finally, he returned to Lenauderie, where the headquarters was closing. He monitored by radio the progress of the division units that were moving to their new staging areas. The attack was to begin the following morning, July 21, and so after the headquarters packed up, he joined the other division commanders at Collins's command post. When the meeting ended, Barton headed south for his new command post at a farmstead north of Le Dézert named Charlemagnerie.[7]

The weather on July 21 remained unacceptable for the planned air attack, and Bradley postponed the assault. While the senior commanders waited, the assault troops and supporting artillery adjusted their positions. Flint's 39th Infantry was one of the few units in contact, fighting to gain good locations along the Périers–Saint-Lô Road. But besides visiting Rodwell, Barton could do little more than wait at his headquarters.[8] The weather on July 22 was no better, and there was little he could do other than visit his units and discuss the attack with Jim Rodwell. That night he returned to VII Corps headquarters, where Collins gave the division and key regimental commanders another update on what was taking place across the First Army sector and what Bradley had in mind as the attack progressed.[9]

Barton continued planning at his Charlemagnerie headquarters during the morning of July 23 as the bad weather continued. Around noon LeRoy Watson delivered his liaison officer to the 4th Division command post. With his 3rd Armored Division passing through the 4th Infantry's penetration, Watson would depend on his representative to keep him appraised of the Ivy Division's progress, help coordinate artillery fire, and help clear the routes as his tanks and mechanized infantry moved against the Germans. That afternoon Ernie Pyle, the columnist and Pulitzer Prize winner for his war reporting, came by the headquarters and interviewed Barton. Then Barton, with

Pyle in tow, took to the road and visited Rodwell and Luckett. Pyle reported, "I went with the infantry because it is my love, and because I suspected the tanks being spectacular, might smother the credit due to the infantry. I teamed up with the 4th Infantry Division since it was in the middle of the forward three and spearheading the attack. The first night behind the front lines, I slept comfortably on a cot in a tent at the division command post and met for the first time the 4th's commander—Major General Raymond O. Barton, a fatherly, kindly, thoughtful, good soldier."[10]

That afternoon Collins came by to pass on any new information on the operation and see how his lead division commander was holding up. On the eve of a significant battle, with all the plans complete, there is little senior commanders can do other than circulate among their units. As the corps commander departed, Larry LeSueur, the CBS radio reporter who had been with the 4th since Utah Beach, dropped by the headquarters to get Barton's comments on this next operation.[11] Later, Lieutenant General Lesley McNair, commander of AGF, visited Barton and his command post. When the attack commenced, McNair planned to be with a regimental command post in Hobbs's 30th Infantry Division.[12]

However, local ground operations continued as the troops on the front line fought to secure favorable ground. That evening it became extremely personal when Tubby got the bad news about his dear friend Paddy Flint. Flint's regiment was trying to clear terrain near the Périers–Saint-Lô Road, where the 8th Infantry would cross the next day. When German fire stopped his attacking unit's advance, he went forward to get his troops moving. Flint was out in front, where a regimental commander should not be, riding on the back deck of a tank and then leading a squad on foot. As he took cover with his soldiers near a farmhouse, a German sniper shot the 56-year-old colonel. He died the next day.[13] For thirty-six years Barton and Flint had been close friends. They had been classmates at West Point and Fort Leavenworth, and the army often stationed them near each other: Eagle Pass, Fort Sill, Coblenz, and Fort Benning. Since June Flint's 39th Infantry had twice been part of the 4th Division, at Crisbecq and now outside Saint-Lô. Barton said little about Flint's death, but it surely affected him. However, he had no time to grieve as his command was about to go into battle.

Early on July 24, the 8th Infantry's assault battalions moved into their attack positions. At 11:00 the 8th Infantry passed through the 39th Infantry, now commanded by Lieutenant Colonel Van H. Bond, its executive officer, in place of Flint. Barton notified Collins that he was returning the unit to Eddy's command and began moving it to the rear. Rodwell's regiment, led by Alfred Yarborough's 2nd Battalion, continued to attack against heavy artillery and mortar fire to a line just north of the Saint-Lô–Périers Road. Then Barton ordered it back about eight hundred meters to await the aerial assault, which was to take place at noon.[14]

At noon the VII Corps headquarters notified the division that the First Army had postponed the operation again. Yet bombs were falling! Rodwell reported heavy bombardment twenty-five minutes after being told the air force had called it off.[15] The Allied Expeditionary Air Force headquarters attempted to cancel the mission at the last minute because of the weather. However, many of the bombers never got the word and dropped about 550 tons of high explosives and 135 tons of fragmentation bombs.[16] Immediately after the aborted bomb run, there was confusion about what the ground units should do. Collins decided he needed to exploit this surprise and sent orders to seize the Périers–Saint-Lô Road and dig in. Marr passed this information to Rodwell and Luckett. But Barton disagreed and convinced the corps commander to stop the units where they were. A little after 13:00, he called Major Oma Bates, the regiment's executive officer, and told him, "The attack beyond the road is definitely canceled. The division will seize, secure, dig in and hold the road in conjunction with the adjacent units-No element forward of the road." Hobbs's 30th Infantry Division took the most friendly-fire casualties: 25 dead and 131 wounded. The 4th Infantry Division suffered 27 killed and 70 wounded, mainly from the 8th Infantry.[17]

That evening Ernest Hemingway arrived at Barton's command post. Barton, distraught over the loss of his good friend and focused on the upcoming assault, had little time for the famous correspondent and award-winning author. He turned him over to Roosevelt's former aide, Marcus Stevenson, who now worked for Garlan Bryant as a public affairs officer. Stevenson took him immediately over to the 8th Infantry's command post. Stevenson spent the next few days driving Hemingway around the division. The correspondent got along well with its officers and would remain an unofficial member until the end of the year.[18]

Barton was not sure the attack would begin on July 25 as scheduled. So he called Rodwell and told him that the cue it was going as expected was when the medium bombers appeared over the target zone. At 08:40 hours corps reported that the operation, code-named Charlie, would take place according to its schedule.[19] An hour later 250 fighter-bombers began attacking preregistered targets and any German positions they could identify. Then they cleared the area as more than 1,500 B-24 and B-17 bombers from the Eighth Air Force saturated the area south of the Périers–Saint-Lô Road. Finally, 400 B26 Marauder medium bombers from the Ninth Air Force struck the southern half of the bombardment rectangle. At 12:15, as the last aircraft departed, dozens of 105 mm and 155 mm artillery battalions from all six divisions and the VII Corps Artillery opened on German positions. Other corps artillery battalions stood by to fire counterbattery fire if German mortars or artillery fired back.[20]

Like the previous day, some bombs landed among the American soldiers. According to a historian interviewing soldiers after the battle, Lieutenant Colonel Erasmus H. Strickland's 3rd Battalion, 8th Infantry, "arrived late and stopped on hedgerow back of the prescribed front line. This proved fortunate; the next hedgerow in front was obliterated by the bombing."[21] Lieutenant Colonel John H. Meyer's 1st Battalion, 8th Infantry, was not as fortunate, as his Company B suffered a direct hit, losing ten killed and twenty-seven wounded. When the attack began, this unit could send only two squads, one machine-gun section, and four men borrowed from battalion headquarters into the assault.[22] Among the dead in the assault area was General McNair, who had spent several hours with Barton the afternoon before and had been with the 30th Infantry Division's 120th Infantry, which received the bulk of the inaccurate bombs.[23]

As the bombing ended, Meyer's 1st Battalion advanced on the left, and Strickland's 3rd Battalion on the right passed through Lieutenant Colonel Langdon Jackson's 2nd Battalion. Jackson (USMA 1936) was new to the division. Barton had placed him in command that morning, as the bombers were approaching, after Rodwell determined that Major Yarborough, who took command after MacNeely's wounding on July 11, was exhausted and unable to continue commanding the battalion. It was challenging to make such a change, but it was better to do it earlier rather than later.[24]

Barton could not sit back at division headquarters and organized a small group of staff officers into an advanced command post. Leaving Captain Huntt to begin dismantling the headquarters, Barton and his team moved forward and set up near Rodwell's 8th Infantry's command post at a farmhouse called La Couture near Amigny. They were close to the front, and around 14:30 an armor-piercing shell, probably from an 88 mm antitank gun, slammed into the regimental headquarters. With a direct fire range of almost nine miles, much farther than the ability of its optical site to locate the target, it could have been a stray shot fired miles away. But the result was the severe wounding of two captains from the 8th Infantry staff and the smashing of much of the command post's equipment.[25]

As Meyer and Strickland's battalions moved forward, they found German troops trying to resist without any logical organization or command. Supporting fires were limited, and when they encountered enemy strongpoints, the assault units moved around them and turned the task over to Jackson's trailing battalion. Trailing behind the advancing regiment, Luckett's 12th Infantry began moving forward and continued to clear isolated strong points and neutralize small groups of enemy troops. By the end of the day, the division had made good progress. It had covered about a third of the distance to the Saint-Lô–Coutances Road.[26]

La Couture (Amigny)

Early on July 26, Rodwell continued his attack. Supported by rocket-firing P47s from the Ninth Air Force, his 1st and 3rd Battalions continued to advance against desperate German soldiers. Around noon the 3rd Battalion encountered a disorganized German infantry battalion and killed or captured most of it. Collins visited Barton at La Couture midafternoon and urged him to keep moving and drive toward Marigny, on the south side of the bombing box. Barton found Rodwell at 15:20, passed on the urging (Rodwell needed little), and watched as the 8th Infantry's command post headed south, followed by Hemingway, who was now shadowing the division's progress. Meanwhile, the remainder of Huntt's division headquarters moved into recently vacated spaces.

For the infantry progress was slow until late afternoon, when German defenses seemed to collapse. Nevertheless, Rodwell's two battalions advanced toward their objectives, and at 17:00 Rodwell committed Jackson's 2nd Battalion into the into a full-fledged assault. The 12th Infantry was still moving behind the 8th Infantry and clearing isolated German soldiers and small units. As the sun went down on July 26, the 4th Division had essentially shattered the German defenses and occupied the enemy positions at Marigny. Barton joined Rodwell around 18:30 and discussed the division's array for the night and plans for the next day.[27]

Although the gains appeared minor on the large maps at Bradley's head-quarters, the 4th Infantry Division and the other attacking infantry had moved relatively briskly through the devastated German defensive line. They found the enemy not organized, not establishing a coherent defense, and not reply-ing with its traditional counterattacks. At VII Corps headquarters, the brain trust of Collins, McKee, Troxel, Palmer, and Carter weighed their options. To commit the exploitation force too early might create chaos if the German forces were still intact and could counterattack. However, it would result in missed opportunities and the ability to exploit if Collins unleashed his armor too late.

To Collins and his staff, it appeared the corps was on the verge of a deci-sive penetration, and they needed to take advantage of enemy disorganization before the enemy could recover. The Germans were no longer counterattack-ing, which indicated their cohesion and confidence were broken. In one of his most important decisions of the war, Collins ordered his armored force into the fray. In short order the 1st Infantry Division (Motorized), 2nd Armored Division, and 3rd Armored Division began moving toward passage routes created by the front-line infantry.[28] By 21:22 hours the lead units of Watson's 3rd Armored Division were moving through the 4th Infantry Division's zone toward Marigny.[29]

Barton's two infantry regiments encountered isolated German soldiers throughout the night. The next morning, July 27, Rodwell adjusted his fighting positions to block any German efforts to retake terrain and cleared the roads through the area so Watson's tanks could move through the 4th Infantry Division's sector with as little interference as possible. Luckett's 12th Infantry also opened routes of enemy dead, equipment, and horses and cleared the division zone of isolated German soldiers and equipment. As usual, Barton was on the move, checking in with Luckett and Rodwell. He then drove to Watson's location to ensure the 4th Division gave his exploiting armor all the support it needed. Late that afternoon, from high ground near Luckett's headquarters, Barton watched as columns of tanks, supporting infantry, and artillery roared down the torn-up road past Marigny. He spent the night in a temporary command post at a farmhouse east of La Chapelle-en-Juger called Bas Marais.[30] That evening the corps chief of staff, McKee, noted in his diary, "Steady Progress—breakthrough complete."[31] Barton and his 4th Infantry had fulfilled all the tasks Collins had assigned him for Operation COBRA.

As the 3rd Armored Division roared past the exhausted infantry from the 8th and 12th Infantries, Barton's command became the corps' reserve.[32] The infantrymen spent the morning clearing the division's zone of any remaining German forces. That afternoon, July 28, Collins ordered it to move about ten miles south to the area near Notre-Dame-de-Cenilly. Luckett's regiment began its foot march at 16:45 hours. Collins wanted the division to mount the unit on jeeps and get it there faster. Barton's chief of staff, Dick Marr, convinced him it was impractical and promised the division would arrive by 22:00 that night. Unfortunately, that proved impossible as the broken vehicles and thousands of trucks, soldiers, and equipment from more than two divisions were using the same damaged roads and trails. Rodwell's soldiers, marching all night, pulled into their assigned area at 04:45 and Luckett's command at 06:22, after a fourteen-hour march. It had been almost four days since anyone had had a decent rest.[33]

That included Barton, who met Brooks from the 2nd Armored Division for a short meeting and then linked up with Collins to discuss the current situation and plans with him. He then joined the column heading south. From time to time, he dismounted from Barton's Buggy and marched with his soldiers. The journey took all night.[34]

Le Bourg (Notre-Dame-de-Cenilly)

The American offensive continued and expanded as the VII Corps exploited its initial success. Following in the tracks of the two armored divisions, the 4th Division had marched all night and began assembling east of the village of Hambye on the morning of July 29. Meanwhile, on Barton's right flank, General Brooks from the 2nd Armored Division realized that many German troops, mainly from SS units, were trying to escape the American encirclement. He was short on infantry to stop them and sent a message to VII Corps headquarters: "Imperative 4th Infantry Division move to support troops southwest Notre Dame [de-Cenilly] to prevent escape."[35] Brooks also visited the 8th Infantry's headquarters to speak to Rodwell directly and ask for help.[36] Barton complied and moved elements of the 8th and 12th Infantries to locations to stop the enemy exfiltration. Rodwell sent Strickland's 3rd Battalion, 8th Infantry. His Company I was instrumental in assisting the 41st Infantry (2nd Armored Division) in stopping German attempts to escape to the east at Pont Brocard. Simultaneously, Luckett's 12th Infantry also occupied escape routes toward Tessy, stopping German movement in that sector.[37]

While the main division command post continued to move south, Barton directed operations with his small command group. It arrived at Le Bourg, about four thousand yards southeast of Notre-Dame-de-Cenilly, not far from the fighting, around dawn. Dave Goodwin set up his operations map and began to plot the locations of the division's two regiments as they moved into position. Barton spent more than an hour with his G-3 discussing the situation and considering the next phase of the operation. He expected Lanham's 22nd Infantry would be under his control soon. As part of Task Force ROSE, Lanham's infantry had performed brilliantly and the War Department would award the regiment a Presidential Unit Citation.[38] In the afternoon Barton headed to Rodwell's command post to discuss the regiment's operations and plans for the following day.[39]

When he gave the 8th Infantry to his chief of staff, rumors among the troops were that he was doing this so Rodwell could "get combat experience, so he could qualify for a star."[40] That is most likely true since a regimental command was required for professional advancement. However, many regimental commanders would fail during the campaign from Normandy to Germany, and Rodwell was not one of them. His leadership during the brutal fighting in the Bocage and commanding the breakthrough on COBRA more than qualified him for advancement. Barton and Collins, who knew his regimental commanders, were satisfied with his performance and would recommend promotion when the time came.

Villedieu-les-Poêles

Almost eighty years later, it is difficult to imagine what that small part of France looked like at the end of July. As planned, Bradley took command of the newly formed Twelfth Army Group. Hodges stepped up to command the First US Army consisting of the V (Gerow), VII (Collins), and XIX (Corlett) Corps. George S. Patton, who had given Barton his brigadier stars back at Fort Benning three years earlier, took command of the Third Army with the VIII (Middleton), XII (Cook), XX (Walker), and XV (Haislip) Corps. It should be obvious to the reader that this group of generals, most of whom were Barton's classmates or good friends, knew each other well. They had worked together for years and, brought up in the army's education system, were experts managing tactical units on the battlefield. This would be essential over the next few weeks as Bradley reshuffled his entire chain of command in reorganizing the Twelfth Army Group.[41]

Over 900,000 American soldiers, in 176,620 vehicles of all kinds, were moving south, seeking to escape the confines of lower Normandy. All this movement took place over a road network designed for horse-drawn carts and light trucks, and everyone was in a hurry. Thunderbolt fighter-bombers from the Ninth Air Force in the sky were adding to the confusion, attacking German and sometimes American troop concentrations. Finally, a fractured but still dangerous German Army continued to fight and contest the American effort to break out from its bridgehead.[42]

In the slogging matches in the Bocage and near Saint-Lô, Barton's role was generally confined to getting artillery and air support to the troops in combat. During the exploitation Barton often became a traffic coordinator and coach—keeping units from colliding on the small French roads and coordinating attacks on German concentrations. His primary role of urging his regimental and battalion commanders to keep moving was at the heart of his responsibilities. He talked to Collins constantly, keeping abreast of mission changes and the general flow of the battle, and communicated it to Marr, Luckett, and Rodwell.

Colonel Truman E. Boudinot's Combat Command B, 3rd Armored Division, was moving past the 4th Division, so he and Barton coordinated operations early on July 31. His regiments needed to keep the main roads open and search for and destroy any pockets of Germans, especially tanks and antitank crews, that could interfere with the armor moving forward. Once the two agreed on the general concept for the next few hours, Barton went to Luckett's headquarters to check on his progress. The 12th Infantry was now moving past Rodwell's troops and marching south toward Saint-Pois. Barton and his small group engaged in a firefight with a German platoon on the way. As his aide noted in his diary, "[Barton] got a great deal of front-line experience."[43] Hemingway was still hanging with the division and had acquired a German Army Mercedes-Benz convertible. Unfortunately, it needed some repairs, so Barton assigned him a mechanic-driver to get the automobile working. That evening, Hemingway and his driver drove by Barton's trailer, providing the commander a sense of levity in the middle of his weighty responsibilities.[44]

The division was on the outskirts of Villedieu-les-Poêles, an important crossroads between Vire and the coast.[45] The next day they were to attack to seize the town. According to the army's official historian at the time, Martin Blumenson, Barton got his regimental and battalion commanders together and moved into the coaching role. After passing out their specific instructions, he told them, "We face a defeated enemy, an enemy terribly low in morale, terribly confused. I want you in the next advance to throw caution to the winds . . . destroying, capturing, or bypassing the enemy, and pressing"—he paused to find the correct word—"pressing recklessly on to the objective."[46]

The division did that, capturing Villedieu-les-Poêles the next day, August 1. While Luckett was leading the attack, Barton made the rounds of the nearby headquarters, including Boudinot's combat command and

Huebner of the 1st Infantry Division. At each stop the senior officers coordinated movement routes and sectors for clearing or blocking. That evening Barton returned to his command post. Then, after another staff call, he was off to corps headquarters to clarify future activities and back to Luckett and Rodwell to inform them of the adjustments to the plan. Everything was fluid, so coordination and communication were essential for the operation's success. The key to a successful division was helping its leaders do their jobs. Barton's veteran Ivy Division had acted as the spearhead for COBRA and had been hugely successful, doing all that Collins asked. [47]

As the armor divisions moved past, the 4th Infantry Division cleared the area of German soldiers and protected the corps' eastern flank from enemy attempts to interfere with its movement south. Barton spent the morning of August 2 at his command post coordinating these issues and then headed south to La Landerie, a farming community near National Route 799, the main road between Saint-Lô and Villedieu. When he arrived, Collins was waiting and the two discussed operations and changes. Barton went to Rodwell's headquarters near Villedieu and directed him to orient to the east to secure the eastern flank. He also told him to attach a battalion to Boudinot's Combat Command B, currently assigned to the 4th Division, to give it more infantry support. Rodwell selected Strickland's 3rd Battalion. Strickland was the only battalion commander remaining from the landing on June 6. As Luckett's regiment continued attacking south, Lanham's 22nd Infantry began returning from its assignment to the 2nd Armored Division. [48]

By August 3 Patton's Third Army had broken into open ground, and his divisions were heading west and southwest toward Brest, Nantes, and Le Mans. Hodges's First Army continued to attack to the east and southeast, generally toward Vire and the crossroads at Mortain. Alarmed by the American success, the German high command began to move some armored units from the Caen area south to prepare for a counterattack against the breakthrough. [49] Collins continued to rearrange his corps, consisting of the 1st, 4th, and 9th Infantry Divisions and the 3rd Armored Division north of Villedieu-les-Poêles. [50] Barton's 8th and 12th Infantries continued to adjust their positions and attack isolated German defenders south and east of Saint-Pois. Lanham's 22nd moved into an assembly area just south of the town to regroup after its recent attachment to the 2nd Armored Division. Task Force Boudinot, still assigned to Barton's command, would be dissolved and return to Watson's 3rd Armored Division.[51]

Now in a relatively stable phase, Barton hit the road to coordinate with the commanders and staff nearby. He started, as usual, with his regimental commanders. Barton spent time in each command post, sharing information from beyond the division and ensuring he understood their situation, then went to Boudinot's command post, where he and Leroy Watson discussed the armored command's operations and prepared to move it on its way. From Collins's perspective, Watson, a classmate of Bradley and Eisenhower, had not done well over the past week and should not have been commanding an armored division. Therefore, he contacted Bradley, and they decided to make the change. Within a few days, Maurice Rose, currently leading Combat Command A, 2nd Armored Division, would replace Watson. Barton spent August 3 at his temporary command post at La Beltiere, southeast of Ville-dieu. The next day, after checking his regiments, he joined Collins, McKee, and Troxel as they planned the next operation.[52]

Les Loges-sur-Brécey

For the first time since the middle of July, Barton had a good night's sleep on August 4–5. Now that the corps had paused the division's rapid offense, he had time to tour his sector, including visiting the division's prisoner-of-war cage, where he questioned a few Luftwaffe crews that American antiaircraft guns had shot down during the night. Then it was off to watch some of the local clearing engagements conducted by the 8th and 12th Infantries. Small German units occupied many of the local hills and wooded areas, and American infantry needed to find and eliminate these pockets before they could do some harm. Next, he met up with Buck Lanham and spent some time talking with him. Lanham had only been in command for a couple of weeks and had performed brilliantly over the last month. Barton needed to get to know him better, and so far he was impressed. Finally, it was off to his new command post at a little village, about two kilometers south of yesterday's temporary location, named Les Loges-sur-Brécey.[53]

After another quiet evening and a morning of catching up on the mountains of paperwork delivered by his adjutant general, Barton had lunch with Brigadier General Benjamin O. Davis. As the senior Black officer in the US Army, he was assigned to the War Department's Inspector General Office and was visiting the African American troops, mainly in supply units, in the battle area. Later in the afternoon, Barton encountered one of those units, an ordnance truck company, lost and heading straight for the German lines and being shot at by the enemy forces. He managed to stop the convoy, disengage it from a potentially dangerous fight, turn it around, and send it off in the right direction. On the way back to his headquarters, he ran into Brigadier General J. Leslie Kincaid, the future supervisor of the army's hotel system, who was searching for potential locations for the First Army's next command post. Back in Le Loges, Barton enjoyed a performance by a USO troupe.[54]

During the day, Leland Hobbs's 30th Infantry Division had replaced the 1st Infantry Division in the area around the town of Mortain, a market town in the southeastern Manche. While the road network is one reason for its importance, the other is its dominating terrain, Hill 314 and its small chapel to Saint Michel, from which observers can see Le Mont-Saint-Michel to the west and the approaches from Flers and Domfront to the east. The 2nd Battalion, 120th Infantry, 30th Infantry Division, occupied this critical location. During the night of August 6–7, the German army launched one of its most significant operations on the western front, Operation Lüttich. With elements of five panzer and two infantry divisions, the XLVII Panzer Corps headed straight for Avranches to cut off the American penetration. The German assault isolated the 2nd Battalion from the remainder of the 120th Infantry. For the next week, this surrounded battalion, supported by massive amounts of artillery and air attacks, beat back many assaults from the 2nd SS Panzer Division and its attached 17th SS Panzer Grenadier Regiment. The battalion held its ground, and its story has become one of the most celebrated US Army exploits during the campaign in France.[55]

Other than disrupting the American operation, the enemy's counteroffensive never had a chance. With only about 150 tanks, it did not have the combat power to do much more than hinder American operations. Moreover, Bradley and Hodges were unconcerned about its long-term prospects since the air power and artillery available to First Army ensured that the American lines would hold, and Patton's tank units were already advancing south of the penetration. Another reason for this confidence was the 4th Infantry Division along the north bank of the See River on the German offensive's right flank. Given its firepower, suitable terrain, and veteran leaders, there was little prospect of a German advance north. Once Barton realized what was going on, he moved his 8th and 22nd Infantries into position to secure all crossing sites. He also ordered his artillery into firing positions to deliver high-explosive rounds deep into the German penetration.[56] In the short term, Hobbs's 30th Infantry Division was hit hard by the assault near Mortain, and Collins ordered Barton to attach his reserve regiment, this time Luckett's 12th Infantry, to Hobbs's division as reinforcements. For the next six days, the regiment fought an intense series of battles against the German 117th Panzer Grenadier Regiment and the 2nd Panzer Division at a crossroads called Saint-Barthélemy.[57]

Meanwhile, Barton continued to adjust his lines and moved the 22nd Infantry east to connect its battle line with the 39th Infantry, Paddy Flint's old unit, which was now on the 4th Infantry Division's left flank. On the night of August 7–8, the regiment had difficulty defeating a German attack, but the division's 20th Artillery Battalion helped stop it. Collins attached this unit to the 4th Infantry Division to better coordinate artillery and air support. Barton and Taylor were soon on the way to its headquarters to ensure they coordinated the defensive fires and provided what it needed to maintain its defensive line.[58]

Once Parks Huntt selected the command post location at Les Loges-sur-Brécey, Captain Phillip Bragar and his 4th Signal Company established the headquarters communications. By 1944 a division command post had an impressive web of AM, FM, and wire lines, all integrated into a series of networks or "nets." A headquarters was responsible for establishing and monitoring each net connecting different units. For example, the 4th Infantry Division headquarters had separate networks for commanders, staff sections, fire support, logistics, and other special functions. Barton would monitor his command net when traveling, talking to Goodwin at the headquarters and Luckett, Rodwell, and Lanham in the field, from his

SCR-300 FM radio. But when his command center was operating, and he was back at headquarters, he could simultaneously listen to several different communications systems.[59]

By the evening of August 8, Bragar's soldiers had it operational with antennas in place and wire laid to key command nodes. The American dominance in artillery and communications now became apparent. That evening the 39th Infantry, now under Barton's direction, reported a German tank battalion of at least seventeen tanks attempting to bypass Mortain and move along the See River toward Le Mesnil-Adelée. Major David Condon, one of the artillery air observers, was soon on the scene, flying up and down the road as he looked for the tanks trying to evade his view. When he discovered some, he contacted the division's fire direction center and requested fire from the batteries in range. Once the explosive rounds landed, Condon would call back and ask for a subsequent mission, with adjustments to move the impact zone. This process repeated until the observer could report on the firing results. Barton could monitor artillery and ground radios simultaneously and get the reports as they arrived. As his aide wrote, it was one "of the most thrilling radio broadcasts."[60] The after-action report noted at least three tanks were knocked out, and the German attack stopped for the time being.[61]

By August 9 the VII Corps had a solid defensive line along the Seé in place with Eddy's 9th Infantry Division in the north, Barton's 4th Infantry Division (minus 12th Infantry) in the center, and Hobbs's 30th Infantry Division, reinforced by Luckett's 12th Infantry and Boudinot's Combat Command B, 3rd Armored Division, around Mortain. In addition, Major General Paul W. Baade's 35th Infantry Division was now part of the VII Corps, attacking on the 30th Infantry's right flank toward the southern portion of Mortain. Barton knew Baade (USMA 1911) from West Point and they were classmates at Fort Leavenworth from 1923–24. Meanwhile, informed from radio intercepts from the super-secret Ultra group and convinced that Collins had the situation in hand, Bradley kept Patton's Third Army attacking to the south and east of the German penetration, heading for Le Mans and Chartres. With the British and Canadian Armies attacking south from Caen, it would only be a matter of time until the Allies encircled the best German forces on the western front in what would become the Falaise Pocket.[62]

Now operating from his advanced command post at the village of Haut Travigny, just northwest of Saint-Pois, Barton's role was to arrange his portion of the battlefield and ensure his forces were tied in with Eddy's and Hobbs's divisions on either flank. The intent was to prevent the Germans from infiltrating through unguarded gaps and defeat their attempts to move to the main crossroads at Brécey. All day he drove throughout his sector, coordinating in person with each division and regimental commander. He and Collins talked several times and made temporary adjustments to ensure the line's integrity and support of the main effort around Mortain.[63]

Buais

While Barton and the division had the situation stabilized north of the Sée River, the 12th Infantry was fighting one of its most brutal battles at Saint-Barthélemy to the south. Hobbs had split the regiment, attaching Lindner's 3rd Battalion to the depleted 117th Infantry. For two days Hobbs had ordered the regiment, plus Lindner's troops, to continue attacking and regain some of the lost ground. The fighting between the regiment and the 2nd Panzer Division units was brutal. The Germans had an adequate supply of artillery and fired much of it at the crossroads, falling on Lindner's battalion.

At 07:00 on August 10, the 3rd Battalion was supposed to join in an assault to secure a crossroads. Lindner's soldiers, however, would not move. The young battalion commander visited his companies, trying to convince them to move forward, and but they would not comply. In addition, his soldiers asked him to stay away from them because they were convinced German forward observers were following him with fire. Although the veteran officers and noncommissioned officers claimed they were ready to move, his infantrymen were mostly replacements and refused to fight. Finally, at 11:00 Lindner reported to the 117th Infantry commander, "[My] troops absolutely will not budge." The immediate effect was that Hobbs called off the attack and ordered the 117th Infantry and Lindner's battalion to dig in and go over to the defense.[64] At 15:20, as Barton was heading to his new command post, Collins called and gave him temporary control of the 117th Infantry. Although the division's journal does not indicate what action its leaders took, most likely George Taylor was with Luckett and Lindner that afternoon. It was a temporary event, as the battalion was back in combat and performed well the following day. The regimental historian, who was the executive officer then, makes no mention of this incident in his narrative.[65]

Meanwhile, Barton was on his way to VII Corps headquarters at Villedieu-les-Poêles. Collins told him the division was to begin repositioning to the south of Mortain to rest and prepare for future operations.[66] He would move the division, minus Rodwell's regiment now attached to the 9th Infantry Division and Luckett's with the 30th Infantry Division. As they talked, Hodges, who was making his rounds of the First Army's corps, arrived, and Barton departed.

Back at Haut Travigny, he instructed Marr and Goodwin to prepare the appropriate movement order to get the division on the road. The new command post would be in the village of Buais, twenty miles south of Travigny and ten miles south of Mortain. This new location would facilitate the division's movement after the current fighting ended. On the way he visited Baade, whose 35th Infantry Division was attacking Mortain's southern area. Barton needed to ensure his division was moving clear of the advancing forces and occupying an assembly area that would not conflict with Baade's troops.[67]

Now that the German attack had ended, the entire Allied effort focused on eliminating German soldiers caught between the advancing Canadians in the north and Patton's Third Army moving east. The VII Corps continued to slide to the southwestern portion of the pocket. Collins's headquarters moved on August 11 to a village southwest of Le Teilleul and set up in the Château de Goué. This was a large home constructed on the top of an ancient castle. It was next to a large lake, suitable for fishing and ensuring the corps staff lived well.[68]

Barton, as usual, was on the road and headed east to the 22nd Infantry's command post and then forward to an outpost five miles from Domfront, which had been the German line of departure only a few days earlier. After spending time with Lanham, he returned to Buais. He met with Brigadier General Dole O. Hickey, whose Combat Command A, 3rd Armored Division, still part of VII Corps, was maneuvering through the new 4th Infantry Division's sector and preparing to counterattack the retreating German forces.[69] Stepping outside

Major General Barton holds a bouquet of flowers presented to him by a French girl, Buais, France, August 8, 1944. US Army photograph, Dwight David Eisenhower Presidential Library.

his compound, he encountered a small group of local citizens. Then, in a touching moment, a young woman came forward, and "a farm girl presented the General with a bouquet of flowers. She was very nicely dressed in new clothes and planted a kiss on him after presenting the posies."[70]

After this pleasant moment, his small command group displaced again, now a few kilometers east to the village of Le Teilleul on the road to Domfront. He was waiting for the return of the 8th and 12th Infantries, which Collins had restored to his control.[71] He was especially concerned about Luckett's command. While unable to influence the action, he monitored its operations carefully, as the division's operations log attests. It had filled the gap between the 30th Infantry's 117th and 120th Infantries for four bloody days. As noted earlier, the 3rd Battalion was attached to the 117th Infantry and took excessive casualties. In only four days, it suffered 1,150 killed, wounded, and missing, about 35 percent of its authorized strength. Almost all of these were combat infantrymen, and this unit would be essentially combat-ineffective for several days.[72]

Nantrail

As the 4th Infantry reassembled and began refitting, the remainder of the Allied armies encircled the withdrawing German army, between eighty and one hundred thousand soldiers, in a triangle marked by the towns of Flers, Falaise, and Argentan. Fighter-bombers and artillery poured over the area as units moved to cut off the withdrawal. While defeating this counterattack was one of Eisenhower's great successes during the war, it was not a complete victory. The inability of Bradley and Montgomery to effectively coordinate their operations allowed at least half of the nearly surrounded Wehrmacht to escape back to Germany. It exposed fractures among Allied commanders that were reflected in questionable decisions for the remainder of the campaign.[73]

Barton adjusted his command post again, moving down the road a few miles to a large farmhouse at Nantrail, not far from Le Teilleul. It was away from the town and its civilian and military traffic but nearby sufficient facilities to accommodate the division headquarters. The Red Cross detachment had caught up with the headquarters, and Barton took its director, Betty Schuler, out to visit the newly returned 8th Infantry, which had experienced a difficult battle when attached to the 9th Infantry Division.[74] Barton spent the next few days at his headquarters, resting from the physical and mental demands of the last month. Except for a short time near Carentan in mid-July, there had been no time for him to relax. As a result, his ulcer was causing him a great deal of pain, and Tubby often had to lie down to alleviate his symptoms. Hemingway, still under the illusion that he was acting as Barton's "irregular cavalry," witnessed his pain firsthand.[75] Meanwhile, Collins again decided to raid the division staff and moved Dave Goodwin from his post as division G-3 to be a deputy G-3, working for former boss Troxel. John Delaney, the deputy, assumed responsibility for this critical position.[76]

After two days of proper rest, Barton emerged from his van on August 14. The 12th Infantry's command group had just arrived, and he went directly to see Jim Luckett, whose command had suffered so much during its attachment to Hobbs's division. Undoubtedly, while we have no transcript of the conversation, the division commander wanted to know the mental status of the regiment's leaders. Since Lindner's troops had effectively rebelled, it would not have been unusual for Barton to relieve him as commander. That did not happen, however, and he would remain with his battalion. Although not mentioned in any narratives, Barton and Luckett probably transferred some of the battalion's lieutenants and sergeants to different units. Meanwhile its soldiers were finally able to relax and take advantage of hot showers, hot food, USO shows, and the "Famous Fourth's Red Cross doughnut girls."[77] Satisfied that Luckett had his command under control, Barton went to the division's small airfield, the base operated for the liaison and artillery aircraft. He wanted to recognize the superb job of David Condon and other members of the division's artillery in their defense of the Sée River line and defeat of the German tank probes. He was able to award several Air Medals and Silver Stars to those who did so much that day.[78]

On August 16 Generals Hodges and Collins arrived at the 4th Infantry Division's command post to pass out awards. It was an impressive ceremony as they presented many medals for battlefield performances in June and early July. Hodges pinned a Distinguished Service Medal on Barton in appreciation for his role in training and commanding the division. Collins awarded him a Silver Star for his heroism outside the Cherbourg airport back in June. The duo of senior commanders awarded a host of medals, including Distinguished Service Medals and Silver Stars for each of the battalion commanders and a host of Bronze Stars and other awards, about fifty medals in all, to recognize some of the many who had performed with distinction over the last few months.[79]

But there was still one issue Barton had to address: the refusal to attack by the 3rd Battalion, 12th Infantry. A few days later, on August 19, after the division recovered, Barton met with senior officers and staff to discuss the campaign's next phase. He took the time to discuss the attitude of "silent mutiny" that had recently affected some soldiers. He believed these men had decided that they were being "pushed around, that nobody cares about them, and they have decided that they are through and will quit trying." Of course, Barton would have none of that, and they had to take the missions, no matter how difficult, as they came. But he wanted his unit commanders to know that "whenever they were detached from the division, they could be sure he

Lieutenant General Hodges pins Distinguished Service Medal on Barton, Nantril, France, August 16, 1944. US Army photograph, Dwight David Eisenhower Presidential Library.

was using all his influence to get them back at the earliest possible date."
According to the division historian, Barton did not mention the 12th Infantry
by name, not meaning the discussion as criticism. But everyone knew what
Luckett and Lindner's commands had been through and how demoralized
they were when the regiment returned to 4th Infantry Division control.[80]

In the First Army's post-breakout reorganization, Bradley assigned the
4th Infantry Division to Gerow's V Corps. Collins, in his farewell letter to
Barton and his division, cited at the beginning of this chapter, acknowledged,
"The ability of the division to absorb almost two-thirds of its initial strength
in replacements and still be able to carry on and take every objective assigned
to it is a remarkable achievement and reflects great credit upon the Division
Commander, his staff and the entire personnel of the division."[81]

However, in his efficiency report, Collins rated Barton superior and
called him "a determined, tenacious fighter who has proven his ability to
command a division in action." Yet he still rated him as "about 75 among
150 Major Generals [that he personally knew]."[82] Since he only had six or
seven ever assigned to his corps, one wonders who the other seventy-five
successful major generals he encountered were. He did not need to explain
this remark, and it implied that Collins believed Barton was not among the
theater's best leaders and he was not qualified for corps command. We will
never know why Collins rated him thus, but it might be Collins's retaliation
for how Barton's mentor, Oscar Griswold, had treated him a year earlier. Was
it because of the incident with Roosevelt's Medal of Honor? We will probably never know. But it certainly had nothing to do with the performance of
Barton or his division on the Normandy battlefield.

Chapter 13

Paris and the Schnee Eifel, August–September

The aggressive courage, unselfish devotion, tenacity of purpose
and outstanding leadership of all ranks is evidenced by the fact that
the 4th Infantry Division has never failed to capture its assigned
objectives and has never lost ground to the enemy.
—Gerow to Barton, September 17, 1944

Rouairie, August

Eisenhower and his advisors never intended to capture Paris after the Allied breakout from Normandy. Indeed, the rapid pace of operations over the previous weeks reinforced that determination. The last thing SHAEF needed was for its divisions to waste away in intensive street fighting against a determined German defender. Associated considerations were the possibility of destroying one of the greatest cities in Europe and the additional costs of feeding and supplying the city's population. So all the senior leaders agreed that the best course of action was for the ground forces to cross the Seine River to the west and the Marne to the city's east and encircle the city. In their view the trapped German defenders would have few options if they chose to remain.[1]

The French, of course, had different ideas. As the Allied armies moved closer to the city, the various factions of the French Resistance were determined to impose a solution to end the city's occupation. Henri Rol-Tanguy, better known during the war as Colonel Rol, the Communist resistance leader, initiated a rebellion on August 14, as the Allied armies cleaned up the Falaise Pocket and headed toward the Seine. The next day the Paris Police began to abandon their posts and prepared to combat the German occupiers, and soon the city was in rebellion. By August 18 the French tricolor was flying over buildings across the city. Of course if the German Army, commanded in Paris by Dietrich von Choltitz, decided to subdue the rebellion, it would have little chance of survival. Most likely unknown to the Paris participants, two weeks earlier a similar uprising had broken out in Warsaw, Poland. By August 20 German forces had finished repositioning and began the city's elimination as the Soviet Army waited a short distance to the east.[2]

After extensive discussions with the Free French leader Charles de Gaulle and French emissaries from Paris earlier in the day, Eisenhower reversed his previous decision and ordered the army group commander to seize the city. Bradley flew to Hodges's First Army headquarters at Couterne, east of Domfront, early in the afternoon on August 22 and gave him the mission. Hodges assigned Gerow's V Corps to supervise the operation. The primary force would be Philippe François Marie Leclerc de Hauteclocque's 2nd French Armored Division. The division had arrived at the beginning of August, with its primary purpose to be the first Allied force to enter Paris. On the way it had contributed to the closing of the Falaise Pocket near Argentan.[3]

Bradley gave Hodges the mission of advancing on Paris. Since Leclerc's command was already part of Gerow's V Corps, he decided to keep that relationship. Gerow's command, streamlined for the mission of liberating Paris, now consisted of the 102nd Cavalry Group, the 2nd French Armored Division, Barton's 4th Infantry Division, and the normally assigned corps troops, including eleven battalions of field artillery. If Leclerc's forces had difficulties, he was confident that Barton's veteran unit would ensure the attack ended well. Gerow's mission was "V Corps will advance without delay on PARIS on two routes to a line of departure which will not be crossed prior to 231200B August, take over PARIS from the FFI (French Forces of the

Interior), seize the crossings of the SEINE south of the city and establish a bridgehead across the SEINE southeast of PARIS."[4]

Meanwhile, focused on restoring his command's fighting power, Barton was only partially aware of what was happening in Paris and at army headquarters. After the fighting near Mortain, the 4th Infantry Division had little to do but rest. Then, beginning August 17, it followed the VII Corps as it moved east, passing through the villages of Passais-Villages, Lassay-les-Châteaux, Pré-en-Pail, and La Doucelle, before arriving at Carrouges on the eastern end of the Orne Department, where the entire division assembled. For his headquarters he selected a small farm with a large house southwest of La Rouairie.[5]

Barton began his routine of visiting every headquarters within a few hours' drive. The first stop was to check in with Collins at his new command post at Château de la Motte, southwest of Argentan, and see what he could anticipate. There was little the VII Corps commander could pass on since the situation was still in flux as the forward troops cleared and closed the Falaise Pocket. With no guidance from above, Barton directed his commanders to train the replacements and prepare for new operations. He picked up another officer, First Lieutenant George F. Marable, to serve as a temporary aide, as he gave York a few days off to relax. As of August 21, after another meeting with Collins, McKee, and Troxel, Barton had no idea what the 4th Infantry Division's next mission would be. However, the following day he was making his rounds when Collins contacted him and told him he was now part of the V Corps and needed to prepare his command to move to Paris.[6]

Paris

Early the following day, August 23, Barton packed his gear and headed to Sées to confer with his new corps commander, Major General Leonard T. Gerow. A 1911 graduate of Virginia Military Institute, Gerow and Eisenhower became best friends during their 1925–26 year at the CGSS. The two spent the year studying together in the attic of Eisenhower's quarters at Otis Hall on Kearney Avenue. In addition, both became close with another classmate and associate of Fox Connor, Eisenhower's mentor, James L. Collins, who

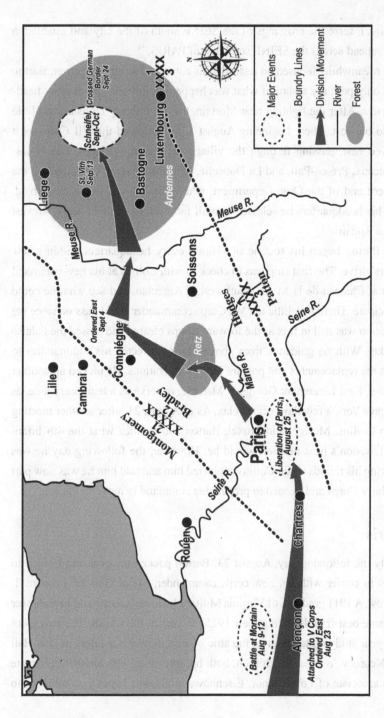

4th Infantry Division, August 9–October 30

lived nearby on Pope Avenue. It might be simply coincidence, but after their association with Pershing's former aide, both Eisenhower and Gerow got plum assignments, and their careers blossomed.[7] Now Gerow was Barton's commander. His orders were simple, approach Paris on the southern route, cross the Seine above and below Orly Airport, and be prepared to support the French 2nd Armored Division in seizing the city. He returned to his command post and issued his order that afternoon at 14:00.[8]

Barton and his command group headed east at 17:30 that afternoon, with Buck Lanham's 22nd Infantry in the lead. That evening the remainder of the division, carried by corps truck companies, departed at 19:00 hours and headed toward Paris. All night it rained as the march route took the division through Alençon, Bellême, and Courville. The convoy passed through Chartres, which Barton had last visited in 1919, but there was no time to stop. The rain soaked everything and everyone. Vehicles full of troops and supplies slid off the road, and maintenance crews had to spend many hours recovering them and their rain-soaked occupants. The convoy had to stop every three hours, allowing its passengers to dismount, stretch, and find a place to urinate or defecate. Back on the trucks, the soldiers were in high spirits, and few slept. Some believed their days at war were ending. In the early morning of August 24, Barton and the 22nd Infantry finished the road march and moved into an assembly area around Ablis, about twenty miles northeast of Chartres. The remainder of the division would continue arriving all day and be ready for an operation that evening if Gerow ordered it to move to Paris.[9]

After establishing his command post, Barton headed north to Rambouillet, where Leclerc had his headquarters. The French leader Charles de Gaulle arrived about the same time, but there is no evidence that Barton encountered him. However, he did spend some time talking to General Joseph Marie-Pierre Koenig, his military chief of staff. Meanwhile, the regiments near Ablis cleaned their equipment, took a brief rest, and prepared to move into the city when given the word. At 18:00 that evening, Barton moved closer to Paris to the ancient château of Bruyères-le-Châtel near Ollainville. He sent the 102nd Cavalry Group (with the 4th Reconnaissance Troop), which Gerow had attached to his command, to conduct a zone reconnaissance of the sector from his assembly area north to evaluate the roads and river crossing sites and locate enemy forces between his unit and the city. By the end of the day, his division had consolidated, recovered from the 145-mile night road march, and was ready to move into Paris.[10]

Meanwhile, Bradley, Hodges, and Gerow were frustrated with the inability of Leclerc's 2nd Armored Division to seize the city. The V Corps commander was also unhappy that the French division was disobeying orders and not remaining within its zone of action and crossing into the 4th Infantry Division's sector. Therefore, at 21:30 on August 24, Gerow ordered the 4th Infantry Division to Paris. Before midnight Barton gave his instructions to his commanders and followed up with Field Order #24.[11] Early the next morning, Delaney, who had been the G-3 for only ten days, sent the movement orders to the regiments. Gerow called Barton to corps headquarters at Limours nearby to get revised instructions, some that came directly from Hodges.[12] Luckett's regiment was the main effort in Paris. At 09:45 hours the 38th Cavalry Squadron, attached to the 12th Infantry mounted in trucks, passed through the Porte d'Italie. Behind the cavalry scouts, the unit moved in a column of battalions. By 11:05 4th Infantry Division soldiers were outside the Cathedral of Notre Dame. At 13:15 Luckett reported he had arrived at his objective, the Prefecture of Police in the center of Paris.[13] His regiment then occupied the Austerlitz, Lyon, and Vincennes railroad stations. Meanwhile, Rodwell's 8th Infantry moved onto Orly Airport, and Lanham's 22nd Infantry fought across the Seine at Corbeil, south of the city. Barton followed his regiment into Paris and then went to confer with Jim Luckett, who had moved with some of his troops to the Hotel de Ville. Everything had worked splendidly.[14]

Now Barton went looking for Leclerc, whose division arrived at about the same time. As was his style, he wanted to coordinate the dispositions of their respective divisions. Leclerc was having lunch at Prefecture of Police and, rather than inviting Barton to join him, held his napkin and appeared annoyed at being disturbed. According to an interview Martin Blumenson conducted with Barton ten years later, he "suggested that he go to the Montparnasse station." Barton, who did not like French officers, was irritated by his attitude and shot back, "I'm not in Paris because I wanted to be here but because I was ordered to be here."[15] Annoyed, Barton received word that

Gerow was at the Gare de Montparnasse and drove over and reported on the status of the division. While there, he briefly met with De Gaulle, who had just arrived in the city. While Barton was making his rounds in Paris, Marr moved the division's command post to Épinay-sur-Orge, south of Paris.[16]

Meanwhile, Luckett's 12th Infantry began clearing the city of German snipers and stay-behind troops. Over the next few days, the 4th Infantry Division continued to patrol Paris's eastern portion and help the local Free French units force the surrender of small pockets of Germans. Besides a few meetings with Gerow, Barton spent most of his time visiting his regiments and talking to his soldiers. Finally, on August 27, he moved to the Bois de Vincennes and set up his new command post, his thirty-first since landing on Utah Beach almost three months earlier. That afternoon the V Corps headquarters ordered Barton to return all truck companies to First Army control.[17] The next day the division began marching to the northeast, and Barton established his advanced headquarters at Montfermeil, north of the Marne and near the airport at Bourget. That afternoon Gerow called Barton back to corps headquarters. The situation was very fluid, and the corps commander wanted to give him directions to head to the German border.[18]

August 29 was the day of the big military parade in Paris. Gerow invited Barton, who brought his G-1, Garlan Bryant, and Jim Luckett from the 12th Infantry, which had done much of the heavy work inside the city. Almost all the principal leaders joined de Gaulle and Eisenhower on the reviewing stand, an upside-down Bailey Bridge, with Leclerc, Koenig, Bradley, Hodges, Gerow, and many others joining the reviewing party. Meanwhile, despite the celebration, Franco-American cooperation had not been especially good. Leclerc's actions toward Barton earlier were only one of many such incidents over the last week. Therefore, according to Eisenhower, when Charles de Gaulle asked him for two US divisions for support and to help him "establish his position," he declined. There was no possibility of him placing American troops under French command.[19]

However, he did order Gerow to have the 28th Infantry Division march through, rather than around, the city on August 29. Therefore, in full combat gear and ready to fight, the troops, tanks, artillery, and a division's equipment marched down the Avenue des Champs-Élysées. Those on the reviewing stand saluted at the appropriate times, and the troops kept marching. Within sixty days more than half of all the infantrymen marching that day would be killed, wounded, missing, or captured in the cesspool of the Hürtgen Forest. After the ceremony Barton returned to his headquarters after checking in with Rodwell and Lanham, who had taken care of their assigned sectors beyond the range of politics and inter-Allied drama.[20]

Over the next two days, the division slid to the northeast. Barton established new command posts on the way, first at Montgé-en-Goële, east of the modern Charles de Gaulle Airport, and then to Nanteuil-le-Haudouin. Finally, Paris was behind them, and now they were headed north. Most soldiers, and indeed the senior officers, believed the war was essentially over. The debate was exactly when, before or after the new year. Little did they know the 4th Infantry Division had some of its most brutal combat yet to come.[21]

Moving North

These were heady days for the Allies as they raced north across France. On August 15, while the drama in Paris was playing out, American and Free French forces landed on the Mediterranean. Within a short time, they had secured Marseille and Toulon and turned north. By September 1 Barton's friend Sandy Patch, now commanding the Seventh Army, and General Jean Joseph De Lattre de Tassigny's First French Army had seized Lyon. These two armies formed the 6th Army Group, commanded by Barton's war college classmate Jake Devers. In the west Montgomery's 21st Army Group, with the Canadian First and British Second Armies, had crossed the Seine and headed north toward the Somme River, where some of their senior leaders had fought in the previous war almost thirty years ago to the day. With Paris left to the French authorities to establish order, Bradley's Twelfth Army Group headed toward the center of the crumbling German line. Patton's Third Army attacked along the Loire in the east, and Hodges's First Army passed on both sides of the capitol, heading for the Belgian border. Finally, William Simpson's Ninth Army arrived over Utah Beach in early September, assigned to capture the port of Brest in Brittany. The Nazis appeared to all as on the verge of decisive defeat.

All the senior commanders believed they were now in a pursuit, "when the enemy is no longer able to maintain his position and endeavors to escape by retreat."[22] While this may have been true at the end of August, it was not a condition that would last. As the Soviets could attest, the Wehrmacht was the master of recovery and ad-hoc defenses. General Field Marshal Walter Model, a proven leader from the eastern front, took command of German Army Group B on August 15, as the Allies destroyed the Falaise Pocket. Two days later, with Hitler's relief of General Field Marshal Günther von Kluge, OB (Supreme Command) West Commander, Model took temporary command of the entire western front. After two weeks of evaluating the situation and arguing with Hitler, he received permission to establish the Third Reich's defenses along the old Siegfried Line along the border. The Reich's human, armament, and engineering resources labored to develop the abandoned fortifications and barriers into a comprehensive and viable defensive system. Behind the barrier belt, staff officers greeted retreating soldiers and units and hastily assembled them into an organized defensive force. By September 15, from the German perspective, the retreat was over.[23]

As the retreating German soldiers fell back on the resources of their new battle line, Allied forces moved increasingly farther away from their supply bases. As a result, logistics were in turmoil. The Germans successfully demolished the ports of Cherbourg, Le Havre, and Brest, which SHAEF badly needed to increase the unloading of cargo from the United States, Canada, and England. Even if the ports were operating, the preinvasion bombardment destroyed most of France's rail centers and tracks. As a result, resupply would be a problem for the next two months.[24]

In addition, operational deficiencies among senior leaders contributed to the Allied field armies' inability to exploit the German disarray. Although the German Army had demonstrated the value of straightforward operational design in the first few years of the war in France, the Balkans, and Russia, it had not become part of the Allied, primarily American, lexicon. Rather than identify an enemy center of gravity and mass forces to defeat it, Eisenhower directed what came to be known as the *broad front* approach to the campaign. He arrayed the three army groups and their armies online and advanced them toward the German border with little consideration of operational maneuver. While he identified that the left flank through the Netherlands was the main effort, he insisted his armies continue to attack across the entire front. While perhaps looking good on SHAEF maps, this approach prevented the massing of precious supplies and material where they could be used to best advantage.

Additionally, because of internal bickering among the senior commanders, especially Bradley, Montgomery, and Devers, nothing decisive would occur on the western front until December after the German counteroffensive in the Ardennes. Before that, both Devers and Montgomery urged Eisenhower to modify his operational approach, take advantage of opportunities to mass forces and exploit German vulnerabilities. In both cases Eisenhower rebuffed the army group commanders. Sadly, the lessons of Operation COBRA—such as mass, the concentration of force, maneuver, operational tempo, and unity of command—disappeared. With the minor exception of the failed Operation MARKET-GARDEN, well-designed large-unit thrusts gave way to all units attacking everywhere. While that might have been appropriate in August, by the middle of September, the German Army was in position on the Siegfried Line and waiting for Eisenhower's infantry assault. For the last eighty years, historians and military strategists have argued over Eisenhower's broad front approach.[25]

However, that was all in the future for the Allied forces moving north in early September. From Bois de Vincennes, where Barton had supervised the last activities in Paris, the 4th Infantry Division began to march northeast in the direction of Compiègne, where the Germans had signed their cease-fire on November 11, 1918, and the French signed their capitulation on June 22, 1940. August 31 opened with Jim Luckett's 12th Infantry moving on the left, Jim Rodwell's 8th Infantry on the right, and Buck Lanham's 22nd Infantry trailing as the division reserve. Gerow attached Brigadier General Eugene A. Regnier, Combat Command A, 5th Armored Division, to speed the advance. Around midday Regnier's tanks passed through the marching infantry, attempting to catch up with the retreating Germans. Unfortunately, it ran into the Retz Forest, a dense, ancient woodland that had not changed much in three hundred years. Small trails, a lack of bridges for water crossing, and a lack of maps conspired to disrupt the combat command's advance. By the end of the day, Ivy riflemen were walking past the immobile tankers. Regnier was very embarrassed at such a lack of progress. Barton told him to find a crossing site anywhere in his sector,[26] then returned to corps head-quarters in Paris to discuss the situation with Gerow. After that conference he decided to reorganize his forces to attempt to move quicker through the dense terrain. That night he and his staff prepared Field Order #29, designed to get the division moving.[27]

The new order for September 1 organized the division into two task forces, each commanded by a brigadier general. The pace of movement over rough terrain on a broad front required more decentralized control, so this advance against a withdrawing enemy made sense. Task Force Taylor, led by his assistant commander, consisted of Lanham's 22nd Infantry, a tank-infantry battalion from the 5th Armored Division (Task Force Burton), most of the 746th Tank Battalion, and the 4th Reconnaissance Troop. Its intended axis of advance was on the division's right flank on a line from Soissons to Coucy and then to Chauny. Task Force Regnier consisted of the remainder of Combat Command A, Luckett's 12th Infantry, and most of the 70th Tank Battalion. It was to cross the Aisne and Somme Rivers on the division's left flank, clearing the Compiègne forest as it advanced. Trailing the two combined arms teams was Rodwell's 8th Infantry. Barton broke his command post into two parts, a mobile command group so he could remain near the advancing regiments and the remainder at the division's rear.[28]

The terrain was the most significant obstacle since the German troops in the 4th Division's zone of advance had no intention of fighting but only of getting away to the developing defenses along the border. Furthermore, the G-2 report noted, "The advance was so rapid front lines, and enemy unit iden-tifications did not exist."[29] The advance was chaotic, as battalions sought to move as rapidly as possible. The rugged terrain and narrow roads in villages caused the troops to attempt some roads and trails, only to backtrack to find better routes.[30] Barton was moving to keep up with the advancing troops. He stopped to meet Gerow near Villers-Cotterêts on the National Route 2 to Soissons. That night, he continued to move toward Soissons, pulling off the road at the village of Cœuvres-et-Valsery for the evening.[31]

Despite everyone's best efforts, the advance on September 2 was slow. Narrow forest trails, numerous streams without bridges, and the occasional German roadblock ensured that the dismounted foot soldier set the pace for its advance. Barton struggled to meet Gerow's demands to move north rapidly. At 10:00 hours he sent out a broadcast to all his commanders. "Imperative you push on and accomplish mission tonight. You must brush aside or bypass resistance and get on. Charge riflemen and MGs with tanks. Take losses if necessary. Report desired from elements that bivouacked last night reasons for doing in face of orders to march during night. If to enemy resistance, rpt what kind, how much, your losses and steps taken to eliminate resistance. Barton."[32]

In addition to demanding his units keep moving, he was working on getting the required division and corps support elements, such as bridge and truck units. Despite enemy resistance, TF Taylor made good progress and by 17:30 had reached the commune of Landrecies on the banks of the Sambre River. However, Barton told Taylor to hold in place before he could cross the river. He had received orders from V Corps headquarters telling him to "halt advance your division on general line Landrecies-Le Cateau-Cambrai and await orders. Continue to close up your command during daylight hours." Barton had disbanded Task Force Regnier and returned it to the 5th Armored Division. It was not the kind of terrain that favored armored advances.[33]

Two issues were affecting the V Corps' advance. One was space, as the American and British forces were converging. As a result, Bradley ordered Hodges to slide to the east, toward Patton's forces moving into Lorraine. The other was the absence of fuel. It was simply impossible for the motorized American Army to advance for any long distance.[34] Gerow's instructions flowed down the chain of command that afternoon and evening. On the afternoon of September 2, Barton reported to Gerow, who, again, told him to consolidate and keep his division where it was. He should prepare to advance to the east as soon as the senior headquarters decided where they wanted contact with the Siegfried Line. Meanwhile, Barton established his next command post at Nampcel, southeast of Noyon. It was not the enemy that stopped the advance. It was the absence of sufficient fuel.[35]

As Taylor's task force assembled between Landrecies and Le Cateau-Cambrai on September 3, it occupied one of the German lines of retreat.

A convoy of a dozen vehicles and forty horse-drawn carts stumbled unaware into the American lines. It did not go well for the enemy, as the 22nd Infantry and its armored support wreaked havoc along the line. It took almost three hundred prisoners and killed so many soldiers and horses that the 4th Engineer Battalion had to bring bulldozers forward to clear the road so the Americans could use it. During the engagement, enemy fire had hit Lanham and Taylor with the same bullet. Fortunately for all involved, the round passed through the colonel's sleeve and then hit the brigadier's jacket, grazing his skin.[36]

Meanwhile, the remainder of the division moved to its new assembly area north of Saint-Quentin and occupied crossings on the Saint-Quentin and Canal de la Sambre. The division headquarters established its new command post, its thirty-eighth since Normandy, at nearby Urvillers. Harry Hansen's G-2 section finally had time to evaluate the enemy the division faced, and it amounted to an assortment of about five infantry divisions and the SS Hitler Youth Division. So far none of them had taken action to delay the 4th Infantry's advance seriously.[37]

After a conference with Montgomery and General Miles Dempsey, commander of the British Second Army, Bradley ordered Hodges to push east rather than continue north. He directed Gerow's V Corps to move on the right flank of the First Army as it headed toward Germany through Luxembourg, and ordered Collin's VII Corps, which had been consolidating south of Hirson, to advance on the left into Belgium toward Liege. Gerow ordered Barton to "alert your command for movement to assembly areas south and east tomorrow; orders will be issued later." Meanwhile, Barton told everyone to consolidate on the terrain he had assigned them and to remain alert. He also ordered his commanders to take a personal interest in fuel conservation.[38]

The Advance East

In twenty-four hours, according to the revised SHAEF plan, the First Army changed its direction of march from north to northeast. Rather than heading toward Lille and Brussels, it now had Aachen and Luxembourg in its sights. Rather than moving through a relatively open country that facilitated rapid maneuver, it entered some of the most challenging terrain in Europe. Within a box generally defined by the Meuse River to the west and north, the Mosel to the south, and the Rhine to the east lay a dark, dense, massive forest: the Ardennes. While armies can traverse this region, it is almost impossible to do it quickly, especially if the defender knows the attacker's approach. Planners at SHAEF intended to block it and concentrate forces to the north and south on the more reasonable routes into Germany. Indeed, as many accomplished students of military history have commented over the last eighty years, there was no need to trap one of the most powerful forces the US Army ever assembled within this region. Eisenhower's decision to overrule his planners and attack on a broad front without consideration of tactical and operational opportunities would be catastrophic for the First Army and the 4th Infantry Division.[39] An unjustified sense of impending victory and operational inflexibility among senior leaders allowed the Germans to reposition to stop the American advance.

On September 4 Barton used his time to rest his command, visit his units, and pass out awards and decorations. The division had run out of Bronze Stars, so he had to issue letters and other commendations. Later that evening he learned of the campaign's new direction and at 17:30 hours jumped into one of his Cub aircraft and flew to the corps command post for his detailed orders.[40] The First Army and its three corps would now demonstrate operational flexibility by rapidly shifting to the east. Within Gerow's V Corps, the 4th Infantry would move on the left, screened by the 102nd Cavalry Group, while Lunsford Oliver's 5th Armored Division advanced on the right flank. Norman Cota's 28th Infantry Division followed Oliver's troops. The first objective was to get across the Meuse River. Barton returned to his command post and began to issue orders. This veteran staff had little difficulty getting instructions to all divisional units.[41]

The Ivy division moved the next day from the area around Saint-Quentin and headed east. Marr's command post took the road through Guise to Tremblois-lès-Rocroi, on the edge of the Ardennes Forest and just west of the Meuse River. The sixty-five-mile journey, over small country roads in increasingly rugged terrain, took most of the day. Truck companies shuttled infantrymen to preclude their marching. As the command post departed, Barton and Delaney boarded their small Cub aircraft and flew to the corps headquarters for a quick discussion. Then they were back into the airplane and headed to Rimogne, three miles east of Tremblois, where he spent the night of September 5–6. During the movement, Barton had warned his commanders to be alert as German soldiers, individually and in small groups, continued to move through the area and shoot unprepared American vehicles. Meanwhile, on the other side of the Ardennes, Field Marshal von Rundstedt returned to command of German forces on the western front.[42]

The advance continued the next day. Colonel Cyrus A. Dolph III's 102nd Cavalry Group, now attached to Barton's command, operated an advanced guard between the advancing division and the Meuse River. It continued to clear the zone of Germans walking, on vehicles, and riding bicycles. Most were headed north, while the cavalry and Barton's troops traveled east, ensuring many unintended clashes. By 17:00 hours the division's headquarters was at Hargnies, across the Meuse and only a short distance from Belgium. Most bridges across the river were either too small or destroyed, so division and corps engineers began improving the local road network so that heavy vehicles and supplies could move into the new area of operations.[43] Meanwhile, Barton also returned Jim Luckett to the rear for a week's leave. Since Red Reeder's evacuation in June, he had commanded the regiment and needed to rest after an intense four months. Colonel Robert H. Chance, who had been one of Barton's battalion commanders in the 8th Infantry back in Georgia, had recently arrived at the 4th Infantry Division headquarters and was ready to assume command of the 12th Infantry. Barton trusted and respected Chance, so it would be an easy transition.[44]

Now across the Meuse, Barton's command continued its advance during the first week of September, but now it traveled even slower, thanks to the daunting Ardennes terrain, destroyed bridges, and a severe gasoline shortage. Rodwell's 8th infantry moved on the left of the zone and Chance's 12th Infantry on the right, with the 102nd Cavalry conducting an advanced screen in front of the marching regiments. Lanham's 22nd Infantry, which Gerow had temporarily attached to the 31st Infantry Division, trailed in trucks as the division reserve.[45] Barton drove throughout the zone, coordinating with his commanders and urging them on. Finally, at nightfall on September 7, he established his temporary forward command post in Graide, twenty-five miles into Belgium and deep into the Ardennes.[46]

As the Ivy Division had approached the Siegfried Line, the Germans became more aggressive, and artillery more accurate and coordinated. Barton spent much of the time with Bob Chance, an experienced officer but new to regimental command. Later, when he caught up with his command post, he told Marr to get the word out about returning empty five-gallon fuel cans, generally called jerry cans, back to supply channels. Soldiers were discarding them by the side of the road when empty. Given the theater-wide shortage, that was not a good policy.[47]

Over the next several days, the division continued to march east over the rugged Ardennes terrain. Unlike in friendly France, the closer the unit moved toward Germany, the greater the possibility became of civilians interfering with the American movement. Barton alerted his commanders to be prepared for civilian interference and noted, "Immediate and stern action will be taken against any civilian or groups of civilians who impede the progress of the division." He also ordered them to resume camouflage of unit areas, having all antiaircraft weapons sited and manned, and to improve their unit's state of alert. While reading the order, the impression was that the Ivy Division had become sloppy in the race to the border, and the veteran leaders needed to regain control. He traveled the forest roads through Libin and then to Saint-Hubert, Belgium. Since it was difficult to travel by Jeep to speak to Gerow, Barton spent much time in the division's small Piper Cub aircraft, flying from one grass strip to another. The V Corps was significantly overextended across a seventy-mile front.[48] In pursuit of the broad front operational approach, the senior commanders were taking risks.

Fortunately, the German Army was not yet offering serious resistance, and the American pursuit continued. During the second week of September, the 5th Armored Division's Combat Command A captured Luxembourg, one of Europe's great cities. The 28th Infantry Division passed Bastogne, and the 4th Infantry Division approached Saint Vith, two towns that would become famous the following December.[49] On September 11 Barton stopped in the village of Givroulle, deep in the Ardennes and northwest of Bastogne.[50] It had been an aggressive advance. However, the internal friction of Allied fuel supplies would be matched by an increasingly determined German defense, bringing the pursuit to an end.

The German Border

For several days the 4th Infantry Division would cross some of Europe's most rugged terrain. From Givroulle it advanced on all the trails and roads available on a northeast axis from Bastogne to Saint Vith, two of the most critical crossroads in the forest and the scene of some of the most intense combat during the German counteroffensive in December. A Belgian Maquis (resistance) group, escorted by a British Special Air Service operative named Frazer, checked into the division command post to let Barton's staff know what they were up to in the division's zone of advance.

Meanwhile, on September 11, back at the First Army Headquarters south of Charleroi, Gerow met with Hodges to discuss the V Corps. The two headstrong commanders argued for three and a half hours. Hodges's diary indicates it was an "occasionally rather tempestuous discussion."[51] Most likely the arguments were about supply and his orders to spread his corps over such a dispersed front. Before he left Gerow called his division commanders to meet him at the corps command post, now located northeast of Sedan. Barton flew by Cub aircraft for guidance and probably insight about Gerow's recent exchange with the army commander. Later, he again boarded his Cub, traveled to the temporary airfield at Bastogne, met up with Richardson and York, and then drove to his new command post at Beho, Belgium, only a few miles from the German border.[52]

As usual the regiments stopped for the night and prepared defensive positions. Then, per Barton's instructions, Chance's 12th and Lanham's 22nd Infantries sent out patrols to investigate the next day's movement route. For the last two weeks, Ernest Hemingway had been commuting between his digs at the Ritz in Paris and Lanham's command post at the front. Somehow, the famous author had the run of the American zone of operations. While Barton was too busy to spend much time with him, Lanham enjoyed the author's company, and he had been at the 22nd Infantry's headquarters for the last few days.[53]

Shortly before 21:30 hours, a reinforced combat patrol from the 22nd Infantry arrived on a plateau above the Our River that defined the Belgian-German border in that area. The Germans had already destroyed the small railroad bridge, but a path led down to what appeared to be a ford. Overwatched by two self-propelled tank destroyers and several Jeeps with mounted machine guns, Lieutenant C. M. Shugart led a small, dismounted patrol across the river and entered the nearby village of Hemmeres in the Rhineland-Palatinate region of Germany. The patrol encountered some civilians, who were probably surprised to see American troops in their town. Shugart then gathered some German soil and returned across the border. At 23:00 Lanham called headquarters to report this success, and Delaney's G-3 staff forwarded it immediately to corps headquarters. The division report noted, "This patrol is believed to have been the first organized allied unit to cross onto German soil during World War II."[54]

Meanwhile, events on the other side of the world now affected the V Corps' progress in the Ardennes. Gerow had been chief of the War Plans Division at the War Department in 1941 when the Japanese attacked Pearl Harbor. The Japanese aviators' success set off a howl in Congress. The investigation into the Pearl Harbor disaster began the following year. By the fall of 1944, the investigators had determined it was time to get Gerow's sworn testimony on record. He would turn over his command to Major General Edward Brooks, the 2nd Armored Division commander, on September 18 and travel back to Washington.[55]

On September 12 Barton started the morning by passing instructions to his commanders and staff. Then he sat down with V Corps Chief of Staff Colonel Henry J. Matchett, who was preparing his subordinate staff officers for the forthcoming change of corps commanders.[56] Meanwhile, Gerow, still in command, contacted Barton and gave him his orders. Barton passed them down: "Regroup units early tomorrow morning; recon in force to the east: Mission: Locate hostile fortified zone, determine hostile strength and dispositions; remainder of division be prepared to resume the march to the east on division order to be issued tonight or early tomorrow." He wanted patrols forward but did not want to get involved among enemy fortifications until they were ready.[57]

Once the orders were on the way, he left the command post to meet with Lanham. Together they crossed the Our and drove into Hemmeres. Barton believed he was the first Allied general officer to cross into Germany. Barton had to depart, but Lanham took Hemingway across. That night the

Barton drives his jeep across the Our River at Hemmeres, Germany,
September 12, 1944. US Army photograph.

regimental commander, Executive Officer Ruggles, his three battalion
commanders, the author, and Roosevelt's former aide and now public affairs
officer Marcus Stevenson sat down to dinner. Hemingway had confiscated
some chickens and wine, and a German woman offered to cook the feast.
Years later Lanham remarked, "The dinner in the farmhouse seemed the
happiest night of the war."[58]

The regiments continued to advance into Germany. Although resistance
was not stiff, it was stronger than it had been since the end of July. Troops also
knew the enemy artillery fire was becoming more accurate and intense.
Barton wanted troops to be cautious and advised his commanders to pay attention to the ground, reconnoiter displacement routes, and keep at least one-third
of the ammunition available to repel counterattacks. Barton moved the division
command post forward, first to Grüfflingen at about noon, and that evening to
a better location about three thousand yards east of Saint Vith.[59]

By the middle of September, Barton faced three significant problems as a division commander. The first was fuel and ammunition; there was very little for the 4th Infantry Division. Logistics shortages were a problem across the front but made worse by Operation MARKET-GARDEN; the Allied ground and airborne assault into the Netherlands was about to begin. Marr and DeYoung, the G-4s (Logistics), investigated every possible avenue for procuring as many supplies as possible. Secondly, the German Army was pouring reinforcements into the Siegfried Line defenses. Occupying the best terrain, these fortifications consisted of concrete pillboxes, entrenchments, concrete dragon teeth, wire, and mines. The often poorly trained troops occupying much of the zone were well armed with machine guns and other automatic weapons. Enemy frontline troops could count on supporting field artillery for the first time in months. In addition, first-class veteran units, reinforced by a few tanks, stiffened the defenders and executed counterattacks against American penetrations. Therefore, in fighting like that in the Bocage and Saint-Lô in July, every move had to be planned, with supporting fires and logistics in the right place. Decentralized operations were no longer possible, and every moment had to be coordinated by the division commander. Casualties increased, creating additional stress and fatigue among the division's leaders.[60]

Poor logistics and an increasingly competent enemy helped to complicate Barton's main problem: he was very sick. The constant demand to make life-and-death decisions, very little sleep, poor food, and excessive smoking inflamed his ulcer and left him in constant pain. Hal Blakeley, one of his best friends and supporters, noted that Barton was making bad decisions because of his illness. He was in too much pain to go forward. Gerow and Ed Brooks visited Barton at his headquarters as part of their change of command tour of the sector. The incoming corps commander had not seen Barton since before COBRA in late July and certainly became aware of his physical condition.[61]

On the ground the division continued to crawl ahead against increasing resistance, but it passed through portions of the Siegfried Line. The 12th Infantry was approaching a ridgeline known as the Schwarzer Mann, one of the highest points in the Eifel. In the south the 22nd Infantry was outside Brandscheid and had achieved an astonishingly quick penetration of this thinly defended sector of the Westwall. Now it appeared an excellent opportunity to exploit the advance.[62] Barton tried to exploit the gap, committing Rodwell's regiment to enter the seemingly open border. But the division was spread out too far, and German soldiers infiltrated between the advancing Americans, slowing the advance even more. Enemy resistance increased, as indicated by more counterattacks, infiltration between units, and artillery pounding the frontline troops. Barton was not happy with the way the fighting went. However, he had three veteran and competent commanders, so if the division could not progress, he knew it was not because of their leadership.[63]

On September 14 Barton talked to both Brooks and Gerow again. Most of it was about the fight in the forest. But behind the scenes the outgoing and incoming corps commanders must have been discussing their subordinate's health. Most likely they contacted Hodges to discuss the situation. Now began a series of personnel moves as the First Army used this potential change to reshuffle leaders as it prepared for what everyone believed would be the march to the Rhine. At Collins's request one of the first changes would be sending his chief of staff, Richard G. McKee, to the 4th Infantry Division to replace Jim Rodwell, who was about to be promoted to brigadier general. In McKee's place Colonel Richard Partridge, the VII Corps G-3 on D-Day and one of the corps commander's favorites recovering from his wounds in Normandy, would assume these duties.[64]

Fighting the next day, September 15, was brutal as the Americans clashed with defenders reinforced by the 2nd SS Panzer Division. While not the quality unit the Americans faced in Normandy in June, its veteran leaders effectively stopped the 4th Infantry Division's advance. It also brought a small number of tanks that improved the German ability to counterattack. Therefore, on September 16 the Ivy Division could not advance farther. German artillery continued to be effective and, in one instance, hit a group of soldiers from the 1st Battalion, 22nd Infantry. The shelling wounded thirty-five and killed sixteen. Among the dead was 26-year-old Lieutenant Colonel John Dowdy, who had been with the regiment since his commissioning. He originally took commanded on June 27 but was wounded on June 28. He had returned to command only two weeks earlier. He was one of Barton's favorite officers, and his death must have contributed to his depressed condition. Robert Latimer, his executive officer, assumed command of the battalion.[65]

On September 15 Barton moved his command group to Auw bei Prüm in Germany. However, German resistance, counterattacks, and artillery fire made it untenable. That night, because of its exposure to hostile artillery, he ordered it back to Belgium to a location near Schönberg, Belgium. As the division historian noted, it was "the first retrograde movement it [the division] had made since Carolina [maneuvers]." Unfortunately, the hasty retrograde also created fits for Blakeley and his artillery, and he protested the redeployment. It was one of those questionable decisions he commented on years later.[66] George Taylor took a more prominent role in the command decisions and went to V Corps' headquarters to argue for halting the attack, especially toward Brandscheid. With his health failing, Barton appears to have lost his drive. He had also lost control of the division, issuing orders that were militarily unsound. The result was an increasing casualty list that undoubtedly affected his decision-making ability. With the corps commander's approval, Barton issued orders to stop the advance.[67] The last week had been costly as the division transitioned from a pursuit to a series of deliberate attacks it was unprepared to conduct. Almost 950 casualties were the price of one week of combat.[68]

Hospitalization, September 19–October 4

On the way back to Schönberg from a visit to Lanham's headquarters, Barton got caught in an artillery barrage and had to take cover. He was becoming careless as he fought off his stomach discomfort. When the artillery briefly stopped, he discovered his Jeep was still working, jumped in, and managed to drive through the fire and back to safety. When he returned to headquarters, he had two messages from Gerow. One was a letter, cited at the beginning of this chapter, thanking him for his dedication and professionalism. The second was a message telling him to report to the local hospital for an evaluation and to plan on being away for more than a few days. That night Dick Marr notified all regimental commanders to report to headquarters at 08:00 the next day, September 18.[69]

After the meeting, in which Barton informed his team that he was departing, he headed down to see Gerow, who had not yet passed the command to Brooks, at the V Corps command post in Luxembourg City. The two had a long talk; most likely it was about Barton's health and not the military operation. He then returned to his headquarters at Schönberg and waited. Finally, at noon Brooks took command of the V Corps, and at 20:00 he called and ordered Barton to stop by his headquarters the next day and then travel to the 44th Evacuation Hospital in Saint-Hubert. Brooks told him that his good friend and former 8th Infantry commander Jim Van Fleet would be his replacement.[70]

Appearing tired and in obvious pain, Barton gathered his principal leaders on the morning of September 19 and told them he was going to the hospital. He did not indicate that he would be away for more than a few days. However, Generals Gerow, Brooks, and Hodges had other plans. When he arrived at Saint-Hubert, the hospital commander, Colonel (Doctor) John F. Blatt, and the First Army Surgeon, Colonel (Doctor) John A. Rogers, were waiting. The three met for a long time, giving the two physicians time to assess Barton's health and physical state. At the end of the meeting, which included dinner, Rogers ordered Barton to report to the American Hospital near Paris and spend the next six weeks resting and recovering. The surgeon's directive would essentially end Barton's tenure as the 4th Infantry Division's commander. His protests did not affect Rogers, whose decision had Hodges's and Bradley's full support.[71]

Anticipating the medical decision, Bradley arranged for Eisenhower to release his G-3 and Barton's old friend Harold R. Bull to assume temporary division command. Bull was a superb staff officer whom Eisenhower depended on, but this would be his only opportunity to lead a division. Unfortunately, Eisenhower would only loan him to the First Army, so Bradley ordered Van Fleet, now serving as assistant commander of the 2nd Infantry Division, to return to the 4th Infantry Division as its next permanent commander.[72]

Barton's first day on hospitalization status was on September 20 and began with visits from the 4th Division's personnel and administrative staff. By late morning he had taken care of all the administrative and judicial actions that went with being a division commander. Then, after an early lunch at the 44th Evacuation Hospital, he departed for Paris. His return route took him through Sedan, Reims, and Meux. Finally, at 19:15 he arrived at the American Hospital in Neuilly-sur-Seine, less than two miles northwest of the Arc de Triomphe. The army had taken over this fine American-financed facility in August, ejected its German collaborating director and staff, and replaced it with the 350th Station Hospital. It was one of Europe's best military hospitals under American control and a fine place to rest worn-out generals.[73]

On Barton's arrival the hospital commander greeted him and turned him over to the staff, who assigned him a room, sent him to "supper, and put him to bed." It was his first night without any responsibilities since the war began. Meanwhile, back at the division, Bull, Van Fleet, and McKee all arrived at Schönberg. Harold Bull would take temporary command the next day. A couple of days later, Van Fleet brought McKee down to the 8th Infantry and started the transition between him and Rodwell.[74]

Of course, Barton began plotting his return after he had a few undisturbed nights of sleep and several days of healthy meals. He dispatched his trusty aide, Bill York, to SHAEF to see what he could arrange for his restless boss. York met with Colonel Ford Trimble, the secretary to the general staff, who was instrumental in gaining access to anyone in the command group. Trimble introduced him to Major General Albert W. Kenner, the SHAEF's chief medical officer and the most influential physician in Europe. Somehow, York convinced Kenner to get him access to daily war room briefings and convinced him to visit Barton at the American Hospital. Kenner came by that evening, and the two generals talked for a long time as Barton made his case for returning to the front.[75]

Meanwhile, Barton could enjoy Paris between resting, eating well, and politicking to return to command. He went shopping and bought some rugs and perfume for Clare. Tubby also had the opportunity to visit Countess Grace de Lesseps, widow of the aviation pioneer Jacques de Lesseps and daughter of a Canadian railway entrepreneur, for a pleasant afternoon tea. He also ate and drank with Hemingway, who was back in Paris at the Ritz. Ernest was in trouble, as the European Command investigated him for his conduct before the liberation of Paris in August. By most accounts he was too free and easy with his role as a civilian journalist.[76] Van Fleet took command of the division on September 30, prepared to lead it forward. But it was not to be.[77]

Soon after taking control, he visited the regimental and separate battalion commanders, many of whom were his old friends from years of serving together. He gave each a gift of a few cognac bottles that he had accumulated over the last few months.[78] He had received a warning order that the 4th Infantry Division was returning to the VII Corps and had dispatched reconnaissance parties to begin checking out the new area.[79] But in Paris Barton was doing more than simply touring monuments and museums, visiting old friends and his hangouts from his early time in Paris, such as Harry's New York Bar. Instead, he was actively politicking his doctors and the chain of command to let him return to the Ivy Division.[80]

As Van Fleet settled in, Barton visited SHAEF in Trianon Hotel in Versailles on October 2. His first meeting was with Harold Bull, who had just returned from the front and was back in his job as Eisenhower's G-3. Bull gave him a thorough report on the division, and then they went to lunch. Bull was a good contact to have at the senior Allied headquarters. Barton then encountered Eisenhower's chief of staff, Lieutenant General Walter Beedle Smith, Bull's boss. Smith, a crusty, no-nonsense staff officer, was probably tired of Barton's maneuvers to get back to the field. Nevertheless, he acquiesced to Barton's request to leave Paris and visit Bradley at 12th Army Group Headquarters, now in Verdun. Barton then returned to Neuilly-sur-Seine to spend his last night in the hospital.[81] The next day he departed Neuilly at 07:45, joining the troops, supplies, and equipment columns moving north. He passed through Meaux, Château-Thierry, and Sainte-Menehould, arriving just after noon. Barton reported to Major General Leven Allen, Bradley's chief of staff and an acquaintance from Fort Leavenworth and Benning. Allen called Bradley, who was making his rounds of the battle area, who told Allen to keep Barton there until he returned. That night Barton slept in the army group's staff billets.[82]

Bradley would not arrive until the afternoon of October 4, so Barton, York, and Richards toured the Verdun battlefield. Barton also visited Fort Douaumont, the nearby cemetery, and the Trench of the Bayonets. He got word that Gerow was returning from Washington and headed back to army group headquarters to meet him. No one yet knew if Bradley would give him back his corps, so both generals had come begging for their old jobs. Gerow and Barton met before their commander returned, and both must have had much to discuss. After returning, Bradley spoke with Gerow first, told him he would return to V Corps, and wanted his opinion on Barton's future. One suspects Bradley would have supported his corps commander in whatever he desired, and Gerow apparently wanted Barton back. After a lengthy conversation with Barton, Bradley reassigned him to his old division. Soon after issuing orders for a division attack to occur a few days later, Van Fleet learned he was on his way out. While Van Fleet was disappointed with the decision, Bradley took care of his classmate and gave him command of the 90th Division within a few days.[83]

Usually a division commander has his choice for a deputy, and with Rodwell now a brigadier, the choice was easy. Within days Rodwell would return to the Ivy Division, replacing Taylor, who would return as the assistant commander to his old unit, the Big Red One.[84]

Barton's two weeks in Paris did not cure him of his stomach problems but only gave him a temporary respite from its painful effects. He had not had sufficient time to heal. Moreover, his campaign to hastily return to the division had several long-term consequences. Barton's return spared Van Fleet the trauma of commanding the division in the Hürtgen Forest, an event that might have affected Van Fleet's rise to four-star command. Another few weeks of rest would also have put Barton in position for corps command, several of which opened up after October. Pete Corlett, John Millikin, Manton S. Eddy, Leonard T. Gerow, Raymond S. McLain, and Lucian Truscott departed their corps positions after Barton's release from the hospital and before the end of the war. All his senior commanders knew he was a fighter, and a healthy Major General Barton would have been on Bradley's shortlist, despite Collins's less than glowing efficiency reports, to fill one of the slots that would open up in the next few months. Indicating the need for corps commanders, Van Fleet, who only briefly served as division commander in the 90th Division, assumed command of the XXIII Corps in March.[85] Because of his haste to return to the 4th Infantry Division, he would never have the opportunity for corps command. As the next few weeks would demonstrate, Barton was not well. Returning him to combat so soon was a poor decision by all concerned.

Chapter 14

The Hürtgen Forest, October–November

*Quentin and I have been reading the news accounts of your division
with the greatest interest. What a tough time you must have had!
I do hope you are now having a rest. Few people in civilian life
can possibly realize the fortitude necessary for this kind of fighting.
Apart from the danger existing at all times, the great discomfort
and fatigue must be terrific, especially when it goes on for so long.
Our thoughts are with you all the time, in pride and sympathy.*
—Eleanor Butler Roosevelt
December 14, 1944[1]

Büllingen

With Barton's return senior leaders began to say good-bye or introduce themselves to the commanders of regiments and separate units. In command for only a few days, Jim Van Fleet made a cursory visit to each headquarters to say good-bye. Leading the 4th Infantry Division, where he had served so many years, was a dream. But he was too good for Bradley to leave on the bench, and in early October he took command of the 90th Infantry Division and led it through the end of the war.[2] With Jim Rodwell's return, George Taylor moved to his old unit, the 1st Infantry Division, and served as its assistant commander until his retirement in 1946.

After he met with Bradley on October 4, Barton spent the night in Verdun. The following day he was up early and traveling back to his division. His first stop was at Saint Vith for lunch with the officers of the division's rear echelon and the logistics and personnel management staff, then V Corps headquarters at Mirfeld. Major General Brooks had not yet departed, so the two discussed what had happened over the last two weeks and the future plans. Then he was off to the small Belgian town of Büllingen, where the division head-quarters had relocated during his absence. Barton spent his first day back calling his regimental commanders, meeting with staff officers, and adjusting to being back in command. He said good-bye to Van Fleet and Taylor and welcomed Jim Rodwell back to the division. The two had worked together for so long, and Barton could, without question, trust "Roddy's" loyalty and judgment. It was the same for Hal Blakeley, who had run his artillery since before D-Day, and Dick Marr, who remained his chief of staff.[3]

Without question it was the strongest command team he had worked with. Jim Luckett was a superb leader who knew how to get the most out of their troops. He had mentored Luckett since he took command of the division and watched him blossom as commander of the 12th Infantry Regiment. He had done well, but he and his regiment still bore the scars from the fighting near Mortain. Barton's other two commanders, Lanham with the 22nd Infantry Regiment and McKee now leading the 8th Infantry Regiment, were Hodges's protégés. Although Barton and Lanham often argued, Lanham was a solid, if not overly dramatic, leader who would get the most out of his regiment. Lanham was glad to see Barton back with the division but told his wife he was not following the doctor's orders on taking care of himself. But, he noted, "Tubby at his worst is better than a lot I know at their best."[4]

McKee was somewhat an unknown element as a commander, but he and Barton had known each other for a long time, beginning with the occupation at Coblenz and, more recently, his role as VII Corps chief of staff. However, McKee had never been in combat, so he needed a strong executive officer. Lieutenant Colonel Erasmus H. Strickland, the former 3rd Battalion commander, fit that role. He had recently returned from the hospital after recovering from wounds he received on COBRA, and everyone knew of his bravery and aggressiveness. Assigning him as McKee's executive gave the new commander a connection with the earlier fighting and an experienced hand in managing the staff, interacting with higher and adjacent teams, and supporting the combat battalions.[5]

Without active combat Barton settled into a routine of visiting his regimental command posts, artillery headquarters, and most independent battalions every day or two. He spent much time with McKee, who would be facing his first test of battle. He visited or welcomed commanders and staff officers from other commands whenever he could. These included Gerow, who was back in control of V Corps and, like Barton, pushing training and recreation since they had no active mission. In nearby Saint Vith, he had lunch with his friend Walt Robertson, still commanding the 2nd Infantry Division, and later with Norm Cota (USMA 1917), the 28th Infantry Division commander. Army Chief of Staff General Marshall arrived on October 8 and visited the troops, which was always a significant event for a frontline unit. Newspaper reporters often found Barton at the division headquarters, especially Hank Gorrell, a reporter for the United Press, who managed to occasionally show up for lunch or dinner. He also dedicated time for the Red Cross Chief Betty Schuler, who provided so many services to his soldiers, and took her on tours of the frontline units, to places where her assigned vehicles could not go.[6]

Background

Meanwhile, Barton got informal notification that his division would soon return to the VII Corps as part of Bradley's attempt to drive from Aachen to the Rhine: Operation QUEEN, conducted by both the First and Ninth Armies. Collins's VII Corps would be General Hodges's First Army's main effort to breach the Rur River line that blocked the route to Köln. On his main avenue of approach, called the Stolberg Corridor, Collins arrayed Allen's 104th Infantry Division on the left and Huebner's 1st Division on the right, supported by Maurice Rose's 3rd Armored Division to the rear. Each infantry division had a sector about two miles wide, narrow enough for the initial penetration, as the main effort. However, unlike the successful Operation COBRA, Collins had no infantry behind these two divisions to help fight through the defenses and urban terrain and open the way for Rose's 3rd Armored Division. The veteran 4th Infantry Division would have been the right unit to widen the penetration and pass the tank division forward. However, one of Collins's problems was the dense Hürtgen Forest on his right flank. He had no idea what the Germans had deployed inside the woods. Since it only had a few routes out of the woods into the corridor, a good, doctrinal, answer would have been to use Tully's 4th Cavalry Group as a flank guard to block any interference from Germans lurking in the Hürtgen Forest.

Sadly, Collins decided to conduct a frontal attack, into the dense, almost impassable terrain. He also wanted to bridge the more than ten-mile gap between the 1st Infantry Division and V Corps to the south, ensuring the attacking division would occupy a front four or five times wider than US Army Doctrine prescribed. The woods would also mitigate against conducting pre-assault reconnaissance, massing armor, precision artillery, or air support, all of which generally made American attacks effective. The corps commander gave this nearly impossible task to Barton's 4th Infantry Division.[7]

Collins's instructions to Barton were relatively vague. The 4th Division:

1. Will attack in conjunction with the 1st Infantry Division on its left to seize crossing on the ROER [Rur] River.
2. Will make its main effort on its right (SOUTH) flank.
3. Will assist the advance of 1st Infantry Division on its left.
4. Will continue the attack within SOUTHERN part of Corps zone of action to seize KÖLN. (Details of attack EAST of ROER will be issued later.)[8]

Collins was sending one of the best combat units in the United States Army into an almost impossible patch of woods, on a broad front, without an attainable objective (seize a river crossing more than ten miles away), and in divergent directions! In his almost daily memos, Collins indicates that neither he nor anyone from his staff understood the nature of the terrain or how the Germans intended to defend it. As the authors of a history of the 4th Division noted, "The commander of VII Corps, would often insist to his fellow officers and subordinates that terrain was all important in any offensive or battle, but sadly he would neglect his own advice when he sent VII Corps into the Hürtgen Forest."[9]

Repositioning and Wasting the 12th Infantry

Barton's battle in the Hürtgen Forest began on November 1, when Gerow, also recently back in command, met him for lunch. Several days earlier Hodges had ordered him to send Norm Cota's 28th Infantry Division to clear the Hürtgen Forest before the beginning of Operation QUEEN later in the month. Although a previous attempt at penetrating this massive forest by the 9th Infantry Division had turned out badly, the First Army commander determined his best course of action was to send his infantry into the woods to clear it rather than block it.[10] Since the 4th Infantry Division was still assigned to the V Corps, Gerow directed Barton to conduct a demonstration in support of his main attack. It would consist of patrols, raids, and artillery strikes to confuse the German defenders.[11] Such a mission was not especially complex, and Barton spent the first evening in November with his staff at a steak dinner in the Hotel Malmedy in Büllingen.[12]

Barton continued to make the rounds for the next few days, visiting each regiment's headquarters and measuring the readiness of his commanders. Finally, after one visit to the 12th Infantry Regiment, he typed up a memorandum concerning Jim Luckett and filed it with his personal papers. The 37-year-old colonel had been in command the longest, and the note probably contained Barton's thoughts on his next step, probably a promotion. But there is also some indication that he and Barton's relationship was becoming strained, the result of both commanders' exhaustion from more than five months of combat. No matter, with Colonel Bob Chance still at headquarters, Barton had some options regarding his senior regimental commander.[13] Meanwhile, Cota's 28th Infantry Division began to move into the Hürtgen, and its liaison officer reported that things were going well.[14]

On November 4 the First Army formally alerted the 4th Infantry Division that it would be assigned to VII Corps effective November 8. Shortly after receiving the alert, Barton visited each of the regiment's staff sections.

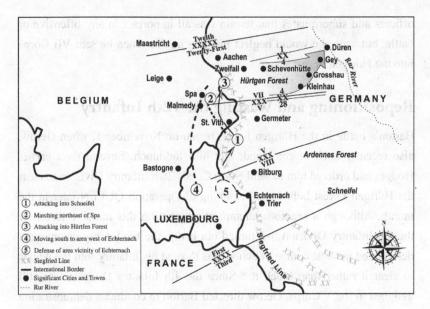

4th Infantry Division, October–December

It had been three months since the command had worked for Collins, so it was essential to remind them of the differences between Collins and Gerow.[15] At their final meeting before he departed, Gerow told Barton he was sorry to see him go. He gave Barton an efficiency rating that placed him among the top third of the generals he knew, rated him as superior in performance and knowledge, and recommended him for corps command.[16] He also gave him a personal letter that ended with, "It is without reservation that I say you have a hard fighting, smooth functioning division. I accept its loss to this command with regret."[17] Meanwhile, the news from the 28th Infantry Division continued to be good as its liaison officer reported the capture of another key town. However, Barton noted that enemy tanks were driving one of the regiments back from their forward outposts by noon. It was an ominous sign since they had not encountered German armor, in any quantity, for several weeks.[18]

On November 5 soldiers from the 9th Division exchanged places with their comrades from the 4th Division, who pulled back to temporary assembly areas and waited for the truck companies from the V and VII Corps to move them north to their new sector.[19] Meanwhile, Barton monitored the alarming reports from the 28th Infantry at his command post. The situation was getting worse, and it was now in contact with the veteran 116th Panzer Division, which had been preparing for Hitler's December offensive but diverted to block the Americans. Rough terrain, enemy defenders, and armored counterattacks were rapidly defeating Hodges's operation.[20]

The situation changed the next day, November 6, as the Ivy Division began its relocation to the 7th Corps Area. It was now apparent that the 28th Infantry Division was in trouble. Two more German infantry divisions had joined the 116th Panzer Division and were driving Cota's troops back. That afternoon Gerow contacted Barton and alerted him that plans might change.[21] Although not indicated in Barton's or Hodges's diary, there must have been a conversation between Hodges and the two corps commanders since Barton's division was transitioning from one corps to the other. When Hodges ordered him to send a regiment to support the 28th Infantry Division, Barton chose Jim Luckett's 12th Infantry since he was his most experienced commander and his regiment was already positioned on the 4th Infantry Division's right flank. Luckett met with General Cota in the early afternoon, who ordered him to relieve the 109th Infantry Regiment on the plateau north of the village of Germeter as soon as possible.[22]

Barton was proud of how Luckett reacted and how quickly he moved to relieve the battered 109th Infantry Regiment. However, a concern for him, Delaney, and Marr was that they had been preparing for the Ivy Division's main attack and had anticipated a combat-ready 12th Infantry Regiment. Based on previous experience over the last five months, they realized that might not be true. However, Collins expected that Barton would get Luckett back soon and in good shape, so he did not change his plans.[23]

So as the 12th Infantry began its struggle in the woods, the rest of the 4th Infantry Division moved into its assemble area centered on Zweifall on the western edge of the Hürtgen Forest and southwest of Aachen. The headquarters commandant, Parks Huntt, moved the command post to the town and took over the recently vacated local Nazi headquarters. He evicted a few German families seeking shelter and set up the command post. Ernest Hemingway, who had abandoned his digs in Paris, had rejoined the division and took over a house nearby. He spent most of this operation with

Buck Lanham's 22nd Infantry command post, located nearby. He also visited Barton on many evenings during the battle.[24] Meanwhile, the soldiers from the 8th and 22nd Infantries continued to move at night in the rain and on muddy roads. At one point thirty-one of the 8th Infantry's vehicles slid off the road, with two turning over and sending six soldiers to the hospital.[25]

On November 8 Barton checked in with Norm Cota and discussed the battle and especially the situation with the 12th Infantry. He then went to see Luckett at the front. There was little Barton could do since he had no authority with the regiment working for the 28th Infantry Division. All he could do was listen and promise to try to get Luckett the assistance he needed. However, nothing was going right; the Germans stopped Luckett's infantry attacks, and he could not get his supporting tanks or tank destroyers into the fight.[26] Meanwhile, Barton visited his other regiments and worked with his staff to prepare for the main attack, Operation QUEEN, which would begin in a few days.[27] But the physical and emotional cost of two separate but related actions were taking a toll on Barton and aggravating his recently subdued ulcer. He knew that, only a few miles away, Luckett was protesting an order to conduct an unfocused attack on either side of a plateau. He believed it made no tactical sense and would result in needless casualties. Cota's response was that it was to "be pushed at all costs."[28]

As Luckett predicted, the 12th Infantry's attack on November 10 did not go well. With a frontage of over four thousand yards in hilly and forested terrain, it was relatively simple for the enemy to infiltrate between his battalions. Throughout the day the individual companies from the 2nd and 3rd Battalions had to fight isolated battles as Germans attacked from all sides. At one point Lieutenant Colonel Franklin Sibert's 2nd Battalion command post came under assault, and the battalion commander and his headquarters company defended it with their small arms. At the end of the evening, Luckett had four of his companies isolated and his 2nd Battalion ineffective and incapable of offensive action. That night the V Corps released the 12th Infantry back to Barton's control, and he sent his G-3, John Delaney, to help get Luckett's regiment back to the division. Meanwhile, Barton spent the day at the VII Corps command post at Kornelimünster with Collins and the division commanders. After the conference, rather than concentrate on the 12th Infantry that needed

General Dwight D. Eisenhower and Barton discuss tactics in the Hürtgen Forest, November 10, 1944. US Army photograph.

his attention, he had to host a meeting in Zweifall with Eisenhower, Bradley, and Collins, looking for briefings on the 4th Infantry Division's role in Operation QUEEN. Then he had to meet with Rodwell, Marr, Lanham, and McKee to ensure they knew all the details of the main attack.[29]

Not until November 13, after heavy fighting, was Luckett able to establish a coherent defensive line on the 4th Infantry Division's right flank. However, the regiment was physically and emotionally drained. It began the fight with a total strength of 3,233 men. In less than a week, it suffered casualties of 75 officers and 1,887 enlisted men, for a total of 1,962. That was almost 61 percent of the total regiment's strength. The losses are even more significant considering that most came from the 2,613 assigned to the three combat battalions. Not all casualties were fatal, and many soldiers, still assigned, were in the hospital system; 500 enlisted soldiers and 7 officers would soon arrive as replacements.[30]

Barton visited each of the 12th Infantry's battalions that afternoon, talking to those who had just been through so much in this wasteful assault and assuring them they were now back with the Ivy Division. After that meeting, Barton, Rodwell, and Luckett met at division headquarters that night to discuss events. Luckett's command was now combat ineffective and needed to be reorganized before it could return to combat. Barton probably alerted Bob Chance to be prepared to return to the 12th Infantry.[31]

Penetration of the Main Line of Resistance

Barton had been in combat for ten days, working with Gerow, Cota, and Luckett. He was always on the road, visiting his nearby regimental command posts. Despite the condition of the 12th Infantry, Collins still wanted Barton, with only his two regiments, to attack in the northern portion of the forest, cross-country, simultaneously protecting the 1st Infantry Division's right flank in the north and linking with the V Corps' left flank in the south.[32] Given the situation, Barton asked for reinforcements, but Collins could spare little.[33]

Therefore, Barton did his best by having Buck Lanham's 22nd Infantry bridge the distance between the reorganizing 12th Infantry in the south and the 8th Infantry in the north. He ordered Lanham's regiment, with its headquarters still near Zweifall, to capture a string of villages (Kleinhau, Grosshau, and Gey) and then continue toward Düren. Because of the weather and terrain, it would have been a challenging mission even without the presence of the German infantry. On the left flank, Dick McKee was about to face his first significant test of battle as the division's main effort. His 8th Infantry would begin the fight just south of the village of Schevenhütte. There, without reconnaissance, it would scale a steep hill onto a heavily wooded plateau and attack in a column of battalions. Then it would continue to the northeast, protecting the 1st Infantry Division's right flank, through the woods to the edge of the forest overlooking Düren.[34]

However, Barton's opponent had almost all the advantages to defend his sector. Generalleutnant Hans Schmidt's 275th Infantry Division had already blooded both the 9th and 28th Infantry Divisions and had become a catchall for almost three dozen smaller commands looking for leadership. He no longer had reserves, such as the 116th Panzer Division, heading to a staging area in preparation for Wacht am Rhein, the Ardennes offensive in December. He had prepared the ground well with hidden fortifications, barbed wire, barriers, and many mines. He had about as many fighters as the 4th Division, about 6,500 men. He also had 106 artillery and mortar tubes, with plenty of ammunition. In addition, he could deploy twenty-one assault guns and twenty-three antitank guns of 75 mm and larger. Fighting from fortifications that protected them from both the weather and direct fire, the German soldier was well equipped with machine guns and automatic weapons. He had already ranged his weapons and established preplanned killing zones.[35] Adding to Barton's problem was the horrible weather that magnified the difficulty of crossing the terrain. And because it was conducting a supporting attack, the 4th Division received almost no air support.[36] Collins had set Barton up for an unequal struggle, violating almost all the tenets of sound tactics.

After a week of rain and snow, the generally miserable weather improved, and Hodges ordered the attack to begin on November 16.[37] Before first light Barton was with Luckett to check on the 12th Infantry's status. The regiment had not yet recovered. Although new replacements had filled the rifle companies to 60–70 percent of authorized strength, most were untrained and unprepared for heavy combat.[38]

In the 8th Infantry's sector, Lieutenant Colonel Langdon A. Jackson's 2nd Battalion led the regiment's assault on the plateau above Schevenhütte. As the assault companies proceeded up the steep slope, German artillery and mortar fire made movement difficult. On schedule at 12:45 hours, under an intense German barrage, the soldiers from the 2nd Battalion scrambled up the steep, five-hundred-yard slope onto the ridgeline. The Americans emerged into the open and found themselves in the prearranged engagement zone. Now accurate rifle, machine-gun, artillery, and mortar fire from a dug-in barrier line hit the prostrate Americans from seemingly all directions.[39] Around 14:00 Jackson, who was still at his observation point and had not yet gone forward with his companies, tried to adjust his plan, calling two of his commanders back to his headquarters. As they approached his command post for instructions, a German artillery barrage caught them on the move, immediately wounding both. Almost simultaneously, enemy fire killed Company E's commander on the plateau facing the barrier. Immediately, Jackson's entire chain of command for his rifle companies disappeared.[40]

The 22nd infantry began its attack on time and moved in a column of battalions with Lieutenant Colonel Glenn D. Walker's 2nd Battalion leading. They moved through the woods, avoiding trails and firebreaks to sidestep mines and enemy kill zones. Six hundred yards beyond the line of departure, the Germans detected the battalion's movement and began firing mortars and machine guns. Hubert Drake's 1st Battalion followed the 2nd, turned north, and advanced on its right flank. By the end of the day, the regiment had driven into the enemy defenses and secured a position on the high ground called Hill 201. Most of the casualties were from artillery and mortar fire.[41] Meanwhile, Barton had no intention of throwing Luckett's 12th Infantry back into the fight and used it on November 16 to protect Lanham's right flank and try to maintain contact with units in the V Corps sector.[42]

Barton had spent the day alternating between the 8th and 22nd Infantries. Lanham, often with Hemingway, who was determined to see the action through the eyes of his favorite commander, kept Barton apprised of the details, and so far Buck had the situation in hand. The same was not true with the 8th Infantry, where it had not been a good day, and the commander and McKee had an intense discussion over what to do next. However, at this point, there was little that the division commander could do other than urge the McKee on and provide any resources he could send.[43]

At 08:05 hours on November 17, Jackson's 2nd Battalion, with new company commanders, emerged from their positions and began moving toward two gaps in the wire they had blown the previous evening.[44] By 09:00 hours things at the front were at a standstill, and because of the effects of rain and moisture, many of the explosives were not working. In F Company platoon leader First Lieutenant Bernard J. Ray had lost more than his share of casualties trying to get bangalore torpedoes under the wire. Ray snapped around 10:00 hours; he grabbed a few more sections of the device, wrapped the primer cord around his body, and placed the explosive caps in his pockets. Under intense rifle and machine-gun fire, he ran to the wire. Suddenly a mortar round burst overhead, and its shrapnel wounded him. He lay at the edge of the wire with the entire explosive cord still wrapped around his body and connected to the explosive caps and torpedo. As his soldiers watched in horror, he pushed down on the plunger, destroying himself in a massive explosion. The 8th Infantry had its first opening in the defensive barrier and the 2nd Battalion its first Medal of Honor recipient.[45] That night McKee ordered Jackson's battalion off the hill and back to the original assembly area and replaced it with Cyril J. Letzelter's 1st Battalion.[46]

While McKee struggled on the division's left flank, the attack was going no better in the 22nd Infantry's sector. Lanham planned to expand the width of the regiment's attack by moving the 1st Battalion alongside the 2nd and then advancing with the two battalions on either side of the main road. The regiment's attack depended on Major James B. Drake's 1st Battalion first attacking north to seize a hill mass and then continuing to the east. Lanham ordered Drake to begin his attack no later than 08:00 hours.[47] As the battalion assembled to move forward, the Germans reacted violently and increased their heavy and accurate artillery and mortar concentrations. Captain Swede Henley, the 1st Battalion's operations officer, recorded in his diary, "All Hell broke loose. . . . Jerry artillery and mortars cutting us to pieces."[48] The fire killed Drake instantly. With the commander down, Henley assumed command and moved the battalion forward to seize the objective, later turning command over to Major George Goforth.[49]

Barton joined Lanham about 13:00 hours after watching the 8th Infantry. As expected, he was unhappy with the regiment's advance, but he could not do much.[50] The regiment's casualties were heavy. With two out of its three battalion commanders out of the fight, and many vital junior leaders killed or wounded, the unit was almost combat ineffective. Ten officers and 162 enlisted were killed and injured that day, mainly from the 1st Battalion. In addition, the 44th Field Artillery lost four of its nine forward observers in the day's struggle. On the right flank, the 12th Infantry continued reorganizing and securing the boundary with V Corps.[51]

Early the following day, November 18, Barton headed to McKee's headquarters and helped him relieve Jackson and replace him with his executive officer, George Mabry. Although only 27, the young major was now the battalion's "old man," and he spent the day rebuilding his badly damaged organization. The daily report to 4th Division headquarters only notes, "The 2nd Battalion had continued its reorganization."[52]

Meanwhile, no longer a meeting engagement, the 8th Infantry was now conducting a deliberate attack. McKee helped Letzelter, the 1st Battalion commander, assemble a reinforced combined arms team around Captain Robert D. Moore's Company C, augmenting it with a platoon of light tanks, a platoon of medium tanks, and three tank destroyers. Once Moore's company was through the barrier, the remainder of the battalion was to follow.[53] The attack was supposed to begin at 08:30, but getting everything in place took longer than expected, and Letzelter asked for an hour's delay. McKee and Barton, monitoring the attack's progress, had no problem with him taking a little more time. However, the Germans had been pounding the line of departure with mortars and heavy artillery since dawn. A little after 09:00 hours, just before the attack, a barrage hit Company A's commander, executive officer, first sergeant, supply sergeant, and the company radio operator, killing them all and wounding several others nearby. Therefore, before it could even cross the line of departure, one-third of Letzelter's company-level leadership was gone, and he needed to conduct a hasty reorganization of that unit.[54] But the attack would go forward, and at 09:15 hours Company C and its supporting armor headed for the wire, was soon through the gap, and requested combat engineers to clear a path for the tanks. They arrived promptly and, under heavy enemy artillery and mortar fire, began clearing antitank mines on the route of advance. By the end of the day, they were on their initial objective.[55]

At the same time McKee was fighting on his plateau, Lanham's 22nd Infantry was attacking with the 1st and 2nd Battalions along the main forest road to Düren. But again the Germans had struck before the Americans were ready. The 44th Field Artillery fired five hundred rounds of 105 mm artillery in one hour in support of the defenders, and by 08:00 the 2nd Battalion reported the attack had stopped. Once underway, George Goforth, now commanding 1st Battalion, had little difficulty, while Glenn Walker's 2nd Battalion, to the south, met determined enemy resistance. Behind the attacking companies, artillery continued to rain.

Just before noon German artillery landed on the 2nd Battalion's forward command post, wounding Walker and most of his staff. Major Joseph Samuels, the battalion executive officer, moved forward to take over but was wounded shortly after. Captain James Clark took command but was killed when he arrived from Fox Company. Easy Company's commander, Captain Arthur Newcomb, was next and directed the unit until Major Howard Blazzard, the regimental intelligence officer, assumed command. In a single hour, five officers commanded the 2nd Battalion; one was dead and two others were wounded. Fox Company, the battalion reserve, covered the regiment's southern flank. Heavily hit by artillery and persistent German attacks on its southern flank, the company had lost two of its officers, four NCOs, and nineteen other ranks, more soldiers than any other company in the 2nd Battalion (which occurred while in battalion reserve). Somehow, the 2nd Battalion managed to keep going and was in line with the 1st Battalion and on the objective by 16:50 hours. The next day Lieutenant Colonel Thomas Kenan took command of the battalion. He was the regiment's operations officer on D-Day but was wounded in July. He had returned just in time to stabilize the 2nd Battalion.[56] Meanwhile, in reserve, Arthur Teague's 3rd Battalion covering the rear against hostile infiltration had no direct contact with the enemy but received heavy casualties from artillery. One volley wounded Teague and a large part of his staff. His executive officer, Major James C. Kemp, assumed command.[57]

Losses among leaders were significant: 28 front-line infantry officers and 110 NCOs, including all 3 battalion commanders, a battalion executive officer, almost the entire 2nd Battalion staff, and large parts of the other two battalion staffs.[58] Meanwhile, the 12th Infantry was strengthening its line but in the middle of reorganization and could not yet join the battle.[59]

Late that afternoon Collins joined Barton at the Zweifall command post. The VII Corps was not making the progress he had expected, and the Germans were resisting fiercely and launching counterattacks against every penetration across his front. However, little did they know at the time, the bloody fighting had caused the German command to realize that the 275th Infantry Division could not stop the 4th Infantry Division and they moved another unit, the 344th Infantry Division, to strengthen the line.[60] The first phase of the fight was over. Now Barton and his commanders had to continue farther into the enemy's defenses.

Expanding the Assault

Continuing the attack on November 19, Barton attempted to coordinate the three separate regimental operations. Rather than attacking as a concentrated force, as McNair and his staff had planned back in 1940, the corps mission forced it to deploy along a wide frontage, with each regiment moving on a different path. Barton was constantly on the road seeking to coordinate his dispersed command. Because of the terrain and the restricted routes, he could not maneuver his regiments to take advantage of opportunities. Rather than directing his units as part of a coherent attack, Barton became the coordinator and cheerleader for his regimental commanders, carrying the fight forward on their divergent axis of advance.[61]

Even massing fires on important targets was difficult, given the distance. But, as the division historians noted months later as they finished their report, "It is possible that had the 4th Division fought as a unit it could have reached and perhaps crossed the [Rur] river, and made a real breakthrough for other units to exploit."[62] Unfortunately, that was not the case, and the regimental commanders fought their battles with little coordination. Meanwhile, Collins was in the same situation as his vision of a rapid advance to the Rur degenerated into a slogging match across the corps front. All he could do for Barton was narrow his sector in the south, allowing the 12th Infantry to narrow its front, and send him a couple of troops from the 24th Cavalry to cover some of the open areas between the two advancing regiments.[63]

In the northern portion of the sector, McKee's 8th Infantry continued to attack in conjunction with the 1st Infantry Division on its left flank and heading toward Düren. By the early morning of November 20, he had all three of his battalions online, oriented to the northeast. The German forces appeared to have an inexhaustible supply of mortar and artillery rounds, and the regiment was constantly under fire. Major Mabry had finished reorganizing his 2nd Battalion and now had a new executive officer, new company commanders, and many new platoon and squad leaders. McKee put his battalion in the center of the regimental line, between the other two battalions and not far from his forward headquarters. At 09:40 the regiment moved forward, and around noon Mabry moved back to confer with his commander.[64]

No sooner had he arrived at McKee's location than he was called back by one of his company commandeers. Machine gun and mortar fire overwatching the minefield was intense, and he could not move. Mabry responded, "Stand by for further orders."[65] Over the next few hours, Mabry personally led the battalion against enemy positions, often engaging in bayonet and close combat with groups of German defenders.[66] As darkness fell, Mabry, unsure of the enemy situation, pulled the battalion close and set up a 360-degree defense, prepared to defeat enemy attacks from all sides. While McKee probably could not see Mabry in action, the reports of the day's actions reached him by nightfall, and he ordered the witnesses to write their observations. The first award recommendation by Captain John C. Swearingen, the regiment's S-3, was for another Distinguished Service Cross. However, someone, probably the regimental commander, changed the proposal to one for the Congressional Medal of Honor.[67] The 8th Infantry continued to advance over the next few days against stiff resistance. By November 24 it had achieved a breakthrough of the defensive line the enemy had constructed before the 4th Infantry division's attack. Now was the time to commit a follow-on battalion or even a regiment into the enemy's depths to secure the route to the Rur River. However, it was not to be, as neither Barton nor Collins had troops available.[68]

Buck Lanham used November 19 to reorganize his 22nd Infantry after losing all three of his original battalion commanders and most of his company commanders. It was difficult as German infantry seemed to be everywhere. That afternoon a bypassed enemy strong point opened fire on the regimental command post with small arms and mortar fire. In response Lanham called up his Company K to clean them out with the ever-present Hemingway's help to drive off the attackers.[69] Meanwhile, the command reorganized, brought up supplies, and repaired roads and trails, mopping up bypassed pockets of resistance and patrolling to the north. Artillery continued heavy and casualties severe. Barton dropped in on Lanham on November 20 and told him he was forwarding his name up the chain for promotion to brigadier general.[70]

Early the following day, the 2nd Battalion began attacking a hill only six hundred yards away and ran into a German counterattack. Nevertheless, it continued to move forward against determined resistance. Heavy enemy artillery fire delayed the 1st Battalion's attack until 09:20 hours but it progressed rapidly and had covered some five hundred yards by midmorning. By 14:20 the 1st and 2nd Battalions occupied their objective. However, casualties were high as heavy artillery and mortar fire continued to rain upon them. Barton told Lanham to take another day for consolidation.[71] The regiment spent November 21 reorganizing, clearing out isolated enemy strongpoints, and improving the supply route. Nevertheless, German artillery and infiltration took their toll, and the 22nd Infantry had 206 casualties that day. Although replacements continued to arrive, the regiment was short 300 men and 40 officers, mainly in the front-line companies.[72]

Meanwhile, after a week of resupply and minimal operations, Robert Chance replaced Luckett as commander of the 12th Infantry on November 21. The former commander then joined Rodwell and Marr at the division command post in Zweifall, helping to manage the division's fight in the Hürtgen. He would remain at headquarters to rest and serve as an extra colonel for Barton to employ in the event of an emergency.[73] At the same time, Barton decided to move Charles Jackson from command of the 1st Battalion, 12th Infantry. Except for a short period when he was recovering from wounds in June, he had been in command since December 1942. He needed a break, and Oma Bates, who had just turned over his executive officer duties to Strickland in the 8th Infantry, was ready to take command.[74]

The attack continued for its seventh day, November 22. In the 22nd Infantry's sector, the 1st and 2nd Battalions advanced online, moving east. Then, in a dramatic move, Kemp's 3rd Battalion, which moved shortly after daylight, passed through the northern flank of the 1st Battalion and turned south, securing the intersection controlling the western edge of the village of Grosshau, the regiment's primary objective. Lanham was close to accomplishing his mission, but the cumulative strain of the battle on personnel, organization, and communications now made it necessary to take two days to consolidate.[75]

In the 12th Infantry's sector, Bob Chance began moving forward, with the 3rd Battalion in the lead. Soon it was online and connected to both the 22nd Infantry on its left and the 121st Infantry, 8th Infantry Division, V Corps, on its right. But other than that, it made little progress. For the next two days it continued to plod ahead, with advances measured in yards.

Headquarters mess, 4th Infantry Division, Zweifall, Germany, Thanksgiving Day, 1944. *Left to right*, Rodwell, Hodges, Barton, Collins, and Lanham. US Army photograph, Dwight David Eisenhower Presidential Library.

The 4th Infantry Division advance slowed but did not stop as Thanksgiving approached. Barton spent most of Thanksgiving Day at his headquarters and dispatched Rodwell to visit the regiments. That afternoon General Hodges, General Kean, his chief of staff, Collins, and Lanham came to the division command post to discuss the attack's progress. Rodwell returned, and they all decided to have Thanksgiving dinner at Barton's mess, one of the nearby houses in the village. However, adding to the ambiance of the holiday was the first floor, flooded with three feet of water. No one appears to have complained. After dinner he hopped into Barton's Buggy and headed off to see McKee for an update.[76] McKee was approaching his original objective and fighting determined defenders of a hunting lodge called Jägerhaus. The 8th Infantry had lost many soldiers but was still in reasonable shape. Lanham's regiment was still far short of its objectives because of its terrain but kept attacking. Chance's 12th Infantry was only beginning to show life and moving to the east.[77]

But while progress looked acceptable on a map, the division was in terrible condition and could not be expected to do much more. Late Thanksgiving evening Barton called Collins to update him on his dire situation. His aide made hasty notes of the conversation about the "status of the 12th and 22nd Infantry . . . so that [the corps] will know what tools [it] has to work with." Barton told Collins that Bob Chance, who had taken over the 12th Infantry several days ago, was doing what he could to repair the unit, which was still somewhat dazed. An artillery bombardment had temporarily knocked out his 2nd Battalion commander, Major Frank P. Burk, who refused to go forward after he recovered; Chance relieved him. After a few days on the job, Chance believed his combat efficiency was about 30 percent, and Barton supported that estimate, as he could not count on it to do much. Lanham and McKee were in better condition, but each regiment had one battalion that might have difficulty, but he was sure they would take their assigned objectives. "We will take our objective tomorrow and we will hold them. But . . . you need to measure how much power we have and to be sure you know that."[78]

Final Advance

The 4th Infantry Division's grinding advance continued November 25. McKee and Lanham had settled into their routines of fighting two separate battles as Barton bridged the divide and sought to allocate and acquire the resources they needed to continue. Finally, on the morning of November 25, he had the regiments arrayed online, with the 8th in the north, the 22nd in the center, and 12th in the south.[79] Division headquarters reported that movement was incredibly slow as the rain rendered the thick matting of the forest and the few roads and trails a mass of mud. It was almost impossible for the tanks and tank destroyers of the units to keep up with the advancing infantry. And the Germans defended their positions with all the small arms, mortars, and mines they had at their disposal.[80]

McKee's regiment was in reasonably good shape and now had a generally straight front from boundary to boundary. It had seized an area 3,000 yards deep by 2,500 yards wide in ten days. It was abreast of the 22nd

Infantry, which was preparing to attack Grosshau at that time, but there was a gap of a mile between the regiments, covered by a light cavalry screen.[81] The 22nd Infantry was exhausted, and Lanham did his best to capture the town. When Kemp's 3rd Battalion attacked toward the north side of the town, the Germans caught it when it entered an open field. Self-propelled guns, mortars, and devastating small-arms fire stopped this attack, disabled four of the supporting tanks and two tank destroyers, and drove the troops back to the edge of the woods. For the next three hours, German artillery bombarded the exposed battalion, preventing any movement. In addition to the armored vehicles, this assault cost Kemp 122 soldiers either killed or evacuated, many of them leaders.[82]

Stung by his losses, and high-strung and somewhat argumentative by nature, Lanham clashed regularly with Barton over his orders. Gruff by nature, exhausted by months of costly combat, and in pain, Barton had little tolerance for his regimental commander's complaints. Lanham's animosity toward Barton, and much of his staff, would continue long after the war.[83]

Meanwhile, Bob Chance's 12th Infantry was regaining its strength and able to participate in the division's offensive scheme. When Collins came by the headquarters, Barton convinced him to adjust his boundaries to allow for a more focused attack. Collins agreed, and Barton notified Chance to move most of his command, leaving a portion to affect a relief by a V Corps unit. He wanted the 12th Infantry to reposition behind the other two regiments and to be prepared to close the gap between them.[84]

On November 26 things slowed as the lead regiments reorganized and adjusted their lines, and the 12th Infantry Regiment continued moving north. After visiting his regimental commanders, Barton returned to his command post around noon and found Gerow, his former corps commander, waiting for him, and the two had lunch. The 8th Infantry Division was advancing on Barton's right flank and Gerow wanted to start the coordination. As Gerow left Collins returned for his daily update. Finally, at the end of a long day, Hemingway arrived, and he and Barton talked late into the night.[85]

Except for Lanham's regiment, November 27 was a slow day as the 8th and 12th continued to adjust. The Germans had committed extensive resources to defend Grosshau, including tanks and self-propelled guns. They had dug in most of their machine guns and heavy weapons and protected them with wire, mines, and booby traps. One engagement was especially noteworthy. Company B, 1st Battalion, attacked at 09:00 to retake the ground to the village's west, which a German counterattack had retaken the previous day. Machine guns and self-propelled artillery fire stopped the American attack. Because of the loss of noncommissioned officers, privates led some squads, one being Private First Class Marcario Garcia, an immigrant from Castaños, Mexico. He was wounded during the initial assault and, after being attended to by a medic, refused evacuation and continued forward. Alone, he crawled forward to a suitable location where he could see the German machine gun. "Hurling grenades, he boldly assaulted the position, destroyed the gun, and with his rifle killed three of the enemy who attempted to escape." When he returned to his squad, a second machine gun opened fire. Ignoring the fire, he attacked the position, destroyed the machine gun, killed three Germans, and captured four. Finally, after the remainder of the company arrived at the objective, the medics evacuated him to the rear to an aid station. Amazed at what he saw, his commander recommended him for the Medal of Honor, and he became the third Ivy Division member to have this recommendation approved. He was also the first Mexican citizen to receive this award, becoming a US citizen in 1947.[86]

Meanwhile, Barton continued his planning sequence, visiting troops and entertaining visitors as he had lunch with Collins, wanting another update on the division's progress. Later, the reporter Hank Gorrell came by for dinner with Barton and his staff to say good-bye. Barton liked Gorrell, who had spent much of his time in Europe with the 4th Division but who was now returning to the United States. When Barton returned home, he would recommend him for an award.[87] The reporter almost did not make it home, as the headquarters came under fire from heavy artillery, killing one of its guards and tearing up some of the command post.[88]

The 12th Infantry started its attack the next day, November 28, and began bridging the large gap between the 8th and 22nd Infantries. Chance's objective was a village north of Grosshau on the Düren road, in the middle of the sector.[89] Since Collins had reduced the division's northern boundary by two thousand yards, its frontage was more in line with US Army doctrine. However, as the division historian noted, "The 4th Div. now had a frontage and disposition appropriate for a strong attack. Unfortunately, the infantry units were no longer in condition to make such an attack."[90] Barton was all over the sector, starting the day with a visit to McKee's command post in the morning, then to the 1st Infantry Division's command post two miles north of Zweifall, where he discussed troop locations and boundaries with Generals Huebner and Taylor. Finally he arrived back at his command post to meet with Collins over the next phase of the operation. On his right flank, the 8th Infantry Division had replaced the 28th Infantry Division. Its new commander was his good friend Bill Weaver, who came by the headquarters to coordinate the joint boundary. Undoubtedly, Barton poured out everything he knew about the previous fight and what Weaver would face in the next week.[91]

The following day, November 29, began the last phase of the division's Hürtgen battle. The 8th Infantry attacked through light resistance and advanced about one thousand yards.[92] The 12th Infantry advanced through the woods toward the Düren road, while the 22nd Infantry finally captured Grosshau.[93] However, Grosshau had been an integral part of the Siegfried Line, and Lanham's troops had needed to storm it in hand-to-hand fighting, clearing out each structure. Once captured, the German artillery continued to pound it with guns of all calibers. The regiment was exhausted.[94] The division command post was busy as Collins and General Oliver, still commanding the 5th Armored Division, came for a conference. Collins left but returned after lunch with Bob Macon, still leading the 83rd Infantry Division. While all this was going on, Gerow entered the command post. Obviously, Barton was unable to get any work done until they all departed.[95]

The attack continued on November 30 as all three regiments moved forward. Fighting in the 8th and 22nd sectors intensified as the Germans resisted. But Grosshau was now in Lanham's hands, and the regiment began moving north on the Hürtgen-Düren road. But Buck Lanham was despondent. "At this time my mental anguish was beyond description. My magnificent command had virtually ceased to exist." Meanwhile, Hemingway felt safe enough to visit Grosshau in person that afternoon. He was stunned and wrote, "One American soldier, lying in the road, had been so flattened by the passage of many vehicles that he was hardly recognizable as human." This and many other sights he never forgot.[96] The arrival of the 12th Infantry Regiment in the division's center surprised the Germans, and the regiment was able to move forward with little resistance toward its objective.[97] Barton started the day monitoring the fight. After lunch he linked up with Bob Chance, who was finally contributing to the division's attack, then down the road to the 22nd Infantry, where Lanham was convinced Barton was ignoring his situation by demanding he keep pushing forward. Obviously, Lanham had little understanding of the pressure Collins was placing on his boss.[98]

By December 1 it was apparent the 4th Infantry Division's attack in the Hürtgen was incapable of continuing. Most of its riflemen were recent replacements, lacking the skill and training they needed for offensive operations. McKee's regiment spent the day adjusting its positions in the north, fighting to ensure all battalions were online and supporting each other. The 12th Infantry had arrived at the woods to the west of the Düren road but could not continue as an artillery barrage scattered two of the 2nd Battalion's companies that needed to be regrouped and reorganized. Lanham's regiment, now in the worst condition of the three, had also managed a short advance. Meanwhile, Kenan's 2nd Battalion, 22nd Infantry, supporting Oliver's Combat Command A and Weaver's 8th Infantry Division units on the right flank, took heavy losses.[99] That evening Barton again called back to Collins and told him the division's combat condition was poor and in no condition to continue its attack the next day.[100] The response was as expected, and at 21:50 hours Barton told Chance and Lanham that "the plan of attack as ordered previously will go as ordered."[101]

December 2 was another day of intense combat by a tired and worn-out division. The regiments fought to capture small pieces of the terrain, defended by dug-in German soldiers who continued to defend and counterattack every gain. In the 8th Infantry's sector, the battalions moved forward, online, against stiff resistance. On the right flank, Letzelter's 1st Battalion was successful in seizing its objective. One of the reasons for that success was Private Pedro Cano's bravery in moving through a minefield, armed with a rocket launcher and hand grenades, taking out several bunkers. Cano, another Mexican immigrant, did not rest and continued his performance the next day, crossing fire-swept terrain and destroying another three machine-gun bunkers. His commander was impressed, and after the war he received a Distinguished Service Cross in the mail. Later, General Jonathan Wainwright rectified that error and presented it in person, noting the impressive citation and that he probably deserved a higher award. Unfortunately, Cano died a few years later in an automobile accident after becoming an American citizen. Meanwhile, many in and out of Texas government petitioned for a review of his military record, and in 2013 a review committee selected Cano to receive the Congressional Medal of Honor, the fourth for Barton's division in only two weeks.[102]

In the early hours of December 2, Generals Hodges, Collins, Gerow, Oliver, Weaver, and Barton were all crowded around Dick Marr's operations map. Finally, Hodges had seen enough and ordered the attack called off, and the 4th Infantry Division to be replaced in the line. In his diary Hodges commented that the division's relief "is not going to happen any too soon as its troops are obviously tired and at the end of their rope."[103] At 16:00 the orders went out: Assume the defensive. Be prepared to be relieved.[104] After everyone left, Barton relaxed and spent the late hours listening to the Army-Navy game on the radio broadcast from the Armed Forces Network.[105]

For the next two days, Barton's regiments tightened their lines, repelled a continuous series of counterattacks, and prepared for relief from Macon's 83rd Infantry Division.[106] Hemingway, who had seen enough action over the last few days, came to see Barton as he left for Paris. He announced that he was returning to the United States after eighteen days in the Hürtgen Forest.[107] Barton was on the road, visiting his regiments, checking their status, and assessing what they needed. He essentially ended his contribution to the fight on December 3, when he came by the 42nd Field Artillery Battalion, supporting the 12th Infantry, to personally fire its one hundred thousandth round toward the German lines.[108]

On his way to visit Bradley in Luxembourg on December 4, Hodges and his chief of staff had to pass the muddy trucks with the dirty, unshaven soldiers from Lanham's 22nd Infantry heading in the same direction. His diarist noted, "The General said later that he wished that everyone had had a chance to see those men."[109] But what men were they? They certainly were not the 3,000 fully trained and equipped veterans that Lanham had marched into the forest over two weeks earlier. Over 2,805 were killed or wounded, an incredible 86 percent of its assigned strength. Not all of these, of course, were the original veterans, as many casualties took place among the untrained and ill-prepared that the army's replacement system threw into battle.[110] The division was in shambles as it had to recover from the 432 dead, 255 missing, and 3,300 wounded soldiers no longer in the ranks. Also absent were another 3,413 soldiers in the hospital suffering from trench foot, sick, or psychologically incapable of further operations.[111]

For the 4th Infantry Division, the poorly planned and executed assault into the Hürtgen Forest was a tactical failure not of its doing. Hodges, Collins, and Gerow surrendered the advantages of American firepower, mobility, and logistics to a dug-in, determined, and resourceful defender. As more than one analyst has reminded us, the correct answer would have been to block the forest by an economy of force unit and concentrate the First Army's tank, infantry, and artillery forces on a narrow front.[112] The reasons for the defeat—and it was a defeat—in these woods are many but generally can be credited to the senior leaders' failure to pay attention to the fundamentals of grand tactics or operational art.[113] Rarely is a frontal attack, without overwhelming force and firepower, a sound course of action. The destruction of the 4th and 28th Infantry Divisions represents one of the most significant failures of American generalship in the Second World War. As a result of this failure, the German high command was able to buy time and mass sufficient forces to launch its offensive in the Ardennes a few weeks later.

Barton writes little about his experiences at the end of the battle, but one can only imagine his level of exhaustion. Under fire every day for a month, he had done his best to accomplish Collins's tasks. Every day, as his diary tells us, he had to justify and explain his actions as a commander to Collins and Hodges, and even Bradley and Eisenhower on occasion. Every day he navigated the muddy roads and logging trails to meet with regimental and battalion commanders. Watching the destruction of his three regiments and constantly needing to attain his mission made his command experience almost unbearable. As a result, he was also putting extreme pressure on his regimental commanders, increasing tension and discord in the command. Finally, the pain from his ulcer seriously reduced his effectiveness as a commander.

Chapter 15

Luxembourg, Relief, and Retirement

My dear General Barton:

So far as I know, no American division in France has excelled the magnificent record of the 4th Infantry Division, which has been almost continuously in action since it fought its way ashore on the 6th day of last June.

Your fight in the Hurtgen Forest was an epic of stark infantry combat; but, in my opinion, your most recent fight—from the 16th to the 26th of December—when, with a depleted and tired division, you halted the left shoulder of the German thrust into the American lines and saved the City of Luxembourg, together with the Headquarters of the Twelfth Army Group, and the tremendous supply establishments and road nets in the vicinity,—is the most outstanding accomplishment of yourself and your Division.

G. S. Patton Jr.
27 December, 1944[1]

Luxembourg, December 8–27

A tired and wounded division moved from the VII Corps to Major General Troy H. Middleton's VIII Corps during the first week of December.[2] Its new location was the southern end of the Ardennes Forest and northeast of Luxembourg City, in a region known as Petite Suisse Luxembourgeoise (Luxembourg's Little Switzerland). Located on the left bank of the Sûre (Saur) River, as its name implies, the region has thick forests and hilly and rough terrain punctuated by many small streams. Middleton had the task of resting and restoring the 4th and 28th Infantry Divisions, both badly bruised from the Hürtgen battle, to fighting form. He also introduced the newly arrived 106th Infantry Division (Major General Alan W. Jones) to the combat environment. As a result, the area had the reputation as "a quiet paradise for weary troops."[3]

Middleton directed the 4th Infantry Division to relieve Bob Macon's 83rd Infantry Division, which had been in that sector for several weeks. Barton arrived on December 8 and joined Rodwell, who had arrived a day earlier, at the new division command post on the eastern edge of Luxembourg City.[4] Barton spent the next few days visiting his regiments, adjusting their sectors, and contacting the other commanders in the area. He and Middleton spent several hours on December 10 discussing the arrival and training of replacements. Later that day Colonel Harry L. Reeder met Barton at his headquarters. Reeder was instrumental in setting up the Ghost Army, which had contributed to the Germans' confusion during the early stages of the Normandy invasion. Finally, as close as he was to Bradley's headquarters, Barton maintained contact with it and invited its staff officers to visit him at the front.[5]

The German troops facing the 4th Infantry Division were a mixture of small units that appeared to pose no threat to the recovering Ivy Division. However, Barton's G-2, Harry Hanson, had read the reports the 83rd Division's G-2 had accumulated and noticed it contained information on a large amount of strange German activity across the Sûre River over the last few weeks.[6] So, based on Hanson's recommendation, he arranged his units in a defensive posture. The 4th Infantry Division Field Order #57 confirmed his verbal instructions and provided for the artillery and logistics support the division required in this new environment. He placed his three regiments along the riverbank, with Chance's combat team on the left flank facing north, McKee's in the center at the river's bend, and Lanham's on the right facing east. The two flank regiments needed to maintain contact with units on both flanks. He wanted all to have minimal contact forward, with positions in depth. Each regiment needed one reserve battalion with one reinforced company ready to move on one hour's notice and the remainder of the battalion four hours later.[7]

Over the next few days, Barton and Hanson, a first-rate and very experienced G-2, discussed several possible German courses of action. These meetings convinced Barton that a large raid on Luxembourg City was the enemy's most probable and dangerous course of action. Bradley had moved the 12th Army Group Headquarters to the city, making it an obvious target, and it was also the home of the massive and powerful Radio Luxembourg broadcasting tower.[8]

Barton hosted his first commander's meeting on December 13. After outlining several contingencies, he was somewhat surprised by their critical reaction. Barton sensed they believed "we are in here for a rest, higher headquarters assures us that the Germans are incapable of assuming any offensive and the old man is simply getting jittery [emphasis original]."[9]

Although sensing some pushback, he continued and directed his regimental commanders to post only outposts along the river and array their battalions in and around the major villages. In addition, he required each regiment to keep one battalion as a mobile reserve, capable of moving on four-hour notice. Finally, he discovered the division's rest centers were too far in the rear. So in an unpopular move, he directed them all to relocate forward of the regimental command posts. Barton then stressed his intent for the next few weeks: (1) being able to meet the tactical situation, (2) conducting a training program, and (3) meeting the recreational and rehabilitation situation of the division.[10] After the meeting he welcomed Major Philip A. Hart, his former aide and later assistant civil affairs officer who had been severely wounded on D-Day. He was now back with the headquarters. Finally, he, Rodwell, and Blakeley visited the reinstated American charge-de-affairs in Luxembourg for a pleasant evening of dinner and conversation.[11]

Daily he continued his program of visiting each regiment and most separate battalions, ensuring each followed his detailed program of restoring discipline, unit sanitation, fixing its broken vehicles, and combat training.[12] All was quiet until the evening of December 14, when frontline outposts captured several enemy soldiers, who indicated that a German battalion had infiltrated across the Sûre and was hiding on the American side of the river. The prisoners offered that a significant attack was about to take place. The warning went forward but was not a cause for concern at higher headquarters.[13]

General Erich Brandenberger's Seventh Army began its assault on December 16, with an early morning artillery and rocket barrage. Brandenberger's army was to serve as a flank guard for the two panzer armies conducting the main attack in the north. Against the 4th Infantry Division he sent the LXXX Corps, consisting of the 275th Volks Grenadier Division in the north. Farther south, General Franz Heinrich Otto Sensfuß's 212th Volksgrenadier Division acted as the southern unit for the entire German counteroffensive and would cross the Sûre in the Echternach sector and drive head-on against the 12th Infantry.[14] Sensfuß had a good picture of Barton's unit locations and combat capability. It was a porous border, and his agents and patrols had little trouble setting up listening posts along the roads and in local bars and restaurants.[15] These initial artillery barrages against the 12th Infantry's company and battalion locations were accurate and disrupted Bob Chance's defense. In addition, the explosives cut the telephone wires, which were essential because most of his radios were in the shop for repair.[16] At 02:30 hours Chance called Barton and let him know he was receiving some artillery fire, but a check with the 12th Infantry headquarters at first light indicated nothing had yet changed. But across the American front, German artillery fire increased, and around 08:00 Barton and Middleton talked by landline, and he warned Barton to be on the look for Germans infiltrating the corps sector.[17]

The first time the 12th Infantry command post knew they were under attack was when Company F at Berdorf, west of Echternach, was able to use an artillery observer's radio to send an alert. Over the next few hours Chance kept division headquarters informed as to the developing German attack across his front. Because of the way Barton had arranged the division, the 8th and 22nd Infantries experienced only limited patrolling.[18] Barton contacted Middleton again and asked if he had any fresh troops to back up his still-tired regiments. All he had to offer Barton as an augmentation was the 159th Combat Engineer Battalion working on the roads. They were his if Barton could find them, which he later did. Because of the German assault, the 4th Infantry Division was effectively cut off from the First Army support and began receiving its supplies from the Third Army.[19]

By late morning Barton, who had been monitoring the attack from his command post, had developed a good idea of what was happening. At 11:45 hours he ordered, "There will be no retrograde movements without authority from this HQ."[20] He authorized Chance to commit the 1st Battalion (Lieutenant Colonel Oma R. Bates), the regimental reserve. At the same time, he gave him eight medium tanks and ten light tanks, leaving the 70th Tank Battalion (Lieutenant Colonel Henry E. Davidson Jr.) with only three mediums and a platoon of light tanks in running order. Small tank-infantry teams quickly formed and went forward to relieve or reinforce the hard-pressed companies. But, unfortunately, rain and snow during the previous days had turned the countryside into mud, and the tanks were restricted to moving on the roads.[21]

Late that afternoon Barton visited the 12th Infantry's command post and discussed the regiment's situation. On an extended front, Chance's depleted regiment faced at least two intact German divisions. He had several of his companies surrounded and now had nothing else to spare. Not wanting to disrupt the defensive posture of his other two regiments, Barton's primary approach on the first day was to find Chance reinforcements, such as Captain Lewis E. Goodrich's 4th Cavalry Reconnaissance Troop, and send them forward.[22]

Barton was also concerned about the valley, called the Mullerthal, that ran along his left flank. Before he retired for the night, he contacted the commander of the 4th Engineer Battalion, Lieutenant Colonel William M. Linton. He ordered him to be prepared to move on an hour's notice to secure the valley and told John Delaney, his G-3, to ensure the required trucks were available. At about 02:30 the following morning, Barton was spooked and told Linton to move. The battalion arrived just before dawn and drove off the German scouts seeking to secure the same key terrain.[23] The night ended with the four companies surrounded, but the reinforced 12th Infantry still held the line.[24]

Barton began the second day of the assault, December 17, looking for reinforcements for Chance's decisively engaged regiment. He scrounged about one hundred officers and soldiers from his headquarters company and formed them to advance to the 12th Infantry. As they were boarding trucks, one of the sergeants could take it no more, went back to his hut, and "blew his own brains out."[25]

Undeterred, but somewhat concerned by "how soft the men around me had become," Barton continued to redirect units from less threatened sectors and attach them to the 12th Infantry, one of the first being the 19th Tank Battalion, 9th Armored Division.[26] Concerned about his left flank, he reinforced the 4th Engineer Battalion in the Mullerthal and sent Jim Luckett, still with the headquarters, to take command. Task Force Luckett had the mission of taking care of the left flank. Barton sent him George Mabry's 2nd Battalion, 8th Infantry, who attacked to block an avenue of approach from the Sûre. He also shifted three battalions of 155 mm howitzers and two batteries of 105 mm howitzers to reinforce the two battalions already supporting the 12th Infantry. Out of reserves, Barton began to consider pulling most of his other two regiments out of line and joining Chance's fight. Of course, he would violate his orders to secure that sector, but he thought he might have to.

Fortunately, he got word that Major General William H. Morris Jr.'s 10th Armored Division was on the way and would provide support to secure the German offensive's southern flank. Morris had graduated a year earlier than Barton from West Point and later was one of his instructors at the Army War College.[27] Morris arrived in the afternoon, and the two commanders, each technically assigned to a different field army, crafted a counterattack to regain key terrain and take pressure off the 12th Infantry. Knowing the terrain, Barton recommended an axis of attack to block the Echternach-Luxembourg road. The attacking unit was Brigadier General Edwin W. Piburn's Combat Command A. Piburn had been one of Barton's captains during the Rhineland Occupation more than twenty years earlier. The first tanks arrived in the late afternoon and would attack early the following day.[28] Meanwhile, Hemingway had not returned to the United States but was back at the front with Barton and Lanham. However, he was sick and spent the next couple of days in bed and partially sedated.[29]

The counterattack moved off on the morning of December 18, with three combined-arms task forces heading toward the isolated 12th Infantry companies. One platoon arrived at Echternach and offered to cover the isolated Company E's withdrawal. First Lieutenant Martin MacDiarmid, commanding the company, refused. His poor communications ensured he had not received any orders changing Barton's no retreat order. Several days later MacDiarmid was forced to surrender his surrounded unit to the Germans.[30] With that exception, the fighting was give-and-take all day as Morris and Barton strengthened the battle lines. On several occasions Blakeley and his other artillery commanders asked to pull back, but Barton refused. It was not simply bravado but the realization that any withdrawal might cause the whole line, manned by exhausted soldiers and new replacements, to break. In addition, German soldiers had infiltrated the area and would disrupt any attempt to withdraw. Of course, as a result, in more than one instance individual artillery batteries had to engage in close battle with small numbers of German soldiers.[31]

Meanwhile, McKee and Lanham, each short a battalion, were nervous and continued pestering the division commander about actions in their sector. The 22nd Infantry commander was especially persistent, calling Barton almost every night around 02:00, reporting hostile tanks moving across his front. Finally, he sent out a patrol and, on December 21, called Barton and "rather sheepishly informed him that what he thought was hostile tanks, turned out to be a German sound truck simulating tank movement."[32]

The next day the fighting continued to be intense as Task Force Luckett, led by Mabry's 2nd Battalion, 8th Infantry, fought for the high ground overlooking the Mullerthal. Again, casualties were high, and Barton called off the attack later in the day.[33] Barton sensed that the Germans had lost their momentum, but with much of the Third Army moving north toward Bastogne, Patton needed to cement his hold on this portion of the German penetration. Accordingly, he formed a provisional corps under Morris's command that included most of the 9th and 10th Armored Divisions, the 4th Infantry Division, and the 109th Infantry (28th Infantry Division). Morris's task was to coordinate the area's defense so it would not interfere with the relief of Bastogne.[34] Meanwhile, more reinforcements were coming as Major General Horace L. McBride (USMA 1916) and his 80th Infantry

Division moved toward the 4th Division's sector. McBride and his advanced party arrived in the evening, and Barton briefed him on the situation and what to expect.[35]

Heavy fighting continued on December 20 in the division sector as the 12th Infantry and its task forces struggled to secure the best offensive line. By the end of the day, Barton's infantry and Morris's tank units had stopped the German assault in their sector. As the US Army official historian noted, "The southern shoulder of the German counteroffensive had jammed."[36] On his way north, General Patton visited the command post and discussed operations with Barton. The Third Army commander had not seen Barton in the last few months and must have noted how worn and tired he looked. That evening Barton got another aide, Lieutenant Schuyler B. Marshall III, from a well-to-do family in Texas.[37]

By December 21 the 4th Infantry Division's operation on the edge of the German bulge was essential over. While it continued to defend and fight, other units, such as the 5th and 80th Infantry Divisions, were moving into the sector to block any renewed effort. That afternoon Patton and many of his corps and division commanders met at the Third Army's new command post in Luxembourg. On the eve of the attack into Bastogne, he wanted to ensure everything was ready for the assault. Patton had assigned Barton to Manton S. Eddy's XII Corps. The two had known each other for a long time and had fought alongside each other in Normandy, when Eddy commanded the 9th Infantry Division and was Paddy Flint's boss.[38] When the meeting was over, Eddy pulled Barton aside and told him, "Tubby, you look worn and tired. Say the word and I will see to it that you go home." Barton argued and protested about his duties and responsibilities, but Eddy concluded with "OK, but if you change your mind, let me know."[39]

The fighting would continue for the next few days and would be intense at moments. But the depleted division had done its part in one of the largest battles the US Army would ever fight. Barton was wrong about the German intentions of seizing Luxembourg City. The enemy assault was much grander than he could have possibly imagined.[40] Hitler intended to capture a prize much more significant than Bradley's headquarters or the Luxembourg Radio tower: Antwerp.

Barton with his aides and assistants, Christmas Eve, 1944. Bill York on far
left and Schuyler Marshall on right. US Army photograph, Dwight David
Eisenhower Presidential Library.

Relief

Although Eddy's XII Corps and Barton's 4th Infantry Division stopped
the German Seventh Army's attack on the southern flank of the bulge
on December 23, the crisis was far from over. Not until the afternoon of
December 26 would the III Corps' 4th Armored Division arrive at Bastogne
to begin the relief of the 101st Airborne Division, which would continue
until the first week in January. German tanks and motorized units continued
moving west for several more days. However, there was now little possibility
of it succeeding, and Allied leaders at all levels began to prepare plans to
drive the Germans back into the Rhineland. Barton had the 10th Infantry,
5th Infantry Division, to help improve his tactical situation.[41]

Barton began Christmas Eve with Eddy arriving at his command post
to discuss tidying up the corps' sector with limited attacks to drive the small

German units back across the Sûre. He again told Tubby that he looked terrible and needed a rest. Barton was getting the message, and it was probably at this meeting that he agreed to start the replacement process. Moving a successful division commander from his unit, especially not for a failure to perform, required a discussion by the chain of command. Patton was busy working the relief of Bastogne and had little time for his quiet sector, but somehow Eddy got through to the army commander. After Eddy left, Barton was off to visit Bob Chance, whose defense of his sector was magnificent. Cool under fire, he was an excellent replacement for Jim Luckett, who had also distinguished himself during the last few days.

That afternoon the 5th Infantry Division had passed through the 4th Division, and Barton could dissolve Task Force Luckett and pull this overworked commander out of line. His orders to the division, the last one he would issue, instructed the division to hold in present positions.[42] That evening after dinner Barton wandered over to the aides' room where Bill York, Schuyler Marshall, Garlan Bryant, and Warrant Officer Bainbridge had a champagne and cake celebration. They talked late into the evening. Since these assistants formed his most intimate group, he probably confided in them the decision he was considering—to ask for relief.[43]

Barton made the rounds of his commands on Christmas morning. Bob Chance's 12th Infantry was now in comfortable billets near Luxembourg City, and the troops were all eating a hot turkey dinner. He invited Chance to join him that night for a dinner party in his honor to acknowledge him for his superb performance. Before dinner, Hemingway, Jim Rodwell, Hal Blakeley, Jim Luckett, Chance, and Barton went to Blakeley's room and consumed large amounts of Scotch, gin, local brandy, and champagne. Notably absent was Buck Lanham, who had continued arguing with the division commander. So Barton ordered him to take temporary command of the 12th Infantry along with his 22nd so that Bob Chance could go to dinner. Also missing, for no apparent reason, was Dick McKee, whose sector was farthest from the headquarters.

For dinner they had turkey with mashed potatoes and cranberry sauce. They were all drinking more than usual, and the strain of months of combat was beginning to show on everyone. Sadly, after two hours Jim Luckett

From left, Rodwell, Chance, Barton, Blakeley, and Marr, Christmas, Luxembourg, 1944. The day before Barton requested relief from command. US Army photograph, Dwight David Eisenhower Presidential Library.

became excessively belligerent and critical of Barton and the division command group. So Barton kicked him out, and Hemingway drove him to another party with the 70th Tank Battalion. After dinner the remaining group headed to Barton's apartment, where the aides had erected a small tree, for more drinks and conversation. While this session was in progress, Hemingway returned, this time with the famous war correspondent Martha Gellhorn, soon to be the ex–Mrs. Hemingway, for a few more drinks and conversation.[44]

By December 26 the 4th Infantry Division was probably the least involved unit in the 12th Army Group. Its three regiments remained in place, resting and refitting as the 5th Infantry Division moved forward of Chance's 12th Infantry and continued attacking to restore the American line along the Sûre River. To the north Patton's Third Army, especially John Millikin's III Corps, struggled to enlarge its corridor into Bastogne from the south.

It would take days before the town's defenders were reinforced along their defensive lines and received the food, medical care, and other supplies they needed. In the northern portion of the Bulge, as it was now called, Hodge's First Army finally defeated the various armored probes from the German Fifth and Sixth Panzer Armies, well short of the Meuse River and their ultimate objective of Antwerp.[45]

Barton decided this was his last day as the division commander. He contacted Eddy, told him he was ready to depart, and recommended that Blakeley, his senior brigadier who knew the division better than anyone else, take command. Jim Rodwell, who was still a new brigadier, would remain his deputy. Eddy got hold of his boss, Patton, and passed on the request.[46] Barton's diary records that he was making plans for the division's move, but that isn't very likely. Later in the day, Buck Lanham came by with his operations officer Earl Edwards, probably to see what he had missed the previous evening and to get instructions for the next few days. Dinner was with Lieutenant Colonel Henry E. Davidson Jr. from the 70th Tank Battalion, which had fought with the 4th Division since Utah Beach in June. As dinner was winding down, George Patton called and told Barton the relief was approved and to get ready to leave. He picked up the telephone and told Hal Blakeley to come on over.[47]

Supply trucks and ambulances continued to roll into the Bastogne on December 27, as the III Corps' 4th and 9th Armored Divisions and the 80th Infantry Division continued to broaden the corridor to the city. Across the front, in both the Twelfth and Twenty-First Army Groups, commanders assessed their status and prepared to resume the offense and drive the German forces from the Bulge. American soldiers fought to restore mid-December's front line for the next two weeks. Throughout this period the 4th Infantry Division remained with the Third Army until it was well across the Rhine and into the heart of Germany.[48] But Barton would experience none of this.

Early in the morning he headed to a schoolhouse in Luxembourg City that served as the Third Army headquarters for an out-brief with an extremely busy George Patton. Patton took the time he needed to reassure Tubby that it had nothing to do with his record as a leader. Nevertheless, it was an emotional meeting. Patton had been a firstie when Barton arrived as a plebe; they got to know each other as students at Fort Leavenworth and maintained contact through assignments in Washington. In addition, Patton had mentored one of his best friends, Paddy Flint, at Fort Benning, welcomed him as a general officer, and gave Barton a set of his brigadier general stars. Behind the scenes, Patton was an emotional man, and his farewell letter said it well: "My purpose in requesting that you be sent to America for medical treatment is, as you know, based on my friendship and affection for you and on my belief that a man who has fought as heroically and as long as you must be given a respite. In closing I desire to reiterate the fact that your present relief is in no way a criticism of your fighting ability, but simply arises from the necessity of saving such a soldier for future operations."[49]

Then Barton headed back to his headquarters to finish the transfer of command to his good friend Hal Blakeley. He said good-bye to his other comrades, especially Jim Rodwell and Dick Marr, who had been with him since his days as division chief of staff. Then he left the headquarters he had created back in 1940 for the last time and drove across town to the XII Corps command post. General Eddy awarded Barton a Bronze Star medal and told him, "No division commander in France has had to bear a greater or a more prolonged strain of battle than yours. Your reluctance to rest, even when given the opportunity, has been admirable but costly. The fact that your mental stamina has outlasted your physical stamina can never be a reflection upon you—it can be only an everlasting credit to your courage, your tenacity, and your high sense of responsibility. You are being given a rest because you have earned it, and because the service must take full advantage of what you have yet to give."[50]

Other than in the category of physical endurance and activity, where he kindly rated Barton as "Satisfactory," Eddy rated him as a superior performer and recommend him for corps command. In the remarks column he noted, "He definitely should not be disregarded for future command."[51] Barton said farewell to several more friends at the headquarters, including Hemingway, and then drove across town to spend the night at the Hotel de Paris in the center of Luxembourg City.[52]

The Journey Home

Before departing Luxembourg on December 28, Barton began his journey by visiting Bradley at Eagle TAC (Twelfth Army Group Tactical Command Post) and paying his respects. After a half-hour meeting, he left and passed through Longwy and Châlons, stopping at a nearby fighter base for lunch. He continued to Meaux and arrived in Paris around 15:30 hours. The SHAEF billeting office assigned him a room in the Ritz Hotel, a significant improvement from his quarters a few days ago. After a great dinner in one of the best dining rooms in the city, he spent his first night without the weight of command in over two years.

The following day he was at the Majestic Hotel for a meeting with Lieutenant General John C. H. Lee, who was still commanding Eisenhower's Communications Zone. Lee turned him over to a staff personnel officer, Colonel Vincent Meyer, whom Barton had taught with back at Fort Leavenworth, to take care of all the details to get him back to the United States. For the next two days, he relaxed in the city and took care of administrative issues, such as changing his orders so he could travel to New York and then to Washington, DC. George Marshall had sent two major generals to France after the Germans attacked in December in case Eisenhower needed to replace division commanders. Ray E. Porter would take command of the 75th Infantry Division in a few days, and Albert E. Brown (USMA 1912), a West Point classmate who had commanded the 7th Infantry Division before Pete Corlett, would get a second command succeeding Stafford Irwin at the 5th Infantry Division, who would soon replace Eddy at XII Corps. Barton spent time with both, who were looking to gather information about commanding in the ETO.

Dinners in the evening were with various officers at restaurants in the Ritz and the King George V. Hotel. On New Year's Eve, his last evening in the city, he took his aides on a tour of Paris and spent one evening at the Follies Bergèr at Montmartre. Josephine Baker had not yet returned, but it must have been quite an evening for this group, nevertheless.[53]

On New Year's morning, the group drove to Orly Field and boarded a C-47 cargo plane to London, arriving at Boyington Airport a little after noon and then staying at Claridge's Hotel in London, one of the world's finest. In London he balanced his meals at Willow Run, the European Command's staff mess hall, and some of the better hotels and restaurants. After dinner on January 3, he headed to Euston Rail Station and took the train to Glasgow, Scotland.[54]

Arriving at 08:30 on January 4, he had breakfast and then drove to the docks at Greenock, where the RMS *Aquitania* was preparing for its crossing. This Cunard Line cruise ship was no stranger to carrying troops back and forth to America, having performed this task in both world wars. By 10:50 he had a stateroom and met his dining companions for the voyage home. That afternoon he was sailing through the Firth of Clyde and into the North Atlantic.[55]

From January 5 through 11, Barton had little to do besides reading, eating at the fine mess, and dropping in on the ship's skipper, Captain Battle, whom Barton enjoyed talking to immensely. The liner had a hospital section, and the general visited it several times to speak to soldiers, especially those from the 4th Infantry who were on their way home. Finally, early on January 12, the *Aquitania* sailed past the Statue of Liberty and docked at a pier on West 50th Street at 09:35. An escort officer met him on the dock, helped him gather his baggage, and took him to the Waldorf Astoria, where his wife and daughter were waiting. He had been gone only a little more than a year, but it might as well have been a lifetime, given their different experiences.[56]

After an evening of family time, Barton obtained a car, drove the two Clares to West Point on Saturday, January 13, and checked in at the Thayer Hotel. They spent the remainder of the day with their son, R. O., who was still at the academy.[57]

On Sunday afternoon they returned to New York and boarded a train for Washington, DC. Bill York was waiting and took Barton to a set of quarters at Fort Myer. Soon after his arrival, Colonel Frank McCarthy, the secretary of the general staff, met him and gave him the background for his visit with Marshall on Tuesday. After the war McCarthy continued to work for the government for a few years and then became a Hollywood producer. Among his credits are *Patton* (1970) and *MacArthur* (1977).

He spent Tuesday at the new Pentagon, visiting General Marshall and joining him at a briefing later that afternoon. The next day he spent time with Robert P. Patterson, undersecretary of war. Thursday he returned to Georgetown University and had a good time meeting with some of the faculty who remained. Of course he had many friends in the area, including Doc Cook, who had turned his XII Corps over to Eddy just before the Bulge. The two major generals had come a long way since they first entered the gates at West Point in 1908.

Detracting from the joy of his homecoming, Clare Conway got sick and needed to be moved to Walter Reed Army Hospital. We have no indication of what it was, but it was severe enough to cause the Bartons to leave the quarters at Fort Myer and move into quarters on the hospital grounds to be nearby for the rest of the week. While at the hospital, Barton visited everyone he knew who was recovering there, and he and Clare had a pleasant visit with George Marshall's wife, Margaret. He also visited the Pentagon and talked to many of his friends and other officers, such as General Joseph Stillwell, whom Roosevelt had just recalled from China and was now head of AGF. Bill York finally left Barton and went on leave, turning his duties over to Schuyler Marshall. Finally, on Friday, January 26, Tubby and the two Clares (Clare Conway by ambulance) drove to Union Station in Washington. They were on their way to the family wartime home in Jacksonville, Florida.[58]

Last Assignment and Retirement Board

After a couple of weeks in Jacksonville, Barton went to a hospital in Miami, where he was diagnosed with a duodenal ulcer and treatment with various medications began. On March 1, 1945, appearing fit to return to duty, he took command of the Infantry Replacement Center at Fort McClellan, Alabama. McClellan was a temporary assignment, so Clare remained in Jacksonville. Although the war was winding down in Europe, it was still in full force in Asia. Oscar Griswold was still commanding the XIV Corps, now finishing the capture of Manila. If, as expected, Griswold would become an army commander for the invasion of Japan, he would probably need a battle-tested officer he trusted to take on one of his corps. Barton certainly fit

From left, Blakeley, Barton and Rodwell, Camp Butner, North Carolina, June 1945. Home of the 4th Infantry Division as it prepared for operations in Japan. US Army photograph, Dwight David Eisenhower Presidential Library.

the bill. However, even in this low-stress position, his ulcer continued to bother him, often with severe attacks making it difficult to function. Often he remained at home rather than reporting to his office. However, he held out, hoping he would get better and the army would send him again to an important position.[59]

Meanwhile, on April 29 he was the guest speaker at the dedication of a memorial at Arlington National Cemetery in memory of Major General George H. Cameron, who had organized the 4th Division and led it through most of World War I. Barton gave a long speech, detailing the legacy of Cameron and identifying many officers who had served with the Ivy Division. After the ceremony Barton was honored at a lunch at the Carlton Hotel. Among the attendees were Doc Cook and Red Reeder, who was still at Walter Reed, recovering from his injury in Normandy almost a year earlier.[60]

In late June the 4th Infantry Division, still commanded by Hal Blakeley and Jim Rodwell as his deputy, returned to the United States at Camp Butner,

North Carolina. Barton visited the division being refitted for possible service in the Pacific and spent some quality time with his two old friends. Hodges, who was on his way to take command of a possible assault on Japan, stopped by Butner to check on the division and how it was progressing.[61]

However, in August the American dropping of two atomic bombs and the subsequent invasion of Manchuria by the Soviet Army induced Japan to surrender. Meanwhile, Barton continued to soldier on until Japan surrendered in August 1945. He realized the War Department would not need him in the peacetime army, so he requested a retirement board.[62]

The board convened on September 21, 1945, at the Regional Hospital at Fort McClellan. After opening the proceedings, the board president invited Barton to make a statement. In it he recited his history of stomach pain throughout his entire career, beginning around 1919. After years of suffering through it, without a war in progress, it was time to seek relief and retire. Questioned by a board member, he explained his relief. He was insistent that it was not because of his performance but because both Generals Patton and Eddy, "both friends of mine of many years standing," determined after several visits that he was sick and needed to return home. When asked why he was not requesting a return to duty, he commented he needed to get control of his stomach pain, "including mental and physical relaxation which might heal that condition, and I know I cannot do that and stay with the job I have."[63]

His physician, Doctor Thad P. Sears, testified that Barton had been in severe pain for six months. He had talked to both of his aides, Captains York and Marshall, who described in some detail his discomfort in the Hürtgen Forest and how the pain continued until he came home. Sears had been treating him since the early summer and could never end the general's discomfort. Seers concluded that "even with the best care and rest and diet, he will still have scar tissue from the ulcer." The result will be "permanent aggravation." Sears also noted Barton was suffering from arteriosclerosis.[64]

Another physician, Doctor Martin G. Goldner, testified that Barton also suffered from pulmonary emphysema and arteriosclerosis besides his ulcer. When asked about whether the general should undergo further hospitalization, Goldner replied, "At the moment, I think General Barton should get away from the Army, of to such a place as he wants to, have relaxation, have a proper diet, be free of responsibility over several months and under the circumstances he doesn't need hospitalization. What he needs is freedom from making decisions and all the things that go along with his executive capacity."[65] On October 15 the board recommended retirement and that he was "considered physically unfit for limited service following retirement."[66]

The proceedings and recommendations worked through the system as fall turned to winter. He took leave over the holidays, spending time at his Jacksonville home with Clare. In the middle of his rest, he received a telegram from the War Department inviting Barton to travel back to Camp Butner to be present at the inactivation of the 8th Infantry. Although we do not have a roster of participants, we can assume that most former commanders—Van Fleet, Rodwell, and McKee—were present, along with its current commander, Erasmus Strickland, who had been with the regiment since 1940. Blakeley left the division in October, followed by Rodwell, who retired.[67] Soon after Barton got home, his orders arrived, putting him on retirement leave, with a retirement date of February 28, 1946. His permanent grade, from before the war, was as a colonel. But his orders confirmed his retirement grade was as a major general with over thirty-seven years of active service.[68]

Chapter 16

Conclusion and Legacy

More so perhaps than any other Augustan, Raymond O. Barton
had touched the lives of Americans from every segment of society.
It was a benign influence he wielded, soothing in its application
yet inspirational in its effect. . . .

Augusta owes much to the colorful and capable general.
So does his country.
—Editorial, *Augusta Chronicle* (Augusta, GA),
March 1, 1963

hile in Jacksonville Barton had been searching for a place to retire.
Jacksonville was a navy town, and he lived there only because he
was assigned to the IV Corps in 1941. Tubby had no reason to return to
Ada, as his family, other than Maude, had all passed on. Indeed, he was not
going north, especially after his years in Alaska, New York, and Europe in the
winter of 1944. But Augusta, where he had lived twice, always had appeal.
The weather was great, and it was not far from the beach on Tybee Island.
He loved to play golf, and some of the best courses in the United States were
nearby. For more practical reasons, Camp Gordon had a good hospital and

facilities such as a commissary and post exchange. It appeared to have an uncertain future as the stream of soldiers outprocessing from overseas ended, and the enemy prisoners of war returned to Germany. However, Barton probably knew that the War Department intended to relocate the Military Police School and the Signal Corps Training Center to Gordon in 1948. So Augusta would be a great place to live the life of a retired general.

He and Clare started house hunting in the winter of 1946. The local newspaper, the *Augusta Chronicle*, quoted him on December 3 as saying, "I have always loved this city and always hoped to come back to live someday."[1] In January 1947 he moved to 938 Hickman Road on the west end of town. But then, like today, it was probably an apartment, and he and Clare wanted something more permanent. A few months later, they moved to a lovely home a little farther west on Helen Street.[2]

Once he left uniform, Tubby continued his practice of extensive correspondence. He and Elenore Butler Roosevelt continued an active correspondence until she died in 1960. Intensifying the mail was her desire to publish the whole story of Collins and Bradley denying her husband the Medal of Honor after D-Day. By 1958 Barton and Collins were on good terms, so he urged her to hold back and not aggravate the relationship. She agreed and decided not to add it to her forthcoming book.[3] In addition, *Time Magazine* published an article that indicated Ted Roosevelt had led the division during the invasion, and Barton fired off a letter, with a copy to Eleanor, telling the magazine that was not the case.[4] For the rest of her life, she pestered the War Department bureaucracy, including Army Chief of Staff J. Lawton Collins, for an accurate accounting of all awards and recognition Ted received during his military service.[5]

In 1959 Cornelius Ryan began researching his signature book, *The Longest Day.* Following an extensive interview, Barton sent Ryan, whom he addressed as "Dear Corney," photographs, a marked map, and a detailed account of his D-Day activities.[6] Similarly, Barton collaborated with the Office of the Chief of Military History in writing the official *History of the United States Army in World War II*, especially *Breakout and Pursuit* (1960), *The Siegfried Line Campaign* (1963), and *The Ardennes* (1965).[7]

Although they never saw each other again after Paris, Barton and Hemingway carried on their correspondence after the war.[8] *Collier's* magazine published what is probably Hemingway's best-known article on the 4th Infantry Division in November 1944, "The GI and the General." Although Barton is never named, one descriptive passage gives the reader an insight into the nature of this long-serving officer:

"The people are very tired, Ernie," he said. "They ought to have a rest. Even one good night's rest would help. If they could have four days . . . just four days. But it's the same old story."

"You're tired yourself," I said. "Get some sleep. Don't let me keep you awake."

"There should never be tired generals," he said. "And especially there should never be sick generals. I'm not as tired as they are."[9]

Hemingway was best friends with Buck Lanham, and they continued writing to each other until just before the writer's suicide in 1961. Lanham had no love for Barton, and it shows in his letters. Hemingway could humor his complaints about Barton, whom Lanham referred to in his letters as L. L. (Living Legend).[10] Hemingway later told Tubby, "I know he is a little SOB—but damn it, I love him."[11] Hemingway sent Clare Conway an autographed copy of *The Old Man and the Sea* as a wedding present. After Hemingway's death, Charles Scribner, who owned most of the author's major works, asked Carlos Baker from Princeton University to write his biography. Barton went out of his way to provide many details on this complex individual.[12] The results of this correspondence are in Baker's biography and also an accompanying collection of letters. No detailed description of the 4th Infantry Division in the Second World War is complete without including Hemingway and his dramatic involvement.[13]

Lanham never got over his grudge with Barton. Although Barton recommended him for promotion to brigadier general, which took place in May 1945, he failed to submit an efficiency report on his 22nd Infantry commander or, most likely, any of his key leaders. Apparently, Barton was so sick when he left that he left it to his staff to take care of the paperwork. But the war was on and nothing was done. We do not know if Lanham contacted Barton directly, but we do know that he petitioned the War Department to no avail in 1949.[14] The US Army promoted McKee just before his retirement, after service in Korea in 1953, also suggesting he was missing an efficiency report.[15] Blakeley also did not receive an efficiency report for his command of the 4th Division artillery from July through December, nor a Distinguished Service Medal that he deeply desired.[16] It is surprising to this author that Barton did not attempt to remedy these administrative omissions before he retired.

Although no longer in uniform, Tubby remained deeply involved in military affairs. One of his first projects was transforming the National 4th (IVY) Division Association, formed by World War I veterans in 1919, into an organization that welcomed the recently returned veterans from the European Campaign. As late as June 1945, its official name was still the National 4th Division Association, AEF.[17] Along with Hal Blakeley, Jim Rodwell, Arthur Teague, Gerden F. Johnson, and other recently returned veterans, the organization quickly became a two-war organization.[18] Barton organized the association's annual reunion in Augusta in September 1948, praising the division's veterans from both world wars.[19] By the following year, Johnson was its president and Parks Huntt ran the significant Atlanta chapter. Both Blakeley and Rodwell would later serve as national presidents. In addition to demobilized veterans, it maintained contacts with others still serving, such as Jim Van Fleet suppressing the insurgency in Greece, Red Reeder coaching at West Point, and John J. McCloy, who served with the division in the First World War and was president of the World Bank and would soon become the US high commissioner in Germany.[20] The association remained a viable and active membership organization in the twenty-first century.

Soon after he settled in Augusta, Barton submitted recommendations for Distinguished Unit Citations for the division's intense combat in the Hürtgen Forest. These included most of the division and its troop units, such as the 4th Infantry Division Artillery, 4th Reconnaissance Troop, 803rd Tank Destroyer Battalion, 4th Signal Company, and the 29th Field Artillery Battalion. Out of his twenty-two recommendations, the War Department approved none of them.[21] Despite its sacrifice, only the 22nd Infantry Regiment received any recognition from the War Department for its bloody three weeks of combat.[22]

He remained an active member of the informal retired general officer's club, corresponding regularly with others in and out of uniform.

These included Van Fleet, Bradley, Harry Collins, Joe Collins, and Ridgway.[23] He gave the main address when the War Department reactivated the 4th Infantry Division at Fort Ord. Breaking with protocol, he asked all troops, both officers and men, to sit down in place rather than stand rigidly at attention or parade rest. After the applause from the appreciative spectators, he began to speak.[24] As the editor of the *Ivy Leaves* noted, "It was stirring and impressive, as only we who had the privilege of serving under his command can know."[25]

> So, gentlemen, as you march behind those bloodied Colors of the 4th Infantry Division in review today and as later see the battle streamers and coat of arms, I want you to march by with pride in our unit, but more than that, I want you to march with a deep responsibility for the men whose blood is scattered to the far reaches of the world. The blood of those young Americans who died to ensure that you and I would continue to have the American way of living calls you. You can make no greater contribution to them than to pass on their spirit and tradition.[26]

Of course, once the North Koreans invaded the south in 1950, Tubby asked to be recalled to active duty. After reading the application from the 61-year-old, rather unhealthy, retired general, the adjutant general noted, "Your tender of service is appreciated and is being made a matter of record."[27] A few years later, at the Normandy invasion's tenth anniversary, he joined eighteen other retired officers, including Eddy and Gerow, to commemorate the event. Before they departed at the beginning of June 1954, they stopped by their former commander, now president, Eisenhower's office to accept the torch they would bring to help commemorate the landing. Barton, Eddy, Gerow, and Quesada then moved to Washington National Airport and boarded Eisenhower's presidential aircraft, the *Sacred Cow*, for their flight to Paris. Met in Normandy by General J. Lawton Collins, the delegation visited during its two days on the ground the new American Cemetery under construction, Utah Beach, Omaha Beach, Carentan, and Saint-Lô, all scenes of division battles only a decade earlier.[28]

Meanwhile, Barton contributed to his new hometown of Augusta. He started as vice president for industrial development of the Augusta

President Eisenhower presents a torch to be lit at ceremonies commemorating
the tenth anniversary of the Allied landings in Normandy to Lieutenant
General Leonard T. Gerow at the White House, June 3, 1954. Barton standing
in center of delegation. Dwight David Eisenhower Presidential Library.

chamber of commerce, seeking to attract industry to the postwar southern
city. Two years later he joined the real estate department of Southern
Finance Corporation and remained with the firm until just before his
death. He served his city in many ways, with the Georgia/Carolina Scout
Council, American Red Cross, the local Community Chest, and the Rotary
Club.[29] During the presidential elections, Tubby supported his former boss,
Dwight D. Eisenhower.[30]

He and Clare's son, Raymond Oscar Jr. (R. O.), graduated from West
Point in 1948, married Anne Claussen from Augusta, and became an air
force fighter pilot. In September 1949, when his son, Rocky, arrived,
Tubby wrote him a letter and sent him, as a birth gift, a rock from the
day he crossed into Germany.[31] RO deployed to Korea after the Communist invasion. During the war he flew over one hundred missions in a F-86

Major General Raymond O. Barton, US Army (retired), civilian portrait, Augusta, 1955. Courtesy Barton family.

Sabre fighter, shooting down three enemy MiG fighters and damaging seven others. He also was part of the first nonstop fighter flights across the Pacific and Atlantic Oceans, where he pioneered in-flight refueling. He ended his military career as an instructor to the first class in the US Air Force Academy, leaving the service in 1958.[32] Clare Conway graduated from the University of Alabama, married Aloysius "Wish" Redd, a veteran and Notre Dame graduate, originally from Augusta, in 1950, and moved first to Mexico and then to Texas.[33]

   Since returning to the United States, Tubby had never been very healthy, continuing to smoke and drink as he had all his life. But it caught up with him, and during the last week in February, he moved to the hospital at Fort Gordon where, on February 27, 1963, he passed away from "acute myocardial infarction of left ventricle"—a heart attack.[34] It had been an eventful seventy-four years.

Raymond and Rocky, Augusta, September 1951. Courtesy Barton family.

We do not know why he did not wish to be buried at Arlington National Cemetery with many of his classmates and friends. His choice was to remain in Augusta, and it was a large ceremony on March 1 at Westover Memorial Park. Accompanying Clare to the funeral were Raymond Jr. and his wife, Anne; Clare Conway and her husband, Wish, Percy's daughter, Barbara; Tubby's older sister Maude; and Helen. Also in the audience was his friend and successor in command, Hal Blakeley, and many of his comrades from his days in the 4th Division. Sadly, Jim Rodwell, his close friend since reactivating the division in 1940, had passed away in Denver a year earlier. They had been quite a team, Barton, Blakeley, and Rodwell, throughout the heavy fighting of 1944.[35]

Raymond's funeral, Westover Cemetery, Augusta, March 1, 1963. Clare receives
the casket flag accompanied by Raymond Jr. and Clare Conway. Barbara Barton
Chambers is seated behind them. Courtesy Barton family.

Many of Barton's mentors, friends and classmates lie buried in Arlington
National Cemetery. Why not him? According to his family, he made it clear he
wanted to remain in Augusta. Despite efforts by the Veterans of the Fourth Infantry Division Association to erect a more prominent monument, he rests today
under a modest, civilian cemetery headstone. Clare continued to live on Helen
Street until she passed away in 1978. After Raymond's death her sister Kiki
(Helen) moved in with her and remained there until her passing in 1983.[36]

Immediately after Barton's death, the Fort Gordon Commander renamed
Parade Field #4 to Barton Field. Two years later, in March 1965, the post held
a formal dedication and placed a large monument at the field's entrance. After
a short recap of Barton's history with the division, it concludes, "He gave
55 years of federal and civic service to his country." In 1980 James Van Fleet
came to Augusta and, in the name of the 4th Infantry Division, presented a
large granite monument to Barton and all 4th Infantry Division members. It is
on Green Street in Augusta's historic district.

Major General Raymond O. Barton's headstone, Westover Memorial Park,
Augusta, Georgia. Author's photograph.

However, despite these city monuments, Raymond O. Barton and his role
in the European Campaign have receded into history. While almost everyone
interested in America and its war against Germany knows about Ted Roosevelt
on Utah Beach, few can name the 4th Infantry Division commander and
describe his leadership over the next seven months. The National Defense
Act of 2021 directed the Department of Defense to remove the names of Civil
War Confederate generals from US Army military bases. Although Barton
had close connections with the city, the renaming commission, with some
comment from the Augusta community, decided to rename Fort Gordon
Fort Eisenhower because the retired supreme commander had "formed ties
to the community during visits to the nearby Augusta National Golf Club."[37]
Fortunately, in May 2022, he joined his colleagues Bradley, Devers, Eddy,
Eisenhower, Gerow, Hodges, Huebner, Middleton, Patton, Van Fleet, and
Walker as a member of the Fort Leavenworth Hall of Fame. Accepting the
award for the family was his great-grandson, T. J. Barton. However, like most
of his fellow division and corps commanders, his contribution to the nation's
history is generally unknown.

Who Was Raymond O. "Tubby" Barton?

This study has attempted to answer the questions posed in the beginning of this book. Raymond, an ambitious, bright, and politically connected young man from a small Oklahoma town, sought and received an appointment to the US Military Academy at West Point. By the time he graduated, he had become a serious student, athlete, and professional soldier. Although not in the least obese, his stocky physique and prowess on the wrestling mat and football field generated his peer-awarded nickname. He was Tubby to his seniors, peers, and friends for the rest of his life.

His assignments were typical of those who entered the US Army early in the twentieth century. Outpost duty in Alaska, training civilians in New York, and securing the border in Texas was typical for the soldiers of the pre–First World War era. Like others such as Omar Bradley and Dwight Eisenhower, Barton was needed by the War Department more at home as a trainer than as a frontline commander. After an eventful assignment in the Rhineland, he returned to the United States. He spent the next seventeen years in intellectually stimulating assignments as a student in the army's service schools, on senior staffs, and as an instructor in the CGSS. In battalion command as the US Army began its Second World War expansion, he was well positioned to rise as a division commander.

Not a member of the famous Pershing-Marshall clique of officers, he nevertheless had important mentors who guided him throughout his career, most notably Asa Singleton, James Ord, and Oscar Griswold. Griswold mainly propelled him from the staff officer role into the elite division command echelon. However, he would not have arrived at this point if he had not earned praise and support from most of his leaders, from Halsey Yates in Alaska to George Duncan in Omaha, to Lloyd Fredendall in the prewar 4th Infantry Division. While never becoming a close comrade with J. Lawton Collins, his other corps commanders, especially Leonard T. Gerow and Manton S. Eddy, considered him an excellent division commander worthy of senior command. By the time he arrived in Europe in 1944, Barton knew most of the senior officers in the infantry and many others in the other services. The core of his friends came from his West Point class and his first assignment in the 30th Infantry Regiment. The names of Flint, Ord, Fechet, and Corlett continue to appear on these pages. Others enter at Fort Leavenworth or the Army War College, such as Huebner, Allen, and Woodruff.

Thanks to his large cache of letters from his twenties and thirties, we have a good picture of him balancing his tough, professional persona with one that demonstrates a caring and loving nature toward his parents, Clare, their children, and his niece and nephew. Both Marshall Holmes and Barbara Barton would live productive lives because of Raymond and Clare's intervention and support.

What emerges from this study is a picture of an aggressive yet balanced leader. In general it appears he got along well with his subordinates until the pressures of months of combat caught up with him. The stress of battle, the loss of so many of his junior officers, and the pain caused by his ulcer caused him to be less tolerant of his subordinates, especially Lanham and Luckett, as his command term ended. However, as many of his raters noted, he was a solid and competent officer. Most likely only his ill-advised effort to return prematurely from the hospital prevented him from ending the war as a corps commander.

His career is a window into the US Army in the critical years between the end of the Spanish-American War and the Second World War. Most history buffs know the names and general stories of the pantheon of American generals who allegedly won the most significant conflict this country ever engaged in. Bookshelves and magazine racks, now often digital, strain with homages to Eisenhower, Bradley, Marshall, and, most prominently, George Patton. But this is a very selective list. We know little about Courtney Hodges, Alexander Patch, and William Simpson, all army commanders. The lives of corps commanders, those who maneuvered combat divisions, such as Gilbert Cook, Manton Eddy, and Wade Haislip, are essentially lost to history.

The historical gap is even more pronounced when considering those commanding combat divisions. Eisenhower commanded approximately sixty American divisions during the campaign in Europe. Few of their names are familiar, but veteran's associations and national governments carved their deeds into the stone markers that populate the French and Belgian countrysides: Clarence Huebner with the 1st Infantry Division, Terry Allen with the 1st and 104th Divisions, Walt Robertson with the 2nd Infantry that held the critical Elsenborn Ridge during the early stage of the Battle of the Bulge, Ira Wyche with the 79th Division that fought alongside the 4th Infantry at Cherbourg, Walton Walker with the 3rd and John Wood with the 4th Armored Divisions that spearheaded the Third Army's race across France.

Also lacking in the historical record is the role of division commanders, and their assistant commanders, during the battle. Although some historians have used oral histories to argue that soldiers seldom saw their senior officers, Barton's story should put an end to thoughts that commanders practiced some kind of chateau generalship. His diary and division and regimental staff logs clearly record Barton's comings and goings. When troops were in contact, he visited each of his regiment, and often battalion, commanders. Often he visited leaders and staffs on his flanks, to mitigate the confusion that takes place along unit boundaries. He was always in contact with his corps commander, Collins or Gerow, who generally met with him at least every other day. To add to the command presence, his assistant commanders—Barber, Roosevelt, Taylor, and Rodwell—were also circulating around the battle area. While there may be some exceptions, Barton's hyperactivity was probably typical of the successful Second World War division commander. When he was no longer able to maintain that pace of operations, it was time for him to depart.

The corps and division commanders mentioned in this book all share one characteristic: they had progressed through the ranks with Tubby Barton. Their shared assignments, promotions, the military school system, and relationships help us appreciate the cast of leaders that took one of the least effective ground forces among the major powers and turned it into one that effectively battled the more experienced German and Japanese forces to a standstill. While we might and should criticize the operational decision making among the senior commanders, those who led combat divisions—Barton's peers—did so with proficiency and tactical prowess. Paraphrasing the editor of the *Augusta Chronicle* noted at the beginning of this chapter, this country owes much to this colorful general and his peers.

Endnotes

Notes

When citing works in the notes, the following abbreviations have been used:

4ID	4th Infantry Division
8IR	8th Infantry Regiment
AAR	after-action report
BPP	Raymond O. Barton Personal Papers
CARL	Ike Skelton Combined Arms Research Library, Fort Leavenworth, KS
CCB	Clare Conway Barton (Raymond and Clare's daughter)
CGSS Press	Command and General Staff School Press, Fort Leavenworth, KS
CMH	US Army Center of Military History, Washington, DC
CMHL	US Army Center of Military History Library, Fort McNair, Washington, DC
CSI	Combat Studies Institute, Fort Leavenworth, KS
DRL	Donovan Research Library, Fort Moore, GA
FM	Field Manual
GPO	US Government Printing Office
NACP	National Archives and Records Administration, College Park, MD
NPRC	National Personnel Records Center, Saint Louis, MO
RG	Record Group
ROB	Raymond O. Barton

Notes for Preface

1. H. W. Blakeley, *4th Infantry Division* (*Yearbook*) (Baton Rouge, LA: Army & Navy Publishing, 1946), 2.
2. Stephen A. Bourque, "Richard G. McKee: A Forgotten U.S. Army Officer of World War II," *On Point, The Journal of Army History* 25, no 1. (Summer 2019): 36–43.
3. See Ty Seidule, *Robert E. Lee and Me: A Southerner's Reckoning with the Myth of the Lost Cause* (New York: St. Martin's Press, 2020).

Notes for Introduction

1. Martin Blumenson, *The European Theater of Operations: Breakout and Pursuit* (Washington, DC: CMH, 1960), 215–18.
2. Ernie Pyle, *Ernie's War: The Best of Ernie Pyle's World War II Dispatches*, ed. David Nichols (New York: Simon & Schuster, 1986), 331.
3. Darryl F. Zanuck, *The Longest Day* (Twentieth Century Fox Films, 1962).

Notes for Chapter 1

1. Letter, Will J. Sims to Mrs. Carrie M. Barton, March 15, 1898, BPP, courtesy Barton family. Unless otherwise noted, all letters are from this collection.
2. US Federal Census–Slave Schedule: CO Barton, *Eighth Census of the United States, 1860*, Series Number M653, RG 29 (Records of the Bureau of the Census), NACP.
3. "Private Josian Lemuel Fields Barton," *Antietam on the Web*, accessed May 2023, https://antietam.aotw.org/officers.php?officer_id=1697; Conway O. Barton, US Census, 1880, Ancestry.com.
4. Orel Busby, "In Memory of Judge C. O. Barton," eulogy, BPP.
5. "Biography: Conway Oldham Barton Jr.," *Oklahoma Genealogy Trails*, accessed August 2022, http://genealogytrails.com/oka/pontotoc/bios.html#barton; "Judge Barton Passes Sunday: Life Covered by Long Span of Service," *Ada Evening News* (Ada, OK), July 14, 1941.
6. Gregory M. Franzwa, *Maps of the Santa Fe Trail* (St. Louis: Patrice Press, 1989), 177; Robert Autobee and Deborah Dobson-Brown, *Colorado State Roads and Highways* (Denver: Colorado Historical Society, 2003), 8–13; Grenada, Colorado, *Legend of America*, accessed February 2020, https://www.legendsofamerica.com/granada-colorado.
7. US Census Reports for Carry [Carrie] Mosher and George Mosher, 1880, Ancestry.com.
8. Carrie M. Mosher, diary entry for January 4, 1937 (BPP); conversations between author and Cathy Barton Clarke.
9. Maude G. Barton and Ann C. Barton, US Census, 1900, Ancestry.com.
10. Raymond O. Barton, "Autobiographical Sketch," 1959, BPP.
11. The name "Daughter" may seem strange to twenty-first-century readers, but the high rate of deaths during childbirth must have created a hesitancy for parents to give a permanent name to their newborn.
12. *Lamar Register* (Lamar, CO), February 22, 1896: 5; *Phillips County Herald* (Holoyoke, CO), March 6, 1896.

13. The stationary header on letters sent by Raymond O. Barton (ROB) to family.

14. Michael Tower, "Pauls Valley," *Encyclopedia of Oklahoma History and Culture*, accessed February 2020, https://www.okhistory.org/publications/enc/entry.php?entry=PA019; Conrooy O. Barton, US Census, 1900, Ancestry.com. The census taker misspelled his first name.

15. Letter, Will J. Simms to Carrie M. Barton, March 15, 1898.

16. "Conway Oldham Barton Jr.," *Oklahoma Genealogy Trails*; Conway Oldham Barton Jr., US Census, 1910, Ancestry.com.

17. Gary Haney and Dare Strickland, *Images of America: Pontotoc County* (Charleston, SC: Arcadia, 2012), 100; Pontotoc County Historical and Genealogical Society, *History of Pontotoc County, Oklahoma*. (Ada, OK: Pontotoc County Historical and Genealogical Society, 1976), 185; Roy S. McKeown, *Cabin in the Blackjacks: A History of Ada, Oklahoma*. (Ada, OK: Self Published, 1980), 29–30; "Major General Charles Carl Chauncey," *Air Force*, accessed December 2021, www.af.mil/AboutUs/Biographies/Display/Article/107457/; "Orel Busby," *Oklahoma Hall of Fame*, accessed November 2021, https://oklahomahof.com/member-archives/b/busby-orel-1963.

18. "Conway Oldham Barton Jr.," *Oklahoma Genealogy Trails*.

19. Busby, "In Memory of Judge C. O. Barton."

20. J. Hugh Biles, *The Early History of Ada* (Ada, OK: Oklahoma State Bank, 1954), 83.

21. Ada Chamber of Commerce, *Ada Oklahoma: The Railroad, Industrial, and Educational Center of Southern Oklahoma* (Ada, OK: Chamber of Commerce: 1914).

22. ROB to Papa and Mamma, August 26, 1905.

23. ROB to Percy, September 3, 1905.

24. ROB to Papa and Mamma, September 2, 1905.

25. *Ada Weekly News* (Ada, OK), September 1, 1905; ROB to Folks, August 26, 1905. From here on, Barton addresses most mail to his parents as "Dear Folks" or "Folx."

26. McKeown, *Cabin in the Blackjacks*, 31; *Ada Evening News*, April 20, 1907; Clipping: "Remember?" (n.d.), BPP.

27. *Ada Weekly Democrat*, May 24, 1907.

28. *Ada Weekly Democrat*, July 19, 1907.

29. Bureau of the Census, "Appointment of Special Agent," August 3, 1907, BPP.

30. ROB to Folks, September 2, 1905; "Orel Busby," *Oklahoma Hall of Fame*.

31. Dom Pedro to CMB, October 13, 1907.

32. ROB to Papa, November 26, 1907.

33. ROB to Charles D. Carter, December 30, 1907.

34. *Ada Weekly Democrat*, January 3, 1908.

35. ROB to Folks, January 12, 21, 25, 1908.

36. *Ada Weekly Democrat*, February 7, 1908, p.8.

37. *Ada Weekly Democrat*, February 21, 1908.

38. ROB to Folks, February 28, 1908.

39. ROB to Folks, February 28, 1908.

40. Henry L. Flynn, ed., *The Howitzer* (New York: Chas. L. Willard, 1912).

41. ROB to Folks, February 28, 1908.

42. *Ada Weekly Democrat*, March 13, 1908, p8; ROB to Folx, February 28, 1908.

43. Hugh L. Scott, *Annual Report of the Superintendent of the United States Military Academy* (West Point, NY: United States Military Academy, 1909), 3–4.

44. Thomas E. Griess, "Dennis Hart Mahan: West Point Professor and Advocate of Military Professionalism, 1830–1871," (unpublished master's thesis, Duke University, 1968), 116–26.

45. William Gardner Bell, *Commanding Generals and Chiefs of Staff, 1775–2013* (Washington, DC: US Army Center of Military History, 2013), 110.

46. Stuart C. Godfrey, ed., *The Howitzer* (New York: Chas. L. Willard, 1909), 119; "Register of Graduates and Former Cadets, 2010," *West Point*, accessed December 2023, https://www.west-point.org/wp/ring_recovery/RRP/RingPix/2010ROG_1802-1931DeceasedClassesRegis-terofGraduatesROGAOGAlumni.pdf.

47. William C. Sylvan, and Francis G. Smith Jr., *Normandy to Victory: The War Diary of General Courtney H. Hodges & the First U. S. Army*, ed. John T. Greenwood (Lexington: University of Kentucky Press, 2008), 472.

48. Scott, *Annual Report*, 4; 1912 Executive Committee, *Ten Year Book: Class of Nineteen-Twelve* (West Point, NY: USMA Class of 1912 Executive Committee, 1922); Flynn, *Howitzer* (1912).

49. Wilson A. Heefner, *Patton's Bulldog: The Life and Service of General Walton H. Walker* (Shippensburg, PA: White Maine Books, 2001); and Paul F. Braim, *The Will to Win: The Life of General James A. Van Fleet* (Annapolis, MD: Naval Institute Press, 2008), for example.

50. Carlo D'Este, *Eisenhower: A Soldier's Life* (New York: Henry Holt, 2002), 486.

51. ROB to Folks, March 25, 1908.

52. ROB to Folks, March 26, 1908.

53. *Ada Weekly Democrat,* April 4, 1908, p.1.
54. ROB to Folks, May 2, 1908.
55. ROB to Mother, August 6, 1908.
56. ROB to Folks, June 17, 1908.
57. ROB to Folks, July 7, 1908.
58. ROB to Folks, July 8, 1908.
59. Godfrey, *Howitzer* (1909), 135–39.
60. ROB to Folks, September 5, 1908.
61. ROB to Folks, August 9, 1908.
62. ROB to Folks, December 12, 1908.
63. Godfrey, *Howitzer* (1909), 128.
64. Godfrey, *Howitzer* (1909), 128.
65. ROB to Folks, March 12, 1909.
66. ROB to Folks, May 20, 1909.
67. Frederick S. Strong Jr., ed., *The Howitzer* (New York: Chas. L. Willard, 1910), 184.
68. ROB to Folks, November 27, 1909.
69. *Ada Weekly Democrat,* October 8, 1909, p. 4; ROB to Folx, October 5, 1909.
70. ROB to Folks, January 2, 1910; ROB to Folks, January 30, 1910.
71. ROB to Folks, February 2, 1910; CMB to ROB, June 10, 1910; Orel Busby to ROB, July 7, 1910.
72. Morris Massey, "What You Are Is Where You Were When," program 1 of *The Original Massey Tapes* (Video Publishing House, 1972).
73. ROB to Folks, September 25, 1910, and October 28, 1910.
74. ROB to Folks, October 23, November 6, and December 11, 1910.
75. ROB to Folks, February 6, 1911; Curtis H. Nance, ed., *The Howitzer* (Philadelphia: Hoskins Press, 1911), 143–44.
76. ROB to Folks, March 16, 1911.
77. ROB to Folks, December 11, 1910.
78. Steven L. Ossad, *Omar Nelson Bradley: America's GI General, 1893–1981* (Columbia: University of Missouri Press, 2017), 33–36; D'Este, *Eisenhower,* 59–65; Braim, *Will to Win,* 10–15; "Register of Graduates and Former Cadets, 2010."
79. Flynn, *Howitzer* (1912), 53, 208–9.
80. William C. Weaver, "Raymond O. Barton 1912," Cullum No. 5085, USMA; *Evening News* (Ada, OK), March 5, 1912, p. 3; Efficiency Record of Barton, Raymond Oscar, [1912–]1917, Raymond O. Barton Official Military Record File, RG 319, NPRC.
81. War Department, "General Orders No. 22, August 3, 1912," BPP.

Notes for Chapter 2

1. ROB to Folks, September 19, 1912.
2. ROB to Folks, October 8, 1912.
3. John K. Mahon and Romana Danysh, *Infantry, Part I: Regular Army*, Army Lineage Series (Washington, DC: CMH, 1972), 40.
4. ROB to Folks, October 8, 1912; Fort Gibbon, "Condition of the Command," September 1912, *Returns from U.S. Military Posts, 1800–1916*; Records of the Adjutant General's Office, 1762–1984, RG 94, NACP; Lyman L. Woodman, *Duty Station Northwest: The U.S. Army in Alaska and Western Canada, 1867–1987*, vol. 1, *1867–1917* (Anchorage: Alaska Historical Society, 1996), 213–19; "Fort Gibbon and the Village of Tanana," *LitSite Alaska*, accessed July 2020, http://www.litsitealaska.org/index.cfm?section=digital-archives&page=Government&cat=Military&viewpost=2&ContentId=2732.
5. ROB to Folks, July 22, 1913.
6. "Leon Roudiez, 86, Expert on French Writers," *New York Times*, June 23, 2004, https://www.nytimes.com/2004/06/23/us/leon-roudiez-86-expert-on-french-writers.html.
7. "Julie Yates, Sculptor, Dies of Pneumonia; Wife of Col. Halsey E. Yates of Governors Island—Was a Pupil of Rodin," *New York Times*, November 6, 1929, accessed February 2022, https://www.nytimes.com/1929/11/06/archives/julie-yates-sculptor-dies-of-pneumonia-wife-of-col-halsey-e-yates.html.
8. ROB to Folks, October 24, 1913.
9. ROB to Folks October 8, 1912.
10. Woodman, *Duty Station Northwest*, 230–31.
11. ROB to Folks, October 8 and December 19, 1912.
12. ROB to Folks, June 26, 1913.
13. ROB to Folks, June 26 and December 7, 1913.
14. Fort Gibbon, "Condition of the Command," December 1912 and April 1913, *Returns*, RG 94, NACP; Special Orders 89, Fort Gibbon, August 14, 1913, BPP.
15. ROB to Folks, September 15, 1913.
16. ROB to Folks, December 7, 1913.
17. Efficiency Report: ROB, December 31, 1912, RG 319, NPRC. This report is a summary of comments by Barton's superior officers from 1912 until 1917; Fort Gibbon, "Condition of the Command," June 1914, *Returns*, RG 94, NACP.

18. Efficiency Report: ROB, December 31, 1913, RG 319, NPRC.
19. ROB to Folks, November 11, 1912, and September 15, 1913.
20. ROB to Folks, September 15, 1913.
21. ROB to Folks, March 9, 1913.
22. Woodman, *Duty Station Northwest*, 307.
23. ROB to Folks, October 24, 1913.
24. Request for Aviation Branch, 1917. "Classmate" refers to USMA graduates a year older and one or two later—essentially, cadets Barton would have encountered when attending.
25. Efficiency Record: ROB, RG 319, NPRC; Presidio of San Francisco, "Condition of the Command," February 1915, *Returns*, RG 94, NACP.
26. ROB to Folks, November 23, 1914.
27. Brian McAllister Linn, *The Echo of Battle: The Army's Way of War* (Cambridge: Harvard University Press, 2007), 92–110.
28. The town spelled its name both "Plattsburg" and "Plattsburgh." For consistency this book uses the latter, which is the modern official spelling.
29. J. Garry Clifford, *The Citizen Soldiers: The Plattsburg Training Camp Movement, 1913–1920* (Lexington: University of Kentucky Press, 2014), 238; Allan R. Millett, Peter Maslowski, and William B. Feis, *For the Common Defense: A Military History of The United States from 1607–2012*, rev. and expanded ed. (New York: Free Press, 1994), 304–8; Edward M. Coffman, *The War to End All Wars: The American Military Experience in World War I* (Lexington: University of Kentucky Press, 2004), 14–18; Russell F. Weigley, *History of the United States Army* (Bloomington: Indiana University Press, 1967), 342–44, 348.
30. Letter, Commander, 30th Infantry Regiment, "Transportation of the 30th Infantry to New York on transport BUFORD," December 7, 1914, Records of the Office of the Quartermaster General, 1774–1985, RG 92, NACP; Woodman, *Duty Station Northwest*, 308. See Charles Dana Gibson, "Ships and Men of the Army Transport Service (ATS)," *American Merchant Marine at War*, accessed March 2023, http://www.usmm.org/atshistory.html.
31. Charles H. Corlett, *Cowboy Pete; the Autobiography of Major General Charles H. Corlett* (Santa Fe, NM: Sleeping Fox, 1974), 34–35.
32. Letter, Quartermaster General, Subject: Passenger List of the Transport BUFORD, December 7, 1914, RG 319, NPRC; *Ada Weekly News*, January 21, 1915, p. 5; Corlett, *Cowboy Pete*, 35.
33. *Ada Weekly News*, January 21, 1915, p. 5.

34. ROB to father and Percy, June 20, 1915.
35. ROB to Mother, June 21, 1915.
36. Clifford, *Citizen Soldiers*, 69–75; Millett, Maslowski, and Feis, *For the Common Defense*, 306; Weigley, *History of the United States Army*, 342–43.
37. Major O. O. Ellis and Major E.B. Garey, *The Plattsburg Manual: A Handbook for Military Training*, 10th ed. (New York: Century Company, 1917); Robert W. Walker, *The Namesake: The Biography of Theodore Roosevelt, Jr.* (New York: Brick Tower Press, 2008), 67–68.
38. Tim Brady, *His Father's Son: The Life of General Ted Roosevelt Jr.* (New York: New American Library, 2017), 72–73.
39. ROB to Folks February 12, 1915; Efficiency Record: ROB, extract from Major Harry H. Bandholtz, 3d Battalion commander, November 15, 1915, RG 319, NPRC.
40. 30th Infantry Regiment, "Condition of the Command," January–November 1915, *Returns*, RG 94, NACP; Bandholtz comments.
41. Fort Niagara, "Condition of the Command," December 1915–May 1916, *Returns*, RG 94, NACP.
42. Fort Niagara, "Condition of the Command," May 1916, *Returns*, RG 94, NACP; Correspondence Between Barton and Eastern Department, re: returning to 30th Infantry, Fort Niagara, May 9, 1916.
43. Mitchell Yockelson, "The United States Armed Forces and the Mexican Punitive Expedition," pts. 1 and 2, *Prologue Magazine* 29, no. 3 (Spring 1997) : 256–62; 29, no. 4 (Winter 1997) : 334–43; Millett, Maslowski, and Feis, *For the Common Defense*, 302–3.
44. Marvin A. Kreidberg and Merton G. Henry, *History of Military Mobilization in the United States Army, 1775–1945* (Washington, DC: Department of the Army, 1955), 198–99; Millett, Maslowski, and Feis, *For the Common Defense*, 302–3; Weigley, *History of the United States Army*, 348.
45. Camp Eagle Pass, "Condition of the Command," July 1916, *Returns*, RG 94, NACP; Braim, *Will to Win*, 23–25, 62. Braim does not indicate who Van Fleet knew when on the Texas border.
46. Mahon and Danysh, *Infantry*, 42; War Department, *Order of Battle of the United States Land Forces in the World War*, vol. 3, pt. 2, *Zone of the Interior: Territorial Departments, Tactical Divisions Organized in 1918, and Post, Camps, and Stations* (Washington, DC: CMH, 1931), 602–3, map 2; *Ada Weekly News*, May 11, 1916, p. 1.

47. Efficiency Summary Report: ROB, James G. Ord, July 1916, RG 319, NPRC.

48. Michael Robert Patterson, "James Garesche Ord—Major General, United States Army," *Arlington National Cemetery*, accessed July 2020, http://www.arlingtoncemetery.net/jamesgar.htm.

49. Efficiency Summary Report: ROB, Edwin A. Root, November 1916, RG 319, NPRC; ROB, "Autobiography of Brigadier General Raymond O. Barton, U.S.A.," (unpublished manuscript, January 1942), BPP (hereafter ROB, "Autobiography").

50. Efficiency Summary Report: ROB, William L. Reed, May 1917 and February 1917, RG 319, NPRC.

51. Corlett, *Cowboy Pete*, 36–38; Allan R. Millett, *The General: Robert L. Bullard and Officership in the United States Army, 1881–1925* (Westport, CT: Greenwood Press, 1975), 288–89.

52. Thomas Fleming, *The Illusion of Victory: Americans in World War I* (New York: Basic Books, 2003), 86; David R. Woodward, *The American Army and the First World War*, Armies of the Great War (New York: Cambridge University Press, 2014), 85.

53. Kreidberg and Henry, *History of Military Mobilization*, 281–82.

54. William Learner, *Historical Statistics of the United States, Colonial Times to 1970* (Washington, DC: Bureau of the Census, 1976), series H 752, 757, 761.

55. "Register of Graduates and Former Cadets, 2010."

56. *Ada Weekly News*, May 17, 1917, p. 5.

57. Robert E. Brennan and Jeannie I. Brennan, *Images of America: Sackets Harbor* (Charleston, SC: Arcadia, 2000), 95–128.

58. Kreidberg and Henry, *History of Military Mobilization*, 198–99; Gordon C. Heiner Jr., *From Saints to Red Legs: The History of a Border Post* (Watertown, NY: A. W. Munk, 1938), 70; Raymond E. Bell Jr. "Madison Barracks New York," *On Point* 23, no. 2 (2017): 46–49.

59. Ellis and Garey, *Plattsburg Manual*.

60. *New York Times*, May 17, 1917; Letter, Edwin B. Terry to ROB, 1917.

61. Promotion to Captain, July 25, 1917, RG 319, NPRC.

62. Efficiency Summary Report: ROB, William R. Sample, August 1917, RG 319, NPRC.

63. *Watertown Harold* (Watertown, NY), August 11, 1917, p. 1, col. 4N.

64. Executive Committee, *The Plattsburger* (New York: Wynkoop Hallenbeck Crawford, 1917), 7.

65. Efficiency Report: ROB, George E. Goodrich, December 1917, RG 319, NPRC; Secretary of War, *Official Army Register* (Washington, DC: GPO, 1926), 230.

66. *Plattsburger*, 89–93; John Keegan, *The Face of Battle* (New York: Penguin Books, 1976), 221–22.

67. Graham A. Cosmas, "San Juan Hill and El Caney, 1–2 July 1898," in *America's First Battles, 1776-1965*, ed. Charles E. Heller and William A. Stoft (Lawrence: University Press of Kansas, 1986), 138–39; Leroy Yarborough and Truman Smith, *History of the Infantry School, Fort Benning, GA* (Fort Benning: Infantry School, 1931), 19.

68. Yarborough and Smith, *History of the Infantry School*, 11–22; Mahon and Danysh, *Infantry*, 38–40.

69. Yarborough and Smith, *History of the Infantry School*, 46, 65–66.

70. *Ada Weekly News*, December 13, 1917, p. 6.

71. Heefner, *Patton's Bulldog*, 16–27; "Register of Graduates and Former Cadets, 2010."

72. Efficiency Report: ROB, William B. Loughborough, May 1918; Jessie C. Drain, August 1918; and Henry E. Eames, 1918, RG 319, NPRC; Secretary of War, *Official Army Register* (Washington, DC: GPO, 1918), 584.

73. ROB to Folks, February 2, 1918.

74. ROB to Folks, January 1, 1918, and March 1, 1918.

75. ROB to Folks, March 1, 1918; "Register of Graduates and Former Cadets, 2010."

76. Percy Barton to Folks, July 7, 1918.

77. *Ada Weekly News*, February 14, 1918, p. 5.

78. Richard A. Tilden and Rosalind Roulston, *History of the Infantry School* (Draft) (Fort Benning: Infantry School, 1944), 41–43.

79. *Ada Weekly News*, September 5, 1918, p. 7; ROB to Folks, September 29, 1918.

80. *Ada Weekly News*, October 10, 1918, p. 6; *Ada Weekly News*, October 17, 1918, p. 4.

81. *Ada Weekly News*, December 8, 1921; note to the author from Cathy Barton Clarke, July 26, 2020.

82. Letter, commander of the Infantry School of Arms to ROB, October 7, 1918.

83. *Pontotoc County, Oklahoma, Genealogy Trails*, accessed February 2020, http://genealogytrails.com/oka/pontotoc.

84. Yarborough and Smith, *History of the Infantry School*, 72–73.

85. Efficiency Report: ROB, Oliver Edwards, August 13, 1919, RG 319, NPRC.
86. ROB to Folks, October 10 [estimated date], 1918.
87. Efficiency Report: ROB, L. A. Kunzig, August 13, 1919, RG 319, NPRC.
88. William J. Woolley, *Creating the Modern Army: Citizen-Soldiers and the American Way of War, 1919–1939*, Studies in Civil-Military Relations, ed. William A. Taylor (Lawrence: University Press of Kansas, 2022), 132; "A History of the Infantry School," (unpublished manuscript, Infantry School Research Library, Fort Benning, GA, 1945–1990), 49, 54, 60–62, 69. This unpublished manuscript, expanded to two volumes based on the Yarborough and Smith 1931 document, was first updated in 1945. Library staff continued to update the material until at least 1990. ROB to Folks, April 5, 1919. The US Army renamed this post Fort Benning in 1922 and Fort Moore in 2023.
89. ROB to Folks, November 24, 1918; ROB to Conway O. Barton, December 4, 1918.
90. *Ada Weekly News*, January 16, 1919, p. 8.
91. Efficiency Report: ROB, Owen R. Meredith, 1919 and 1920, RG 319, NPRC; ROB to Folks, December 1, 1918.
92. ROB to Folks, June 13, 1919.
93. ROB to Folks, April 20, 1919.
94. ROB to Folks, June 15, 1919.
95. Memo, Alexander M. Patch, re: Overseas Service, June 13, 1919, RG 319, NPRC.

Notes for Chapter 3

1. ROB to Folks, January 28, 1920.
2. Fleming, *Illusion of Victory*, 307.
3. Peter J. Schifferle, *America's School for War: Fort Leavenworth, Officer Education, and Victory in World War II* (Lawrence: University Press of Kansas, 2010), 14–15.
4. Dean A. Nowowiejski, *The American Army in Germany, 1918–1923: Success against the Odds* (Lawrence: University Press of Kansas, 2021).
5. ROB to Folks, July 25, 1919.
6. Richard G. McKee, "Memoirs (Draft)," (unpublished manuscript, 1960), 10–11, Richard G. McKee Personal Papers; Leonard L. Lerwill, *The Personnel Replacement System in the United States Army,*

Department of the Army pamphlet no. 20-211 (Washington, DC: Department of the Army, 1954), 187–88.

7. McKee, "Memoirs," 10.

8. Gordon W. Prange, *At Dawn We Slept: The Untold Story of Pearl Harbor* (New York: McGraw-Hill, 1981), 314–19, 346; ROB to Folks, July 28, 1919.

9. "World War 2 ship Sunk by US Submarine Discovered off Japan Coast," *Express*, September 7, 2018, https://www.express.co.uk/news/uk/1014491/world-war-2-ship-wreck-japan-us-submarine; "Transport *Taiyo Maru*: Tabular Record of Movement," CombinedFleet.com, accessed July 2020, http://www.combinedfleet.com/TaiyoM_t.htm.

10. Headquarters, Camp Meade Replacement Unit No. 10, Passenger List, Cap Finisterre, July 19, 1919, Record Group 92, Records of the Office of the Quartermaster General, 1774–1985 (hereafter RG 92), NACP.

11. ROB to Folks, July 25, 1919.

12. American Battle Monuments Commission, *American Armies and Battlefields in Europe* (1938; repr., Washington DC: CMH, 1992), 437–38.

13. ROB to Folks, August 12, 1919.

14. ROB to Folks, August 12, 1919.

15. ROB to Folks, August 12, 1919.

16. *American Armies and Battlefields in Europe*, 437–47; ROB to Folks, August 12, 1919.

17. ROB to Folks, August 26, 1919.

18. Memorandum for Chief Claims Officer, October 23, 1919; Memorandum for Executive Officer, Subj: Reclassification Civilian Employees, October 23, 1919, BPP.

19. ROB to Folks, September 1, 15, and 19, 1919.

20. Investigation, incident with French chauffeur, November 12, 1919, RG 319, NPRC.

21. ROB to Folks, October 11, 1919.

22. Alfred E. Cornebise, *The* Amaroc News: *The Daily Newspaper of the American Forces in Germany, 1919–1923* (Carbondale: Southern Illinois University Press, 1981), xvii; Nowowiejski, *American Army in Germany*, 25–34, 82–86.

23. ROB to Folks, January 3, 1920.

24. Hosfield, *American Representation*, 347–48.

25. Henry T. Allen, *My Rhineland Journal* (New York: Houghton Mifflin, 1923), 161.

26. *Ada Weekly News*, October 21, 1920, p. 11.

27. Allen, *My Rhineland Journal*, 160.

28. Allen, *My Rhineland Journal*, 441.

29. Efficiency Report: ROB, Keck, February 1920, RG 319, NPRC; ROB to Folks, April 25, 1920.

30. Efficiency Report: ROB, Thomlinson, July 1920, RG 319, NPRC; ROB to Folks, April 4, 1920; Steven Clay, *U.S. Army Order of Battle, 1919–1941*, 4 vols. (Fort Leavenworth, KS: CSI, 2010), 4:2179.

31. ROB to Folks, June 5 and 15, 1920.

32. Medical Board Report, September 5, 1920.

33. Oath of Office, November 20, 1920.

34. ROB to Folks, January 3, 1920.

35. Cornebise, *Amaroc News*, 41–55; Henry Hossfeld, *American Representation in Occupied Germany, 1922–1923* (Coblenz, Germany: American Forces in Germany, 1923), 304–20.

36. Richard G. McKee, McKee Personal Papers; Alfred Cornebise, *Typhus, and Doughboys: The American Polish Typhus Relief Expedition, 1919–1921* (Newark: University of Delaware Press, 1982), 104, 116–18.

37. J. Lawton Collins, *Lightning Joe: An Autobiography* (Baton Rouge: Louisiana State University Press, 1979), 34–41.

38. Efficiency Report: ROB, Hall, November 1920, RG 319, NPRC; Nowowiejski, *American Army in Germany*; Clay, *Order of Battle*, 4:2720.

39. *Army Register, 1926*, 35; Allen, *My Rhineland Journal*, 163.

40. Efficiency Report: ROB, Bates, June 1921, RG 319, NPRC; Allen, *My Rhineland Journal*, 163.

41. ROB to Folks, November 28, 1920.

42. James Fitzpatrick, US Census, 1910, Ancestry.com.

43. Clare Elliott Fitz Patrick, passport application, October 17, 1917, Passport Applications, *January 2, 1906–March 31, 1925, NACP*; *Brooklyn Citizen* (Brooklyn, NY), September 28, 1917, p. 7. Note: In some documents, clerks recorded her name as "Claire," which is a mistake. Interestingly, her passport application lists her name as "Fitz Patrick." As time went on, clerks adjusted it to Fitzpatrick.

44. *Ada Evening News*, November 7, 1921, Page 3; Clare E. Fitz Patrick Barton, passport application, May 17, 1921; *World-Herald* (Omaha, NE), April 21, 1926, p. 11; *Sunday-World Herald* (Omaha, NE), Social and Women's Affairs, March 14, 1926.

45. ROB to Folks, November 28, 1920.

46. ROB to Folks, January 23, 1921.
47. Clare Fitzpatrick Barton (CFB) to Folks, May 1, 1921.
48. Packet, movement of Mrs. Barton to Germany, August 18, 1921, RG 319, NPRC.
49. Jay Winter, *Sites of Memory, Sites of Mourning: The Great War in European Cultural History* (New York: Cambridge University Press, 1998), 22–28.
50. McKee Papers, photographs. Most likely he only participated in the London ceremony.
51. Allen, *My Rhineland Journal*, 259; "Splendid Reception for General Pershing," *Daily Free-Lance* (Henryetta, OK), September 28, 1921, p. 2.
52. ROB to Folks, November 13, 1921.
53. ROB to Folks, November 13, 1921; "Ce Matin, Revue franco-américaine aux Champs-Élysées," *Le Journal* (Paris), October 2, 1921, p. 1; "Le général Pershing remet au soldat francais inconnu la Médaille d'honneur du Congrès américain," *Le Journal* (Paris), October 8, 1921; Allen, *My Rhineland Journal*, 262.
54. Allen, *My Rhineland Journal*, 262; "Ada Man Chosen for Commanding Special Escort," *Ada Evening News* (Ada, OK), November 7, 1921, p. 3.
55. Allen, *My Rhineland Journal*, 267.
56. "London Crowds Hail Pershing and Men: General and Picked Battalion Arrive for Conferring Medal on Unknown Soldier," *New York Times*, October 17, 1921, p. 14.
57. "Americans in London," *New York Herald*, October 24, 1921, p. 8.
58. "Unknown Warrior," *Westminster Abbey*, accessed May 2022, https://www.westminster-abbey.org/abbey-commemorations/commemorations/unknown-warrior.
59. Efficiency Report: ROB, Bates, June 1922, RG 319, NPRC; Cornebise, *Amaroc News*, 98.
60. CFB to Folks, December 2, 1921.
61. ROB, request to study Japanese, November 25, 1921, RG 319, NPRC.
62. CFB to Folks, January 31, 1922.
63. ROB to Max Lough, February 3, 1922.
64. ROB to Folks, February 24, 1922, and April 9, 1922; CFB to Folks, August 11, 1922.
65. ROB to Folks, June 11, 1922, and August 28, 1922; CFB to Folks, July 24, 1922, and December 8, 1922.
66. Allen, *My Rhineland Journal*, 502
67. Allen, *My Rhineland Journal*, 506, 511–34.

68. Allen, *My Rhineland Journal*, 536–40; Alexander Barnes, *In a Strange Land: The American Occupation of Germany, 1918–1923* (Atglen, PA: Schiffer Military History, 2011), 280–81.

69. CFB to Folks, February 5, 1923; ROB, "Autobiography."

70. Memorandum, army officers arriving at Brooklyn on USAT *St. Mihiel*, February 23, 1923, RG 319, NPRC.

71. ROB to Folks, February 9, 1923; memorandum, army officers arriving at Brooklyn on USAT *St. Mihiel*.

72. ROB to Folks, April 22, 1923; Letter, Edna Kelly to ROB, April 27, 1923.

73. ROB and CFB to Folks, May 31, 1923; CFB to Folks, March 16, 1923; Marshall H. Kelly, US Census, 1930, Ancestry.com.

74. Edna Kelly to ROB, April 24, 1923; ROB to Folks, May 6, 1923; ROB and CFB to Folks, May 31, 1923.

75. Clay, *Order of Battle*, 1:363.

76. Kevin M. McCarthy, *Georgia's Lighthouses and Historic Coastal Sites* (Sarasota, FL: Pineapple Press, 1998), 30; Weigley, *History of the United States Army*, 284–85; Linn, *Echo of Battle*, 33–39.

77. ROB to Folks, March 23, 1923, and February 9, 1923; James Mack Adams, *Images of America: Tybee Island* (Charleston, SC: Arcadia, 2000), 45–50.

78. ROB to Folks, February 12, 1923.

79. Efficiency Report: ROB, Bates, March 1923, RG 319, NPRC.

80. *Army Register*, 1945; "Walter Trotter Bates," *Find a Grave*, accessed August 2020, https://www.findagrave.com/memorial/35248274/walter -trotter-bates.

81. US Department of Commerce, *Official Register of the United States, 1921* (Washington, DC: GPO, 1921), 62–63.

82. ROB to Folks, May 13, 1923, and March 23, 1923; Barton, detail to the CGSS, school year 1925–1926, RG 319, NPRC.

83. Efficiency Report: ROB, Gilbert R. Cook, April 21, 1923; and George H. McManus, August 2, 1923, RG 319, NPRC; ROB to Conway O. Barton, July 6, 1923.

Notes for Chapter 4

1. ROB to Folks, April 30, 1927.

2. Timothy K. Nenninger, *The Leavenworth Schools and the Old Army* (Westport, CT: Greenwood Press, 1978), 113–30; J. P. Clark, *Preparing for War: The Emergence of the Modern U.S. Army, 1815–1917* (Cambridge, MA: Harvard University Press, 2017), 196–230.

3. Nenninger, *Leavenworth Schools*, 150.
4. Boyd L. Dastrup, *The US Army Command and General Staff College: A Centennial History* (Manhattan, KS: Sunflower University Press, 1982), 64.
5. Harry A. Smith, *Annual Report of the Command and General Staff School, 1923–1924* (Fort Leavenworth, KS: CGSS Press, 1924), appendix 3; Elvid Hunt, *History of Fort Leavenworth*, 2nd ed. (Fort Leavenworth, KS: CGSS Press, 1937), 165.
6. Hugh A. Drum, *Troop Leading: An Infantry Division in the Attack* (Fort Leavenworth, KS: General Services Schools Press, 1921); Robert H. Allen, *Combat Orders*. (Fort Leavenworth, KS: General Service Schools Press, 1922).
7. Dastrup, *US Army Command*, 65.
8. Schifferle, *America's School for War*, 100.
9. George S. Patton, *The Patton Papers, 1895–1940*, ed. Martin Blumenson (Boston: Houghton Mifflin Company, 1972), 841–46; Mark C. Bender, "Watershed at Leavenworth: Dwight D. Eisenhower and the Command and General Staff School," (master's thesis, US Army Command and General Staff College, 1988), 60; Dwight D. Eisenhower, *Eisenhower: The Prewar Diaries and Selected Papers, 1905–1941*, ed. Daniel D. Holt and James W. Leyerzapf (Baltimore: Johns Hopkins University Press, 1998), 47–48.
10. *Eisenhower:Prewar Diaries*, "On the Command and General Staff School, August 1926," 43–58.
11. Adams, *Tybee Island*, 74–78.
12. ROB to Folks, August 23 and 24, 1923; ROB to Mother, August 28, 1923.
13. Quentin W. Schillare, *Fort Leavenworth: The People Behind the Names* (Fort Leavenworth, KS: CSI, 2015), 42.
14. "100 Years," *Union Station*, accessed August 2020, https://www. unionstation.org/timeline; Sarajane Sandusky Aber, "An Architectural History of the Liberty Memorial in Kansas City, Missouri, 1918–1935," (master's thesis, University of Missouri–Kansas City, 1988), 38–39.
15. Schillare, *Fort Leavenworth*, 44.
16. Hunt, *History of Fort Leavenworth*, 204; Officer's Residence List, Class 1923–24, CARL; Schillare, *Fort Leavenworth*, 49.
17. ROB to Folks, August 24 and September 27, 1923.
18. ROB to Mother, August 28, 1923.
19. Smith, *Annual Report*; 1912 Executive Committee, *Ten Year Book*.

20. *Patton Papers*, 842.
21. Steven Rabalais, *General Fox Connor: Pershing's Chief of Operations and Eisenhower's Mentor* (Philadelphia: Casemate, 2016), 177–201; Matthew F. Holland, *Eisenhower between the Wars: The Making of a General and Statesman* (Westport, CT: Praeger, 2001), 100–104; Bender, "Watershed at Leavenworth," 61.
22. ROB to Folks, March 24, 1924.
23. ROB to Folks, September 5, 1923.
24. ROB to Folks, December 27, 1923.
25. ROB to Father, January 9, 1924; "Roddie Judged Not Guilty by Tecumseh Jury," *Ada Weekly News*, January 31, 1924, p. 4; "Former State Legislator Dies," *Daily Oklahoman*, September 22, 1943, p. 11.
26. ROB to Folks, February 3, 1924.
27. ROB to Folks, April 4 and May 4, 1924.
28. Efficiency Report: ROB, Bundel, June 1924, RG 319, NPRC; CGSS: Academic Report, July 1, 1924, RG 319, NPRC.
29. Smith, *Annual Report*, 3.
30. Requests for details to Syracuse, Staunton, and 8th Inf. Brigade, March–May 1924, RG 319, NPRC.
31. General Staff Corps Eligible, 1924, RG 319, NPRC; Schifferle, *America's School for War*, 138–39
32. ROB and CFB to Folks, March 16, 1924; Major General Duncan to ROB, March 4, 1924.
33. ROB to Folks, June 20, 1924; "Maj. Raymond Barton Given Important Post Under New Assignment," *Ada Weekly News*, July 24, 2024.
34. Postcard, ROB to Folks, July 31, 1924.
35. "Historic Fort Omaha," *Omaha History* (archive), accessed August 2020, https://web.archive.org/web/20070206215748/ http://www.omahahistory. org/fort_omaha.htm.
36. Clay, *Order of Battle*, 1:59, 423, 478.
37. Author's visit, August 2020.
38. Wooley, *Creating the Modern Army*, 43–46; Clay, *Order of Battle*, 1:11–12; Millett, Maslowski, and Feis, *For the Common Defense*, 343–45.
39. Clay, *Order of Battle*, 1:12, 59–64.
40. War Department, *Field Manual 101–5, Staff Officers' Field Manual, Staff and Combat Orders* (Washington, DC: GPO, 1940), 6–16.
41. US Adjutant General, *The Army List, and Directory, September 1, 1925* (Washington, DC: GPO, 1925), 5, 49.

42. ROB to Folks, August 24, 1924; *Lincoln Journal Star*, July 14, 1924, p. 9.
43. ROB to Father, October 12, 1924; Clare Conway Barton, Social Security Index, 1936–2007, Application (SS-5) Files, 1936–2007, NACP.
44. Edna Kelly to CMB, November 16, 1924
45. *World-Herald*, December 25, 1924, p. 17.
46. Medical Officer, Fort Omaha, *Report of Physical Examination, Raymond O. Barton*, January 26, 1925; Hospitalization-Clinical Abstract, 1939, RG 319, NPRC.
47. *Lincoln Journal Star*, April 5, 1925, p. 30.
48. Efficiency Report: ROB, Harry A. Eaton, June 1925, RG 319, NPRC.
49. Duncan, letter of commendation, October 9, 1925, RG 319, NPRC.
50. Efficiency Report: ROB, Tenney Ross, June 1927, RG 319, NPRC.
51. *Lincoln Journal Star*, May 20, 1926, p. 6.
52. *World Herald-Omaha*, June 1, 1926, p. 17.
53. Barton, flying record, 1925–1927, RG 319, NPRC.
54. *Ada Weekly News*, July 15, 1926, p. 8.
55. *World Herald-Omaha*, April 21, 1926, p. 11; *Sunday World-Herald*, March 14, 1926, social section.
56. CFB to "Everybody," October 16, 1926.
57. John M. Barry, *Rising Tide: The Great Mississippi Flood of 1927 and How It Changed America* (New York: Simon & Schuster, 1997), 282–89; Risk Management Solutions, *RMD Special Report: The 1927 Great Mississippi Flood: 80-Year Retrospective* (Newark, CA: Risk Management Solutions, 2007), https://forms2.rms.com/rs/729-DJX-565/images/fl_1927_great_mississippi_flood.pdf; Kevin R. Kosar, *Disaster Response and Appointment of a Recovery Czar: The Executive Branch's Response to the Flood of 1927* (Washington, DC: Congressional Research Service, Library of Congress 2005); Leland R. Johnson, *Situation Desperate: U.S. Army Engineer Disaster Relief Operations, Origins to 1950* (Alexandria, VA: US Army Corps of Engineers, 2011), 147–57; *Nebraska State Journal* (Lincoln, NE), April 26, 1927, p. 1.
58. *World Herald-Omaha*, April 21, 1927, p. 1; *World Herald-Omaha*, April 23, 1927, p. 2; ROB to Folks, April 30, 1927.
59. Efficiency Report: ROB, Tenney Ross, June 1927, RG 319, NPRC.
60. ROB to Folks, December 3, 1927; Medical Report, January 27, 1927, RG 319, NPRC; CFB to ROB, November 22, 1926; ROB to Folks, November 27 and December 3, 1927.
61. *World Herald-Omaha*, October 12, 1927, p. 2.
62. *Lincoln Journal Star*, March 23, 1928, p. 17.

63. *Sunday World-Herald,* March 18, 1928, p. 17; *World Herald-Omaha,* April 19, 1928, p. 14.

64. *Sunday World-Herald,* June 10, 1928, section E; Weaver, "Raymond O. Barton 1912," Cullum 5085, USMA.

65. Special Orders 60, 1928, Orders to Fort Leavenworth, BPP; Efficiency Report: ROB, Ross, June 1928, RG 319, NPRC.

66. Hunt, *History of Fort Leavenworth,* 20; Schillare, *Fort Leavenworth,* 29–30.

67. ROB to Folks, October 20, 1928; Raymond O. Bratton, US Census, 1930, Ancestry.com. The census taker misspelled the Barton name. All the other information is correct.

68. Corlett, *Cowboy Pete,* 41–43.

69. "Register of Graduates and Former Cadets"; D'Este, *Eisenhower,* 486–87.

70. Stuart Heintzelman, *Annual Report of the Command and General Staff School, 1929–1930* (Fort Leavenworth, KS: CGSS Press, 1930), 28.

71. Robert H. Berlin, *US Army World War II Corps Commanders: A Composite Biography* (Fort Leavenworth, KS: CSI, 1989), 11; Schifferle, *America's School for War,* 92–93.

72. "Clarence R. Huebner, Lieutenant General, USA," CGSC.Leavenworth.Army.mil (archive), accessed July2021, https://web.archive.org/web/20070520225856/ http://cgsc.leavenworth.army.mil/carl/resources/ftlvn/ww2.asp#huebner.

73. Clay, *Order of Battle,* 1:197–98.

74. CGSS, *Schedule for 1929–1930: First Year Course* (Fort Leavenworth, KS: CGSS Press, 1929); Roger Cirillo, *Memorandum for the Deputy Commander: 2-Year Course, 1930–1936* (Fort Leavenworth, KS: CARL, 1984), Incl 3.

75. Edward L. King, *Annual Report of the Command and General Staff School, 1928–1929.* (Fort Leavenworth, KS: CGSS Press, 1929), 8.

76. Clay, *Order of Battle,* 1:98–100, 137–40.

77. CGSS, *Schedule for 1933–1934: Second-Year Class* (Fort Leavenworth, KS: CGSS Press, 1933).

78. J. Lawton Collins, "The Conduct of the Secondary Attack" and "Did the German Enveloping Maneuver through Belgium in 1914 Surprise the French General Staff?" (Fort Leavenworth, KS: CGSS, 1933).

79. Cirillo, *Memorandum.*

80. Collins, *Lightning Joe,* 56–57; J. Lawton Collins, interview by Charles C. Sperow, Senior Officers Oral History Program, Project 72–1, Edited

Transcript #720112, 1972, US Army Heritage and Education Center Carlisle, PA, 118–25.

81. Efficiency Reports: Collins, 1921–1931, J. Lawton Collins Official Military Records, NPRC.
82. Forrest C. Pogue, *George C. Marshall: Education of a General, 1880–1939* (New York: Viking Press, 1963), 248–49.
83. Collins, interview by Sperow, 118, 122.
84. Collins, interview by Sperow, 124.
85. *St. Joseph Gazette* (St. Joseph, MO), July 31, 1931, p. 5.
86. *Kansas City Times* (Kansas City, MO), October 21, 1931, p. 5.
87. *St. Joseph News-Press/Gazette* (St. Joseph, MO), January 4, 1930, p. 1.
88. *Ada Weekly News*, July 17, 1929, p. 3.
89. ROB to Folks, October 21 and November 18, 1929.
90. ROB to Folks, April 6, 1932.
91. Edward M. Coffman, *The Regulars: The American Army, 1898–1941* (Cambridge, MA: Belknap Press, 2004), 242.
92. ROB to Folks, December 1, 1930.

Notes for Chapter 5

1. ROB to CCB, May 10, 1940.
2. USAWC Alumni Association, *Directory of U.S. Army War College Graduates* (Carlisle, PA: USAWC Alumni Association, 2000), 114.
3. See Henry G. Gole, *The Road to Rainbow: Army Planning for Global War, 1934–1940* (Annapolis, MD: Naval Institute Press, 2003), on the role of Army War College students in preparing for the Second World War.
4. David M. Kennedy, *Freedom from Fear: The United States, 1929–1945.* Oxford History of the United States (New York: Oxford University Press, 1996), 65–87, 160–89.
5. Coffman, *Regulars*, 239–42.
6. Clayton D. Laurie and Ronald H. Cole, *The Role of Federal Military Forces in Domestic Disorders, 1877–1945* (Washington, DC: US Army Center of Military History, 1997), 367–89; Kennedy, *Freedom from Fear*, 92.
7. ROB to Folks, December 2, 1932.
8. "National Register of Historic Places Registration Form: Old Woodley Park Historic District," planning.dc.gov, accessed August 2022, https://planning.dc.gov/sites/default/files/dc/sites/op/publication/attachments/Woodley%20Park%20HD%20nom.pdf; ROB to Folks, August 29, 1932.

9. Coffman, *Regulars*, 284–85.

10. D. K. Crosswell, *Beetle: The Life of General Walter Bedell Smith* (Lexington, KY: University Press of Kentucky, 2010), 197–98; D'Este, *Eisenhower*, 191–92.

11. ROB to Folks, September 27, 1932.

12. ROB to Folks, November 1, 1932.

13. ROB to Folks, December 2, 1932.

14. Forrest C. Pogue, *The European Theater of Operations: The Supreme Command*, United States Army in World War II (Washington, DC: CMH, 1954), 3.

15. Dewitt S. Copp, *Frank M. Andrews: Marshall's Airman* (Washington, DC: Air Force History and Museums Program, 2003).

16. *Directory of U.S. Army War College Graduates*, 114.

17. John A. Adams, *General Jacob Devers: World War II's Forgotten Four Star* (Bloomington: Indiana University Press, 2015), 26–27; Mark T. Calhoun, *General Lesley J. McNair: Unsung Architect of the US Army* (Lawrence: University of Kansas, 2015), 127–35.

18. Forrest C. Pogue, *George C. Marshall: Education of a General, 1880–1939* (New York: Viking Press, 1963), 313; Forrest C. Pogue, *George C. Marshall: Organizer of Victory, 1944–1945* (New York: Viking Press, 1973), 119–20; Henry G. Gole, *Exposing the Third Reich: Colonel Truman Smith in Hitler's Germany* (Lexington: University of Kentucky Press, 2013), 103–16, 268–69.

19. Coffman, *Regulars*, 285.

20. Adams, *Devers*, 27; Ossad, *Omar Nelson Bradley*, 73–74; Crosswell, *Beetle*, 197, for example.

21. Gole, *Road to Rainbow*, appendix H; *Directory of U.S. Army War College Graduates*, 114.

22. Calhoun, *McNair*, 99–100, 116–23; Michael R. Matheny, *Carrying the War to the Enemy: American Operational Art to 1945* (Norman: University of Oklahoma Press, 2011), 57–68; Coffman, *Regulars*, 285–86.

23. Harry P. Ball, *Of Responsible Command: A History of the U.S. Army War College*, rev. ed. (Carlisle Barracks, PA: Alumni Association of the United States Army War College, 1994), 212–15; Coffman, *Regulars*, 285–86.

24. Efficiency Report: ROB, Simonds, June 1933, RG 319, NPRC.

25. ROB to Folks, August 15, 1933.

26. ROB to Mother, December 6, 1935.

27. ROB to Folks, January 20, 1936

28. ROB to Folks, August 15, 1933; *Register of Faculties and Students of Georgetown University, 1933–1934* (Washington, DC: Georgetown University, 1933).

29. John Gilmary Shea, *Memorial of the First Century of Georgetown College, D.C.: Comprising a History of Georgetown University* (Washington, DC: Georgetown University, 1891), 41–45.

30. Millett, Maslowski, and Feis, *For the Common Defense*, 344–45; Arthur T. Coumbe and Lee S. Harford, *U.S. Army Cadet Command: The 10 Year History*, Cadet Command Historical Study Series (Fort Monroe, VA: US Army Cadet Command, 1996), 4–18; Weigley, *History of the United States Army*, 398–401, 28.

31. *Evening Star* (Washington, DC), April 23, 1933, p. 18; *Evening Star*, May 2, 1933, p. 24.

32. Gallagher, *Ye Domesday Booke*, 60–63.

33. *Evening Star*, May 27, 1934, p. 31; Gallagher, *Ye Domesday Booke*, 60–63.

34. *Evening Star*, May 18, 1934, p. 20; "Brigadier General Robert W. Hall," *Air Force*, accessed September 2020, https://www.af.mil/About-Us/Biographies/Display/Article/106876/brigadier-general-robert-w-hall/.

35. *Evening Star*, September 8, 1935, p. 36.

36. Gallagher, *Ye Domesday Booke*, 60–63.

37. ROB to Folks, August 27, 1934.

38. "Obituary, Col. Gregory Hosington," *Harvey County Genealogical Database*, accessed October, 2023, https://www.hcgsks.org/harcodatabase/showmedia.php?mediaID=10932&tngpage=4596&sitever=standardm.

39. Gerden F. Johnson, *History of the Twelfth Infantry Regiment in World War II* (repr., Athens, GA: Deeds, 2017), 38.

40. Efficiency Report: ROB, Edward H. Bertram, July 1935, RG 319, NPRC; Commendation (J. G. Ord), Fort Washington, July 25, 1935; Commendation of Officers, July 1935, RG 319, NPRC.

41. *Evening Star*, May 18, 1934, p. 19; Kennedy, *Freedom from Fear*, 749–60.

42. Orders, promotion to lieutenant colonel, Raymond O. Barton, August 31, 1935, RG 319, NPRC.

43. ROB to Folks, March 27, 1936

44. Woolley, *Creating the Modern Army*, 133–35.

45. Tilden and Roulston, *History of the Infantry School*, 142–49, 159; Woolley, *Creating the Modern Army*, 138.

46. Neil M. Maher, *Nature's New Deal: The Civilian Conservation Corps and the Roots of the American Environmental Movement*

(New York: Oxford University Press, 2008), 77–97; Kennedy, *Freedom from Fear*, 144–47.

47. *Atlanta Constitution* (Atlanta, GA), July 5, 1936, p. 14; John C. Paige, *The Civilian Conservation Corps and the National Park Service, 1933–1942: An Administrative History* (Washington, DC: National Park Service, 1985), 132; Charles E. Heller, "The U.S. Army, the Civilian Conservation Corps, and Leadership for World War II, 1933–1942," *Armed Forces & Society* 36, no. 3 (2010): 447–48.

48. Woolley, *Creating the Modern Army*, 182–83; Coffman, *Regulars*, 242–45;

49. Heller, "U.S. Army, the Civilian Conservation Corps," 442–44; Paige, *Civilian Conservation Corps*, 68, 70–72; Harry H. Woodring, *Report of the Secretary of War to the President, 1937* (Washington, DC: GPO, 1937), 32.

50. Paige, *Civilian Conservation Corps*, 54–55.

51. For example, the *Columbus Ledger* (Columbus, GA), February 1, 1937, p. 8; *Columbus Enquirer* (Columbus, GA), August 2, 1937, p. 3.

52. *Columbus Enquirer*, October 1, 1936, p. 1; Efficiency Report: ROB, Asa L. Singleton, June 30, 1937, and June 30, 1938, RG 319, NPRC; "Infantry School Officer's Roster, 1938," DRL; *Columbus Enquirer*, September 1, 1936, p. 12; *Columbus Enquirer*, October 1, 1936, p. 1.

53. *Columbus Ledger*, November 25, 1936, p. 1.

54. ROB to Folks, August 31, 1936.

55. *Columbus Enquirer*, July 3, 1937, p. 3.

56. Efficiency Report: ROB, Asa L. Singleton, June 30, 1937, and June 30, 1938, RG 319, NPRC.

57. "Asa Leonidas Singleton," *Find a Grave*, accessed August 2021, https://www.findagrave.com/memorial/19357090/asa-leonidas-singleton.

58. ROB to Folks, June 27, 1938; *Columbus Enquirer*, August 2, 1937, p. 3; ROB to Mother, July 31, 1937; "John Harlan Chambers," *Find a Grave*, accessed December 2021, https://www.findagrave.com/memorial/481394/john-harlan-chambers.

59. Accident investigation, November 28, 1936.

60. Memorandum from adjutant general to assistant chief of staff, G-1, September 2, 1938, RG 319, NPRC; ROB Folks, June 27 and August 12, 1938.

61. ROB to Mother, December 4, 1938.

62. *Columbus Ledger*, November 2, 1938, p. 5.

63. Richard Cloues, "Fort Screven: National Register of Historic Places Inventory–Nomination Form" (Atlanta: Historic Preservation Section, Georgia Department of Natural Resources, 1980).

64. Robert A. Ciucevich, "City of Tybee Island Historic Resources Survey Phase II" (Savannah, GA: Quatrefoil Historic Preservation Consulting, 2017); Adams, *Tybee Island*; Pogue, *Education of a General*, 272–73;

65. ROB to Folks, December 27, 1938; Chambers to his parents, January 15, 1939, BPP.

66. Flynn, *Howitzer* (1912), 53.

67. Barton, reports of physical examination, 1920–1943, RG 319, NPRC.

68. Brief Medical History, Raymond O. Barton, August 1945, RG 319, NPRC (hereafter cited as Brief Medical History: ROB); "Antacids," NHS.uk, accessed October 2020, https://www.nhs.uk/conditions/antacids/.

69. ROB to Mother, February 25, 1939.

70. ROB to Folks, March 3, 1939.

71. Barton, report of physical exam, January 1939, RG 319, NPRC.

72. ROB to Parents, May 26, 1939, BPP (letter is mistakenly dated 1937); Charles T. Lanham, Efficiency Report, Robert H. Chance, January 10, 1941, Charles T. Lanham Official Military Records (hereafter Lanham Records), NPRC.

73. Henry L. Stimson, *Report of the Secretary of War to the President, 1937* (Washington, DC: GPO, 1940), 26.

74. Forrest C. Pogue, *George C. Marshall: Education of a General, 1880–1939* (New York: Viking Press, 1963), 326–30; Eric Larrabee, *Commander in Chief: Franklin Delano Roosevelt, His Lieutenants, and Their War* (New York: Harper & Row, 1987), 106–7.

75. Geoffrey Perret, *There's a War to Be Won: The United States Army in World War II* (New York: Ivy Books, 1991), 25.

76. Calhoun, *McNair*, 226–27; Gary H. Wade, *CSI Report No. 7: World War II Division Commanders* (Fort Leavenworth, KS: CSI, 1983), 3.

77. Kennedy, *Freedom from Fear*, 426–38.

78. Forrest C. Pogue, *George C. Marshall: Ordeal and Hope, 1939–1942* (New York: Viking Press, 1966), 132–33.

79. Francis G. Smith. "History of the Third Army, Study No. 17," Army Ground Forces Studies (Fort Leavenworth, KS: CARL, 1946), 7. Note: These are the Third Army Louisiana Maneuvers, not to be confused with the General Headquarters Louisiana Maneuvers of 1941.

80. Tilden and Roulston, *History of the Infantry School*, 184–85.

81. War Department, *FM 101-5*, 22.

82. Efficiency Reports: ROB, Stanley Embick, 1940, RG 319, NPRC.

83. Letter, Bush to commander, 7th Corps Area, June 17, 1940, RG 319, NPRC.

Notes for Chapter 6

1. ROB to CCB, February 26, 1942 (with transcript of War Department phone conversation).
2. John B. Wilson, *Maneuver and Firepower: The Evolution of Divisions and Separate Brigades*, Army Lineage Series (Washington, DC: CMH, 1998), 52–55; Glen R. Hawkins and James Jay Carafano, *Prelude to Army XXI: U.S. Army Division Design Initiatives and Experiments, 1917–1995* (Washington, DC: CMH, 1997), 5–6.
3. John B. Wilson, *Armies, Corps, Divisions and Separate Brigades*, Army Lineage Series, (Washington, DC: CMH, 1987), 187.
4. War Department, *Order of Battle of the United States Land Forces in the World War*, vol. 2, *American Expeditionary Forces: Divisions* (Washington, DC: GPO; repr., Washington, DC: CMH, 1988), 59–73; Wilson, *Armies*, 187–89.
5. Calhoun, *McNair*, 153–70; Jonathan M. House, *Combined Arms Warfare in the Twentieth Century* (Lawrence: University Press of Kansas, 2001), 96–103; Shelby L. Stanton, *World War II Order of Battle: An Encylopedic Reference to U.S. Army Ground Force Units from Battalion through Division, 1939–1946* (Mechanicsburg, PA: Stackpole Books, 2006), 8–10.
6. Tilden and Roulston, *History of the Infantry School*, 182–84; Stanton, *World War II Order of Battle*, 81, 200–204; Raymond O. Barton, *The 4th Motorized Division* (Augusta, GA: Walton Printing, 1942), 13–17.
7. Tilden and Roulston, *History of the Infantry School*, 198–99, 201.
8. *Atlanta Constitution*, July 30, 1940, p. 9.
9. Braim, *Will to Win*, 259; Bourque, "Richard G. McKee."
10. War Department, *Technical Manual-E 30-451: Handbook on German Military Forces* (Washington: GPO, 1945), 98–101.
11. Wilson, *Maneuver and Firepower*, 172.
12. Barton, *4th Motorized Division*, 13, 20; Stanton, *World War II Order of Battle*, 81; War Department, "Table of Organization No. 77, Infantry Division (Triangular, Motorized)," November 1, 1940, DRL.
13. *Atlanta Constitution*, September 14, 1940, p. 11.
14. Letter of commendation, Walter E. Prosser to ROB, October 5, 1940, RG 319, NPRC; Blakeley, *4th Infantry Division (Yearbook)*, 16.
15. *Atlanta Constitution*, September 25, 1940, p. 4.
16. Efficiency Report: ROB, Walter E. Prosser, 1940, RG 319, NPRC.
17. Rick Atkinson, *An Army at Dawn: The War in Africa, 1942–1943* (New York: Henry Holt, 2002), 272–73.

18. ROB to Folks, February 18, 1941.
19. Kent Roberts Greenfield, Robert R. Palmer, and Bell I. Wiley, *The Army Ground Forces: The Organization of Ground Combat Troops* (1947; repr., Washington, DC: CMH, 1987), 106; Christopher R. Gabel, *The U.S. Army GHQ Maneuvers of 1941* (Washington, DC: CMH, 1991), 41; *Atlanta Constitution*, May 21, 1941, p. 25.
20. News clippings, Ada, OK papers, June 1941, BPP.
21. ROB to Folks, June 30, 1941.
22. Clippings from Ada newspapers, July 1941.
23. George F. Howe, *The Mediterranean Theater of Operations: Northwest Africa: Seizing the Initiative in the West* (Washington, DC: CMH, 1957), 35n11.
24. Efficiency Reports: ROB, Fredendall, 1940, RG 319, NPRC. With the war on the horizon, officer's efficiency reports received attention from Marshall and McNair, who were searching for aggressive officers for command billets. The positive comments from Barton's raters helped him meet the criteria for his subsequent advance.
25. Gabel, *U.S. Army GHQ Maneuvers*, 27–29; *Arizona Daily Star* (Tucson), August 12, 1941, p. 3.
26. Barton, *4th Motorized Division*, 5; *Town Talk* (Alexandria, LA), August 12, 1941, p. 8.
27. ROB to CFB, September 13, 1941.
28. ROB to CCB, November 9, 1941.
29. ROB to CCB, September 20, 1941.
30. ROB to CFB, November 13, 1941.
31. ROB to CCB, September 9, 10, 17, 1941.
32. ROB to CFB, August 17, 1941 (letter is misdated April 17).
33. ROB to CFB, August 17, 1941.
34. ROB to Mother, September 13, 1941.
35. Barton, *4th Motorized Division*, 5, 16.
36. Smith, "History of the Third Army," 17; Pogue, *Ordeal and Hope*, 97–103; Calhoun, *McNair*, 243–44; Gabel, *U.S. Army GHQ Maneuvers*, 115–18.
37. Efficiency Report: ROB, Oscar W. Griswold, October 1941, RG 319, NPRC.
38. ROB to CCB, October 6, 1941.
39. ROB to CCB, October 7, 1941.
40. *Tampa Bay Times* (St. Petersburg, FL), October 11, 1941, p. 6.
41. ROB to CCB, October 12, 1941.
42. Gabel, *U.S. Army GHQ Maneuvers*, 127–28.

43. ROB to family, October 14, 1941; Gabel, *U.S. Army GHQ Maneuvers*, 127, 133, 199–200.
44. Greenfield, Palmer, and Wiley, *Army Ground Forces*, 361.
45. ROB to CFB, November 15, 1941.
46. Gabel, *U.S. Army GHQ Maneuvers*, 132.
47. Gabel, *U.S. Army GHQ Maneuvers*, 127, 133.
48. ROB to family, October 24, 1941; Gabel, *U.S. Army GHQ Maneuvers*, 135.
49. ROB to family, October 14, 1941; ROB to CFB, October 27, 1941; ROB to family, October 24, 1941.
50. ROB to Mother, October 27, 1941.
51. ROB to family, October 31, 1941; ROB to CCB, November 1 1, 1941.
52. Also known as torticollis or loxia; see Bethany Cadman, "What Is Wry Neck and How Is It Treated?," *Medical News Today*, October 12, 2018, https://www.medicalnewstoday.com/articles/323332; ROB to CFB, November 13, 1941.
53. ROB to CCB, November 5, 1941.
54. ROB to family, November 6, 1941.
55. ROB to CCB, November 9, 1941.
56. ROB to CFB, November 13, 1941.
57. Gabel, *U.S. Army GHQ Maneuvers*, 133–34.
58. Gabel, *U.S. Army GHQ Maneuvers*, 149–50.
59. Gabel, *U.S. Army GHQ Maneuvers*, 155.
60. Efficiency Report: ROB, Lanham, June 15, 1940, RG 319, NPRC; Efficiency Report: Courtney Hodges, Lanham, June 30, 1941, AF Form 66, Officer's, Warrant Officer's, and Flight Officer's Qualification Record, Lanham Records; ROB to Family, November 25, 1941.
61. ROB to Family, November 25, 1941.
62. ROB to Family, November 27, 1941.
63. Gabel, *U.S. Army GHQ Maneuvers*, 166.
64. Letter, Griswold to adjutant general, December 26, 1941, RG 319, NPRC.
65. Smith, "History of the Third Army," 23–24.
66. Letter, ROB to CCB, December 12, 1941; Letter, ROB to family, December 13, 1941.
67. Louis Morton, *The War in the Pacific: The Fall of the Philippines*, United States Army in World War II (Washington, DC: CMH, 1993).
68. ROB to CCB, December 17, 1941.
69. News clipping, December 1941 (BPP).
70. ROB to CCB, December 23, 1941; ROB to CCB, December 31, 1941.

71. ROB to CCB, January 6, 1942; ROB to CCB, January 16, 1942; ROB to CCB, January 22, 1942.

72. *Ivy Leaf*, January 9, 1942; Barton, *4th Motorized Division*, 5. Renamed Fort Eisenhower in 2023.

73. ROB to CCB, Feb 10, 12, 15, 1942.

74. ROB to CFB, February 23, 1942. Smith, "History of the Third Army," chap. 3.

75. ROB to CCB, February 5, 1942; Letter, ROB to CCB, February 17, 1942.

76. ROB to CCB, February 15, 1942.

77. ROB to CFB, February 20, 1942.

78. ROB to CCB, February 2, 1942; Letter, ROB to CCB, February 17, 1942.

79. Griswold to commander, Third Army, February 23, 1942, RG 319, NPRC.

80. ROB to CCB, February 26, 1942 (with transcript of War Department phone conversation).

81. ROB to CCB, February 28, 1942.

82. ROB to CCB, February 28, 1942.

83. Tilden and Roulston, *History of the Infantry School*, 214; board results: Barton to brigadier general, n.d.; ROB to CCB, March 5, 1942.

84. ROB to CFB, March 13, 1942.

85. "Wade H. Haislip," *Solid Brass*, accessed December 2020, http://www.solidbrass.com/UncHam.html.

86. Sylvan and Smith, *Normandy to Victory*, 411n67.

87. Tilden and Roulston, *History of the Infantry School*, 160.

88. ROB to CFB and Raymond O. Barton Jr., March 15, 1942; ROB to CFB, March 17, 1942.

89. ROB to CFB, March 27, 1942.

90. ROB to family, April 7, 1942; ROB to CFB, April 8, 1942.

91. ROB to CCB, March 5 and March 25, 1942.

92. ROB to CFB, March 13, 1942,

93. ROB to family, with a note to CCB, May 12, 1942.

94. ROB to CCB, May 25, 1942.

95. Clippings, Colorado Springs newspapers, June 1942.

96. Ronald H. Spector, *Eagle against the Sun: The American War with Japan* (New York: Vintage Books, 1985).

97. ROB to family, April 15, 1942.

98. ROB to family, April 30, 1942.

99. ROB to family, with a note to CCB, May 12, 1942.

100. ROB to CFB, May 8, 1942; Technical Services Division, *Administrator's Guide, Motor Transport Special Service School Course "F"* (Baltimore: Holabird Quartermaster Motor Base, 1942), table of contents.
101. ROB to family, with a note to CCB, May 12, 1942.
102. ROB to CFB, May 8, 1942.
103. "Roster of Allied Prisoners of War believed aboard *Shinyo Maru* When Torpedoed and Sunk 7 September 1944," *West Point*, accessed December 2020, https://www.west-point.org/family/japanese-pow/ShinyoMaruRosterJPW.html.
104. 85th Infantry General Orders 6, June 10, 1942, BPP.
105. Memo for the chief of staff, Subject: General Officer, June 17, 1942.
106. Special Orders 161, June 25, 1942; Assumption of Command, 4th Motorized Division, General Orders No. 38, July 1, 1942, BPP.

Notes for Chapter 7

1. *Atlanta Chronicle,* July 5, 1942, p. 1.
2. Letter, CG VII Corps to commander, Second Army, Brig. Gen. O'Brien, January 28, 1943, BPP.
3. Sylvan and Smith, *Normandy to Victory,* 427.
4. "LTC Richard Cathcart Hopkins," *Find a Grave,* accessed December 2020, https://www.findagrave.com/memorial/49207066/richard-cathcart-hopkins.
5. Braim, *Will to Win,* 23, 35, 43–48, 93.
6. Stephen P. Cano, ed., *The Last Witness: The Memoirs of George L. Mabry, Jr. From D-Day to the Battle of the Bulge* (Fresno, CA: Linden, 2021), 22–23.
7. "Regimental and 1st Battalion Commanders," 1-22infantry.org, accessed December 2020, https://1-22infantry.org/commanders/commanders.htm; Hossfeld, *American Representation,* 319; AFG Report, 319, CARL; William S. Boice, *History of the Twenty-Second United States Infantry World War II* (self-published, 1959), 2.
8. *Ivy Leaf,* February 5, 1943; Johnson, *History of the Twelfth Infantry,* 28, 36–39. Note: a related publication, the *Ivy Leaves* is the publication of the National 4th (Ivy) Division Association.
9. "Carroll Armstrong Bagby," *Assembly,* June 1974, 98–99.
10. Jacob L. Devers, *Report of Army Ground Forces Activities* (Washington, DC: Army Ground Forces, 1946), 19; Bell I. Wiley, *Training in the*

Ground Army, 1942–1945, Study XI (Washington, DC: Army Ground Forces Historical Section, 1948), 12.

11. *Charlotte Observer* (Charlotte, NC), July 19, 1942, p. 30; *Times and Democrat* (Orangeburg, SC); July 14, 1942, p. 1; *Tampa Bay Times* (Tampa, FL), July 14, 1942, p. 14; *Panama City News-Herald* (Panama City, FL), July 14, 1942, p. 6.

12. Barton, *4th Motorized Division*, 19.

13. Howe, *Mediterranean Theater*, 13–14; Maurice Matloff and Edwin M. Snell, *The War Department: Strategic Planning for Coalition Warfare, 1941–1942*, The United States Army in World War II (1953; repr., Washington, DC: CMH, 1999), 313–15.

14. *Ivy Leaf* (4ID), December 1, 1942, 18, 23.

15. ROB to CCB, January 26, 1943.

16. ROB to CCB. February 14, 1943.

17. ROB to CCB, January 30, 1943.

18. Chief of staff to division commanders, March 3, 1943, BPP.

19. *Tampa Bay Times*, January 14, 1943, p. 20.

20. Greenfield, Palmer, and Wiley, *Army Ground Forces*, 337–39.

21. *Index-Journal* (Greenwood, SC), March 10, 1943, p. 1.

22. Information Office, *History of Fort Dix: Part 1, 1917–1967* (Fort Dix, NJ: United States Army Training Center, 1967), chap. 9.

23. Johnson, *History of the Twelfth Infantry*, 39.

24. Phil Hunt to CCB, April 23, 1943; ROB to CCB, May 3, 1943.

25. Efficiency Report: ROB, Reinhardt, July 26, 1943, RG 319, NPRC.

26. ROB to CCB, May 2, 1943. At this point the collection of Barton's personal letters terminates. He wrote his mother often, and she kept most of his correspondence. From here on family details become increasingly scarce.

27. *Daily Oklahoman*, August 7, 194, p. 5.

28. Greenfield, Palmer, and Wiley, *Army Ground Forces*, 338–39; Wilson, *Armies*, 187.

29. Ray E. Porter, "Memorandum for Commanding General, Army Ground Forces, 18 August 1943, Subject: Amphibious Training," War Department, Organization and Training Division G-3, Record Group 337, Records of Headquarters Army Ground Forces, 1916–1956 (hereafter cited as RG 337), Entry 55, Box 661, AGF Amphibious Bundle #2, NACP.

30. Marshall O. Becker, *The Amphibious Training Center: Study No. 22* (Washington, DC: Historical Section, Army Ground Forces, 1946), 4.

31. *Ivy Leaf* (4ID), October 14, 1943; Efficiency Report: ROB, Lloyd Fredendall, December 1943, RG 319, NPRC; "Summary of 27 letters sent home by Pvt. Frank Brown 12th Regiment, 4th Infantry Division while training at Camp Gordon Johnston, Oct-Nov 1943," Camp Gordon Johnston World War II Museum, Camp Gordon Johnston, Carrabelle, FL.

32. Medical Board Proceedings, Barton statement, September 9, 1945, RG 319, NPRC.

33. G-3, 4th Infantry Division, "Training Memorandum 73: Training Directive, 18 October 1943–16 March 1944," 14 October 1943, RG 338 (Army Organizations), Entry 37042, Box 3320, NACP; Charles H. Briscoe, "Commando & Ranger Training, Part III: Forging Junior Leaders to Toughen Men to Win in Combat," *Veritas: Journal of US Army Special Operations History* 16, no. 1 (2020): 47–48.

34. Headquarters, Amphibious Training Center, "Training Memorandum Number 2: Training Program: Effective January 15, 1943," January 6, 1943, Carrabelle, FL, Amphibious Training Center, RG 337, Entry 29B, Box 107, NACP.

35. Shore to Shore Amphibious Training School, "Syllabus, 1 October 1943," Camp Gordon Johnston, FL, RG 337, Entry 29B, Box 106, NACP.

36. Johnson, *History of the Twelfth Infantry*, 40; Boice, *History of the Twenty-Second*, 2.

37. Sylvan and Smith, *Normandy to Victory*, 498.

38. Official Personal Military Records File: Blakeley, Harold W. (1883–1966), NPRC; George P. Hayes, "Fact Sheet on the 4th Infantry Division," United States Army 4th Infantry Division, RG 407 (WWII Operational Reports, 1941–48), NACP. Primary location for most of the 4th Infantry Division's Second World War official documents, including those for all regiments and division troops, is this record group, Entry 407, Boxes 5663–5888. Researchers may also locate most of these documents in the Adjutant General, WWII Microfilm Collection, available at many US Army libraries and the Dwight D. Eisenhower Presidential Library. Unless otherwise noted, all 4th Infantry Division records come from this collection in either original or microfilm form. "Harold Whittle Blakeley – Major General, United States Army," *Arlington Cemetery*, accessed January 2020, http://www.arlington-cemetery.net/hwblakeley.htm. Blakeley's papers were at the Patton Museum at Fort Knox, KY. However, these papers are missing since the relocation of the Armor School to Fort Moore (Benning) in 2011.

39. *Ivy Leaf* (4ID), November 11, 1943.
40. Boice, *History of the Twenty-Second*, 2–3; Braim, *Will to Win*, 66–67.
41. Johnson, *History of the Twelfth Infantry*, 41; Boice, *History of the Twenty-Second*, 3; "Camp Kilmer," globalsecurity.org, accessed December 2020, https://www.globalsecurity.org/military/facility/camp-kilmer.htm; Boice, *History of the Twenty-Second*, 3; H. W. Blakeley, *Special Troops (Yearbook)* (Baton Rouge, LA: Army & Navy Publishing, 1946), 75.
42. 42. Boice, *History of the Twenty-Second*, 3.
43. Boice, *History of the Twenty-Second*, 3, 41–44; Johnson, *History of the Twelfth Infantry*, 41.
44. Letter, Findlater Stewart to John Maude, Minister of Health, "Subject: American Forces in the United Kingdom: reception and liaison arrangements BOLERO Combined Committee, 13 May, 1942," UK National Archives, Kew Gardens, UK, MH 79/571; Roland G. Ruppenthal, *Logistical Support of the Armies*, vol. 1, *May 1941–September 1944* (1953; repr., Washington, DC: CMH 1995), 54, 61–65.
45. Norma Jean Lutz, *J. D. Salinger*, Bloom's Biocritiques Series (Philadelphia: Chelsea House, 2002), 3–44.
46. Blakeley, *4th Infantry Division (Yearbook)*, 78.
47. Lutz, *J. D. Salinger*, 18.
48. Johnson, *History of the Twelfth Infantry*, 45.
49. UK Station List, June 1944, Historical Reference Collection, CMHL.
50. Boice, *History of the Twenty-Second*, 4.
51. Headquarters, 4th Infantry Division (hereafter HQ 4ID), Narrative History, June 1940–March 1946, Entry 427, Box 5663, RG 407, NACP.

Notes for Chapter 8

1. T. Roosevelt to CFB, May 14, 1944.
2. HQ 4ID, "History of the 4th Infantry Division 1 January–31 December 1943," 7, Box 5663, RG 407, NACP.
3. Stephen C. Kepher, *COSSAC: Lt. Gen. Sir Frederick Morgan and the Genesis of Operation Overlord* (Annapolis, MD: Naval Institute Press, 2020), 214; Cable, Eisenhower to Combined Chiefs of Staff, January 23, 1944, in Dwight D. Eisenhower, *The Papers of Dwight David Eisenhower: The War Years*, ed. Alfred D. Chandler Jr. and Stephen E. Ambrose (Baltimore: Johns Hopkins Press, 1970), 1673–674.
4. Cable, Eisenhower to George C. Marshall, January 29, 1944, in *Papers of Eisenhower*, 1695–696.

5. Efficiency Report: Collins, Alexander Patch, May 29, 1943, Official Military Personnel File for Joseph L. Collins, RG 319, NPRC.

6. Efficiency Report: Collins, Oscar W. Griswold, June 30, 1943, Collins File, RG 319, NPRC.

7. Letter: Oscar W. Griswold to Leslie McNair, Re: Potential Corps Commanders, 30 November 1943, RG 337, General Correspondence, 1940–1944, Box 9, NACP.

8. Efficiency Report: Collins, Griswold, December 1, 1943, Collins File, RG 319, NPRC.

9. Brig. Gen. A. J. Barnett to J. Lawton Collins, December 13, 1943, J. Lawton Collins Papers, Eisenhower Presidential Library (hereafter cited as Collins Papers).

10. Collins *Lightning Joe*, 177.

11. DA Form 66, Officer Qualification Record, J. Lawton Collins, May 13, 1964, Collins File, RG 319, NPRC.

12. Personal correspondence between author and Nancy McKee Smith, April 2017. At both Fort Benning and Fort Sam Houston, Hodges and his wife spent much of their off-duty time with the McKee family.

13. 4ID, "History of the 4th Infantry Division 1 January–31 December 1943;" Joseph Balkoski, *Utah Beach: The Amphibious Landing and Airborne Operations on D-Day* (Mechanicsburg, PA: Stackpole Books, 2005), 35.

14. Stanton, *World War II Order of Battle*, 8–10.

15. 4ID, "History of the 4th Infantry Division 1 January–31 December 1943;" Johnson, *History of the Twelfth Infantry*, 46.

16. Johnson, *History of the Twelfth Infantry*, 45.

17. Harry C. Butcher, *My Three Years with Eisenhower: The Personal Diary of Captain Harry C. Butcher, USNR, Naval Aide to General Eisenhower, 1942–1946* (New York: Simon and Schuster, 1946), 487–88.

18. Johnson, *History of the Twelfth Infantry*, 46; "Devon D-Day Assault Training Center," *US Military in South Wales*, accessed June 19, 2024, https://sites.google.com/site/usmilitaryinsouthwales/devon-d-day-assault-training-center.

19. "Narrative History, 4th Infantry Division, June 1940–March 1946," 7, Entry 427, Box 5663, RG 407, NACP.

20. "Narrative History, June 1940–March 1946."

21. Clifford L. Jones, *The Administrative and Logistical History of the ETO*, part VI, *Neptune: Training, Mounting, the Artificial Ports* (Fort McNair, Washington, DC: CMH, 1946), 240.

22. Raymond O. Barton, "War Diary, March 1944–December 1945,"
    compiled by William B. York, BPP.
23. Collins to ROB, March 2, 1944, Collins Papers.
24. Beverly W. Brannan, "Eleanor Butler Roosevelt (1889–1960)," *Library
    of Congress*, accessed February 8, 2020, https://www.loc.gov/rr/print/
    coll/womphotoj/rooseveltessay.html.
25. Michelle Cannon, ed., "D-Day's Oldest Soldier: Theodore Roosevelt
    Jr.," news.va.gov, September 26, 2019, https://www.blogs.va.gov/
    VAntage/66542/d-days-oldest-soldier-theodore-roosevelt-jr/;
    "Theodore Roosevelt Jr.," *Theodore Roosevelt Center at Dickinson
    State University*, accessed Feb. 7, 2000, https://www.theodoreroosevelt-
    center.org/Learn-About-TR/TR-Encyclopedia/Family-and-Friends/
    Theodore-Roosevelt-Jr.aspx.
26. Rick Atkinson, *The Day of Battle: The War in Sicily and Italy,
    1943–1944* (New York: Henry Holt, 2007), 159–60; Albert N. Garland,
    Howard McGaw Smyth, and Martin Blumenson, *The Mediterranean
    Theater of Operations: Sicily and the Surrender of Italy*, The United
    States Army in World War II (Washington, DC: CMH, 1965), 46–47;
    Ossad, *Omar Nelson Bradley*, 139–42; Raymond O Barton, "Recom-
    mendation for Award: Medal of Honor, Roosevelt, Theodore, Jr.," BPP.
27. Brady, *His Father's Son*, 27–28; Walker, *Namesake*, 294–96.
28. Johnson, *History of the Twelfth Infantry*, 47–49; Jones, *Neptune*, 240.
29. Barton, "War Diary."
30. Johnson, *History of the Twelfth Infantry*, 47–49; Jones, *Neptune*, 240.
31. Boice, *History of the Twenty-Second*, 4–5; Jones, *Neptune*, 240.
32. Jones, *Neptune*, 241.
33. Barton, "War Diary," March 21, 1944.
34. Barton, "War Diary."
35. Collins, *Lighting Joe*, 184–85; Collins, interview by Sperow, 123–24.
36. Barton, "War Diary."
37. Jones, *Neptune*, 211–39; Ruppenthal, *Logistical Support of the Armies*,
    345–49.
38. Barton, "War Diary."
39. Barton, "War Diary"; Jones, *Neptune*, 241–43; Peter Caddick-Ad-
    ams, *Sand & Steel: The D-Day Invasion and the Liberation of France*
    (Oxford, UK: Oxford University Press, 2019), 203
40. Christopher D. Yung, *Gators of Neptune: Naval Amphibious Planning
    for the Normandy Invasion* (Annapolis, MD: Naval Institute Press,
    2006), 159–60; Barton, "War Diary."

41. Barton, War Diary; "1997 Distinguished Graduate Award Recipients," *West Point*, accessed January 2020, https://www.westpointaog.org/ DGARussellReederJr1926. At Fort Leavenworth Barton worked with Reeder's father, who was the director of the extension course.

42. Barton, "War Diary."

43. Barton, "War Diary."

44. Corlett, *Cowboy Pete*, 88–89; Crosswell, *Beetle*, 587.

45. D'Este, *Eisenhower*, 483; Barton, "War Diary."

46. Caddick-Adams, *Sand & Steel*, 244; Barton, "War Diary."

47. Barton, "War Diary."

48. Alexander G. Lovelace, "Hughes' War: The Allied High Command through the Eyes of General Everett S. Hughes" (master's thesis, George Washington University, 2013), 74; Barton, "War Diary."

49. Barton, "War Diary."

50. Johnson, *History of the Twelfth Infantry*, 51; Barton, "War Diary."

51. Barton, "War Diary."

52. Michael Connelly, *The Mortarmen* (Victoria, BC: Trafford, 2005), 5–9.

53. HQ 4ID, Field Order #1 (TIGER), April 18, 1944, Entry 427, Box 5763, RG 407, NACP (note: Orders NEPTUNE and TIGER are both listed as Field Order #1); Barton, "War Diary."

54. Barton, "War Diary."

55. HQ 4ID, Field Order #1 (TIGER).

56. Barton, "War Diary."

57. Carl von Clausewitz, *On War*, ed. and trans. Michael Howard and Peter Paret, indexed ed. (Princeton: Princeton University Press, 1984), 119.

58. Yung, *Gators of Neptune*, 161.

59. Raymond O. Barton, interview by Cornelius Ryan, June 7, 1958, Cornelius Ryan Collection of World War II Papers, "The Longest Day: Interviews and Correspondence," Box 13.7, Ohio University Library, Athens, OH (hereafter cited as Baron, interview by Ryan).

60. Yung, *Gators of Neptune*, 161; Barton, "War Diary."

61. War Office, Secretary General Staff Records, Exercise "Tiger," April– May 1944, WO 219/186, National Archives, Kew Gardens, UK; Charles B. MacDonald, "Slapton Sands: The Cover-up That Never Was," *Army* 38, no. 6 (June 1988): 64–67; Craig L Symonds, *Neptune: The Allied Invasion of Europe and the D-Day Landings* (New York: Oxford University Press, 2014), 210–19; Yung, *Gators of Neptune*, 165–67; Ruppenthal, *Logistical Support of the Armies*, 351–52.

62. Moon to Collins, April 29, 1944, Collins Papers.

63. Barton, "War Diary."
64. Barton, "War Diary"; Roosevelt to CFB, May 14, 1944.
65. Barton, "War Diary."
66. Barton, "War Diary."
67. Caddick-Adams, *Sand & Steel*, xxxviii.

Notes for Chapter 9

1. Raymond O. Barton, overlay (and comments for Cornelius Ryan, 1958) to accompany Maj. Gen. R. O. Barton's personal D-Day Opn's map, Normandy Invasion, June 6, 1944, BPP (hereafter cited as Barton, overlay and comments).
2. Wade, *World War II Division Commanders*, 2.
3. Barton, interview by Ryan.
4. Barton, "War Diary."
5. Raymond O. Barton, "Recommendation for Award: Medal of Honor, Roosevelt, Theodore, Jr." July 4, 1944, BPP.
6. Barton, interview by Ryan.
7. Barton, "Recommendation for Award: Roosevelt"; War Department, Official Statement of the Military Service and Death of Theodore Roosevelt Jr., August 29, 1958, Theodore Roosevelt Jr. File, RG 319, NPRC.
8. Zanuck, *Longest Day*, scene 3.
9. Balkoski, *Utah Beach*, 231.
10. *Globe-Gazette* (Mason City, IA), June 13, 1944, p. 1.
11. Adam Bernstein, "Newsman Larry LeSueur Dies," *Washington Post*, accessed June 2021, https://www.washingtonpost.com/archive/local/2003/02/07/newsman-larry-lesueur-dies/871e4420-5da8-4a35-945b-8482c27f50da/.
12. Marc Lancaster, "D-Day: Utah Beach With Kenneth Crawford," *World War II on Deadline*, March 29, 2020, https://ww2ondeadline.com/2020/03/29/d-day-utah-beach-kenneth-crawford/.
13. Barton, interview by Ryan.
14. Barton, "War Diary."
15. Barton, interview by Ryan. Ryan indicates this incident occurred on June 5, but Barton's war diary confirms it was on June 2.
16. Barton, "War Diary."
17. Barton, "War Diary."
18. Barton, "War Diary"; HQ 4ID, "Action Against Enemy, Reports After/Action After Reports (June 1944)," Box 5663, RG 407, NACP (hereafter cited as 4ID, AAR, June 1944).

19. Sandy Gall, "Yogi Berra's U. S. Navy Service Came before Baseball Fame," *The Sextant*, September, 23, 2015, https://usnhistory.navylive.dodlive.mil/Recent/Article-View/Article/2686629/yogi-berras-u-s-navy-service-came-before-baseball-fame/.

20. Historian, 4th Infantry Division (hereafter 4ID Historian), "The Invasion of France," Box 5664, NACP.

21. Balkoski, *Utah Beach*, 231.

22. Barton, "War Diary"; Richard McKee diary, McKee Personal Papers; 4ID Historian, "Invasion of France," Box 5664, NACP; Robert O. Babcock, *War Stories*, vol. 1, *D-Day to the Liberation of Paris* (Atlanta: Deeds, 2001), 22; "Welcome to Atlantikwall: WW2 defences from 1941–1944," *Atlantikwall*, accessed August 2021, http://www.atlantikwall.co.uk.

23. Barton, interview by Ryan.

24. Recommendation for Award: Roosevelt, Statements by James Van Fleet and Carlton O. MacNeely, in Raymond O. Barton, "Recommendation for Award: Medal of Honor, Roosevelt, Theodore, Jr.," July 4, 1944, BPP.

25. Russell P. (Red) Reeder, *Born at Reveille: Memoirs of an American Soldier*, rev. ed. (Quechee, VT: Vermont Heritage Press, 1994), 276.

26. George L. Mabry, "The Operations of the 2nd Battalion 8th Infantry (4th Inf. Div.) in the Landing at Utah Beach, 5–7 June 1944 (Normandy Campaign), Personal experience of a Battalion S-3," (Infantry Officer Advanced Course, US Army Infantry School, Fort Benning, GA, 1947), 21, DRL.

27. Braim, *Will to Win*, 78–79.

28. Recommendation for Award: Roosevelt, Statements by James Van Fleet and Carlton O. MacNeely, in Raymond O. Barton, "Recommendation for Award: Medal of Honor, Roosevelt, Theodore, Jr." July 4, 1944, BPP.

29. Babcock, *War Stories*, 118.

30. Balkoski, *Utah Beach*, 32–33.

31. Barton, interview by Ryan.

32. Barton, interview by Ryan; Barton, overlay and comments; 4ID Historian, "Invasion of France," Box 5664, NACP.

33. Barton, overlay and comments.

34. Barton, overlay and comments.

35. Babcock, *War Stories*, 16–17.

36. The G-5 position is not identified in the US Department of War, *FM 101-5, Staff Officers' Field Manual*.

37. Barton, overlay and comments. After law school and private practice in Detroit, Hart became active in local and state politics. By 1954 he was Michigan's lieutenant governor and in 1958 became a member of the United States Senate, remaining in office until his death from melanoma in 1976. In 1982 the US Senate voted to name its new building the Hart Senate Office Building.

38. Barton, overlay and comments.

39. Roland G. Ruppenthal, *Utah Beach to Cherbourg* (*6 June–27 June 1944*), American Forces in Action (Washington, DC: CMH, 1984), 52; Barton, overlay and comments.

40. Barton, overlay and comments.

41. Barton, overlay and comments.

42. Barton, interview by Ryan.

43. Barton, interview by Ryan; Barton, overlay and comments.

44. Barton, overlay and comments.

45. Ruppenthal, *Utah Beach to Cherbourg*, 43–47.

46. Barton, overlay and comments.

47. Reeder, *Born at Reveille*, 279.

48. Sylvan and Smith, *Normandy to Victory*, 13.

49. House, *Combined Arms Warfare*, 96–100.

50. War Department, *FM 100-5, Field Service Regulations: Operations* (Washington, DC: War Department, 1941), 103–4.

51. Babcock, *War Stories*, 25; 4ID Historian, "Invasion of France," Box 5664, NACP.

52. Marcus O. Stevenson, Roosevelt's aide, maintained a war diary and a set of notes. He passed these down to his son and they were utilized by Robert W. Walker when researching his biography published in 2008. However, I have been unable to locate this important source. See Walker, *Namesake*, 331.

53. Ruppenthal, *Utah Beach to Cherbourg*, 62–63; Collins, *Lightning Joe*, 203–4.

54. Mabry, "2nd Battalion 8th Infantry," 29-30; Officer's Advanced Course Committee 10, "Armor in Operation Neptune (Establishment of the Normandy Beachhead)" (Armor School, Fort Benning, GA, 1949), 58–59, DRL. Ruppenthal, *Utah Beach to Cherbourg*, 63–65; John C. McManus, *The Americans at Normandy: The Summer of 1944—The American War from the Normandy Beaches to Falaise* (New York: Forge Books, 2004), 66–67; 4ID Historian, "Invasion of France," Box 5664, NACP.

55. Reeder, *Born at Reveille*, 151–52.

56. Johnson, *History of the Twelfth Infantry*, 65–66. Ruppenthal, *Utah Beach to Cherbourg*, 62–63; 4ID Historian, "Invasion of France," Box 5664, NACP.

57. "Hervey Aldrich Tribolet," 1-22infantry.org, accessed March 2020, http://1-22infantry.org/commanders/triboletpers.htm.

58. "Azeville Battery: German Batteries of the Atlantic Wall in Normandy," *D-Day Overlord*, accessed March 2021, https://www.dday-overlord. com/en/d-day/atlantic-wall/batteries/azeville.

59. Boice, *History of the Twenty-Second*, 18; Ruppenthal, *Utah Beach to Cherbourg*, 66; McManus, *Americans at Normandy*, 70; Paul Carell, *Invasion! They're Coming! The German Account of the D-Day Landings and the 80 Days Battle for France*, trans. David Johnston (Atglen, PA: Schiffer Military History, 1995), 134–35.

60. Ruppenthal, *Utah Beach to Cherbourg*, 66–68.

61. Steven J. Zaloga, *D-Day Fortifications in Normandy*, Fortress 37 (Oxford, UK: Osprey, 2005).

62. Ruppenthal, *Utah Beach to Cherbourg*, 71, Boice, *History of the Twenty-Second*, 16–17; Clifford "Swede" Henley Diary, 1973, MSS 0428, George A. Smathers Libraries, Gainsville, FL (hereafter cited as Henley diary); 4ID Historian, "Invasion of France," Box 5664, NACP.

63. HQ 4ID, "Field Order #2, June 7, 1944," Box 5763, NACP (hereafter cited as 4ID, Field Order #2); chief of staff, VII Corps, "Ops Memo #10, June 11 (Instructions given between 7 and 10 June)," Entry 427, Box 3382, RG 407, NACP (hereafter cited as VII Corps, Ops Memo #10); Barton, "War Diary"; Collins, *Lightning Joe*, 203–4; Ruppenthal, *Utah Beach to Cherbourg*, 103.

64. Ruppenthal, *Utah Beach to Cherbourg*, 77–90; G-3, VII Corps, "Capture of Cherbourg and Cotentin Peninsula by VII Corps, U.S. Army (6 June to 1 July 1944)," Box 3275, RG 407, NACP (hereafter cited as VII Corps, AAR, June 1944); VII Corps, Ops Memo #10.

65. VII Corps, Ops Memo #10.

66. 4ID, AAR, June 1944.

67. War Department, *FM 100-5: Operations* (1941), 97.

68. Barton, "War Diary."

69. "Azeville (Manche): The Cities of Normandy during the 1944 Battles," *D-Day Overlord*, accessed March 2021, https://www.dday-overlord. com/en/battle-of-normandy/cities/azeville; Ruppenthal, *Utah Beach to Cherbourg*, 103.

70. Boice, *History of the Twenty-Second*, 19; Ruppenthal, *Utah Beach to Cherbourg*, 103; Henley diary, June 7, 1944; "Thomas C. Shields," 1-22infantry.org, accessed April 2021, http://1-22infantry.org/kia/shieldspers.htm.
71. Ruppenthal, *Utah Beach to Cherbourg*, 103.
72. Ruppenthal, *Utah Beach to Cherbourg*, 95–97.
73. Ruppenthal, *Utah Beach to Cherbourg*, 94–97; Barton, "War Diary"; 4ID, AAR, June 1944.
74. Ruppenthal, *Utah Beach to Cherbourg*, 125–36; VII Corps, AAR, June 1944; VII Corps, Ops Memo #10.
75. Ruppenthal, *Utah Beach to Cherbourg*, 97–100; Barton, "War Diary."
76. Ruppenthal, *Utah Beach to Cherbourg*, 101–2; Barton, "War Diary."
77. Ruppenthal, *Utah Beach to Cherbourg*, 104–7.
78. Ruppenthal, *Utah Beach to Cherbourg*, 107; Barton, "War Diary"; 4ID, Field Order # 2, Entry 427, Box 5763, RG 407, NACP.

Notes for Chapter 10

1. Boice, *History of the Twenty-Second*, 21; "Robert Trueheart Foster," 1-22infantry.org, accessed May 2022, http://1-22infantry.org/commanders/fosterpers.htm.
2. VII Corps, AAR, June 1944; Barton, "War Diary."
3. 4ID, AAR, June 1944.
4. Ruppenthal, *Utah Beach to Cherbourg*, 107; 4ID, AAR, June 1944.
5. Ruppenthal, *Utah Beach to Cherbourg*, 107; 4ID, AAR, June 1944; Barton, "War Diary."
6. Ruppenthal, *Utah Beach to Cherbourg*, 108; Barton, "War Diary."
7. Reeder, *Born at Reveille*, 285; Johnson, *History of the Twelfth Infantry*, 78.
8. Johnson, *History of the Twelfth Infantry*, 78.
9. Reeder, *Born at Reveille*, 287–25; Collins, *Lighting Joe*, 206.
10. Chief of staff, VII Corps, "Ops Memo #11, June 12," Box 3382, RG 407, NACP.
11. Carell, *Invasion!*, 135–37; Ruppenthal, *Utah Beach to Cherbourg*, 108; G-3, VII Corps, "Journal file 9–17 June," Box 3304, RG 407, NACP.
12. "VII Corps, G-3 Journal File, 9–17 June 1944," June 12, entry 45, RG 407, NACP.
13. VII Corps, "G-3 Journal File, 9–17 June 1944," June 12, entry 11, RG 407, NACP; Barton, "War Diary."
14. Ruppenthal, *Utah Beach to Cherbourg*, 110.

15. 4ID, AAR, June 1944; Barton, "War Diary."
16. HQ 4ID, "Field Order #5, June 26, 1944," Box 5763, NACP (hereafter cited as 4ID, Field Order #5).
17. McKee, personal diary.
18. VII Corps, AAR, June 1944; Collins, interview by Sperow, 172–76. Collins, *Lightning Joe*, 209.
19. Andrew Z. Adkins III, "History of the 80th Division," *80th Division Veterans Association*, accessed June 2021, https://www.80thdivision.com/history.html.
20. Collins, interview by Sperow; Collins, *Lightning Joe*, 210; Collins to Mrs. Partridge, July 22, 1944, Collins Papers. In his autobiography and an extensive Army War College interview, Collins seldom mentions McKee and never indicates that Troxel became his G-3 and would serve in that capacity until the war's end. He does mention Partridge six times. It is a cautionary tale about the accuracy and completeness of memoirs and personal accounts.
21. G-1, 4ID, "G-1 Journal, May–June 1944," Entry 427, Box 5669, RG 407, NACP (hereafter cited as 4ID, G-1 Journal, May 1944 [or June 1944]).
22. McKee, personal diary.
23. Barton, "War Diary."
24. 4ID, AAR, June 1944; 4ID, G-1 Journal, June 1944.
25. Barton, "War Diary."
26. McKee, personal diary.
27. Chief of staff, VII Corps, "Ops Memo #16: June 17, " Box 3382, RG 407, NACP; HQ 4ID, "Warning Order, June 17," Box 5763, NACP.
28. Barton, "War Diary"; Braim, *Will to Win*, 89.
29. G-3, 12th Army Group, "G-3 Periodic Report #12 (18 June 1944)," 427, Box 1330, NACP; Sylvan and Smith, *Normandy to Victory*, 23.
30. Jonathan Trigg, *D-Day through German Eyes: How the Wehrmacht Lost France* (Gloucestershire, UK: Amberley, 2020), 222–23; chief of staff, VII Corps, "Ops Memo #17: June 19," Box 3382, RG 407, NACP; Ruppenthal, *Utah Beach to Cherbourg*, 145, 150.
31. Barton, "War Diary"; Ray W. Barker Papers, 1942–46, Dwight D. Eisenhower Presidential Library, Abilene, KS.
32. HQ 4ID, "Field Order #6, June 18,1944," Box 5763, NACP; Ruppenthal, *Utah Beach to Cherbourg*, 151–52.
33. Press releases and related records, compiled 1942–1945, RG 337, NACP; 4ID Historian, "4th Infantry Division, Miscellaneous Statistical Data," Box 5669, NACP (hereafter cited as 4ID, Misc. Data).

34. Barton, "War Diary"; Ruppenthal, *Utah Beach to Cherbourg*, 152–53.

35. Boice, *History of the Twenty-Second*, 21–24.

36. Johnson, *History of the Twelfth Infantry*, 87–88; Ruppenthal, *Utah Beach to Cherbourg*, 152–53.

37. Johnson, *History of the Twelfth Infantry*, 88.

38. Collins, *Lightning Joe*, 207; Sylvan and Smith, *Normandy to Victory*, 427; Babcock, *War Stories*, 25; "Welcome to Atlantikwall."

39. Barton, "War Diary"; Mitchel P. Roth, *Historical Dictionary of War Journalism* (Westport, CT: Greenwood Press, 1997), 169; "BG Henry Anson Barber Jr.," *Find a Grave*, accessed April 2021, https://www.findagrave.com/memorial/37941255/henry-anson-barber.

40. Ruppenthal, *Utah Beach to Cherbourg*, 152–53; Michael Boivin, *Les Manchois dans la tourmente de la seconde guerre mondiale (1939–1945)* (Marigny, Manche, France: Eurocibles, 2004), 6:40, 95.

41. Ruppenthal, *Utah Beach to Cherbourg*, 159.

42. Barton, interview by Ryan.

43. Sylvan and Smith, *Normandy to Victory*, 50.

44. Ruppenthal, *Utah Beach to Cherbourg*, 159; Steven J. Zaloga, *Cherbourg 1944: The First Allied Victory in Normandy* (Oxford, UK: Osprey, 2015), 58–60.

45. Barton, "War Diary"; Johnson, *History of the Twelfth Infantry*, 89–90.

46. Ruppenthal, *Utah Beach to Cherbourg*, 159.

47. Barton, "War Diary."

48. Ruppenthal, *Utah Beach to Cherbourg*, 165–66, map XII.

49. Barton, "War Diary."

50. Barton, "War Diary"; Ruppenthal, *Utah Beach to Cherbourg*, 165–69.

51. S-3, 8IR, "S-3, 8th Infantry Regiment Journal Log, June 1944," Box 5663, RG 407, NACP (hereafter cited as 8IR, Journal Log, June 1944); Barton, "War Diary"; Ruppenthal, *Utah Beach to Cherbourg*, 165–69.

52. Boivin, *Les Manchois*, vol. 6, map 5.

53. 4ID, AAR, June 1944; Ruppenthal, *Utah Beach to Cherbourg*, 165–69.

54. Collins, *Lightning Joe*, 222–23; Barton, "War Diary"; McKee, personal diary; VII Corps, AAR, June 1944.

55. G-3, VII Corps, "VII Corps Field Order #3, June 22, 1944," Box 3277, NACP.

56. Ruppenthal, *Utah Beach to Cherbourg*, 171; Thomas Alexander Hughes, *Over Lord: General Pete Quesada and the Triumph of Tactical Air Power in World War II* (New York: Free Press, 1995), 165–66.

57. "The 22nd Infantry in World War II," 1-22infantry.org, accessed May 2010, http://1-22infantry.org/pics2/wwpagethree.htm.
58. VII Corps, AAR, June 1944; Barton, "War Diary."
59. Barton, "War Diary."
60. Collins, *Lightning Joe*, 219.
61. VII Corps, AAR, June 1944; Ruppenthal, *Utah Beach to Cherbourg*, 172; Wesley Frank Craven and James Lea Cate, *The Army Air Forces in World War II*, vol. 3, *Europe, Argument to V-E Day, January 1944– May 1945* (Chicago: University of Chicago Press, 1951), 200; Hughes, *Over Lord*, 1164–65.
62. 4ID, AAR, June 1944.
63. Ruppenthal, *Utah Beach to Cherbourg*, 173; Johnson, *History of the Twelfth Infantry*, 94, 388.
64. Ruppenthal, *Utah Beach to Cherbourg*, 175; 4ID, AAR, June 1944; VII Corps, AAR, June 1944; "Oscar L. Joyner Jr.," *American Battle Monuments Commission*, accessed March 2024, https://www.abmc.gov/decedent-search/joyner%3Doscar.
65. McKee, personal diary; Barton, "War Diary"; G-3, VII Corps, "Sitrep # 33 from 221201 to 222400 June," Box 3376, NACP.
66. 4ID, AAR, June 1944.
67. Sylvan and Smith, *Normandy to Victory*, 29.
68. 4ID, AAR, June 1944.
69. Barton, "War Diary."
70. Ruppenthal, *Utah Beach to Cherbourg*, 184. Barton, Silver Star Citation, July 1944, RG 319, NPRC.
71. Johnson, *History of the Twelfth Infantry*, 100, 106
72. Johnson, *History of the Twelfth Infantry*, 100–102; Ruppenthal, *Utah Beach to Cherbourg*, 184; 4ID, "Advance to Cherbourg."
73. 4ID, "Advance to Cherbourg."
74. 4ID, "Advance to Cherbourg."
75. Barton, "War Diary."
76. Chief of staff, VII Corps, "Ops Memo #19, June 25," Box 3382, RG 407, NACP.
77. Barton, "War Diary"; 4ID, AAR, June 1944; Ruppenthal, *Utah Beach to Cherbourg*, 92; Johnson, *History of the Twelfth Infantry*, 102.
78. Johnson, *History of the Twelfth Infantry*, 110.
79. 4ID, AAR, June 1944; Barton, "War Diary."
80. Barton, "War Diary"; Ruppenthal, *Utah Beach to Cherbourg*, 194. McKee, personal diary.

81. Samuel Eliot Morison, *The Invasion of France and Germany, 1944–1945*, vol. 11, *History of the United States Naval Operations in World War II* (Boston: Little, Brown, 1957), 205–12; Barton, "War Diary"; 4ID, "Advance to Cherbourg."

82. 4ID, "Advance to Cherbourg"; G-3, 4ID, "Journal Logs, June 1944," Entry 427, Box 5708, RG 407, NARA, entries 11, 15; Barton, "War Diary."

83. Carell, *Invasion!*, 206–7.

84. 4ID, AAR, June 1944; 4ID, "Journal Logs, June 1944."

85. 4ID, "Journal Logs, June 1944;" Barton, "War Diary."

86. "The Terrible Tale of the Ravalet Children, from Tourlaville," *Normandy Then and Now*, accessed June 2021, https://www.normandythenandnow.com/the-terrible-tale-of-the-ravalet-children-from-tourlaville/.

87. McKee, personal diary; Ruppenthal, *Utah Beach to Cherbourg*, 199; 4ID, "Journal Logs, June 1944"; chief of staff, VII Corps, "Ops Memo #23, June 28," Box 3382, RG 407, NACP.

88. 4ID, "Journal Logs, June 1944," entry 58.

89. "Chaplain Julian S. Ellenberg," *Chaplain Kit*, accessed June 2021, https://thechaplainkit.com/history/stories/chaplain-julian-s-ellenberg/; Barton, "War Diary."

90. 4ID, "Journal Logs, June 1944," entry 59; Johnson, *History of the Twelfth Infantry*, 117.

91. Barton, "War Diary."

92. Barton, "War Diary"; 4ID, "Advance to Cherbourg;" McKee, personal diary.

93. Letter from Collins, July 2, 1944, RG 319, NPRC.

94. Efficiency Report: ROB, Collins, July 1944, RG 319, NPRC.

95. 4ID, AAR, June 1944.

96. 4ID Historian, "The Carantan Periers Sector," Box 5664, NACP.

97. Blumenson, *Breakout and Pursuit*, 86; TRADOC Historical Office, Normandy—June and July 1944: "Battle Casualties, US Divisions," 1976, Historical Reference Collection, CMHL.

98. G-3, 4ID, "G-3 Journal, June 1944," Box 5708, NACP (hereafter cited as 4ID, G-3 Journal, June 1944); 4ID, "Advance to Cherbourg."

Notes for Chapter 11

1. Blumenson, *Breakout and Pursuit*, 37–38, map 1.

2. Department of Army, *FM 100-5, Operations* (Washington, DC: Department of the Army, 1986), 10. This 1986 manual has, in this author's view, the cleanest definition of operational art.

3. Blumenson, *Breakout and Pursuit*, 36–39.

4. Blumenson, *Breakout and Pursuit*, 38.

5. Blumenson, *Breakout and Pursuit*, 39.

6. Blumenson, *Breakout and Pursuit*, 39.

7. HQ 4ID, "Action Against Enemy, Reports After /Action After Reports (July 1944)," Box 5663, RG 407, NACP (hereafter cited as 4ID, AAR, July 1944); Blumenson, *Breakout and Pursuit*, 78–82.

8. Stuart Heintzelman, *Annual Report of the Command and General Staff School, 1930–1931* (Fort Leavenworth, KS: CGSS Press, 1931).

9. Ruppenthal, *Utah Beach to Cherbourg*, 199; TRADOC, "Battle Casualties."

10. Barton, "War Diary."

11. Headquarters, VII Corps, "History of the VII Corps for the period of 1–31 July, 1944," Box 3275, NACP (hereafter cited as VII Corps, AAR, July 1944).

12. Barton, "War Diary"; VII Corps, Field Order #4, July 3, 1944, Box 3277, NACP.

13. 4ID, AAR, July 1944.

14. "Earl G. Paules papers , 1942–1963," *Archives West*, accessed May 2022, http://archiveswest.orbiscascade.org/ark:/80444/xv11764; Barton, "War Diary."

15. Barton, "War Diary."

16. Barton, "War Diary." Blumenson, *Breakout and Pursuit*, 83–85; McKee, Personal Diary; 4ID, G-3 Journal, July 1944; McManus, *Americans at Normandy*, 214–15.

17. Chief of staff, VII Corps, "Ops Memo #28, July 6," Box 3382, RG 407, NACP; Collins, *Lightning Joe*, 228–30; McManus, *Americans at Normandy*, 216–17.

18. Sylvan and Smith, *Normandy to Victory*, 39.

19. Chief of staff, VII Corps, "Ops Memo #30, July 6," Box 3382, RG 407, NACP; McKee, Personal Diary.

20. Barton, "War Diary"; G-3, 4th Infantry Division, "G-3 Journal, July 1944," Box 5708, NACP (hereafter cited as 4ID, G-3 Journal, July 1944); HQ 4ID, Field Order #5.

21. HQ 4ID, "Field Order #8, July 5, 1944," Box 5763, NACP; Barton, "War Diary."

22. McManus, *Americans at Normandy*, 217.

23. 4ID, G-3 Journal, July 1944; Blumenson, *Breakout and Pursuit*, 86; Johnson, *History of the Twelfth Infantry*, 121–22.

24. Charles T. Lanham Efficiency Report, Major Bird Little and Raymond O. Barton, April 2, 1940, Lanham Records; 4ID, Misc. Data: Leadership.

25. 4ID, G-3 Journal, July 1944; VII Corps, AAR, July 1944; Blumenson, *Breakout and Pursuit*, 86–87, 128–30; Johnson, *History of the Twelfth Infantry*, 125; Barton, "War Diary."

26. 4ID, AAR, July 1944.

27. Blumenson, *Breakout and Pursuit*, 129.

28. Walker, *Namesake*, 317–18. Few details of what he was doing.

29. 8IR, Journal Log, July 1944.

30. Blumenson, *Breakout and Pursuit*, 129; Barton, "War Diary"; Brady, *His Father's Son*, 304.

31. Barton, "War Diary"; S-3, 8IR, S-3 Journal, July 1944, Entry 427, Box 5840, RG 407, NACP (hereafter cited as 8IR, S-3 Journal, July 1944).

32. Barton, "War Diary"; Boice, *History of the Twenty-Second*, 25.

33. Boice, *History of the Twenty-Second*, 26.

34. Charles T. Lanham Efficiency Report, Lieutenant Colonel Paul J. Mueller and Major General Courtney H. Hodges, July 2, 1941, Lanham Records; Infantry School, *Infantry in Battle* (1934; repr., Washington, DC: GPO, 1981).

35. "Charles Trueman Lanham," 1-22infantry.org, accessed July 2022, http://1-22infantry.org/commanders/lanhampers.htm.

36. 4ID, AAR, July 1944.

37. Barton, "War Diary."

38. Boice, *History of the Twenty-Second*, 27; 4ID, AAR, July 1944.

39. 4ID, Misc. Data: Command Posts; Barton, "War Diary"; Blumenson, *Breakout and Pursuit*, 129; 4ID, AAR, July 1944.

40. Johnson, *History of the Twelfth Infantry*, 126–27.

41. HQ 4ID, "Field Order #9, July 11, 1944," Box 5763, NACP; G-3, VII Corps, "G-3 Periodic Report #35 (12 July 1944)," Box 3277, NACP.

42. 4ID, Misc. Data: Commanders and Staffs; Barton, "War Diary."

43. 8IR, S-3 Journal, July 1944.

44. Walker, *Namesake*, 317.

45. Walker, *Namesake*, 317; 8IR, S-3 Journal, July 1944.

46. Boice, *History of the Twenty-Second*, 27–28; 4ID, AAR, July 1944; Johnson, *History of the Twelfth Infantry*.

47. Sylvan and Smith, *Normandy to Victory*, 48; Barton, "War Diary."

48. Brady, *His Father's Son*, 305.

49. Barton, "War Diary."

50. Omar N. Bradley, *A Soldier's Story* (New York: Holt, Rinehart and Winston, 1951), 332–33; Butcher, *My Three Years with Eisenhower*, 612; Eisenhower to Eleanor Butler Roosevelt, July 22, 1944, in *Papers of Eisenhower*, 2024.

51. Johnson, *History of the Twelfth Infantry*; 4ID, AAR, July 1944.

52. Boice, *History of the Twenty-Second*, 28; HQ 4ID, "History of the 4th Infantry Division, 1 January–31 December 1943," Box 5663, RG 407, NACP.

53. Letter, ROB to Eleanor Butler Roosevelt, July 15, 1944.

54. Sylvan and Smith, *Normandy to Victory*, 52; Blakeley, *4th Infantry Division (Yearbook)*; Blakeley, *Special Troops (Yearbook)*, 58.

55. Barton, "War Diary"; Scott Harrison, "How a Soldier Photographed a Famous General's Funeral in Normandy after D-day," *LA Times*, June 18, 2019, https://www.latimes.com/visuals/photography/la-me-fw-how-a-soldier-shot-a-famous-generals-funeral-in-normandy-after-d-day-20190618-story.html; Babcock, *War Stories*, 8; D-Day Overlord, "Theodore Roosevelt, Jr., Funérailles Burial, Sainte Mère Eglise, 14/07/1944, DDay-Overlord," *YouTube*, August 10, 2015, https://www.youtube.com/watch?v=OaPAeMD03lw.

56. ROB to CCB, July 19, 1944.

57. HQ 4ID, Recommendation for Award, Roosevelt, Theodore Jr, Memorandum to Barton from McKee, 4 July 1944, Subject: Returned without action, BPP.

58. Roosevelt Jr., Recommendation for Award, First Endorsement, VII Corps, August 1, 1944, Official Personnel Records of Theodore Roosevelt Jr., RG 319, NPRC (hereafter cited as Roosevelt Records).

59. First Army, General Orders No. 41, 2 August 1944, Roosevelt Records.

60. "Henry Lewis Stimson," *Dictionary of American Biography* (New York: Charles Scribner's Sons, 1974).

61. Sylvan and Smith, *Normandy to Victory*, 54–55.

62. Eleanor Butler Roosevelt to ROB, March 5, 1958.

63. George C. Marshall, *The Papers of George Catlett Marshall*, ed. Larry I. Bland and Sharon Ritenour Stevens, vol. 4, "Aggressive and Determined Leadership," June 1, 1943–December 31, 1944 (Baltimore and London: Johns Hopkins University Press, 1996), 533–34.

64. Memorandum from Eisenhower to War Department, 15 August 1944, Roosevelt Records.

65. *Papers of George Catlett Marshall*, 533–34.

66. "Theodore Roosevelt Jr.," *Congressional Medal of Honor Society*, accessed August 2023, https://www.cmohs.org/recipients/theodore-roosevelt-jr.

67. Blumenson, *Breakout and Pursuit*, 130; Barton, "War Diary"; chief of staff, VII Corps, "Ops Memo #39, July 16," Box 3382, RG 407, NACP.

68. Johnson, *History of the Twelfth Infantry*, 132.

69. 4ID, Misc. Data: Casualties; 4ID, AAR, July 1944; VII Corps, AAR, July 1944; Blumenson, *Breakout and Pursuit*, 128–30.

70. Barton, "War Diary."

71. Flynn, *Howitzer* (1912), 12.

72. Barton, "War Diary"; 4ID, Journal Log, July 1944.

73. Johnson, *History of the Twelfth Infantry*, 132; 4ID, Journal Log, July 1944.

74. Barton, "War Diary."

75. ROB to CCB, July 19, 1944.

Notes for Chapter 12

1. Harrison, *Cross-Channel Attack*, 457.

2. Blumenson, *Breakout and Pursuit*, 217.

3. C. J. Dick, *From Victory to Stalemate: The Western Front, Summer 1944* (Lawrence: University Press of Kansas, 2016), 121–33, 146; Blumenson, *Breakout and Pursuit*, 217.

4. VII Corps, AAR, July 1944, 24; G-3, VII Corps, "VII Corps Field Order #6, July 20, 1944," Box 3277, NACP.

5. Dick, *From Victory to Stalemate*, 121–33, 46; Blumenson, *Breakout and Pursuit*, 217.

6. HQ 4ID, "Field Order #11, July 20, 1944," Box 5763, NACP; Barton, "War Diary."

7. Barton, "War Diary"; VII Corps, AAR, July 1944.

8. Barton, "War Diary"; VII Corps, AAR, July 1944; 4ID, G-3 Journal, July 1944.

9. Barton, "War Diary"; VII Corps, AAR, July 1944; 4ID, G-3 Journal, July 1944.

10. Pyle, *Ernie's War*, 329.

11. Barton, "War Diary"; 4ID, G-3 Journal, July 1944

12. Calhoun, *McNair*, 320–21; Barton, "War Diary."

13. Blumenson, *Breakout and Pursuit*, 231; "COL Harry Albert 'Paddy' Flint," *Find a Grave*, accessed November 2022, https://www.finda-grave.com/memorial/42924752/harry-albert-flint.

14. 4ID, G-3 Journal, July 1944.

15. 8IR, S-3 Journal, July 1944.
16. Blumenson, *Breakout and Pursuit*, 230–31.
17. 8IR, S-3 Journal, July 1944; 4ID, G-3 Journal, July 1944.
18. Carlos Baker, *Ernest Hemingway: A Life Story* (New York: Charles Scribner's Sons, 1969), 401–2; 8IR, S-3 Journal, July 1944.
19. 8IR, S-3 Journal, July 1944; 4ID, G-3 Journal, July 1944.
20. Jacob E. Fickel, *The Effectiveness of Third Phase Tactical Air Operations in the European Theater of Operations* (Orlando, FL: Orlando Army Air Base, 1945), 85–94, CARL Digital Library, https://cgsc.contentdm.oclc.org/digital/collection/p4013coll8/id/1477/rec/3; Kenneth W. Hechler, *VII Corps in Operations "Cobra,"* 1945, Historical Manuscripts Collection, CMHL, 45–50; VII Corps, AAR, July 1944.
21. Hechler, *"Cobra,"* 58.
22. 8IR, S-3 Journal, July 1944; 4ID, G-3 Journal, July 1944; Hechler, *"Cobra,"* 58–65, 91.
23. Calhoun, *McNair*, 320–22.
24. 4ID, Misc. Data: Command Posts; 4ID, AAR, July 1944.
25. 8IR, S-3 Journal, July 1944; Barton, "War Diary."
26. 8IR, S-3 Journal, July 1944; Hechler, *"Cobra,"* 95; Barton, "War Diary."
27. 8IR, S-3 Journal, July 1944; 4ID, AAR, July 1944.
28. Blumenson, *Breakout and Pursuit*, 249–50, 306; chief of staff, VII Corps, "Ops Memo #48, July 25, 1944," Box 3382, RG 407, NACP.
29. 8IR, S-3 Journal, July 1944.
30. Barton, "War Diary"; Johnson, *History of the Twelfth Infantry*, 135.
31. McKee, Personal Diary.
32. Chief of staff, VII Corps, "Ops Memo #50, July 28, 1944," Box 3382, RG 407, NACP; 4ID, G-3 Journal, July 1944.
33. 4ID Historian, "The St. Lo Breakthrough," Box 5664, NACP; 4ID, G-3 Journal, July 1944; chief of staff, VII Corps, "Ops Memo #51, July 29," Box 3382, RG 407, NACP.
34. Barton, "War Diary."
35. VII Corps, AAR, July 1944.
36. 8IR, S-3 Journal, July 1944.
37. Blumenson, *Breakout and Pursuit*, 277; VII Corps, AAR, July 1944.
38. Mahon and Danysh, *Infantry*, 460; Stephen L. Ossad and Don R. Marsh, *Major General Maurice Rose: World War II's Greatest Forgotten Commander* (New York: Taylor Trade, 2006), 168–88.
39. Barton, "War Diary"; 8IR, S-3 Journal, July 1944; 4ID, AAR, July 1944.

40. John C. Ausland, *Letters Home: A War Memoir* (Oslo, Norway: Land Productions, 1993), 37.
41. Brian North, *Making the Difficult Routine: US Army Task Organization at the Army and Corps Level, Europe, 1944* (Fort Leavenworth, KS: CSI, 2016), 19–74.
42. Russell F. Weigley, *Eisenhower's Lieutenants: The Campaign of France and Germany, 1944–1945* (Bloomington: Indiana University Press, 1981), 170–71.
43. Barton, "War Diary."
44. Baker, *Ernest Hemingway*, 403.
45. Blumenson, *Breakout and Pursuit*, 306.
46. Blumenson, *Breakout and Pursuit*, 249–50, 306–8.
47. Barton, "War Diary"; Blumenson, *Breakout and Pursuit*, 329.
48. Headquarters, VII Corps, "History of the VII Corps for the period of 1–31 August, 1944," Box 3275, NACP (hereafter cited as VII Corps, AAR, August 1944); Barton, "War Diary."
49. Mark J. Reardon, *Victory at Mortain: Stopping Hitler's Panzer Counteroffensive* (Lawrence: University Press of Kansas, 2002), 50–54.
50. VII Corps, AAR, August 1944.
51. HQ 4ID, "Action Against Enemy, Reports After/Action After Reports (August 1944)," Box 5663, RG 407, NACP (hereafter cited as 4ID, AAR, August 1944); Barton, "War Diary."
52. Barton, "War Diary"; Collins, *Lightning Joe*, 246–47; Ossad and Marsh, *Major General Maurice Rose*, 191–92.
53. Barton, "War Diary."
54. Barton, "War Diary."
55. Blumenson, *Breakout and Pursuit*, 462; Reardon, *Victory at Mortain*, 293–94; Weigley, *Eisenhower's Lieutenants*, 197–200.
56. Weigley, *Eisenhower's Lieutenants*, 197; Barton, "War Diary"; 4ID, AAR, August 1944; Sylvan and Smith, *Normandy to Victory*, 87.
57. Chief of staff, VII Corps, "Ops Memo #62, August 10," Box 3382, RG 407, NACP; Reardon, *Victory at Mortain*, 185–95, 243–48, 52–64.
58. Barton, "War Diary"; 4ID, AAR, August 1944; G-3, 4ID, "G-3 Journal, August 1944," Box 5708, NACP (hereafter cited as 4ID, G-3 Journal, August 1944).
59. HQ 4ID, "Annex 5 (Signal Communications) to Field Order #1 (Neptune), May 12, 1944," Entry 427, Box 5763, RG 407, NACP; George Raynor Thompson and Dixie R. Harris, *The Technical Services,*

the Signal Corps: The Outcome (Mid-1943 through 1945) (Washington, DC: CMH, 1966), 490–92.

60. Barton, "War Diary."

61. 4ID, G-3 Journal, August 1944; 4ID Historian, "St. Pois," Box 5664, NACP.

62. VII Corps, AAR, August 1944; Rick Atkinson, *The Guns at Last Light: The War in Western Europe, 1944–1945* (New York: Henry Holt, 2013), 155–59; Blumenson, *Breakout and Pursuit*, 474.

63. Barton, "War Diary."

64. Reardon, *Victory at Mortain*, 245, 333n42.

65. 4ID, G-3 Journal, August 1944; Johnson, *History of the Twelfth Infantry*, 163–64.

66. Chief of staff, VII Corps, "Ops Memo #63, August 11," Box 3382, RG 407, NACP; 4ID, G-3 Journal, August 1944.

67. Barton, "War Diary."

68. McKee, Personal Diary.

69. Chief of staff, VII Corps, "Ops Memo #64, August 12," Box 3382, RG 407, NACP (hereafter cited as VII Corps, Ops Memo #64).

70. Barton, "War Diary."

71. VII Corps, Ops Memo #64.

72. Johnson, *History of the Twelfth Infantry*, 155–64, 68.

73. Weigley, *Eisenhower's Lieutenants*, 207–9; Martin Blumenson, *The Battle of the Generals* (New York: William Morrow, 1993), 261–73; McKee, Personal Diary.

74. Blumenson, *Breakout, and Pursuit*, 490; Barton, "War Diary."

75. Brief Medical History: ROB; Baker, *Ernest Hemingway,* 404; Barton, "War Diary."

76. 4ID, AAR, August 1944.

77. Craig S. Chapman, *Battle Hardened: An Infantry Officer's Harrowing Journey from D-Day* (Washington, DC: Regnery History, 2017), 148; Johnson, *History of the Twelfth Infantry*, 168; Barton, "War Diary."

78. Barton, "War Diary."

79. Award Citations, RG 319, NPRC; Sylvan and Smith, *Normandy to Victory*, 96; Barton, "War Diary."

80. 4ID Historian, "St. Pois," 53, Box 5664, NACP.

81. Collins to ROB, August 28, 1944.

82. Efficiency Report: ROB, Collins, August 22, 1944, RG 319, NPRC.

Notes for Chapter 13

1. Blumenson, *Breakout and Pursuit*, 590–91; Weigley, *Eisenhower's Lieutenants*, 249.

2. Michael Neiberg, *The Blood of Free Men: The Liberation of Paris, 1944* (New York: Basic Books, 2012), 103, 22–31; Weigley, *Eisenhower's Lieutenants*, 249–50.

3. Jean-Paul Michel and Monique Brouillet Seefried, *Le general Dio: Le connétable de Leclerc, 1940–1946* (Paris: Foundation Maréchal Leclerc de Hauteclocque, 2022).

4. G-3, V Corps, "Field Order #21, 23 August 1944," Entry 427, Box 2790, RG 407, NACP (V Corps records are all contained in this record group at NACP); Sylvan and Smith, *Normandy to Victory*, 104–5; Bradley, *Soldier's Story*, 391.

5. Barton, "War Diary"; 4ID, AAR, August 1944.

6. Barton, "War Diary"; 4ID, G-3 Journal, August 1944.

7. Edward L. King, *Annual Report of the Command and General Staff School, 1925–1926* (Fort Leavenworth, KS: CGSS Press, 1926); *Eisenhower: Prewar Diaries*, 103; D'Este, *Eisenhower*, 179–83.

8. HQ 4ID, "Field Order #22 (Paris), August 23, 1944," Box 5763, NACP; 4ID, G-3 Journal, August 1944.

9. Barton, "War Diary"; Boice, *History of the Twenty-Second*; 4ID, AAR, August 1944; Johnson, *History of the Twelfth Infantry*, 168; 4ID, G-3 Journal, August 1944; Chapman, *Battle Hardened*, 153–54.

10. Barton, "War Diary"; 4ID, G-3 Journal, August 1944.

11. Leonard T. Gerow, "Memorandum: For Record, 24 August 1944," Box 2791, NACP; HQ 4ID, "Field Order #24, August 25, 1944" (confirming verbal orders issued 242400B Aug 44), Box 5763, NACP.

12. 4ID, G-3 Journal, August 1944.

13. Raymond O. Barton, "Message to CG V Corps (Entered Paris), 25 August 1944)," Box 2791, NACP; HQ 4ID, "Situation Report, 250930, 25 August,1944," Box 2791, NACP; 4ID, G-3 Journal, August 1944, entry #83.

14. G-3, V Corps, "G-3 Journal: 11:40 hrs, 25 August to (12:00 hrs 25 August), Box 2791, NACP; Chapman, *Battle Hardened*, 156; Martin King, Michael Collins, and Jason Nulton, *To War with the 4th: A Century of Frontline Combat with the US 4th Infantry Division, from the Argonne to the Ardennes to Afghanistan* (Philadelphia: Casemate, 2016), 138; Johnson, *History of the Twelfth Infantry*, 168.

15. Blumenson, *Breakout and Pursuit*, 622.
16. 4ID, G-3 Journal, August 1944.
17. 4ID, G-3 Journal, August 1944.
18. Barton, "War Diary."
19. Dwight D. Eisenhower, *Crusade in Europe* (Garden City, NY: Garden City Books, 1948), 297–98.
20. Barton, "War Diary."
21. Barton, "War Diary"; 4ID, G-3 Journal, August 1944.
22. War Department, *FM 100-5, Operations* (1941), 130.
23. Jochim Ludewig, *Rückzug: The German Retreat from France, 1944*, trans. David T. Zabecki (Lexington: University of Kentucky Press, 2012), 87, 172–76.
24. Pogue, *European Theater of Operations*, 256–59; Stephen A. Bourque, *Beyond the Beach: The Allied War Against France* (Annapolis, MD: Naval Institute Press, 2018), 177–78.
25. Weigley, *Eisenhower's Lieutenants*, 253–54; Atkinson, *Guns at Last Light*, 375.
26. 4ID, G-3 Journal, August 1944; 4ID Historian, "Action North of Paris," Box 5664, NACP.
27. Barton, "War Diary."
28. HQ 4ID, "Field Order #29, September 1, 1944," Box 5763, NACP (hereafter cited as 4ID, Field Order #29); HQ 4ID, "Action Against Enemy, Reports After/Action After Reports (September 1944)," Box 5663, RG 407, NACP (hereafter cited as 4ID, AAR, September 1944); G-3, 4ID, "G-3 Journal, September 1944," Box 5708, NACP (hereafter cited as 4ID, G-3 Journal, September 1944).
29. 4ID, AAR, September 1944.
30. Boice, *History of the Twenty-Second*, 43–44; Johnson, *History of the Twlefth Infantry*, 174–77.
31. Barton, "War Diary."
32. 4ID, G-3 Journal, September 1944.
33. 4ID, G-3 Journal, September 1944.
34. Blumenson, *Breakout and Pursuit*, 679–84, 92; Sylvan and Smith, *Normandy to Victory*, 117.
35. Barton, "War Diary"; 4ID, AAR, September 1944; 4ID, G-3 Journal, September 1944.
36. 4ID Historian, "Action North of Paris," Box 5664, NACP; Boice, *History of the Twenty-Second*, 45.
37. Barton, "War Diary"; 4ID, AAR, September 1944.

38. Sylvan and Smith, *Normandy to Victory*, 118; 4ID, G-3 Journal, September 1944.
39. Weigley, *Eisenhower's Lieutenants*, 320–21.
40. Barton, "War Diary"; HQ 4ID, "Action Against Enemy, Reports After/ Action After Reports (September 1944)," Box 5663, RG 407, NACP; 4ID, G-3 Journal, September 1944.
41. 4ID, Field Order #29.
42. Barton, "War Diary"; 4ID, G-3 Journal, September 1944; HQ 4ID, "Field Order #31, September 5, 1944," Box 5763, NACP; 4ID, G-3 Journal, September 1944; Ludwig, *Rückzug*, 207.
43. 4ID, Field Order #29; Barton, "War Diary."
44. Charles T. Lanham Efficiency Report, Robert H. Chance, January 10, 1941, Lanham Records; Johnson, *History of the Twelfth Infantry*, 387.
45. HQ 4ID, "Field Order #32, September 7, 1944," Box 5763, NACP; 4ID, G-3 Journal, September 1944.
46. 4ID, Misc. Data; Barton, "War Diary."
47. Barton, "War Diary"; HQ 4ID, "Field Order #33, September 8, 1944," Box 5763, NACP; 4ID, G-3 Journal, September 1944.
48. HQ 12th Army Group, "Situation Map September 9, 1944," Library of Congress Geography and Map Division Washington, DC, accessed February 2023, http://hdl.loc.gov/loc.gmd/g5701s.ict21096.
49. Sylvan and Smith, *Normandy to Victory*, 124.
50. Barton, "War Diary."
51. Sylvan and Smith, *Normandy to Victory*, 125.
52. Barton, "War Diary."
53. Baker, *Ernest Hemingway*, 420–24.
54. Barton, "War Diary"; Boice, *History of the Twenty-Second*, 48; 4ID, G-3 Journal, September 1944, entry 137.
55. Ray S. Cline, *The War Department: Washington Command Post: The Operations Division*, United States Army in World War II (1951; repr., Washington, DC: CMH, 1990), 75–79; Jade E Hinman, "When the Japanese Bombed the Huertgen Forest," (master's thesis, US Army Command and General Staff College, 2011), 11–12.
56. Interview with Henry J. Matchett, by Thomas F. Soapes, 1976, 20–24, Oral History Collection, Dwight D. Eisenhower Presidential Library, Abilene, KS; Barton, "War Diary."
57. 4ID, G-3 Journal, September 1944.
58. Barton, "War Diary"; Baker, *Ernest Hemingway*, 425.

59. Barton, "War Diary"; 4ID, G-3 Journal, September 1944; 4ID, Field Order #37, September 13, 1944, Box 5763, NACP (hereafter cited as 4ID, Field Order #37).

60. 4ID, G-3 Journal, September 1944; Ludewig, *Rückzug*, 253–62.

61. Barton, "War Diary."

62. Charles B. MacDonald, *The European Theater of Operations: The Siegfried Line Campaign*, United States Army in World War II (1963; repr., Washington, DC: CMH, 1993), 50–52; 4ID, G-3 Journal, September 1944.

63. MacDonald, *Siegfried Line Campaign*, 50–52.

64. Barton, "War Diary"; VII Corps, Chief of Staff, History of the VII Corps for the period September 1–30, 1944, Entry 427, Box 3267, RG 407, NACP (hereafter cited as VII Corps, AAR, September 1944).

65. MacDonald, *Siegfried Line Campaign*, 54–55.

66. Letter, H. W. Blakeley to office of the chief of military history, RG 319, NPRC; 4ID Historian, "The First Penetration of the Siegfried Line into the Schnee Eifel," Entry 427, Box 5664, RG 407, NACP, Narrative 3.

67. MacDonald, *Siegfried Line Campaign*, 55; 4ID, Field Order #37.

68. 4ID Historian, "The Attack into Belgium," Box 5664, NACP.

69. 4ID, G-3 Journal, September 1944; Letter, Leonard T. Gerow to ROB, September 17, 1944.

70. Barton, "War Diary."

71. Barton, "War Diary"; Graham A. Cosmas and Albert E. Cowdrey, *The Medical Department: Medical Service in the European Theater of Operations*, United States Army in World War II: The Tehnical Services (Washington, DC: CMH, 1992), 67.

72. Barton, "War Diary"; G-3, 4ID, G-3 Journal, September 1944; Sylvan and Smith, *Normandy to Victory*, 140.

73. Cosmas and Cowdrey, *Medical Department*, 337–38; Barton, "War Diary"; Brief Medical History: ROB.

74. Barton, "War Diary"; 4ID Historian, "Attack into Belgium," Box 5664, NACP; 4ID, G-3 Journal, September 1944; McKee, Personal Diary.

75. Cosmas and Cowdrey, *Medical Department*, 64–66; Barton, "War Diary."

76. Letter, Hemingway to Lanham, October 8, 1944, in *Ernest Hemingway: Selected Letters, 1917–1961*, ed. Carlos Baker (New York: Charles Scribner's Sons, 1981), 572–73; Baker, *Ernest Hemingway*, 427–28; Barton, "War Diary."

77. 4ID, G-3 Journal, September 1944; 4ID Historian, "Attack into Belgium," Box 5664, NACP.
78. McKee, Personal Diary.
79. McKee, Personal Diary.
80. Barton, "War Diary."
81. Barton, "War Diary."
82. Barton, "War Diary."
83. Braim, *Will to Win*, 98–99; Sylvan and Smith, *Normandy to Victory*, 140.
84. Elizabeth Rieman, *Unpacking Yesterday: Brotherhood's Legacy* (Athens, GA: Deeds, 2020), 164–65.
85. Berlin, *World War II Corps Commanders*, 18–19.

Notes for Chapter 14

1. Eleanor Butler Roosevelt to ROB, December 14, 1944.
2. Braim, *Will to Win*, 99–131.
3. Barton, "War Diary"; McKee, Personal Diary.
4. Charles T. Lanham to his wife, October 6, 1944, Charles T. Lanham Papers, 1916–1978 (Lanham Papers), Mudd Manuscript Library, Princeton University, Princeton, NJ.
5. Connelly, *Mortarmen*, 46.
6. Barton, "War Diary."
7. G-3, VII Corps, "VII Corps Field Order #12, November 8, 1944," Box 3277, NACP (hereafter cited as VII Corps, Field Order #12); MacDonald, *Siegfried Line Campaign*, 408–9; Weigley, *Eisenhower's Lieutenants*, 364–65; War Department, *FM 100-5, Operations* (1941), 49, 97, 103–4. The decision to attack into, rather than bypass, the Hürtgen Forest remains a matter of debate and speculation eighty years later.
8. VII Corps, Field Order #12.
9. King, Collins, and Nulton, *To War with the 4th*, 155.
10. Charles B. MacDonald, *The Battle of the Huertgen Forest* (Philadelphia: J. B. Lippencott, 1963), 88–90; Edward G. Miller, *A Dark and Bloody Ground: The Hürtgen Forest and the Roer River Dams, 1944–1945* (College Station: Texas A&M Press, 1995), 45–46.
11. HQ 4ID, "Letter of Instruction (Demonstration), 2 November 1944," Box 5763, NACP.
12. G-3, 4ID, "G-3 Periodic Report #150, 22 November 1944," Box 5730, RG 407, NACP; Barton, "War Diary."

13. Barton, "War Diary"; HQ 4ID, "Action Against Enemy, Reports After/ Action After Reports (November 1944)," Box 5663, RG 407, NACP. Baker, *Ernest Hemingway*, 440–41.

14. G-3, 4ID, "G-3 Journal, November 1944," Box 5708, NACP (hereafter cited as 4ID, G-3 Journal, November 1944).

15. Barton, "War Diary."

16. Efficiency Report: ROB, Leonard T. Gerow, November 8, 1944, RG 319, NPRC.

17. Leonard T. Gerow to ROB, November 9, 1944.

18. 4ID, G-3 Journal, November 1944.

19. 4ID, G-3, Warning Order 032300A, November 1944.

20. Barton, "War Diary"; HQ 4ID, "Action Against Enemy, Reports After/ Action After Reports (November 1944)," Box 5663, RG 407, NACP (hereafter cited as 4ID, AAR, November 1944); MacDonald, *Siegfried Line Campaign*, 353; 4ID, G-3 Journal, November 1944.

21. MacDonald, *Siegfried Line Campaign*, 360, 66; 4ID, G-3 Journal, November 1944; G-3, 4ID, "G-3 Periodic Report #154 (052400 Nov. to 062400 Nov. 44)," Entry 427, Box 5730, RG 407, NACP.

22. James S. Luckett, "Battle of the Hurtgen Forest, Action of 12th Infantry November 7–21. Account Written for his Personal File by Colonel James S. Luckett, INF. (C. O. 12th Infantry June 15 to November 21, 1944)," Entry 427, Box 24021, RG 407, NACP; William T. Gayle and Kenneth W. Hechler, "4th Infantry Division, Hurtgen Forest Battle, November 7 to December 3, 1944," Entry 427, Box 19030, RG 407, NACP.

23. Chief of staff, VII Corps, "Ops Memo #115, November 7," Box 3382, RG 407, NACP.

24. 4ID, "Field Order #53, November 7, 1944," Box 5765, NACP (hereafter cited as 4ID, Field Order #53); 4ID, AAR, November 1944; Johnson, *History of the Twelfth Infantry*, 196; Baker, *Ernest Hemingway*, 433.

25. 8th Infantry S-3, Action Against Enemy, Reports After/Action Reports, period 1 November 1944–30 November 1944, NACP.

26. Luckett report.

27. Barton, "War Diary"; 4ID, AAR, November 1944.

28. Luckett report; Johnson, *History of the Twelfth Infantry*, 204.

29. Luckett report; Johnson, *History of the Twelfth Infantry*, 203–6; Barton, "War Diary."

30. 4ID, AAR, November 1944; Luckett report; Johnson, *History of the Twelfth Infantry*, 222; Barton, "War Diary."

31. Barton, "War Diary"; King, Collins, and Nulton, *To War with the 4th*, 159; Johnson, *History of the Twelfth Infantry*, 223–24.
32. VII Corps, Field Order #12.
33. MacDonald, *Siegfried Line Campaign*, 430–31.
34. 4ID, Field Order #53; Gayle and Hechler, "Hurtgen Forest Battle," 23.
35. James W. Haley, "Operations of the 2nd Battalion, 8th Infantry, 4th Infantry Division, in the Hurtgen Forest, Germany, 16–22 November 1944 (Rhineland Campaign) (Personal Experience of a Battalion Executive Officer)," (Infantry Officer Advanced Course, Fort Benning, GA, 1947–1948), 23, DRL.
36. MacDonald, *Siegfried Line Campaign*, 430–33; Haley, "2nd Battalion, 8th Infantry," 8–9.
37. 4ID, G-3 Journal, November 1944.
38. Johnson, *History of the Twelfth Infantry*, 217; 4ID, G-3 Journal, November 1944.
39. VII Corps, adjutant general, history of the VII Corps for the period November 1–30, 1944, Entry 427, Box 3267, RG 407, NACP (hereafter cited as VII Corps, AAR, November 1944); Gayle and Hechler, "Hurtgen Forest Battle," 23; Haley, "2nd Battalion, 8th Infantry," 22–23.
40. Haley, "2nd Battalion, 8th Infantry," 25.
41. Robert Sterling Rush, *Hell in Hürtgen Forest* (Lawrence: University Press of Kansas, 2001), 131–42; Gayle and Hechler, "Hurtgen Forest Battle," 25–26; 4ID, G-3 Journal, November 1944; Frederick T. Kent, "The Operations of the 22nd Infantry (4th Infantry Division) in the Hurtgen Forest, Germany, 16 November–3 December 1944 (Rhineland Campaign) (Personal Experience of a Regimental S-4)," (Infantry Officer Advanced Course, Fort Benning, GA, 1948), 9, DRL.
42. 4ID, AAR, November 1944, 18.
43. 4ID, AAR, November 1944, 18; Barton, "War Diary."
44. James N. McNutt and John C. Swearingen, interview with S-3 and Arty LNO, 2nd Battalion, 8th Infantry, in Gayle and Hechler, "Hurtgen Forest Battle"; Headquarters, 8IR, "Action Against Enemy, Reports After/Action Reports, period 1 November 1944–30 November 1944," Box 5838, NACP (hereafter cited as 8IR, AAR, November 1944); Haley, "2nd Battalion, 8th Infantry;" Gayle and Hechler, "Hurtgen Forest Battle," 28.
45. Haley, "2nd Battalion, 8th Infantry," 28–29; McNutt and Swearingen, interview; King, Collins, and Nulton, *To War with the 4th*, 169.
46. 8IR, AAR, November 1944; Haley, "2nd Battalion, 8th Infantry," 29.
47. 4ID, G-3 Journal, November 1944; Rush, *Hell in Hürtgen Forest*, 145–52.

48. Henley diary, November 17, 1944.

49. Gayle and Hechler, "Hurtgen Forest Battle," 26–27.

50. Rush, *Hell in Hürtgen Forest*, 151; Barton, "War Diary."

51. 4ID, G-3 Journal, November 1944; Rush, *Hell in Hürtgen Forest*, 151–52.

52. 8IR, AAR, November 1944; W. Haley, "2nd Battalion, 8th Infantry," 29–30.

53. Gayle and Hechler, "Hurtgen Forest Battle," 26–27; Robert D. Moore, "The Operations of Company C, 8th Infantry (4th Inf. Div) in the attack of the Hurtgen Forest, Germany, 19–21 November 1944 (Personal Experience of a Rifle Company Commander)," (Infantry Officer Advanced Course, US Army Infantry School, Fort Moore, GA, 1949), 15, DRL; Robert D. Moore, interview with commander, Company C, 1st Battalion, 8th Infantry, in Gayle and Hechler, "Hurtgen Forest Battle" (hereafter cited as Moore interview).

54. 8IR, AAR, November 1944. The Fields of Honor database lists both officers with Silver Stars. However, I have not been able to locate the citations as to when and when, which is not unusual as many of these records have vanished over time.

55. 8IR, AAR, November 1944; Moore interview; Moore, " Operations of Company C," 17; 4ID, G-3 Journal, November 1944.

56. Rush, *Hell in Hürtgen Forest*, 160–61, 73; 4ID, G-3 Journal, November 1944.

57. Gayle and Hechler, "Hurtgen Forest Battle," 26–27.

58. Rush, *Hell in Hürtgen Forest*, 163; Gayle and Hechler, "Hurtgen Forest Battle," 27.

59. VII Corps, AAR, November 1944; 4ID, AAR, November 1944.

60. Barton, "War Diary"; 4ID, G-3 Journal, November 1944; MacDonald, *Siegfried Line Campaign*, 417, 437.

61. 4ID, G-3 Journal, November 1944; Message, Barton to Delaney, 24 November, Box 5732, RG 407, NACP.

62. Gayle and Hechler, "Hurtgen Forest Battle," 21; Barton, "War Diary."

63. Chief of staff, VII Corps, "Ops Memo #118, November 19," Box 3382, RG 407, NACP; 4ID, G-3, "Sitrep #64, 29 November, 1944," Box 5732, RG 407, NACP.

64. 4ID, G-3 Journal, November 1944; 4ID, AAR, November 1944; Haley, "2nd Battalion, 8th Infantry," 32.

65. Headquarters, 8IR, "Recommendation for Award of Medal of Honor: Mabry, George L. (7 March 1945)," Entry 427, Box 5846, RG 407, NACP (hereafter cited as Mabry recommendation).

66. Mabry recommendation.

67. Mabry recommendation, cover letter, R. G. McKee to commander, 4ID, March 7, 1945.

68. 4ID, G-3, "Sitrep #68, 20 November 1944," Box 5732, RG 407, NACP; 4ID, AAR, November 1944; Sylvan and Smith, *Normandy to Victory*, 185.

69. Rush, *Hell in Hürtgen Forest*, 164; 4ID, AAR, November 1944; Miller, *Dark and Bloody Ground*, 131.

70. Gayle and Hechler, "Hurtgen Forest Battle," 30; Letter, Lanham to his wife, November 20, 1944, Lanham Papers.

71. Boice, *History of the Twenty-Second*, 61; George D Wilson, *If You Survive: From Normandy to the Battle of the Bulge to the End of World War II—One American Officer's Riveting True Story* (New York: Ballantine Books, 1987), 140–42; Rush, *Hell in Hürtgen Forest*, 173–78.

72. Gayle and Hechler, "Hurtgen Forest Battle," 31; 4ID, AAR, November 1944; 12th Army Group, "G-3 Periodic Report #55, 30 July 1944," Box 1330, NACP.

73. Barton, "War Diary"; Chapman, *Battle Hardened*, 207.

74. Johnson, *History of the Twelfth Infantry*, 223–24.

75. Baker, *Ernest Hemingway*, 436.

76. Barton, "War Diary"; Sylvan and Smith, *Normandy to Victory*, 184.

77. G-3, 4ID, "Confirmation of verbal orders 241630 Nov.," Entry 427, Box 5732, RG 407, NACP; 4ID, "G-3 Periodic Report #167, November 24, 1944," Box 5730, RG 407, NACP; 4ID, G-3, "Sitrep #95, 24 November 1944," Box 5732, RG 407, NACP.

78. Telephone conversation between J. Lawton Collins and Raymond O. Barton, 20:35 Hours, November 24, 1944, BPP.

79. 4ID, "G-3 Periodic Report #172," and "Overlay to Accompany G-3 Periodic Report #172, 24 November 1944," Box 5730, RG 407, NACP.

80. 4ID, AAR, November 1944.

81. Gayle and Hechler, "Hurtgen Forest Battle," 35.

82. 4ID, AAR, November 1944; Rush, *Hell in Hürtgen Forest*, 205–7.

83. Letter, Charles T. (Buck) Lanham to Ernest Hemingway, April 19,1946, Ernest Hemingway Collection, John F Kennedy Library, Boston, MA; Robert Rush, note to author, May 16, 2023.

84. Barton, "War Diary"; G-3, 4ID, "Plan of action, 26 November 1944," Box 5765, NACP; G-3, 4ID, fragmentary orders issued November 26, 1944, Entry 427, Box 5688, RG 407, NACP.

85. Barton, "War Diary"; 4ID, AAR, November 1944.

86. 4th Infantry "Ivy" Division Association, *Steadfast and Loyal* (Paducah, KY: Turner, 1987); 4ID, AAR, November 1944; "Marcario Garcia," *Congressional Medal of Honor Society*, accessed May 2023, https://www.cmohs.org/recipients/marcario-garcia; Jack Patterson, "Veteran of the Day: Army Veteran Marcario Garcia," news.va.gov, May 5, 2022 https://news.va.gov/103159/veteranoftheday-army-veteran-marcario-garcia/.

87. Raymond Oscar Barton, Recommendation for Award (Gorrell, Henry T.), BPP.

88. Barton, "War Diary."

89. 4ID, "Fragmentary Orders Issued November 28, 1944;" HQ 4ID, "Field Order #55, November 29, 1944," Box 5765, NACP; Gayle and Hechler, "Hurtgen Forest Battle," 40.

90. Gayle and Hechler, "Hurtgen Forest Battle," 41.

91. Barton, "War Diary."

92. VII Corps, AAR, November 1944.

93. G-3, 4ID, "Plan of action, 29 November 1944," Box 5765, NACP; Gayle and Hechler, "Hurtgen Forest Battle," 46.

94. Baker, *Ernest Hemingway*, 437.

95. Barton, "War Diary."

96. Baker, *Ernest Hemingway*, 437.

97. 4ID, AAR, November 1944; Gayle and Hechler, "Hurtgen Forest Battle," 44.

98. Baker, *Ernest Hemingway*, 437–38.

99. Gayle and Hechler, "Hurtgen Forest Battle," 42–49; 4th Inf. Div, Fragmentary Orders Issued December 1, 1944; Barton, "War Diary."

100. Gayle and Hechler, "Hurtgen Forest Battle," 49.

101. HQ 4ID, "Action Against Enemy, Reports After/Action After Reports (December 1944)," Box 5663, RG 407, NACP (hereafter cited as 4ID, AAR, December 1944); Rush, *Hell in Hürtgen Forest*, 262; "Pedro Cano," *Congressional Medal of Honor Society*, accessed May 2023 https://www.cmohs.org/recipients/pedro-cano.

102. Stephen P. Cano, *Unsung Hero: Private Pedro Cano, WWII Medal of Honor Recipient* (Fresno, CA: Linden, 2018).

103. Sylvan and Smith, *Normandy to Victory*, 194.

104. 4th Inf. Div., Fragmentary Orders Issued December 2, 1944; 4ID, "Field Order #56, December 3, 1944," Box 5765, NACP (hereafter cited as 4ID, Field Order #56).

105. Barton, "War Diary."

106. Chief of staff, VII Corps, "Ops Memo #124, December 3 1944,"
     Box 3382, RG 407, NACP; 4ID, AAR, December 1944; 4ID, Field
     Order #56.
107. Baker, *Ernest Hemingway*, 438; Barton, "War Diary."
108. Barton, "War Diary."
109. Sylvan and Smith, *Normandy to Victory*, 197.
110. Rush, *Hell in Hürtgen Forest*, 280.
111. Gerald Astor, *The Bloody Forest: Battle for the Huertgen: September
     1944–January 1945* (Novato, CA: Presidio Press, 2000), 298.
112. Miller, *Dark and Bloody Ground*, 203.
113. Weigley, *Eisenhower's Lieutenants*, 432–33.

Notes for Chapter 15

1. George S. Patton, Letter to ROB, December 27, 1944.
2. Focusing on Barton, this narrative only summarizes the battle from
   his perspective. For a more complete analysis, consult other sources,
   such as Peter Caddick-Adams, *Snow & Steel: The Battle of the Bulge,
   1944–45* (Oxford, UK: Oxford University Press, 2013).
3. Hugh M. Cole, *The European Theater of Operations: The Ardennes:
   The Battle of the Bulge.* United States Army in World War II (1965; repr.,
   Washington, DC: CMH, 1993), 238; Letter, ROB to Hugh M. Cole, chief
   of military history, Subj.: Ardennes Campaign, November 17, 1956.
4. Cole, *European Theater of Operations*, 55, 238; Barton, "War Diary";
   HQ 4ID, "Action Against Enemy, Reports After /Action After Reports
   (December 1944)," Box 5663, RG 407, NACP.
5. Barton, "War Diary."
6. ROB to chief of military history, November 17, 1959; Barton, "War Diary."
7. ROB to chief of military history, November 17, 1959; HQ 4ID, Field
   Order #57, December 3, 1944," Box 5765, NACP (hereafter cited as
   4ID, Field Order #57).
8. Caddick-Adams, *Snow & Steel*, 175–76.
9. ROB to chief of military history, November 17, 1959.
10. ROB to chief of military history, November 17, 1959; Barton, "War
    Diary"; 4ID, Field Order #57.
11. Barton, "War Diary"; Cole, *European Theater of Operations*, 239.
12. HQ 4ID, "Letter of Instruction (Rehabilitation), 14 December, 1944,"
    Box 5689, NACP; Barton, "War Diary."
13. Cole, *European Theater of Operations*, 60; ROB to chief of military
    history, November 17, 1959.

14. Cole, *European Theater of Operations*, 213; Caddick-Adams, *Snow & Steel*, 268–69.

15. Cole, *European Theater of Operations*, 240.

16. Johnson, *History of the Twelfth Infantry*, 232; 4ID, AAR, December 1944.

17. ROB to chief of military history, November 17, 1959; G-3, 4ID, "G-3 Journal, December 1944," Box 5708, NACP (hereafter cited as 4ID, G-3 Journal, December 1944).

18. Cole, *European Theater of Operations*, 241–43; 4ID, G-3 Journal, December 1944.

19. ROB to chief of military history, November 17, 1959.

20. 4ID, G-3 Journal, December 1944.

21. Cole, *European Theater of Operations*, 243.

22. ROB to chief of military history, November 17, 1959.

23. ROB to chief of military history, November 17, 1959; 4ID, G-3 Journal, December 1944.

24. 4ID, AAR, December 1944.

25. ROB to chief of military history, November 17, 1959.

26. Cole, *European Theater of Operations*, 248.

27. ROB to chief of military history, November 17, 1959; Cole, *European Theater of Operations*, 244.

28. Cole, *European Theater of Operations*, 249; Caddick-Adams, *Snow & Steel*, 280–81.

29. Baker, *Hemingway*, 439–40.

30. Johnson, *History of the Twelfth Infantry*, 235; Cole, *European Theater of Operations*, 54, 249; ROB to chief of military history, November 17, 1959.

31. ROB to chief of military history, November 17, 1959; 4ID, AAR, December 1944.

32. ROB to chief of military history, November 17, 1959.

33. Cole, *European Theater of Operations*, 253; 4ID, G-3 Journal, December 1944.

34. Cole, *European Theater of Operations*, 255.

35. Barton, "War Diary."

36. Cole, *European Theater of Operations*, 256–58.

37. Barton, "War Diary."

38. Barton, "War Diary"; *Patton Papers*, 602–3.

39. ROB to chief of military history, November 17, 1959.

40. ROB to chief of military history, November 17, 1959.

41. Cole, *European Theater of Operations*, 489–91; 4ID, AAR, December 1944.

42. 4ID, AAR, December 1944.

43. Barton, "War Diary."

44. Baker, *Ernest Hemingway*, 440–41; Barton, "War Diary"; ROB to chief of military history, November 17, 1959.

45. Caddick-Adams, *Snow & Steel*, 622–23.

46. Barton, "War Diary"; ROB to chief of military history, November 17, 1959; Army Retirement Board, September 29, 1945, RG 319, NPRC (hereafter cited as Retirement Board Proceedings).

47. Barton, "War Diary"; George S. Patton to his wife, December 26, 1944, George S. Patton Collection, Library of Congress, Washington, DC.

48. Sylvan and Smith, *Normandy to Victory*, 238–41.

49. Patton to ROB, December 27, 1944.

50. Manton S. Eddy to ROB, 27 December 1944.

51. Efficiency Report: ROB, Manton S. Eddy, January 22, 1945, RG 319, NPRC.

52. Barton, "War Diary."

53. Barton, "War Diary."

54. Barton, "War Diary."

55. Barton, "War Diary."

56. Barton, "War Diary."

57. Barton, "War Diary."

58. Barton, "War Diary."

59. Retirement Board Proceedings, Barton statement.

60. *Ivy Leaves*, vol XVIII, no. 2 (June 1945).

61. *Ivy Leaves*, vol XVIII, no. 3 (September 1945); *Ivy Leaves*, vol 4, no. 4., November 1945.

62. Retirement Board Proceedings, Barton statement; ROB to Joe N. Dalton, re: retirement, September 24, 1945.

63. Retirement Board Proceedings, Barton statement.

64. Retirement Board Proceedings, Sears testimony.

65. Retirement Board Proceedings, Goldner testimony.

66. Retirement Board Proceedings, Medical Retirement Board Findings, Raymond O. Barton.

67. Orders, Barton to Camp Butner, February 8, 1946, RG 319, NPRC.

68. War Department, preretirement leave; War Department, Retirement Orders; War Department, Resume of Service, Raymond O. Barton, RG 319, NPRC.

Notes for Chapter 16

1. *Augusta Chronicle*, December 3, 1946.
2. Raymond O Barton, autobiographical sketch, BPP.
3. Eleanor Butler Roosevelt to ROB, March 5, 1958; Eleanor Butler Roosevelt, *Day Before Yesterday: The Reminiscences of Mrs. Theodore Roosevelt, Jr* (New York: Doubleday, 1959).
4. ROB, Letter to the editor, *Time Magazine*, March 3, 1958.
5. War Department, correspondence with Mrs. Theodore Roosevelt Jr., Roosevelt, Official Military Personnel Records, NPRC.
6. Barton, overlay and comments; Barton, interview by Ryan; ROB to Ryan, 1959; Cornelius Ryan, *The Longest Day* (New York: Simon & Schuster, 1959).
7. Barton, "Comments on the Siegfried Line," 1956, and "Comments on Ardennes," 1959, RG 319, NACP.
8. Ernest Hemingway letters to Barton, 1945, 1948.
9. Ernest Hemingway, "The G. I. and the General," *Collier's*, November 4, 1944, 46–47.
10. Hemingway to Lanham, October 8, 1944, in *Hemingway: Selected Letters*; Lanham to Hemingway, May 7, 1946, Hemingway Collection.
11. ROB to Baker (2), March 20, 1963 (there are two letters on this date).
12. ROB to Baker (1), March 20, 1963.
13. Baker, *Ernest Hemingway*; *Hemingway: Selected Letters*.
14. Lanham, AE Form 66 and correspondence with the adjutant general, October 1949, Lanham, Official Military Personnel File, NPRC; Lanham to Hemingway, 19 April 1946, Hemingway Collection.
15. McKee, War Department Form 66, McKee Personal Papers.
16. Harold W. Blakeley, correspondence with War Department Staff, Subject: Award to Major General H. W. Blakeley, April 1948, Official Military Personnel File, NPRC. File also did not contain an efficiency report from Barton for the second half of 1944.
17. AEF 4th Division Association, "Major General Raymond O. Barton speaks at memorial dedication at Arlington Cemetery Virgina, Sunday, April 29, 1945," *Ivy Leaves*, June 1, 1945.
18. *Ivy Leaves* 1947, 8.
19. *Ivy Leaves*, 1948.
20. *Ivy Leaves*, 1949, 1951.
21. Barton, Recommendations for Unit Awards, 1951, BPP.

458 Notes for Chapter 16

22. Wilson, *Armies*, 187–88; Mahon and Danysh, *Infantry*, 459–61.
23. Omar N. Bradley to ROB, October 4, 1951; Harry J. Collins to ROB, June 11, 1951; James Van Fleet to ROB, June 12, 1951; J. Lawton Collins to ROB, August 12, 1952.
24. *Ivy Leaves*, 1947, 8.
25. *Ivy Leaves*, 1947, 10.
26. *Ivy Leaves*, 1947, 10.
27. Barton, application for active duty, 1950, RG 319, NPRC.
28. Army chief of information to ROB, invitation to D-Day ceremony, May 5, 1954; office of the adjutant general, amendment to invational travel orders, June 2, 1954, BPP.
29. Barton, autobiographical sketch; editorial, "Raymond O. Barton," *Augusta Chronicle*, 1963; Bill Kirby, "The Way We Were: R. O. Barton one of Augusta's D-Day connections," *Augusta Chronicle*, 2018.
30. Lee Ann Caldwell, Augusta University, to author, "Barton in Augusta," March 27, 2018.
31. ROB to Rocky Barton, September 30, 1949.
32. Obituary, *San Angelo Standard-Times* (San Angelo, TX), October 8, 1995.
33. Obituary, *San Angelo Standard-Times*, January 16, 2005.
34. Office of the adjutant general, report of casualty, 1963, RG 319, NPRC.
35. *Ivy Leaves*, 1963, 4–6.
36. Cathy (Barton) Clarke to author, January 2024.
37. Karli Goldenberg, "Post Renaming Complete," *Army* 74, no. 1 (January 2024): 20–21.

Bibliography

Archives, Libraries, and Collections

Ada Public Library, Ada, OK.

Army Retirement Board, Fort McClellan, AL.

Camp Gordon Johnston World War II Museum. Camp Gordon Johnston, Carrabelle, FL.

Charles T. Lanham Papers, 1916–1978. Mudd Manuscript Library, Princeton University, Princeton, NJ.

Cornelius Ryan Collection of World War II Papers. Ohio University Library, Athens Ohio.

Donovan Research Library, Fort Moore, GA

Ernest Hemingway Collection. John F. Kennedy Library and Museum, Boston, MA.

George A. Smathers Libraries, Gainesville, FL.

George S. Patton Collection. Library of Congress, Washington, DC.

Ike Skelton Combined Arms Research Library, Fort Leavenworth, KS.

Imperial War Museum, London, UK.

J. Lawton Collins Papers. Eisenhower Presidential Library, Abilene, KS.

Mudd Manuscript Library. Princeton University, Princeton, NJ.

Musée de la Libération de Paris-musée du général Leclerc-musée Jean Moulin, Paris, FR.

National Archives at College Park, College Park, MD.

National Archives, Kew Gardens, United Kingdom.

National Personnel Records Center, St. Louis, MO.

Oral History Collection. Dwight D. Eisenhower Presidential Library, Abilene, KS.

Ray W. Barker Papers. Dwight D. Eisenhower Presidential Library, Abilene, KS.

Raymond O. Barton Personal Papers. Possession of author and courtesy of Barton family.

Richard G. McKee Personal Papers. Possession of author and courtesy of Nancy G. (McKee) Smith.

US Army Center of Military History Library, Fort McNair, Washington, DC.

US Army Heritage and Education Center, Carlisle, PA.

US Military Academy Library, West Point, NY.

Van Fleet Digital Archive. Van Fleet Foundation, Hobe Sound, FL.

Published Papers and Documents

Eisenhower, Dwight D. *Eisenhower: The Prewar Diaries and Selected Papers, 1905–1941.* Edited by Daniel D. Holt and James W. Leyerzapf. Baltimore: Johns Hopkins University Press, 1998.

Eisenhower, Dwight D. *The Papers of Dwight David Eisenhower: The War Years.* Edited by Alfred D. Chandler Jr. and Stephen E. Ambrose. Baltimore: Johns Hopkins Press, 1970.

Hemingway, Ernest. *Ernest Hemingway: Selected Letters, 1917–1961.* Edited by Carlos Baker. New York: Charles Scribner's Sons, 1981.

Marshall, George C. *The Papers of George Catlett Marshall.* Edited by Larry I. Bland and Sharon Ritenour Stevens. Vol. 4, *"Aggressive and Determined Leadership," June 1, 1943–December 31, 1944.* Baltimore and London: Johns Hopkins University Press, 1996.

Patton, George S. *The Patton Papers, 1895–1940.* Edited by Martin Blumenson. Boston: Houghton Mifflin Company, 1972.

Pyle, Ernie. *Ernie's War: The Best of Ernie Pyle's World War II Dispatches.* Edited by David Nichols. New York: Simon & Schuster, 1986.

Sylvan, William C., and Francis G. Smith Jr. *Normandy to Victory: The War Diary of General Courtney H. Hodges & the First U. S. Army.* Edited by John T. Greenwood. Lexington: University of Kentucky Press, 2008.

War Department. *Order of Battle of the United States Land Forces in the World War.* Vol. 2, *American Expeditionary Forces: Divisions.* Washington, DC: GPO, 1931. Reprint, Washington, DC: CMH, 1988.

War Department. *Order of Battle of the United States Land Forces in the World War.* Vol. 3, pt. 2, *Zone of the Interior: Territorial Departments, Tactical Divisions Organized in 1918, and Post, Camps, and Stations.* Washington, DC: GPO, 1931.

War Department. *The United States Army in the World War, 1917–1919.* 17 vols. Washington, DC: CMH 1988.

Field and Technical Manuals

Department of the Army. *FM 7-20, The Infantry Battalions.* Washington, DC: Department of Army, 1969.

Department of the Army. *FM 100-5, Operations.* Washington, DC: Department of the Army, 1986.

Technical Services Division. *Administrator's Guide, Motor Transport Special Service School Course "F."* Baltimore: Holabird Quartermaster Motor Base, 1942.

War Department. *Field Service Regulations*. Washington, DC: GPO, 1923.

War Department. *FM 6-20 Field Artillery Tactical Employment*. Washington, DC: GPO, 1944.

War Department. *FM 7-20, Infantry Field Manual: Rifle Regiment*. Washington, DC: GPO, 1944.

War Department. *FM 7-40, Infantry Field Manual: Rifle Regiment*. Washington, DC: GPO, 1942.

War Department. *FM 10-35 Quartermaster Truck Companies, W/Change 1*. Washington, DC: GPO, 1945.

War Department. *FM 30-5: Basic Field Manual of Military Intelligence-Combat Intelligence*. Washington, DC: GPO, 1940.

War Department. *FM 100-5, Tentative Field Service Regulations: Operations*. Washington, DC: GPO, 1939.

War Department. *FM 100-5, Field Service Regulations: Operations*. Washington, DC: War Department, 1941.

War Department. *FM 100-10, Field Service Regulations: Administration*. Washington, DC: GPO, 1943.

War Department. *FM 100-20, Field Service Regulations: Command and Employment of Air Power*. Washington, DC: GPO, 1943.

War Department. *FM 100-15, Field Service Regulations: Larger Units*. Washington, DC: GPO, 1942.

War Department. *FM 101-5, Staff Officers' Field Manual, Staff and Combat Orders*. Washington, DC: GPO, 1940.

War Department. *Technical Manual-E 30-451: Handbook on German Military Forces*. Washington, DC: GPO, 1945.

Publications

1912 Executive Committee. *Ten Year Book: Class of Nineteen-Twelve*. West Point, NY: USMA Class of 1912 Executive Committee, 1922.

Aber, Sarajane Sandusky. "An Architectural History of the Liberty Memorial in Kansas City, Missouri, 1918–1935." Master's thesis, University of Missouri–Kansas City, 1988.

Ada Chamber of Commerce. *Ada Oklahoma: The Railroad, Industrial, and Educational Center of Southern Oklahoma*. Ada, OK: Chamber of Commerce: 1914.

Adams, James Mack. *Images of America: Tybee Island*. Charleston, SC: Arcadia, 2000.

Adams, John A. *General Jacob Devers: World War II's Forgotten Four Star*. Bloomington: Indiana University Press, 2015.

Allen, Henry T. *My Rhineland Journal.* New York: Houghton Mifflin, 1923.

Allen, Robert H. *Combat Orders.* Fort Leavenworth, KS: General Service Schools Press, 1922.

American Battle Monuments Commission. *American Armies and Battlefields in Europe.* 1938. Reprint, Washington, DC: CMH, 1992.

Astor, Gerald. *The Bloody Forest: Battle for the Huertgen: September 1944–January 1945.* Novato, CA: Presidio Press, 2000.

Atkinson, Rick. *An Army at Dawn: The War in Africa, 1942–1943.* New York: Henry Holt, 2002.

Atkinson, Rick. *The Day of Battle: The War in Sicily and Italy, 1943–1944.* New York: Henry Holt, 2007.

Atkinson, Rick. *The Guns at Last Light: The War in Western Europe, 1944–1945.* New York: Henry Holt, 2013.

Ausland, John C. *Letters Home: A War Memoir.* Oslo, Norway: Land Productions, 1993.

Autobee, Robert, and Deborah Dobson-Brown. *Colorado State Roads and Highways.* Denver: Colorado Historical Society, 2003.

Babcock, Robert O. *War Stories.* Vol. 1, *D-Day to the Liberation of Paris.* Atlanta: Deeds, 2001.

Baker, Carlos. *Ernest Hemingway: A Life Story.* New York: Charles Scribner's Sons, 1969.

Balkoski, Joseph. *Utah Beach: The Amphibious Landing and Airborne Operations on D-Day.* Mechanicsburg, PA: Stackpole Books, 2005.

Ball, Harry P. *Of Responsible Command: A History of the US Army War College.* Revised ed. Carlisle Barracks, PA: Alumni Association of the United States Army War College, 1994.

Barbier, Mary Kathryn. "George C. Marshall and the 1940 Louisiana Maneuvers." *Louisiana History: The Journal of the Louisiana Historical Association* 44, no. 4 (Autumn 2003): 389–410.

Barnes, Alexander. *In a Strange Land: The American Occupation of Germany, 1918–1923.* Atglen, PA: Schiffer Military History, 2011.

Barry, John M. *Rising Tide: The Great Mississippi Flood of 1927 and How It Changed America.* New York: Simon & Schuster, 1997.

Barry, Thomas H. *Annual Report of the Superintendent of the United States Military Academy.* West Point, NY: United States Military Academy, 1912.

Barton, Raymond O. *The 4th Motorized Division.* Augusta, GA: Walton Printing, 1942.

Becker, Marshall O. *The Amphibious Training Center: Study No. 22.* Washington, DC: Historical Section, Army Ground Forces, 1946.

Bell, Raymond E., Jr. "Madison Barracks New York." *On Point* 23, no. 2 (2017): 46–49.

Bell, William Gardner. *Commanding Generals and Chiefs of Staff, 1775–2013.* Washington, DC: CMH, 2013.

Bender, Mark C. "Watershed at Leavenworth: Dwight D. Eisenhower and the Command and General Staff School." Master's thesis, US Army Command and General Staff College, 1988.

Berlin, Robert H. *US Army World War II Corps Commanders: A Composite Biography.* Fort Leavenworth, KS: CSI, 1989.

Biles, J. Hugh. *The Early History of Ada.* Ada, OK: Oklahoma State Bank, 1954.

Blakeley, H. W. *4th Infantry Division (Yearbook).* Baton Rouge, LA: Army & Navy Publishing, 1946.

Blakeley, H. W. *8th Infantry Regiment (Yearbook).* Baton Rouge, LA: Army & Navy Publishing, 1946.

Blakeley, H. W. *12th Infantry Regiment (Yearbook).* Baton Rouge, LA: Army & Navy Publishing, 1946.

Blakeley, H. W. *22nd Infantry Regiment (Yearbook).* Baton Rouge, LA: Army & Navy Publishing, 1946.

Blakeley, H. W. *Division Artillery (Yearbook).* Baton Rouge, LA: Army & Navy Publishing, 1946.

Blakeley, H. W. *Famous Fourth: The Story of the 4th Infantry Division.* Whitefish, MT: Kessinger Publishing, 1945.

Blakeley, H. W. *Special Troops (Yearbook).* Baton Rouge, LA: Army & Navy Publishing, 1946.

Blumenson, Martin. *The Battle of the Generals.* New York: William Morrow, 1993.

Blumenson, Martin. *The European Theater of Operations: Breakout and Pursuit.* The United States Army in World War II. Washington, DC: CMH, 1960.

Boesch, Paul. *Road to Huertgen: Forest in Hell.* Houston, TX: Gulf, 1962.

Boice, William S. *History of the Twenty-Second United States Infantry World War II.* Self-published, 1959.

Boivin, Michael. *Les Manchois dans la tourmente de la seconde guerre mondiale (1939–1945).* 6 vols. Marigny, Manche, France: Eurocibles, 2004.

Bourque, Stephen A. "Barton on Utah Beach: His Best Day in Combat." *Army History*, Fall 2022, 6–37.

Bourque, Stephen A. *Beyond the Beach: The Allied War against France.* Annapolis, MD: Naval Institute Press, 2018.

Bourque, Stephen A. "Richard G. McKee: A Forgotten U.S. Army Officer of World War II." *On Point, The Journal of Army History* 25, no. 1 (Summer 2019): 36–43.

Bradley, Omar N. *A Soldier's Story.* New York: Holt, Rinehart and Winston, 1951.

Brady, Tim. *His Father's Son: The Life of General Ted Roosevelt Jr.* New York: New American Library, 2017.

Braim, Paul F. *The Will to Win: The Life of General James A. Van Fleet.* Annapolis, MD: Naval Institute Press, 2008.

Brennan, Robert E., and Jeannie I. Brennan. *Images of America: Fort Drum.* Charleston, SC: Arcadia, 2002.

Brennan, Robert E., and Jeannie I. Brennan. *Images of America: Sackets Harbor.* Charleston, SC: Arcadia, 2000.

Briscoe, Charles H. "Commando & Ranger Training, Part III: Forging Junior Leaders to Toughen Men to Win in Combat." *Veritas: Journal of US Army Special Operations History* 16, no. 1 (2020): 41–51.

Butcher, Harry C. *My Three Years with Eisenhower: The Personal Diary of Captain Harry C. Butcher, USNR, Naval Aide to General Eisenhower, 1942–1946.* New York: Simon and Schuster, 1946.

Caddick-Adams, Peter. *Sand & Steel: The D-Day Invasion and the Liberation of France.* Oxford, UK: Oxford University Press, 2019.

Caddick-Adams, Peter. *Snow & Steel: The Battle of the Bulge, 1944–45.* Oxford, UK: Oxford University Press, 2013.

Calhoun, Mark T. *General Lesley J. McNair: Unsung Architect of the US Army.* Lawrence: University of Kansas, 2015.

Cano, Stephen P., ed. *The Last Witness: The Memoirs of George L. Mabry, Jr., from D-Day to the Battle of the Bulge.* Fresno, CA: Linden, 2021.

Cano, Stephen P. *Unsung Hero: Private Pedro Cano, WWII Medal of Honor Recipient.* Fresno, CA: Linden, 2018.

Cantwell, Melissa. "The Rhineland Occupation and Its Legacy." Master's thesis, Marine Corps University, 2011.

Carell, Paul. *Invasion! They're Coming! The German Account of the D-Day Landings and the 80 Days Battle for France.* Translated by David Johnston. Atglen, PA: Schiffer Military History, 1995.

CGSS. *Schedule for 1929–1930: First Year Course.* Fort Leavenworth, KS: CGSS Press, 1929.

CGSS. *Schedule for 1933–1934: Second-Year Class.* Fort Leavenworth, KS: CGSS Press, 1933.

Chapman, Craig S. *Battle Hardened: An Infantry Officer's Harrowing Journey from D-Day.* Washington, DC: Regnery History, 2017.

Cirillo, Roger. *Memorandum for the Deputy Commander: 2-Year Course, 1930–1936*. Fort Leavenworth, KS: CARL, 1984.

Ciucevich, Robert A. "City of Tybee Island Historic Resources Survey Phase II." Savannah, GA: Quatrefoil Historic Preservation Consulting, 2017.

Clark, J. P. *Preparing for War: The Emergence of the Modern US Army, 1815–1917*. Cambridge, MA: Harvard University Press, 2017.

Clausewitz, Carl von. *On War*. Edited and translated by Michael Howard and Peter Paret. Indexed ed. Princeton: Princeton University Press, 1984.

Clay, Steven E. *US Army Order of Battle, 1919–1941*. 4 vols. Fort Leavenworth, KS: CSI, 2010.

Clifford, J. Garry. *The Citizen Soldiers: The Plattsburg Training Camp Movement, 1913–1920*. Lexington: University of Kentucky Press, 2014.

Cline, Ray S. *The War Department: Washington Command Post: The Operations Division*. United States Army in World War II. 1951. Reprint, Washington, DC: CMH, 1990.

Cloues, Richard. "Fort Screven: National Register of Historic Places Inventory–Nomination Form." Atlanta: Historic Preservation Section, Georgia Department of Natural Resources, 1980.

Cobb, Matthew. *Eleven Days in August: The Liberation of Paris in 1944*. New York: Simon & Schuster, 2015.

Coffman, Edward M. *The Regulars: The American Army, 1898–1941*. Cambridge, MA: Belknap Press, 2004.

Coffman, Edward M. *The War to End All Wars: The American Military Experience in World War I*. Lexington: University of Kentucky Press, 2004.

Cole, Hugh M. *The European Theater of Operations: The Ardennes: The Battle of the Bulge*. United States Army in World War II. 1965. Reprint, Washington, DC: CMH, 1993.

Collins, J. Lawton. "The Conduct of the Secondary Attack." Fort Leavenworth, KS: CGSS, 1933.

Collins, J. Lawton. "Did the German Enveloping Maneuver through Belgium in 1914 Surprise the French General Staff?" Fort Leavenworth, KS: CGSS, 1933.

Collins, J. Lawton. *Lightning Joe: An Autobiography*. Baton Rouge: Louisiana State University Press, 1979.

Collins, J. Lawton. *Mission Accomplished: The Story of the Campaigns of the VII Corps, United States Army in the War against Germany, 1944–1945*. Leipzig, Germany: J. J. Weber, 1945. Reprint, Hoosick, NY: Merriam Press, 2008.

Connelly, Michael. *The Mortarmen*. Victoria, BC: Trafford, 2005.

Copp, Dewitt S. *Frank M. Andrews: Marshall's Airman.* Washington, DC: Air Force History and Museums Program, 2003.

Corlett, Charles H. *Cowboy Pete; the Autobiography of Major General Charles H. Corlett.* Santa Fe, NM: Sleeping Fox, 1974.

Cornebise, Alfred. *The Amaroc News: The Daily Newspaper of the American Forces in Germany, 1919–1923.* Carbondale: Southern Illinois University Press, 1981.

Cornebise, Alfred. *Typhus and Doughboys: The American Polish Typhus Relief Expedition, 1919–1921.* Newark: University of Delaware Press, 1982.

Cosmas, Graham A. *An Army for Empire: The United States Army in the Spanish American War.* College Station: Texas A&M Press, 1994.

Cosmas, Graham A. "San Juan Hill and El Caney, 1–2 July 1898." In Heller and Stoft, *America's First Battles,* 109–48.

Cosmas, Graham A., and Albert E. Cowdrey. *The Medical Department: Medical Service in the European Theater of Operations.* United States Army in World War II: The Technical Services. Washington, DC: CMH, 1992.

Coumbe, Arthur T., and Lee S. Harford. *US Army Cadet Command: The 10 Year History.* Cadet Command Historical Study Series. Fort Monroe, VA: US Army Cadet Command, 1996.

Craven, Wesley Frank, and James Lea Cate. *The Army Air Forces in World War II.* Vol. 3, *Europe, Argument to V-E Day, January 1944–May 1945.* Chicago: University of Chicago Press, 1951.

Crosswell, D. K. *Beetle: The Life of General Walter Bedell Smith.* Lexington: University Press of Kentucky, 2010.

Dapp, Rick. "Stackpole Books." *Harrisburg Magazine,* 2016. https://harrisburg magazine.com/community/did-you-know/did-you-know-stackpole.

Dastrup, Boyd L. *The US Army Command and General Staff College: A Centennial History.* Manhattan, KS: Sunflower University Press, 1982.

Department of Commerce. *Official Register of the United States, 1921.* Washington, DC: GPO, 1921.

D'Este, Carlo. *Decision in Normandy.* New York: W. Collins & Sons, 1983.

D'Este, Carlo. *Eisenhower: A Soldier's Life.* New York: Henry Holt, 2002.

Devers, Jacob L. *Report of Army Ground Forces Activities.* Washington, DC: Army Ground Forces, 1946.

Dick, C. J. *From Victory to Stalemate: The Western Front, Summer 1944.* Lawrence: University of Kansas, 2016.

Dickson, Paul. *The Rise of the GI Army, 1940–1941: The Forgotten Story of How America Forged a Powerful Army before Pearl Harbor.* New York: Atlantic Monthly Press, 2020.

Dolski, Michael, Sam Edwards, and John Buckley, eds. *D-Day in History and Memory: The Normandy Landings in International Remembrance and Commemoration*. Denton: University of North Texas Press, 2014.

Drum, Hugh A. *Troop Leading: An Infantry Division in the Attack*. Fort Leavenworth, KS: CGSS Press, 1921.

Eisenhower, Dwight D. *Crusade in Europe*. Garden City, NY: Garden City Books, 1948.

Eisenhower, Dwight D. *Report by the Supreme Commander to the Combined Chiefs of Staff on the Operations in Europe of the Allied Expeditionary Force, 6 June 1944–8 May 1945*. Reprint, Washington, DC: CMH, 1994.

The Eisenhower Foundation. *D-Day: The Normandy Invasion in Retrospect*. Lawrence: University Press of Kansas, 1971.

Ellis, Major O. O., and Major E. B. Garey. *The Plattsburg Manual: A Handbook for Military Training*. 10th ed. New York: Century Company, 1917.

English, John A., and Bruce I. Gudmundsson. *On Infantry*. Revised ed. Westport, CT: Praeger, 1994.

Executive Committee. *The Plattsburger*. New York: Wynkoop Hallenbeck Crawford, 1917.

Ferrell, Robert H. *America's Deadliest Battle: Meuse-Argonne, 1918*. Lawrence: University Press of Kansas, 2007.

Fleming, Thomas. *The Illusion of Victory: Americans in World War I*. New York: Basic Books, 2003.

Flynn, Henry L., ed. *The Howitzer*. New York: Chas. L. Willard, 1912.

Franzwa, Gregory M. *Maps of the Santa Fe Trail*. St. Louis: Patrice Press, 1989.

Gabel, Christopher R. *The US Army GHQ Maneuvers of 1941*. Washington, DC: CMH, 1991.

Garland, Albert N., Howard McGaw Smyth, and Martin Blumenson. *The Mediterranean Theater of Operations: Sicily and the Surrender of Italy*. The United States Army in World War II. Washington, DC: CMH, 1965.

Gallagher, James McD., ed. *Ye Domesday Booke*. Washington, DC: Georgetown University, 1936.

Gersdorff, V. *Battle of Hürtgen Forest, Nov–Early December 1944 (German Viewpoint)*. Fort Leavenworth, KS: CARL, 1945.

Godfrey, Stuart C., ed. *The Howitzer*. New York: Chas. L. Willard, 1909.

Goldenberg, Karli. "Post Renaming Complete." *Army* 74, no. 1 (January 2024): 20–21.

Gole, Henry G. *Exposing the Third Reich: Colonel Truman Smith in Hitler's Germany*. Lexington: University of Kentucky Press, 2013.

Gole, Henry G. *The Road to Rainbow: Army Planning for Global War, 1934–1940*. Annapolis, MD: Naval Institute Press, 2003.

Greenfield, Kent Roberts, Robert R. Palmer, and Bell I. Wiley. *The Army Ground Forces: The Organization of Ground Combat Troops.* 1947. Reprint, Washington, DC: CMH, 1987.

Griess, Thomas E. "Dennis Hart Mahan: West Point Professor and Advocate of Military Professionalism, 1830–1871." Unpublished master's thesis, Duke University, 1968.

Haney, Gary, and Dare Strickland. *Images of America: Pontotoc County.* Charleston, SC: Arcadia, 2012.

Harrison, Gordon A. *The European Theater of Operations: Cross-Channel Attack.* The United States Army in World War II. 1951. Reprint, Washington, DC: CMH, 1993.

Hawkins, Glen R., and James Jay Carafano. *Prelude to Army XXI: US Army Division Design Initiatives and Experiments, 1917–1995.* Washington, DC: CMH, 1997.

Heefner, Wilson A. *Patton's Bulldog: The Life and Service of General Walton H. Walker.* Shippensburg, PA: White Maine Books, 2001.

Heiner, Gordon C., Jr. *From Saints to Red Legs: The History of a Border Post.* Watertown, NY: A. W. Munk, 1938.

Heintzelman, Stuart. *Annual Report of the Command and General Staff School, 1929–1930.* Fort Leavenworth, KS: CGSS Press, 1930.

Heintzelman, Stuart. *Annual Report of the Command and General Staff School, 1930–1931.* Fort Leavenworth, KS: CGSS Press, 1931.

Heintzelman, Stuart. *Annual Report of the Command and General Staff School, 1931–1932.* Fort Leavenworth, KS: CGSS Press, 1932.

Heller, Charles E. "The US Army, the Civilian Conservation Corps, and Leadership for World War II, 1933–1942." *Armed Forces & Society* 36, no. 3 (2010): 493–53.

Heller, Charles E., and William A. Stoft, eds. *America's First Battles, 1776–1965.* Lawrence: University Press of Kansas, 1986.

Hemingway, Ernest. "The GI and the General." *Collier's,* November 4, 1944, 46–47.

Hinman, Jade E. "When the Japanese Bombed the Huertgen Forest." Master's thesis, US Army Command and General Staff College, 2011.

Hofmann, George F. *Through Mobility We Conquer: The Mechanization of US Cavalry.* Lexington: University of Kentucky Press, 2006.

Hogan, David W. *A Command Post at War: First Army Headquarters in Europe, 1943–1945.* Washington, DC: CMH, 2001.

Holland, Matthew F. *Eisenhower between the Wars: The Making of a General and Statesman.* Westport, CT: Praeger, 2001.

Hossfeld, Henry. *American Representation in Occupied Germany, 1922–1923*. Coblenz, Germany: American Forces in Germany, 1923.

House, Jonathan M. *Combined Arms Warfare in the Twentieth Century*. Lawrence: University Press of Kansas, 2001.

Howe, George F. *The Mediterranean Theater of Operations: Northwest Africa: Seizing the Initiative in the West*. United States Army in World War II. 1957. Reprint, Washington, DC: CMH, 1993.

Hunt, Elvid. *History of Fort Leavenworth*. 2nd ed. Fort Leavenworth, KS: CGSS Press, 1937.

Hughes, Thomas Alexander. *Over Lord: General Pete Quesada and the Triumph of Tactical Air Power in World War II*. New York: Free Press, 1995.

Information Office. *History of Fort Dix: Part 1, 1917–1967*. Fort Dix, NJ: United States Army Training Center, 1967.

Infantry School. *Infantry in Battle*. 1934. Reprint, Washington, DC: GPO, 1981.

Johnson, Gerden F. *History of the Twelfth Infantry Regiment in World War II*. Reprint, Athens, GA: Deeds, 2017.

Johnson, Leland R. *Situation Desperate: US Army Engineer Disaster Relief Operations, Origins to 1950*. Alexandria, VA: US Army Corps of Engineers, 2011.

Jones, Clifford L. *The Administrative and Logistical History of the ETO*. Part VI, *Neptune: Training, Mounting, the Artificial Ports*. Washington, DC: CMH, 1946.

Keegan, John. *The Face of Battle*. New York: Penguin Books, 1976.

Kennedy, David M. *Freedom from Fear: The United States, 1929–1945*. Oxford History of the United States. New York: Oxford University Press, 1996.

Kepher, Stephen C. *COSSAC: Lt. Gen. Sir Frederick Morgan and the Genesis of Operation Overlord*. Annapolis, MD: Naval Institute Press, 2020.

King, Edward L. *Annual Report of the Command and General Staff School, 1925–1926*. Fort Leavenworth, KS: CGSS Press, 1926.

King, Edward L. *Annual Report of the Command and General Staff School, 1928–1929*. Fort Leavenworth, KS: CGSS Press, 1929.

King, Martin, Michael Collins, and Jason Nulton. *To War with the 4th: A Century of Frontline Combat with the US 4th Infantry Division, from the Argonne to the Ardennes to Afghanistan*. Philadelphia: Casemate, 2016.

Kirby, John J., Jr, ed. *Ye Doomsday Book*. Washington, DC: Georgetown University, 1934.

Kosar, Kevin R. *Disaster Response and Appointment of a Recovery Czar: The Executive Branch's Response to the Flood of 1927*. Washington, DC: Congressional Research Service, Library of Congress, 2005.

Kreidberg, Marvin A., and Merton G. Henry. *History of Military Mobilization in the United States Army, 1775–1945.* Washington, DC: Department of the Army, 1955.

Kretchik, Walter E. *US Army Doctrine: From the American Revolution to the War on Terror.* Lawrence: University Press of Kansas, 2011.

Larrabee, Eric. *Commander in Chief: Franklin Delano Roosevelt, His Lieutenants, and Their War.* New York: Harper & Row, 1987.

Laurie, Clayton D., and Ronald H. Cole. *The Role of Federal Military Forces in Domestic Disorders, 1877–1945.* Washington, DC: CMH, 1997.

Learner, William. *Historical Statistics of the United States, Colonial Times to 1970.* Washington, DC: Bureau of the Census, 1976.

Lengel, Edward G. *To Conquer Hell: The Meuse-Argonne, 1918: The Epic Battle That Ended the First World War.* New York: Henry Holt, 2009.

Lerwill, Leonard L. *The Personnel Replacement System in the United States Army.* Department of the Army, pamphlet no. 20-211. Washington, DC: Department of the Army, 1954.

Linn, Brian McAllister. *The Echo of Battle: The Army's Way of War.* Cambridge: Harvard University Press, 2007.

Lovelace, Alexander G. "Hughes' War: The Allied High Command through the Eyes of General Everett S. Hughes." Master's thesis, George Washington University, 2013.

Ludewig, Jochim. *Rückzug: The German Retreat from France, 1944.* Translated by David T. Zabecki. Lexington: University of Kentucky Press, 2012.

Lutz, Norma Jean. *J. D. Salinger.* Bloom's Biocritiques Series. Philadelphia: Chelsea House, 2002.

MacDonald, Charles B. *The Battle of the Huertgen Forest.* Philadelphia: J. B. Lippencott, 1963.

MacDonald, Charles B. *The European Theater of Operations: The Last Offensive.* The United States Army in World War II. 1973. Reprint, Wasington, DC: CMH, 1993.

MacDonald, Charles B. *The European Theater of Operations: The Siegfried Line Campaign.* United States Army in World War II. 1963. Reprint, Washington, DC: CMH, 1993.

MacDonald, Charles B. "Slapton Sands: The Cover-up That Never Was." *Army* 38, no. 6 (June 1988): 64–67.

Maher, Neil M. *Nature's New Deal: The Civilian Conservation Corps and the Roots of the American Environmental Movement.* New York: Oxford University Press, 2008.

Mahon, John K., and Romana Danysh. *Infantry, Part I: Regular Army.* Army Lineage Series. Washington, DC: CMH, 1972.

Mansoor, Peter R. *The GI Offensive in Europe: The Triumph of American Infantry Divisions, 1941–1945.* Lawrence: University Press of Kansas, 1999.

Matheny, Michael R. *Carrying the War to the Enemy: American Operational Art to 1945.* Norman: University of Oklahoma Press, 2011.

Matloff, Maurice. *American Military History.* Washington, DC: CMH, 1973.

Matloff, Maurice, and Edwin M. Snell. *The War Department: Strategic Planning for Coalition Warfare, 1941–1942.* The United States Army in World War II. 1953. Reprint, Washington, DC: CMH, 1999.

McKeown, Roy S. *Cabin in the Blackjacks: A History of Ada, Oklahoma.* Ada, OK: Self Published, 1980.

McManus, John C. *The Americans at D-Day: The American Experience at the Normandy Invasion.* New York: Forge Books, 2004.

McManus, John C. *The Americans at Normandy: The Summer of 1944— The American War from the Normandy Beaches to Falaise.* New York: Forge Books, 2004.

McCarthy, Kevin M. *Georgia's Lighthouses and Historic Coastal Sites.* Sarasota, FL: Pineapple Press, 1998.

Michel, Jean-Paul, and Monique Brouillet Seefried. *Le general Dio: Le connétable de Leclerc, 1940–1946.* Paris: Foundation Maréchal Leclerc de Hauteclocque, 2022.

Miller, Edward G. *A Dark and Bloody Ground: The Hürtgen Forest and the Roer River Dams, 1944–1945.* College Station: Texas A&M Press, 1995.

Millett, Allan R. "Cantigny, 28–31 May 1918." In Heller and Stoft, *America's First Battles*, 149–85.

Millett, Allan R. *The General: Robert L. Bullard and Officership in the United States Army, 1881–1925.* Westport, CT: Greenwood Press, 1975.

Millett, Allan R., Peter Maslowski, and William B. Feis. *For the Common Defense: A Military History of The United States from 1607–2012.* Revised and expanded ed. New York: Free Press, 1994.

Morison, Samuel Eliot. *The Invasion of France and Germany, 1944–1945.* Vol. 11, *History of the United States Naval Operations in World War II.* Boston: Little, Brown, 1957.

Morton, Louis. *The War in the Pacific: The Fall of the Philippines.* United States Army in World War II. Washington, DC: CMH, 1993.

Moss, James A. *Officer's Manual, 5th Edition.* Leavenworth, KS: The US Cavalry Association, 1917.

Nance, Curtis H., ed. *The Howitzer.* Philadelphia: Hoskins Press, 1911.

Neiberg, Michael. *The Blood of Free Men: The Liberation of Paris, 1944.* New York: Basic Books, 2012.

Nenninger, Timothy K. *The Leavenworth Schools and the Old Army.* Westport, CT: Greenwood Press, 1978.

Ney, Virgil. *Evolution of the US Army Infantry Battalion: 1939–1968.* Fort Belvoir, VA: United States Army Combat Developments Command, 1968.

North, Brian. *Making the Difficult Routine: US Army Task Organization at the Army and Corps Level in Europe, 1944.* Fort Leavenworth, KS: CSI, 2016.

Nowowiejski, Dean A. *The American Army in Germany, 1918–1923: Success against the Odds.* Lawrence: University Press of Kansas, 2021.

Oklahoma Historical Society. "Judge Conroy O. Barton." *Chronicles of Oklahoma* 20, no. 1 (1941).

Oncken, William, Jr. *Managing Management Time.* Englewood Cliffs, NY: Prentice-Hall, 1984.

Ossad, Steven L. *Omar Nelson Bradley: America's GI General, 1893–1981.* Columbia: University of Missouri Press, 2017.

Ossad, Steven L., and Don R. Marsh. *Major General Maurice Rose: World War II's Greatest Forgotten Commander.* New York: Taylor Trade, 2006.

Paige, John C. *The Civilian Conservation Corps and the National Park Service, 1933–1942: An Administrative History.* Washington, DC: National Park Service, 1985.

Perret, Geoffrey. *There's a War to Be Won: The United States Army in World War II.* New York: Ivy Books, 1991.

Pogue, Forrest C. *The European Theater of Operations: The Supreme Command.* United States Army in World War II. Washington, DC: CMH, 1954.

Pogue, Forrest C. *George C. Marshall: Education of a General, 1880–1939.* New York: Viking Press, 1963.

Pogue, Forrest C. *George C. Marshall: Ordeal and Hope, 1939–1942.* New York: Viking Press, 1966.

Pogue, Forrest C. *George C. Marshall: Organizer of Victory, 1944–1945.* New York: Viking Press, 1973.

Pontotoc County Historical and Genealogical Society. *History of Pontotoc County, Oklahoma.* Ada, OK: Pontotoc County Historical and Genealogical Society, 1976.

Prange, Gordon W. *At Dawn We Slept: The Untold Story of Pearl Harbor.* New York: McGraw-Hill, 1981.

Prucha, Francis Paul. *The Sword of the Republic: The United States Army on the Frontier, 1783–1846.* Macmillan Wars of the United States. Lincoln: University of Nebraska Press, 1969.

Rabalais, Steven. *General Fox Connor: Pershing's Chief of Operations and Eisenhower's Mentor.* Philadelphia: Casemate, 2016.

Reardon, Mark J. *Victory at Mortain: Stopping Hitler's Panzer Counteroffensive.* Lawrence: University Press of Kansas, 2002.

Reeder, Russell P. (Red). *Born at Reveille: Memoirs of an American Soldier.* Rev. ed. Quechee, VT: Vermont Heritage Press, 1994.

Register of Faculties and Students of Georgetown University, 1933–1934. Washington, DC: Georgetown University, 1933.

Reynolds, David. *Rich Relations: The American Colonization of Britain, 1942–1945.* New York: Random House, 1995.

Rieman, Elizabeth. *Unpacking Yesterday: Brotherhood's Legacy.* Athens, GA: Deeds, 2020.

Risk Management Solutions. *RMD Special Report: The 1927 Great Mississippi Flood: 80-Year Retrospective.* Newark, CA: Risk Management Solutions, 2007. https://forms2.rms.com/rs/729-DJX-565/images/fl_1927_great_mississippi_flood.pdf.

Roth, Mitchel P. *Historical Dictionary of War Journalism.* Westport, CT: Greenwood Press, 1997.

Ruppenthal, Roland G. *Utah Beach to Cherbourg (6 June–27 June 1944).* American Forces in Action. Reprint, Washington, DC: CMH, 1984.

Ruppenthal, Roland G. *Logistical Support of the Armies.* Volume 1, *May 1941–September 1944.* 1953. Reprint, Washington, DC: CMH, 1995.

Rush, Robert Sterling. *Hell in Hürtgen Forest.* Lawrence: University Press of Kansas, 2001.

Ryan, Cornelius. *The Longest Day.* New York: Simon & Schuster, 1959.

Schifferle, Peter J. *America's School for War: Fort Leavenworth, Officer Education, and Victory in World War II.* Lawrence: University Press of Kansas, 2010.

Schillare, Quentin W. *Fort Leavenworth: The People Behind the Names.* Fort Leavenworth, KS: CSI, 2015.

Scott, Hugh L. *Annual Report of the Superintendent of the United States Military Academy.* West Point, NY: United States Military Academy, 1909.

Secretary of War. *Official Army Register.* Washington, DC: GPO, 1918.

Secretary of War. *Official Army Register.* Washington, DC: GPO, 1926.

Secretary of War. *Official Army Register.* Washington, DC: GPO, 1945.

Seidule, Ty. *Robert E. Lee and Me: A Southerner's Reckoning with the Myth of the Lost Cause.* New York: St. Martin's Press, 2020.

Shea, John Gilmary. *Memorial of the First Century of Georgetown College, D.C.: Comprising a History of Georgetown University.* Washington, DC: Georgetown University, 1891.

Shirer, William L. *The Collapse of the Third Republic: An Inquiry into the Fall of France, 1940.* New York: Simon and Schuster, 1969.

Smith, Francis G. "History of the Third Army, Study No. 17." Army Ground Forces Studies. Fort Leavenworth, KS: CARL, 1946.

Smith, Gene. *Until the Last Trumpet Sounds: The Life of General of the Armies John J. Pershing.* New York: John Wiley & Sons, 1998.

Smith, Harry A. *Annual Report of the Command and General Staff School, 1923–1924.* Fort Leavenworth, KS: CGSS Press, 1924.

Spector, Ronald H. *Eagle against the Sun: The American War with Japan.* New York: Vintage Books, 1985.

Stanton, Shelby L. *World War II Order of Battle: An Encylopedic Reference to US Army Ground Force Units from Battalion through Division, 1939–1946.* Mechanicsburg, PA: Stackpole Books, 2006.

Stimson, Henry L. *Report of the Secretary of War to the President, 1937.* Washington, DC: GPO, 1940.

Strickland, Dare. *Images of America: Ada.* Charleston, SC: Arcadia, 2010.

Strong, Frederick S., Jr., ed. *The Howitzer.* New York: Chas. L. Willard, 1910.

Symonds, Craig L. *Neptune: The Allied Invasion of Europe and the D-Day Landings.* New York: Oxford University Press, 2014.

Thompson, George Raynor, and Dixie R. Harris. *The Technical Services, the Signal Corps: The Outcome (Mid-1943 through 1945).* Washington, DC: CMH, 1966.

Trauschweizer, Ingo. *The Cold War US Army.* Lawrence: University Press of Kansas, 2008.

Trigg, Jonathan. *D-Day through German Eyes: How the Wehrmacht Lost France.* Gloucestershire, UK: Amberley, 2020.

US Adjutant General. *Army Battle Casualties and Nonbattle Deaths in World War II.* Washington, DC: Department of the Army, 1946.

US Adjutant General. *The Army List, and Directory, September 1, 1925.* Washington, DC: GPO, 1925.

USAWC Alumni Association. *Directory of US Army War College Graduates.* Carlisle, PA: USAWC Alumni Association, 2000.

Votaw, John F., and Steven Weingartner, eds. *The Greatest Thing We Have Ever Attempted: Historical Perspectives on the Normandy Campaign.* Cantigny Military History Series. Wheaton, IL: Cantigny First Division Foundation, 1998.

Wade, Gary H. *CSI Report No. 7: World War II Division Commanders.* Fort Leavenworth, KS: CSI, 1983.

Walker, Robert W. *The Namesake: The Biography of Theodore Roosevelt, Jr.* New York: Brick Tower Press, 2008.

Watson, Mark Skinner. *The War Department: Chief of Staff: Prewar Plans and Preparations*. 1950. Reprint, Washington, DC: CMH, 1991.

Weigley, Russell F. *Eisenhower's Lieutenants: The Campaign of France and Germany, 1944–1945.* Bloomington: Indiana University Press, 1981.

Weigley, Russell F. *History of the United States Army.* Bloomington: Indiana University Press, 1967.

Weinberg, Gerhard L. *A World at Arms: A Global History of World War II.* Revised ed. New York: Cambridge University Press, 2005.

Wheeler, James Scott. *Jacob L. Devers: A General's Life.* Lawrence: University Press of Kansas, 2015.

White, Richard. *The Republic for Which It Stands: The United States during Reconstruction and the Gilded Age, 1865–1896.* Oxford History of the United States. New York: Oxford University Press, 2017.

Wiley, Bell I. *Training in the Ground Army, 1942–1945, Study XI.* Washington, DC: Army Ground Forces Historical Section, 1948.

Williams, Mary H., ed. *Special Studies: Chronology 1941–1945.* United States Army in World War II. Washington, DC: CMH, 1989.

Wilson, George D. *If You Survive: From Normandy to the Battle of the Bulge to the End of World War II—One American Officer's Riveting True Story.* New York: Ballantine Books, 1987.

Wilson, John B. *Maneuver and Firepower: The Evolution of Divisions and Separate Brigades.* Army Lineage Series. Washington, DC: CMH, 1998.

Wilson, John B. *Armies, Corps, Divisions and Separate Brigades.* Army Lineage Series. Washington, DC: CMH, 1987.

Wilson, Theodore A., ed. *D-Day, 1944.* Modern War Studies. Lawrence: University Press of Kansas, 1971.

Winter, Jay. *Sites of Memory, Sites of Mourning: The Great War in European Cultural History.* New York: Cambridge University Press, 1998.

Woodman, Lyman L. *Duty Station Northwest: The US Army in Alaska and Western Canada, 1867–1987.* Vol. 1, *1867–1917.* Anchorage: Alaska Historical Society, 1996.

Woodring, Harry H. *Report of the Secretary of War to the President, 1937.* Washington, DC: GPO, 1937.

Woodward, David R. *The American Army and the First World War.* Armies of the Great War. New York: Cambridge University Press, 2014.

Woolley, William J. *Creating the Modern Army: Citizen-Soldiers and the American Way of War, 1919–1939.* Studies in Civil-Military Relations. Edited by William A. Taylor. Lawrence: University Press of Kansas, 2022.

Works Progress Administration. *Georgia: The WPA Guide to Its Towns and Countryside.* Athens: University of Georgia Press, 1940.

Wyant, William K., *Sandy Patch: A Biography of Lt. Gen. Alexander M. Patch.* New York: Praeger, 1991.

Yarborough, Leroy, and Truman Smith. *History of the Infantry School, Fort Benning, GA.* Fort Benning: Infantry School, 1931.

Yockelson, Mitchell. "The United States Armed Forces and the Mexican Punitive Expedition." Pts. 1 and 2. *Prologue Magazine* 29, no. 3 (Spring 1997): 256–62; 29, no. 4 (Winter 1997): 334–43.

Yung, Christopher D. *Gators of Neptune: Naval Amphibious Planning for the Normandy Invasion.* Annapolis, MD: Naval Institute Press, 2006.

Zaloga, Steven J. *Cherbourg 1944: The First Allied Victory in Normandy.* Oxford, UK: Osprey, 2015.

Zaloga, Steven J. *D-Day Fortifications in Normandy.* Fortress 37. Oxford, UK: Osprey, 2005.

Zaloga, Steven J. *Liberation of Paris 1944: Patton's Race for the Seine.* Oxford, UK: Osprey, 2008.

Media and Web Resources

"Alphabetical Locator of Graduates and Former Cadets." United States Military Academy, 2010. https://www.west-point.org/wp/ring_recovery/RRP/RingPix/2010ROG_1802-1931DeceasedClassesRegisterofGraduatesROGAOGAlumni.pdf.

Army Map Service. France 1:100,000, 1943, Series M661 (GSGS 4249), Second Edition. University of Texas: Perry-Castañeda Library. http://legacy.lib.utexas.edu/maps/ams/france_100k/.

Massey, Morris. "What You Are Is Where You Were When." Program 1 of *The Original Massey Tapes.* Video Publishing House, 1972.

Zanuck, Darryl F. *The Longest Day.* Movie. 178 min. United States: Twentieth Century Fox, 1962.

Index

A

Aachen, GE, 52, 68, 317, 333, 337
Ada, OK, 1, 4–10, 23, 25, 36, 40, 46–47,
    49, 53, 79, 98–99, 160–61, 164
AEF (American Expeditionary Force),
    34, 44–45, 49, 51, 53, 55, 62, 64,
    71, 95, 102
AFG (American Forces in Germany),
    57–60, 64, 94, 104
AGF (Army Ground Forces), 133,
    145, 147, 149, 154, 159, 164–65,
    284, 374
aircraft, Piper Cub, 318, 320–21
Air Force
    Ninth, xxi, 187, 212, 243, 246, 252,
      261, 267–68, 286–87, 291
    Twelfth, 12
Alaska, 22–23, 25, 28–31, 33, 35–36,
    48, 50, 114, 117–18, 379, 389
Allen, Henry T., 53, 104
Allen, Leven C., 147
Allen, Terry de la Mesa, 38, 390
American Expeditionary Force. *See* AEF
American Forces in Germany. *See* AFG
American Red Cross (ARC), 51, 61–62,
    91, 171, 194–95, 384
Anding, James G., 260, 280
Andrews, Frank M., 104–5
Anti-Aircraft Artillery, 377th (automatic
    weapons), 181, 187, 261, 282
antitank/antiaircraft gun, 88 mm Flak,
    230, 241, 246, 287
Ardennes Forest, 314, 318–20, 322, 341,
    356, 360, 380
Arlington National Cemetery, 64, 74,
    110, 115, 375, 386–87
armored car, M-8, 252
Armored Division
    1st, 134
    2nd, 134, 147, 160, 233, 275, 281,
      288–90, 293–94, 309–10, 322

2nd French, xxiii, 306
3rd, 260–61, 275, 281–83, 288–89,
    292–94, 297, 299, 333–34
4th, 276, 367, 370, 391
5th, 168, 188, 314–16, 318, 320, 353
9th, 364–65, 370
10th, 364–65
13th, 147
Army
    First US, xxi, 120, 135, 178, 191,
      206, 219, 258, 260, 263, 272,
      274, 280, 282–83, 285, 291, 293,
      295–96, 299, 304, 306, 311–12,
      317–18, 321, 325, 327, 333, 335,
      356, 363, 370
    Ninth US, 312, 333
    Sixth US, 86
    Third US, xxi, 52, 57, 86, 121, 123,
      128–30, 132, 135, 139–40, 144,
      181, 273, 282, 291, 293, 297,
      299, 312
Army Ground Forces. *See* AGF
Army Group
    Sixth, 105
    Twelfth, 19, 291, 312, 359, 370, 372
    Twenty-First, 192, 370
Army War College, 48, 94, 101, 105,
    110, 143, 145, 157–58, 364, 390
Audouville-la-Hubert, FR, 216, 232
Augusta, GA, 45, 132, 143, 155,
    379–80, 382–88

B

Baade, Paul W, 11, 297, 299
Bagby, Carroll A. (Jake), 11, 110,
    158–59, 188–89
Barber, Henry A., Jr., 156, 187, 189,
    191, 194, 196, 202–3, 206, 208,
    214–15, 220, 227–30, 232,
    237–38, 254
Barker, Ray, 237

477